CONFLICT AND CONTEXT
Hermeneutics in the Americas

A Report on the Context and Hermeneutics
in the Americas Conference
Sponsored by
Theological Students Fellowship
and the
Latin American Theological Fraternity
Tlayacapan, Mexico,
November 24-29, 1983

Edited by

Mark Lau Branson
and C. René Padilla

WILLIAM B. EERDMANS PUBLISHING COMPANY
GRAND RAPIDS, MICHIGAN

Library of Congress Cataloging-in-Publication Data

Context and Hermeneutics in the Americas Conference
    (1983 : Tlayacapan, Mexico)
    Conflict and context.

    1. Bible—Hermeneutics—Congresses.   I. Branson,
Mark Lau.   II. Padilla, C. Rene.   III. Theological
Students Fellowship.   IV. Fraternidad Teológica
Latinoamericana.   V. Title.
BS476.C594   1986   220.6'01   86-19854

ISBN 0-8028-0172-2

Contents

Conference Participants

Frank Alton, formerly associate pastor at the Bel Air Presbyterian Church in Los Angeles, recently began working with the Mexican Association for Rural and Urban Transformation (AMEXTRA) and the Center for Advanced Interdisciplinary Studies (CESIC) in Mexico City.

Mark Lau Branson, formerly general secretary of Theological Students Fellowship, is now dean of the Fellowship Bible Institute in San Francisco and associate editor of *Radix* and *Transformation*.

Orlando Costas, formerly professor of missions at Eastern Baptist Theological Seminary, is now dean and professor of missions at Andover-Newton Theological Seminary near Boston.

Virgil Cruz, formerly professor of New Testament Studies at Western Theological Seminary in Holland, Michigan, is now professor of New Testament at Louisville Presbyterian Theological Seminary.

George Cummings, formerly assistant professor of theology at Chicago Theological Seminary, is a doctoral candidate in theology at Union Theological Seminary in New York.

Pablo Deiros is professor of church history at the International Baptist Seminary in Buenos Aires.

Samuel Escobar, formerly president of the Latin American Theological Fraternity, is professor of missiology at Eastern Baptist Theological Seminary in Philadelphia.

Elouise Renich Fraser is assistant professor of systematic theology at Eastern Baptist Theological Seminary in Philadelphia.

Athol Gil is professor of New Testament at Whitley Baptist Theological College in Melbourne, Australia.

Rolando Gutiérrez-Cortés is the pastor of the Mount Horeb Baptist Church in Mexico City, professor of philosophy at the Polytechnical Institute of Mexico City, and president of the Latin American Theological Fraternity.

Richard Hays is associate professor of New Testament at Yale Divinity School.

Robert Hubbard, Jr., is associate professor of Old Testament at Denver Seminary.

Thomas McAlpine, formerly an editor of *Theological Students Fellowship Bulletin,* is now a senior research associate with the MARC division of World Vision International in Monrovia, California.

Linda Mercadante recently received a Ph.D. in theology and history of doctrine from Princeton Theological Seminary.

Emilio Antonio Nuñez is professor of systematic theology at the Central American Theological Seminary in Guatemala City.

Grant Osborne is associate professor of New Testament at Trinity Evangelical Divinity School near Chicago.

C. René Padilla, currently general secretary of the Latin American Theological Fraternity, is pastor of La Lucila Baptist Church in Buenos Aires and the editor of *Misión.*

Samuel Pagán, formerly dean of the Evangelical Seminary of Puerto Rico, is now the pastor of the University Hispanic Christian Church in Miami and affiliated with the Division of Overseas Ministries of the Christian Church (Disciples of Christ).

Clark Pinnock is professor of theology at McMaster Divinity College in Hamilton, Ontario.

Stephen Reid is associate professor of Old Testament at Pacific School of Religion in Berkeley, California.

J. Deotis Roberts, formerly president of the Interdenominational Theological Center in Atlanta, is now distinguished professor of philosophical theology at Eastern Baptist Theological Seminary, Philadelphia.

Edesio Sánchez-Centina was recently appointed director of the Bible Society of Costa Rica.

Pedro Savage, formerly general secretary of the Latin American Theological Fraternity, is currently engaged in doctoral studies in psychology at Andover-Newton Theological Seminary and is affiliated with the United Church Board of World Ministries.

David M. Scholer is dean of the seminary and professor of New Testament at Northern Baptist Theological Seminary near Chicago.

Gerald Sheppard, formerly associate professor of Old Testament at Union Theological Seminary in New York, is now associate professor of Old Testament at Emmanuel College of Victoria University in Toronto.

Moisés Silva is professor of New Testament at Westminster Theological Seminary in Philadelphia.

Aída Bescançon Spencer is assistant professor of New Testament at Gordon-Conwell Theological Seminary.

William David Spencer teaches in the areas of theology, prayer, and the arts at Gordon-Conwell Theological Seminary.

John Stam is professor of systematic theology at the Baptist Theological Seminary of Nicaragua and at the Ecumenical School of Religion at the National University of Heredia, Costa Rica.

Valdir Steuernagel, a Lutheran pastor from Brazil, is currently a Th.D. student at the Lutheran School of Theology in Chicago and professor-elect at the Lutheran Theological Seminary in Cao Leopoldo, Brazil.

Sze-kar Wan is a Ph.D. student in New Testament at Harvard University.

David Lowes Watson, formerly associate professor of evangelism and missions at Perkins School of Theology in Dallas, is now executive director for covenant discipleship at the General Board of Discipleship of the United Methodist Church.

Douglas Webster is professor of theology and ethics at Ontario Theological Seminary in Willowdale, Ontario.

John Howard Yoder is professor of theology at the University of Notre Dame in Indiana.

C. Hugo Zorrilla, formerly dean of the Latin American Biblical Seminary of San Jose, Costa Rica, and then associate professor of New Testament at the Mennonite Brethren Biblical Seminary in Fresno, California, is now a missionary with the Mennonite Brethren Church and director of the Program of Biblical Studies in Spain.

Foreword

Few today would argue that it is possible to read Scripture without cultural bias. Scholars and laypeople know that their environment affects the way they understand Scripture. Satisfaction with the traditional approaches that have produced a one-way flow of biblical interpretation and theology from the North Atlantic to the rest of the world is slowly giving way to a recognition of the need for a two-way, more circular approach that respects the insights, values, and understandings of each participant in the dialogue. As the church seeks to work and witness effectively, the issues of interpreting Scripture and doing theology are becoming increasingly complex.

In November of 1983, thirty-five scholars from Latin America and North America gathered for five days near Cuernevaca, Mexico, under the sponsorship of the Latin American Theological Fraternity and the Theological Students Fellowship (TSF, a division of Inter-Varsity Christian Fellowship). The conference, entitled "Context and Hermeneutics in the Americas," was designed to examine some of the issues that theologians, biblical scholars, and pastors are facing: How does a church's cultural context affect its interpretation of the Bible? What impact does this have on such basic theological concepts as Christology, soteriology, and ecclesiology? How can such culturally conditioned insights be a strength not only for the originating church but also for churches in other contexts? What dangers exist in contextual hermeneutics? What checks can be helpful?

The conference approached its task along three avenues: plenary theological presentations, Bible study in smaller groups, and open plenary discussions. Each of the four theological sessions involved the reading of a paper followed by several prepared responses from a variety of different contexts and then a general discussion of the paper and the responses. The five Bible study groups incorporated papers written prior to the conference and provided the participants with over twelve hours of on-site study and paper writing. A number of critical topics emerged from the theological presentations and Bible study sessions, each calling for extended plenary discussion time.

At times simultaneous or consecutive translation was provided between the major languages. Often the bilingual abilities of the Latin Americans allowed open discussions to proceed largely in English. At times, however, conversations were rapid and passionate, temporarily hindering some from understanding. As is too often true in such situations, we missed out on valuable contributions from those who had to strain to follow the debate. Of course this was more a problem in the formal meetings whose substance is transcribed in this volume than it was in the hours of informal discussions that took place, but regrettably the latter were not recorded.

As the sessions progressed, it became obvious that we would not be able to give the larger issues substantive treatment without first working to clarify cultural issues. We had to work at developing a better understanding of our own cultural "baggage" before we could proceed. And because the conference was multicultural rather than bicultural, the process was so much the more complicated and profound. Typically a process like this involves explaining oneself "over against" another group, but the many groups present—black, Anglo, Hispanic, native American, male and female, Pentecostal, Lutheran, Reformed, Methodist, Mennonite, Baptist, mainline evangelical, and so on—demanded our making all manner of distinctions. Each of these contexts offers a different perspective on the world and on the gospel. But in order to make the distinctions, one had to acquire a sufficient understanding of both one's own culture and that of the other. As we made the attempt, stereotypes began to fall rapidly. We learned, among other things, that there are more than two cultures in the Americas and that none of the cultures has a monopoly on either radical or conservative politics/economics. By observing the conference room it was clear that women were underrepresented among the delegates from the North and completely unrepresented among the delegates from the South. Theologians attending were all middle-class, although some work closer to poverty than others. "Evangelicals" from the North were not necessarily associated with mainstream American evangelicalism. The character of liberation theologies depends significantly on their roots (European, African, South American, etc.) and the occupation of the theologian defining them (pastor, academic theologian, bureaucrat, etc.). Power struggles within American evangelicalism affect hermeneutics. Paternalism from earlier missionary relationships is still present in many church and parachurch structures.

Throughout all the sessions we sought to learn about the variety of contexts we work in and how they affect the task of interpreting Scripture. We offered one another encouragement and critique to clarify issues and facilitate scholarship. We reflected constantly on how scholarly pursuits are related to ministry. And times of prayer, singing, as well as Sunday worship in Mexico City churches kept us mindful that our work was not primarily academic. Our goal was to glorify our Lord and to become increasingly faithful to the task he has given us.

As preconceptions gave way to new information concerning Latin American realities, TSF delegates gained a new respect for their Latin American colleagues. Many of them are active as both pastors and professors. They, more than the majority of the U.S. and Canadian participants, are ministering in the midst of poverty and revolutionary political struggle. Their theological abilities have been strengthened by years of corroborating, arguing, writing, responding, worshiping, praying, and fellowshiping. Their differences are sharp at times, but their unity is also remarkable.

Latin American delegates were able to see with new eyes the varieties of peoples and theologies from the North. The account given by women of the struggles they are facing led some to new perceptions of their own settings. The image of a monolithic evangelicalism in continuity with fundamentalistic mission enterprises gave way to an understanding of the more complex reality of efforts at reform. And the pervasive and not always helpful influence of academia on the ministry of the church and the work of theologians helped to explain the pressures under which work must be done.

As we explored the papers, Bible expositions, and other topics in our discussions, it became apparent that no consensus document was forthcoming. We were only beginning to grasp relevant concerns and had little to offer others in the way of guidelines. Yet the richness of the event needed to be passed on. So this edited collection is offered to serve classroom discussions, the work of professors, and the questions of missiologists.

Quito   Mark Lau Branson
Christmas 1984   C. René Padilla

Acknowledgments

When so many students, professors, and pastors contribute to and participate in a conference, those deserving words of appreciation are many. No
doubt each person named in the book would wish to express gratitude to
families, secretaries, colleagues, and institution leaders.

Memories of the conference itself are especially treasured because of the
hospitality of the Mount Horeb Baptist Church of Mexico City. Pastor
Rolando Gutiérrez-Cortés and his congregation took care of us for five
days—encouraging us, praying for us, serving us.

Several organizations in the United States shared the vision for this
consultation and gave generously: the Lilly Endowment, Bel Air Presbyterian Church of Los Angeles, First Presbyterian Church of Henderson-
ville, North Carolina, and University Presbyterian Church of Seattle. Also
the Lutheran Welt (World) Mission of Hamburg, West Germany, helped
underwrite expenses.

Samuel Escobar extended an invitation for Mark Lau Branson to work in
Peru during 1984. Dr. Escobar's office, with the friendship and helpful
management of Maxine Jones, was a productive environment for much of the
editorial work. And the extended Padilla family gathered in Quito, Ec-
uador, for Christmas, providing an opportunity for the editors to finalize
their work.

I

Papers

1.1.1

Our Hermeneutic Task Today

SAMUEL ESCOBAR*

> Praise be to the God and Father of our Lord Jesus Christ, who in his great mercy gave us new birth into a living hope by the resurrection of Jesus Christ from the dead! (1 Pet. 1:3)

We start our exercise in this doxological moment. There is no other way to do theology but starting with praise to God. This praise is also an affirmation of the divine initiative that we confess by faith. It is acknowledging that God was there before, that there is a divine priority before our own Christian experience and our reflection.

1. Divine Initiative and Christian Identity

By stating divine initiative, we are confessing our condition as creatures—our "creatureliness." Because of Jesus Christ and from him we have learned that God is our Father. The Father that Jesus Christ reveals is not just a name that theologians have given to the forces of history in a Hegelian fashion. Nor is he the name that we give to the human drive in Promethean fashion like the Peruvian poet Vallejo, who writes to God reproaching him for his aloofness:

> But you have always been well
> you feel nothing for your creation,
> and man does suffer you:
> He is god!
>   "Los dados eternos"

* Samuel Escobar was unable to attend the conference. This paper was read to participants by a colleague.

Right at the start of his letter marked by a clear pastoral intention, Peter affirms the divine existence and the initiative of the Father that has given him and the communities that will read his letter their origin and their meaning in Christ. God is the Father to whom we owe our existence as people that listen to his Word and can understand it. This conviction is foundational for the hermeneutical task that Peter carries on in his epistle. God has acted by resurrecting Christ and, in his mercy, by giving new birth to those that are part of his church, his people. This is the confession with which the interpreter of God's Word begins.

Christian existence springs up from the experience of the new, which is described by the expression "new birth." In Jewish-Greek circles, the original Greek term meant "any decisively new stage in nature, history or personal life."[1] It was a term that, like others in the Pauline theology, had not only a personal reference but a communal and cosmic reference as well. The second part of the expression, "into a living hope," adds strength to the meaning if we take into account the atmosphere of imperial persecution that was already becoming perceptible in the Asia Minor regions where those who received the letter were living at the time it was written. These small communities (the apparently insignificant presence of the *new* that constituted the kingdom in history) had to understand their deepest call (1 Pet. 2:9-10) and fix their eyes upon their Lord (1 Pet. 3 and 4) in order to face the adversary with hope. To be born again into a living hope is to enter into a form of existence that in every century becomes necessary in a different way.

This affirmation of divine initiative and of the Christian identity or existence corresponds to a pattern of preaching and arguing that we also see in Peter's style in the book of Acts. When onlookers attributed the miracles at Pentecost to purely human causes, mockingly suggesting that "They must have been drinking," Peter cries, "This is what the prophet spoke of . . ." (Acts 2:12-16). "God promised . . . God spoke . . . God did . . . we are witnesses" is the constant pattern of Peter's preaching in those initial days.

Paul Minear asks, "What is the minimum rapport that is essential between an ancient author and a modern exegete?" and he hazards five answers, the first two being,

1. An interpreter must believe (believe in the most profound sense) in the God of the prophets as a God who calls and gives specific tasks to special individuals.

2. An interpreter must belong (and belong in the most profound sense) to a community which has been called into existence and given a distinctive vocation by that same God.[2]

1. R. G. Selwyn, *The First Epistle of St. Peter* (New York: St. Martin Press, 1969), p. 122.

2. Minear, *New Testament Apocalyptic* (Nashville: Abingdon Press, 1981), p. 31.

Consequently, this confession places us in a position from which we see the world, we see ourselves, and we can try to hear and understand the Word of God. Beginning from his confessing doxology, Peter goes on to expound in a Christological fashion the nature and meaning of the Christian life (vv. 4-9).

2. The Great Divine Acts and Their Interpretation

This salvation was the theme which the prophets pondered and explored, those who prophesied about the grace of God awaiting you. They tried to find out what was the time and what the circumstances to which the Spirit of Christ in them pointed, foretelling the sufferings in store for Christ and the splendors to follow; and it was disclosed to them that the matter they treated of was not for their time but for yours. And now it has been openly announced to you through preachers who brought you the Gospel in the power of the Holy Spirit sent from heaven. These are things that angels long to see into. (1 Pet. 1:10-12)

We come here with Peter to the specific hermeneutical injunction. It has a Christological center, and around it are integrated both the prophetic announcement and the apostolic preaching. Throughout the entire passage, divine action is said to have a saving intention. Past and present alike are joined in a *kairos* loaded with meaning.

Notice the way in which Peter treats equally the human work of the messenger who "ponders and explores" and the action of the Spirit who inspires the messenger, revealing things to the prophet and the apostle and driving them both. Along with the other things he is presenting in his epistle, Peter not only shares some facts about Christ that he can personally corroborate, having been a witness (they are not "tales artfully spun"— 2 Pet. 1:16), but he also "ponders and explores" the writings of Isaiah, explaining their meaning and deducing their consequences. The apostle moves naturally within a vision of the unity and cohesiveness of the divine talk, its hermeneutic key being the person and work of Christ and the saving intention of God.

An evangelical hermeneutics starts from a conviction about the basic unity of the text of the Bible. It refuses to begin by establishing polarities between the Old and New Testaments, between Gospel and epistle, between Jesus and Paul, between prophets of the left and kings of the right. The key for the unity of the text is Christological. The polarities usually come from ideologies or philosophic systems foreign to the text, to the world of the Bible, worldviews that are opposed in content and intention to the saving purpose of God. This does not mean that we should ignore a plurality of emphases or perspectives that go along with the human and historic side of revelation. But we should be aware that as there are ways of reading the text that end by eliminating a God who has taken the initiative, there are also ways of approaching the text that end by destroying its Christological core.

It is especially important to note in this passage from Peter that there is a reference not only to the fact of Christ but to the prophetic announcement that preceded it and to the gospel that explained it. As René Padilla has put it,

> the acts of God in the history of salvation are not simply events: they are *interpreted events, inseparable from their interpretation.* In themselves they are not able to communicate their significance. They are like a silent film. Therefore God not only acts, but he also speaks. He does not leave the interpretation of his mighty acts to chance, as the object of human speculation; rather, he reveals it to his messengers. . . . The word of interpretation is as much a part of salvation history as are the events themselves. Event and interpretation form an inseparable whole.[3]

An evangelical hermeneutics does not separate a so-called "factual core" from its interpretation, putting in its place an interpretation that better suits whatever scientific or philosophical vogue happens to express the mood of the interpreter's age. Rather, it strives to grasp the deep spirit of each Bible author and of the totality of the message—and in that endeavor some scientific disciplines may be able to help.

3. The Word as an Instrument of Transforming Grace

> Now that by obedience to the truth you have purified your souls until you feel sincere affection toward your brother Christians, love one another wholeheartedly with all your strength. You have been born anew, not of mortal parentage but of immortal through the living and enduring word of God. (1 Pet. 1:22-23)

This reference to the Word is a climax of the exposition that has presented the grace of divine initiative that brings a new birth in the origin of Christian existence. The context for the saving purpose refers now to love as it had referred to hope before. The new life is life for love, a love that is concrete because it is obedience to truth rather than mere sentimentalism. It is a love that is exercised first in the context of the Christian community, but it transcends that context, as can be seen in the rest of the epistle. The references to *purity, purification, sincerity,* and *immortality* point to the divine action in the process, and the reference to the Word of God (the following verses use Isaiah's language) likewise stress the divine action, the graceful nature of that initiative.

3. Padilla, "The Authority of Scripture," *Occasional Bulletin LATF* 1 (March 1972): 4.

There is a creative power in God's Word, creating new life in the new birth as well as in the creation (Heb. 11:3, Ps. 33, Gen. 1). By the instrumentality of his Word, God regenerates—that is, gives new life. In the story in John 6 of the many disciples who retreat, having been scandalized by some of Jesus' words, Peter cries, "Lord, to whom shall we go? Your words are words of eternal life." He, a bearer of the Word, acknowledges the power of the Word as an instrument through which God gives new life. The principle is established that before there was a Christian community there was a God who acted and a Word that was used to bring this community to life.

In the Latin American context, the history of evangelical people reconfirms this principle. Even before the missionaries came the Word had penetrated in many places, and in open contrast to the ritualism of tired nominal Roman Catholicism, churches appeared forming that people from which we who are here come. It is within this experience, in which we have seen relived again that reality about which Peter writes that we have stated the Reformed principle of *sola Scriptura*, though not always understanding it in its full meaning.

The Bible is not the property of any one church in particular, as certain types of Catholic argumentation maintained in the past (and want to maintain even today). Strictly speaking, it was not the church that produced the Bible; it was the preaching of the Word that produced the church. By the instrumentality of the Word that announces Jesus Christ, God gave life to his church. As René Padilla has said,

> from the perspective of the history of the Church and the place accorded the apostles within it, it is absurd to attempt to base the authority of the Bible on the authority of the Church. As the Reformers of the sixteenth century stated, *the Church itself is founded on the testimony of the prophets and apostles.* Apart from the fact of Christ and the apostolic tradition this creates, the Church has no basis. If it is argued that the Church defined the canon, the only possible answer is that authority precedes canonicity, not vice versa. The closing of the canon, far from being an affirmation of the authority of the Church, was the Church's act of submission to the Word of God "given once for all" to the apostles.[4]

A historical overview allows us to see how God has renewed his church in its darkest and most dramatic moments with his Word. I am not referring here only to the sixteenth-century Reformation or to the way in which the Reformers conceived the *Semper Reformanda*. Reformation remains a possibility and a necessity today, and although contemporary tensions among the churches that have come out of the Reformation show how difficult this task is, we can nevertheless be thankful that those churches have not formu-

4. "The Authority of Scripture," p. 9.

lated dogmas that would completely close the way to further reformation. Catholicism, on the other hand, *has* closed the way to a true reformation. As José Míguez Bonino said in 1960,

> when Roman Catholicism sets Scripture and tradition on the same level, it destroys the only possibility to listen to that voice that calls her, judges her, and pardons her. It has been rightly said that there can be reforms *in* the Church of Rome but not a reform *of* the Church of Rome. By putting tradition and Bible at the same level, the Church has put her own voice at the same level with the voice of the Apostles; in the final analysis, she has put her voice at the same level with the voice of Jesus Christ, has put her humanity, her faith, her experience in the place where only the redemptive humanity of Jesus Christ, of whom the Bible is a witness, should be put. Who will be able to reform a church that does not listen any more to the voice of her pastor but only to her own voice?[5]

It is clear that this final question from Míguez Bonino is especially relevant for Latin American evangelicals. We are part of a people inside which there is an explosion of Pentecostal growth that is shedding a blinding light on entrenched forms of missionary colonialism that are either already mired in presumptions of infallibility or in danger of becoming so. Hence the urgency of the hermeneutical task.

5. Míguez Bonino, "Escritura y Tradicion: Un antiguo problema en una nueva perspectiva," *Cuadernos Teológicos* 9 (Junio 1960): 107.

1.1.2

Response to Escobar by Mark Lau Branson

I am grateful for Samuel's opening comments. I regret that passport difficulties prevented him from joining us. As usual, Samuel is the pastor-theologian, and he provides an appropriate direction for our conference. It is not a technical paper, so a technical response is not needed. Rather, I will respond with several "yes . . . also" comments. A "yes . . . but" approach would not work because generally I simply affirm Samuel's comments and then push them a bit further.

1. Our hermeneutics must be formulated in the context of doxology and community. The Christian scholar must be immersed in the church, which is a community of worship and fellowship. Worship provides the needed center, the focus, the orientation for all labors. Geoffrey Wainwright has helped reintroduce this concern into the seminary context of the U.S. Worship provides the reminder of our commitment. It makes us aware that our earthbound scholarship can never be more than partial. It hopefully inserts humility into our souls.

And the fellowship of the church provides the environment for our work. It is the abundance of relationship that offers accountability, encouragement, resources, and complementary skills. These ingredients are necessary if our hermeneutics is to be accurate (careful, appropriate) and relevant. The separation between scholar and church is more severe in the North than in the South. Even those few professors in the North who have had the insight to reread Scripture in light of issues of power, wealth, and justice are themselves often separated both from the church of the poor and from their own traditions. And too often institutions in the South that receive support from the North Atlantic are separated from those people of the barrios that they claim to serve. We stand to learn much from our friends from the South this week. They often have more integrity in linking scholarship to mission because their work is done in the context of God's church.

2. The Bible provides more than historical accounts; it also reveals the meaning of those events. We do not have simply a string of discontinuous events. Rather, the meaning is furnished through the writers of Scripture

and ultimately through Jesus Christ. Samuel rightly calls on us to see the variety but also to begin with that unity provided by the Christological center.

I agree that Jesus is the interpretive key, and I pray that we will not fail to see that in all of our deliberations. Too often contemporary churches and theological traditions hold to some kind of unity, and Jesus is often claimed to be that center, but examination reveals other overriding influences and priorities. Perhaps a particular juridical reading of Paul becomes the final hermeneutic while Jesus' own interpretation of his messiahship, as he clarified it for the messengers of John the Baptist, is omitted. At other times the teachings of Scripture are narrowly defined so issues of systemic evil and political evangelism are ruled out. Often the words and works of Jesus concerning women, the poor, and the oppressed are conveniently forgotten. All such measures are taken to defend some power base, some particular status quo, whether it is a church-based, theologically defined, or politically oriented system.

In this regard, we cannot leave the Christological interpretation of events stalled in the first century. Though we must proceed with caution and humility, the Scriptures and the Spirit provide the church with the ability to look at events in our own environments and offer interpretations that can help the church be God's agent for the work of the kingdom.

3. Finally, the Word continues to be a powerful force of grace in today's world. And Samuel has indicated important ways in which the Scriptures have breathed God's life into people at various times. In fact, it is this conviction that caused this conference's conveners to choose hermeneutics as the focus.

I would suggest that the Word is more powerful than Samuel suggests here. The twenty-year-old quotation from Míguez Bonino has been superseded by the Spirit as the Word has invaded the Roman Catholic Church all over the Americas. But even with these renewals, the thwarting of the Word characteristic of authoritarian churches remains today not only in Roman Catholic settings but equally in evangelical groups. Pentecostal revivalism, missionary colonialism, and doctrinaire evangelicalism have often created their own systems of human infallibility while paying lip service to the Bible. Samuel accurately points to this in his final paragraph, and I add my voice in hoping that our proceedings can begin to unpack such issues in this multicultural dialogue.

As in Jesus' day, when the hermeneutics of the powerful prevented them and many others from understanding the Bible's words about Jesus, today's established authorities skew biblical interpretation and prevent many from following the Lord. May God grant grace to us so that the Spirit opens our eyes to the Word, that we may see Jesus.

1.1.3

An Overview of the Hermeneutical Situation of Biblical and Theological Studies in the United States

GERALD T. SHEPPARD*

At the outset, I want to say that I agree with church historian Sydney Ahlstrom that it is impossible to understand the Christian situation in North America within this century without coming to terms with the fundamentalism/liberalism controversy after the 1900s. I see the contemporary "evangelical movement" as basically the progeny of fundamentalism, which, despite its internal variety, still finds its point of departure in the options set in the 1920s. Like its counterpart among some liberal and neoliberal groups, evangelicalism forms a highly significant part of Christianity in North America. Because of the nature of this conference, I will focus my remarks on evangelicals in the United States rather than trying to deal with the admittedly different situation in Canada.[1]

Much of what follows builds on the implications of an article I wrote earlier, "Biblical Hermeneutics: The Academic Language of Evangelicals" (*Union Seminary Quarterly Review* 32 [1977]: 81-94). In that article, I argue that the term *inerrancy* does not simply entail a "high" affirmation of Scripture. At a more basic level, it is preferred by some conservative evangelicals over such other terms as *infallibility* because it functions rhetorically as a password to admit them into the confidence of a particular set of institu-

---

* Gerald Sheppard was unable to attend the first two days of the conference. His paper was read by a colleague, and some discussion followed. More extensive discussion continued upon his arrival.

1. For information on the differences between the American and Canadian situations, see Robert Handy's *History of the Churches in the United States and Canada* (New York: Oxford University Press, 1978).

tions, presses, and professional associations. Unfortunately, it does a poorer job expressing any precise theological and hermeneutical claims than it does expressing a political loyalty to a predominantly white, northern evangelical establishment. This establishment generally continues the political heritage of fundamentalism in the United States, characterized by a wedding of patriotism (the United States being "this chosen nation") and a pre-millenarian pessimism, often with an accompanying reluctance to confront the social evils in the world.

Even the more progressive evangelicals tend to hold on to a hermeneutics centered on an intentionality theory of meaning. The more liberal members of this group tend to define their position on Scripture by producing nuanced analyses of what part of a biblical author's intent is infallible or subject to the test of error. Jack Rogers and Donald McKim conclude, for example, that Scripture is infallible in its "central saving message" and can err only if a biblical writer willfully intended to lie or to deceive. Clark Pinnock suggests that "the Bible *contains* errors but *teaches* none." While this hermeneutical emphasis dominates even the most progressive evangelical views, it has not gained much of a foothold outside evangelical circles. As a result, debates on related issues often seem peculiar to outsiders.

The evangelical hermeneutical emphasis has remained approximately the same for some time now. It is possible that the controversy surrounding the older issue of "inerrancy" and the role of historical criticism has deepened, as evidenced, for example, by the recent resignation of J. Ramsey Michaels from the faculty of Gordon-Conwell Theological Seminary after twenty-five years of teaching, before a letter of dismissal was drafted by the president, Robert Cooley. That issue turned officially on the question of "the extent to which the methodology of form criticism and/or redaction criticism may be employed in the interpretation of Scripture" that Michaels produced in his book *Servant and Son: Jesus in Parable and Gospel* (John Knox, 1981).[2] While not doubting Michaels's "integrity in signing the [seminary's] Statement of Faith," which included a confession of the "infallibility" of Scripture, the faculty senate found that his interpretation of Scripture too heavily empha-sized the humanity of Christ and that "the benefits of a firm stand on inerrancy were thereby lost."[3] In an immediate response, Michaels stated that

> the Senate's report on my book makes the assumption that inerrancy implies a hermeneutic, or at least a set of certain hermeneutical guide-lines. It is more than a commitment to Scripture's absolute authority and accuracy, with an accompanying commitment to obedience; it also dic-tates to some degree the methods by which Scripture should be interpreted.[4]

2. The quoted material is taken from Cooley's letter dated 28 April 1983.
3. From a letter by Professor Roger Nicole dated 25 March 1983.
4. Michaels, in a letter dated 25 March 1983.

On one level, this debate may indeed seem to be purely one of hermeneutical methods. After all, the faculty senate did not otherwise doubt Michaels's orthodoxy; it stated that it was fully aware that "Prof. Michaels does not wish to impugn or deny the deity of Christ." However, the merely hermeneutical issue also has a distinctly political and theological dimension. On the one hand, the specter of Harold Lindsell surely lies behind the "uneasiness which some people sense toward GCTS to this kind of fluttering hermeneutic"; it was said to pose "a very real threat in *the evangelical constituency* at large and not simply at Gordon-Conwell Theological Seminary."[5] Likewise, Cooley stated that he was concerned about any weakening of the seminary's relation "to numerous evangelical and conservative constituencies." It would seem that the socio-economic future of Gordon is linked to and controlled by a primarily white, North American, fundamentalist/conservative evangelical "constituency" with influence enough to be able to limit what orthodox faculty can write.

On the other hand, it is not an issue merely of "methods" that cross some debatable line among these organized "inerrancy" activists. Michaels was led to acknowledge in his final letter that "I now realize that more is at stake in the issues that divide us than I had at first thought—nothing less, in fact, than the true humanity and historicity of Jesus Christ." In my own opinion, it is not an accident that the only defense for Michaels on the seven-person faculty senate committee came from Professor Stephen Mott, the well-known social ethicist at the seminary. At least in much of traditional Christian theology, and certainly in liberation theology, an emphasis on the humanity of Jesus offers a corrective to a docetic portrayal of the Christ as a heavenly visitor who transcends history and thus does not fully share in the plight of the poor, the oppressed, and the disinherited. A peculiar emphasis on the atonement of Christ leads some believers almost to discount the "human" suffering in his passion story. Such a perspective weakens the degree to which the victims of contemporary Antichrists can, like the apostle Paul, understand themselves to be actually sharing in the suffering of Jesus—who was himself viewed as a political criminal ("king of the Jews") and who on the cross felt himself to be forsaken by his disciples and even by God.

I suspect that on the basis of this hermeneutical perspective, evangelicals are more confident of their theology of culture than of the implicit cultural and political character *of their own theology.* The issue of "inerrancy" in North America—and in Latin America through the influence of evangelical missions—involves more than just a transcultural view of Scripture. It is no more a purely theological topic than "culture" is a purely neutral factor that reflects no claims about ultimate reality. I fear that these debates in the United States have already been exported, along with their political and economic content, to the Latin American evangelical seminaries, and that

5. From Nicole's letter; italics mine.

the missions thus influenced may be seeking to control unduly the biblical hermeneutics and theological creativity within such institutions.

I do not mean to underestimate the resources and the potential of "evangelical" institutions; I mean only to question how adequately those resources have really been used to promote Christianity rather than to appeal to a reactionary "evangelicalism." "Church growth" may itself be disappointing to the degree that it depends primarily on an obfuscation of these same political and economic biases and plays into the prejudices of all those who may confuse the kingdom of God with the white, North American values of the so-called "middle class"—neither too rich nor too poor, neither too political nor too pious.

Of course, there are many voices on the boundary of the northern evangelical establishment. The so-called "young" evangelical activists have begun to explore the extent to which some biblical texts are culturally conditioned in order to secure the liberating message in others. Here I would like to argue that *all* of Scripture is culturally conditioned. Still, the impressive criticism of society by groups such as the Sojourners and the evangelical feminists is a hopeful sign. In a different manner, groups such as the Pentecostals are strongly divided between those who have adopted fundamentalism/evangelicalism (the Assemblies of God is the largest member denomination of the National Association of Evangelicals) and others who have retained a more indigenous approach.

Of course, the Hispanic population in the United States comprises highly diverse nationalities. That portion of the Hispanic population that is Christian is predominantly Roman Catholic, but it also includes strong evangelical and Pentecostal Protestant presences. The situation of Hispanics in the United States is significantly different from that of Hispanics in Latin America. In most of Latin America the Protestant options are not so diverse and public as in the United States. Successful evangelicals have been able to dominate Protestant seminary education in much of Latin America, while in the United States a much greater pluralism may exist, unattached to the presence of a "constituency" from another country. Moreover, North American Hispanics may begin to relate even more easily to black church or Pentecostal/holiness groups than to the politicized evangelical establishment. Evidence of racism and a modernistic form of rationalism within the fundamentalist/evangelical "constituency" has made it more difficult for many black scholars/pastors to identify themselves as "evangelical." In any case, there is reason to hope that North American Hispanics may eventually produce their own fresh perspective, distinct from the indigenous "evangelicalism" of the United States. In this way, the Hispanic community could come to serve as an important bridge between Anglo-Christianity and the confessing church in Latin America.

Evangelicals continue to constitute a significant portion of the population and to make important contributions to the ecumenical church, although I must admit that I do not see many signs of real creativity within evangelicalism as a politicized "continuency." On the other hand, there has been a maturing at most evangelical seminaries in the use of critical methodologies, in an awareness of the social implications of the gospel, and in the energy behind new Bible commentaries. Nevertheless, it remains for even the more ecumenically sensitive North American "evangelicalism" to redefine itself in distinction from its historic ties to fundamentalism. In hermeneutical terms, evangelical options must somehow seek to remain robustly confessional without being politically naive and without implicitly affirming a docetic Scripture, Christ, or nation.

The Hermeneutical Situation among Christians Not Politicized as "Evangelical" in North America

My comments in this area are admittedly highly subjective and selective. But, granting that my observations are by no means evenhanded, I still think some such observations may serve the purposes of this conference.

Perhaps one of the most exciting and mixed situations currently exists in the Roman Catholic church. In light of the more open attitude towards various hermeneutical approaches since Vatican II, a rich plurality of academic theological contributions has flooded the church. It is too soon to know where within this pluralism of fresh analysis the strongest points of consensus will arise. Many older distinctions between Catholics and Protestants in biblical and theological hermeneutics have lost their significance, so that a difference of communions may not be as important as other more general dogmatic issues. Roman Catholic biblical scholars such as Raymond Brown and Roland Murphy are as likely to be mentors of Protestant clergy as their Protestant counterparts in a few ecumenical Protestant seminaries.

Apparently, the emphasis on the teaching magisteria of the Roman Catholic church has often served to protect biblical-critical scholarship from some of the more idiosyncratic impulses found within "liberal" Protestantism. For example, Raymond Brown has on the one hand tried to speak of the "literal sense" of Scripture in terms of the reconstructed intents of the authors and redactors of a given book and has on the other hand spoken of a "canonical sense" as the meaning of that book in the context of the whole of Scripture. This latter sense exceeds the "literal" in much the same way that his earlier use of the concept of *sensus plenior* did: it is his understanding that the teaching of the ongoing church tradition is ever "formative of its [normative] meaning." Similarly, such scholars as David Tracy continue to forge ahead in producing a "fundamental theology," a project that may still seem too apologetic or prone to "natural theology" to many Protestant scholars who in the Biblical Theology movement stood opposed to various social scientific interpretations of the biblical message such as Schleiermacher's "anthropology" on the grounds that they are reductionistic.

I do not pretend to grasp the full range of implications for hermeneutics among Hispanic Roman Catholics in North America. I suspect that the charismatic movement will be attractive to many within this massive group, and in some cases their involvement may lead to the development of a neofundamentalism. However, the cultural and multinational diversity of Hispanic communities in the United States has already given birth to an indigenous "liberation theology" that in some respects parallels, though with its own unique perspective, the black theology movement.

The black church in the United States deserves its own special recognition. James Cone has become perhaps the most incisive, controversial and prolific of the black liberation theologians. He has recently shifted his focus away from polemical analyses of conditions in the United States and developed a multifaceted liberation theology that addresses the concerns of women, Latin Americans, Africans, Asians, and peoples from other parts of the world. Aside from a consistent focus on the social location of the biblical reader and those on whose behalf the gospel speaks most plainly, Cone's biblical interpretation may appear almost precritical. Yet, his Bible is a "text" shared by black laity and ministers alike, not the reconstructed "text" of some historical critic. In this regard he stands in a Barthian or post-Barthian tradition in which the theological interpretation is finally more important than that of technical exegesis.

Such scholars as Gayraud Wilmore, Cecil Cone, and Cornel West, along with many others in the black church, offer fully confessional Christian challenges to white North American biblical scholars and theologians. Their critique in racial, philosophical, and theological interpretation reminds us that biblical interpretation must ever go beyond the limits of the best methods of exegesis—and their critique reminds us that if the gospel as the subject matter of Scripture is ever separated from the the biblical text, it will be rendered just as ineffective for the church as glossolalia separated from the fruits of the spirit. In their critique of the reader they render suspect any North American "modernist" claim to objectivity—whether from fundamentalism to the right or liberalism to the left. I believe that the use of Marx and other postmodern analysis to demystify the situation of the interpreter can be enormously creative and presents one of the most challenging sources for Christian renewal in North America. In saying that, however, I do not mean to underestimate the equally significant new work in church history and other disciplines in which black scholars in particular are breaking new ground.

Again, without getting into particulars, I would like to mention a fresh foment within many sectors of the holiness and Pentecostal communities in North America. Cultural and racial prejudices have traditionally kept these groups out of any direct participation in the older fundamentalist-liberal controversy. My colleague James Washington has suggested that rather than calling these groups "premodern," we might better think of them as "submodern," operating in the lower classes below the social turmoil of the modernist controversy yet accepting elements of it that trickle down to them through popular religious culture. Of course these groups may be prone, like some white Pentecostals, to imitate subsequently the same "orthodoxy" of the fundamentalists that either ignored or condemned them in previous generations. In the past, some Pentecostal groups (especially the Assemblies of God) had hoped that if they could prove their orthodoxy, fundamentalists or conservative evangelicals would come to appreciate Pentecostal views regarding spirit baptism. Ironically, it was the so-called "liberal" denominations that turned out to be the most receptive and that helped usher the charismatic movement into the United States in the 1960s.

Despite a certain poverty of imagination, these "submodern" groups have taken advantage of the fact that they stand on the margins of society and have explored new avenues, in some instances transcending modernist options in a search for alternative models for confessional Christianity. To the extent that they continue to uncover the economic, theological, and political roots of their own neglected histories, they may demonstrate more acumen in ecumenical theology than is typical of politicized "evangelicals" and thereby make increasingly significant contributions to the theology and hermeneutical understanding of Christian faith. Because of the multiracial character of these churches, the growing number of scholars coming from their ranks, the relationship they often have with the churches among the lower classes, and their closeness to certain massive international forms of Christianity among the poor, I think that their significance for the future of biblical and theological hermeneutics is worthy of note.

Finally, I should say a few words about other hermeneutical debates commonplace at the American Academy of Religion and the Society of Biblical Literature. If in the last century the universities were often considered to stand in the shadow of the more prestigious seminaries, the opposite is now the case. "Divinity schools" that were originally the most honored part of a university have been forced to rethink the legitimacy of their offering Christian ministerial training within a public institution that is in every other sense pluralistic. Standards of competence in various disciplines prerequisite for theological discourse may be controlled by the university and taught to prospective seminary teachers in university Ph.D. programs in religion. Accordingly, the seminary teacher can postpone certain church confessional work almost indefinitely while seeking through publications to gain a reputation as a competent scholar under the particular academic and pluralistic terms put forward by the university. For these reasons one no longer finds among the academy of professional theologians in the 1980s the high percentage of pastor/theologians typical in the previous century.

The fact that the life of churches and their pragmatic needs are relegated to a secondary importance in this fashion may account in part for the theological and pastoral dullness of much modern commentary. Such treatment would also seem to invite a reductionism of theology in terms of public discourse about its political, sociological, philosophical, or historical value. It becomes easy to view Scripture either as one text among many in a study of comparative religious canons or as a literary "classic" within the body of Western or ancient Near Eastern literature. Though some serious theological questions should be raised about this tendency in seminary education, we should note that it has not been without some substantial benefits as well. Theological hermeneutics will no longer let piety compensate for slipshod use of the disciplines it shares with the university. It is forced to be the "queen of the sciences" in a real sense rather than merely a privatized discipline within the church. The university has challenged theologians to demystify their language and see the material and social implications of God-talk from the perspective of the world. From a hermeneutical perspective, we must indeed recognize that the goal of a rich and efficacious theological interpretation of biblical texts can be lost just as surely by uncritical piety as it can be forfeited to the historicism of some modern critical methods. At the same time, the elitism of the universities (especially the ivy league schools) and the theological myopia of these concerns may introduce almost as many problems as it tends to solve.

For the above reasons, I want to suggest three "descriptive" directions within the university/seminary debates over hermeneutics that have held special promise in North America in the last few decades. Behind this highly subjective survey lies my assumption that the older Biblical Theology movement is essentially dead, surviving only in a handful of evangelical seminaries. Its hermeneutical consensus, first delineated by J. H. Gabler in the eighteenth century—namely, that there is a clear difference between what a text "meant" (so-called "biblical theology") and what a text "means" (dogmatic or systematic theology)—no longer rules our thinking. The largely negative postmodern critique has, with the aid of Freud, Nietzsche, and Marx, dismantled the "historicism" of a now dated "neo-orthodoxy." Frank Lentricchia's description of the situation in literary criticism is easily applicable to the hermeneutical circumstances current in biblical and theological studies: he characterizes the past two decades as a period that is "the richest and most confusing in our critical history." Because the seminary is linked to the university disciplines as we have noted, it shares in this richness and confusion.

The aspect of contemporary hermeneutics I'd like to consider first is the disarray in the canons of the historical pragmatism touted as typically "American" that has resulted during the past two decades from the arrival of a semiotic shock wave generated in large part by the French (e.g., C. Levi-Strauss, R. Barthes, and F. de Saussure) but also by renewed attention to older philosophers of language (e.g., Kierkegaard and Wittgenstein). This assault on the theories of intentionality and on the idea that the meaning of a text lies primarily in its reference to a world of the really real outside of the text—the world in which the symbols of the text must find their "translation"—has led to a confusing variety of "literary" approaches to the Bible and theology. The fresh attention to the Bible given by major literary critics (e.g., N. Frye and F. Kermode) has stimulated similar conversation among more theological critics in the areas of narrative analysis (e.g., H. Frei, R. Ricoeur, and S. Hauerwas), rhetorical criticism (e.g., P. Trible and W. Holladay), structuralism (e.g., D. Patte and R. Polzin), and so forth. At a minimum this is leading to a rediscovery of the aesthetic dimension in Scripture (as witness, for example, R. Alter's *The Art of Biblical Narrative*) and a fresh appreciation for the "story" of Scripture as its own closed system of signs with its own message. In positive terms, we can once more read the biblical text without having to atomize it into various antiquarian units of ancient tradition. How well these approaches illuminate the biblical text *theologically* remains highly controversial. At least potentially, the Bible could belong as a story to the public discourse of literary criticism at the university and as a religious text to the poor, who could compete to illuminate its meaning alongside the privileged scholar.

Another equally significant set of hermeneutical approaches entails the recent application of social scientific methods to the biblical text and the ancient world. We might roughly distinguish typological or "functionalist" anthropological-sociological interpretation from perspectives giving more emphasis to class struggle (e.g., Marxist), which seek to assess the material ramifications of social change. Examples of functionalist interpretation can be found in the new work on the phenomenology of ancient Israelite prophecy (e.g., that of R. Wilson and D. Peterson), on the role of women in the Bible (e.g., that of P. Bird), on the social determinants within peasant society (e.g., that of H. Kee and B. Malina), on the underlying causes behind apocalyptic thought (e.g., that of P. Hanson and R. P. Carroll), and so forth. The most significant work in the class struggle approaches has been done by such scholars as N. Gottwald in Old Testament studies (on a revolutionary premonarchial Israel) and G. Thiessen in New Testament studies (on the role of early Christians as wandering radicals). These studies tend to move away from the Bible per se to the ancient world that gave rise to it, a world that is often obscured in the later formation of a scriptural canon. The obvious strength in this investigation is its ability to vivify an ancient world, to cause us to see again a real world of flesh and blood people like ourselves who were subject to the social and political conditions in their day as we are subject to the conditions in ours. The effect may be to humanize the Bible against any docetic assumption that it may have suddenly dropped into our hands from heaven. Some of the more radical implications of early Israelite and Christian faith may indeed have been lost or ignored in the formation of Scripture. At the very least, vague and perplexing texts take on more clarity when, for example, we realize that an emphasis on honor and shame in a peasant society underlies its choice of religious vocabulary and laws. These insights check the synchronic enthusiasm of semiotic interpretation by showing how the biblical traditions, even in the context of a normative Scripture, still reflect the material culture in the ancient Near East, even as we might want it to address our own material culture. This kind of reading can clearly be helpful in exposing the sorts of political and sociological assumptions that have been retained in the Bible, but of course it could also be argued that as "biblical" interpretation it often becomes a highly technical and speculative reconstruction of an ancient world that in and of itself is not canonized as a normative guide within the faith of Judaism and Christianity.

Finally, I see great potential in the fresh effort to describe how Scripture was shaped by and has functioned as the bread of life within the major religions of Christianity and Judaism. Wilfred C. Smith has helped this discussion by his work in comparative religions, as has James Sanders in his "comparative midrashic" studies under the theme of "canon criticism." Above all, Brevard Childs has sought to raise radically new questions about how Scripture has meaning within a community of faith. I am closely associated with Childs in this inquiry. We have both been trying to describe the shape or edited character of biblical books in which noncanonical traditions became contextually viewed as a Scripture. In one sense, we have taken up Bonhoeffer's question regarding the Psalter: how can the ordinary words of human prayer to God become God's word to me?

A wide variety of scholars (e.g., R. Clements, R. Brown, and P. Ackroyd) has begun to consider some of these same issues. We have attempted to show the way in which a canonical context can change the meaning of earlier traditions, even to invite a reading against an author's original intent. I have argued, for example, that there is evidence of "canon-conscious redactions," which imply the reader is to hold together, in a common context, books not originally written or edited to be read together. So, for instance, Luke's hellenistic memoir about Jesus is subsequently read as a "Gospel" and the deutero-Pauline epistles present a Paul informed by these later developments in early Christianity. In this sense, to separate out the original letters of Paul from deutero-Pauline letters is implicitly to decanonize Paul's genuine letters. In our attempts to describe this new vision of the biblical text, we may have erred by blurring at times the descriptive with a theologically prescriptive formula for interpretation and perhaps sounded too pejorative in our estimation of traditional historical criticism. A "canonism" will certainly be no less reductionistic than the very "historicism" to which it seeks to offer a corrective. Our concern is that historical criticism not be a pretentious theory that ends interpretation with a pious reading of a reconstructed history rather than offering a historical reading of a constructed text.

As one with my roots both in Pentecostal communities and in an ecumenical seminary, my theological hope is for hermeneutical proposals that allow the biblical text to be competitively illuminated by both intellectuals and laity, both the university-trained and the life-trained, both the privileged and the poor. Far too often the scholar not only claims an elite understanding but substitutes for the Bible of the church a speculatively reconstructed text that only the academy can possess. I think that in our present "postmodern" search for a new hermeneutical future, we may be able to turn again to the older debates in church history over the nature of what constitutes the "literal sense" (*sensus literalis, sensus proprius,* or plain sense) of the Bible. We may ask in a different, postmodern manner the most basic questions of how a text of Scripture has a "context" at all. From this vision of a "canonical context" we can begin to find help to govern the dialectical relationship between the synchronic and the diachronic dimensions of a "Scripture" within Christianity. In this task we are helped by both the literary critical and the anthropological-sociological approaches.

My own proposal calls for more sociological, anthropological, and economic demystification of both the ancient world, out of which the Bible received its shape, and of our own communities of faith. This demystification should help us acknowledge the pragmatic theological-political terms by which we each look through a darkened glass to find our way in the world. At the same time, it is finally a Scripture that provides the common arena in which, as Christians, we do theology. For me, one of the most basic hermeneutic issues concerns how one uses the results of social scientific analysis of texts in order to illuminate a given biblical context without simply atomizing it into various subtexts. Another, perhaps more significant, matter involves the liberation theologian's demystification of the interpreter. For whom you do your theology may indeed be more important initially than how you do it. Our sisters and brothers in Latin America have helped many of us become aware of the blindness that, because of the poverty of our own cultural and racial history, limits our theological exegesis. When our hermeneutical speculation must cease and interpretation must begin, we again are left to pray in the fear of God that the Holy Spirit will lead us to the source of all truth, to which even Scripture is but a human witness.

1.1.4

Response to Sheppard by C. René Padilla

Jerry has taken into account the main trends in hermeneutical thinking in the U.S. I do agree that the history of evangelicalism in the U.S. seems to be largely determined by the fundamentalism/liberalism controversy. Unfortunately, much of what is going on in terms of theological thinking in Latin America bears the same mark. I was interested to hear that theology in the States is largely ideologically conditioned. That is quite a finding for an evangelical. In Latin America of course we are quite used to hearing that kind of thing, but it seems to me that not many evangelicals in the U.S. would begin to recognize it. And because of that, much of what is going on in the name of theology does not really challenge people to obedience to Jesus Christ. Such theology is often developed in evangelical circles to help people feel good with the status quo. Middle-class evangelicalism has its own particular way of rationalizing all kinds of reactionary positions.

I would have liked to hear about the influence that Latin American theology has in the U.S. I know that several liberation theologians, for instance, have been translated and published, and that they do have some kind of influence. Jerry could have helped us by discussing this.

Toward the end, a number of issues were raised that I would love to discuss during this conference. We have ourselves seen the tremendous importance of interdisciplinary theological reflection. That is one of the main emphases in the context of the Latin American Theological Fraternity. Those of you who come from the North may be interested to know that not all the members of the Theological Fraternity are theologians in the classical sense by any means. In fact, a number of our members are professional people who are trying to think theologically within a specific field of humanities.

And finally, just one observation on the matter of making theology more an enterprise in which both the "laity" and the clergy or the professional theologians are engaged: in Latin America we have no other choice. Very, very few people have the theological training to do the kind of theological exercise that entertains many Americans. We are forced into relating—

constantly relating—theology to life, to the practical life of the church. Because of that, we have emphasized the importance of the whole of the church becoming a theological community. People must learn to think theologically. Theology does not belong to an elite.

1.1.5

Discussion

Costas: Number one, evangelical hermeneutics as Samuel has described it—that's Samuel's formulation. There's been a lot of discussion in Latin America in the last two years at least. People right here in this very room have been engaged in hermeneutical thinking, and unfortunately that has not come through in the paper. I think we should bear that in mind. The evangelical question with regard to hermeneutics in Latin America is not closed. It's very much open.

Second, liberation hereneutics is a vital issue for us, and that has not been mentioned by Samuel. And in that connection, we should note that the input of base communities—particularly the poor and the oppressed, as interlocutors in relationship to the biblical text, to the preached text, to the reflected text—is a major issue in evangelical hermeneutics. Liberation hermeneutics is a major issue for us in Latin America, especially in light of the situation in Nicaragua and the recent events in Granada. That is critical.

Cummings: I would simply like to make a comment and then perhaps raise a question with Samuel Escobar and any others within the Latin American Fraternity who are meeting here. Samuel seems to indicate in his paper that one of the central contradictions within Latin American life is the issue of Catholicism and Protestantism. He identifies it as perhaps the most central in his paper. And since the question of the relationship between the text and the context has been raised by Gerald Sheppard in a very cogent way, and since I have just three days ago returned from a ten-day meeting in Cuba on the Latin American reality, I want to ask this question: What is the social context of Latin America? Of course, it's a rhetorical question. And what is the central contradiction that shapes, defines, or conditions the Christians in Latin America as they approach the text?

Pinnock: I would like to put before people the possibility that there's a new racism right here. It seems that no fairness is required in speaking of people. Sheppard is in effect, of course, hating his own white, North, Anglo-Saxon background. I don't hate it. I think there's a new racism in the world and it has to be faced here. If you want to talk about liberation and justice, then show a little justice to the people you are assaulting here in the beginning of this paper. I wish there was some doxology here. This conference has started with controversy rather than doxology. We should have praised God together first.

Cummings: You're saying Jerry Sheppard hates himself?

Pinnock: I'm getting the message that you can say anything you like about successful white Anglo-Saxon Protestants without caring about justice or honesty. They evidently don't deserve much fairness. Just my feeling.

Stam: From the perspective of Central America, I find important Samuel's comment about the community in which the Scripture is read, interpreted, and believed. Because I find in our experience in general through Central America there does not exist a hermeneutical community—that is, there aren't any common criteria for understanding Scripture. This has two consequences. One is an orgy of arbitrary interpretation: it is virtually impossible to bring minds and interpretations together in a framework of understanding about principles and methods. Second, in the Latin America situation there has been a good bit of attention paid to linguistic theory, as Jerry suggests in his paper. But another aspect of great importance is the sociology of knowledge. This helps us understand that every interpretation *in* Scripture and *after* Scripture is brought to expression within the context of society, within a particular social and historic situation. I think this throws some light on the question whether the issue is Catholic/Protestant or modernist/fundamentalist. Behind it all is a historical situation, a human situation, and a sociological situation. It's significant that right at this moment, in light of all the situations that Orlando mentioned, situations that we bleed over every day in Nicaragua, extreme fundamentalism is resurgent—not for theological or hermeneutical reasons but for *social* reasons. This is certainly not to say that sociological exegesis should take the place of historical or grammatical exegesis, but it is a factor that we must be very much aware of.

Nuñez: I believe that the purpose of Sheppard's paper is to help us know more about what's going on in the northern part of America. So I think that for me it is very profitable to listen to this discussion on hermeneutics. At the same time, as Orlando said, we need to listen more to what's going on in Latin America. As John Stam says, there is a revival of fundamentalism in Nicaragua. There is a also revival of traditional nineteenth-century Roman Catholicism in Guatemala. Especially after the visit of the Pope, when posters and papers said "Blessed is the one who comes in the name of the Lord." Evangelicals are considered to be members of sects by the Catholics. We are supposed to come back to mother church.

Stam: I wasn't speaking only about Nicaragua; there's also El Salvador and many other countries. But for me it's even more significant that the same kind of resurgence is occurring in the Catholic Church. And I thoroughly agree with your analysis. We saw in the newspaper a full-page picture of

John Paul II and no other text than this: "I am the way, the truth, and the life." And there is also a sociology of knowledge behind all of that. They're parallel tracks, Protestantism and Catholicism. I don't see them as exclusively antagonistic.

Cummings: I'm not an expert on Central America. I watched the videotape of the Pope's visit to Nicaragua. There is real disagreement about whether the people, the laity of the Catholic Church, are behind the Pope. Within the Catholic Church there is much division with respect to whether the Pope is the way, the truth, and the life. Many of the people stand more consistently with Daniel Ortega, who has associated himself with the struggle of the poor people.

Stam: Actually, Nicaragua is the one exception here. The Pope was received with virtual adoration in every other country. The only country where he was challenged so frontally was Nicaragua.

Costas: I think we should also be paying attention to the Spanish north of the border. Jerry Sheppard was pointing in that direction. The hermeneutical task is closely linked with very complex social, cultural, and religious traditions. From the point of view of evangelicals, we have barely begun to raise the question of how all of that affects the understanding of the message. For example, here in Mexico and north of the border, you don't have to go very far without interacting, confronting, or being confronted by the cult of Guadalupe. Guadalupe is *it* in Mexico and in the Mexican-American setting. Of course some of Jerry's references to the indigenous Catholic discussion are related to the place of Guadalupe in the new Catholic hermeneutic. But we have yet to come to terms with that.

There is a good deal of significance for Mexican history in Guadalupe, this Aztec woman who represents the Virgin Mary, the Virgin Mary with a face of an Aztec Indian speaking the native tongue—a symbol of the mestizos, the mixture that emerges from the conquering Spanish and the aboriginal community. For a theologian such as Virgilio Elizondo it constitutes a hermeneutical nucleus. Evangelicals are very concerned about evangelizing in the Mexican-American culture, and yet they have not raised the question of what Guadalupe means in relation to the interpretation of the gospel. And the same sort of thing is true throughout the Caribbean. Bill Spencer has done some work on the Rastafarian movement, which is important in the black community of Jamaica (at least in Philadelphia) as well as to the people of the eastern Caribbean—Cuba, the Dominican Republic, and Puerto Rico. The whole world of santaría and the African religious motif has decisively affected the way the people perceive the gospel.

I think that we in the Latin American world, the Hispanic world, the Afro-Caribbean world, need to play close attention to the narrative aspect of the gospel. That is already determining the people's perception of the text, and it should be determining our approach as theologians. The academic theology of North America gives us theoretical tools but does not enable us to have the kind of encounter that is decisive for the understanding of the Word of God for today.

Within six months we will be here in Mexico to help evangelical theologians of the Two Thirds World deal with "the Spirit and the spirits." To what extent do we find in contemporary spirituality a point of contact, a point for discussion with, say, white evangelical theology in North America? Those in the established evangelical mainstream and in the Pentecostal mainstream have tried to emphasize the Holy Spirit in regeneration and in piety, or in praise and worship.

Watson: I would agree with that with two provisos. Several comments have stuck with me during the presentation of the papers and the responses. The first was Jerry Sheppard's very astute insight that too many of our schools of theology in North America are tied into university settings that predetermine all of our curricula. That was just a *crie de coeur* for me. Then there was the comment René made to the effect that many Latin American theologians are not equipped to do the sort of theology that entertains people in the North. I like your use of the word *entertain*. It does help to pass the time, and I think this touches on a very important point. But I am concerned, Orlando, about the fact that you seem to criticize North American theology because it appears to work from the top rather than from the grass roots. This is an important critical insight that comes from Latin American theology, which listens more to the grass roots than North America does. But if North America were to listen to its own grass roots, we'd be listening to precisely the things that offend Latin Americans. There is the sort of popular piety that gives a Jerry Falwell such a large following. This is an issue I'd like us to get into this week: Why is it that Latin American theologians listen to the grass roots and come up with something that at least at first glance appears to be more authentically scriptural than we would get from listening to the grass roots of North America?

Cummings: René's comment about the impact of liberation theology on U.S. evangelicalism again touches on the point that Jerry raised and that many theologians in Latin America and North America have been raising in recent years. When we speak of U.S. evangelicalism, Orlando has pointed out that we have to specify *which* evangelicalism. The black churches, the Hispanic churches, have always been deeply evangelical institutions, but they have never been identified with the mainstream evangelicalism of, say, the National Association of Evangelicals or Wheaton. The reference to grass roots raises the question about social locations which Jerry identified. Again, the question is which grass roots? Black theologians have been theologizing from the grass roots of our community. And it's not just piety; its liberating theology, coming out of the eighteenth century, critical of the ideological status of Christianity in the North America. Why haven't we been listening to that? And it would be appropriate to ask whether U.S. evangelicalism has been affected at all by Latin American liberation theology. I think that in many cases North American theologians view Latin American liberation theology as a passing fad.

Mercadante: I'd like to add something that seems obvious to me but might not seem obvious to other people: another grass-roots group that obviously isn't being listened to is women. A good deal of theology has been coming out of that group for at least a hundred years, and probably much longer— probably through the whole history of the church. There was, for instance, Julian of Norwich. She was lucky: some people read her work. But there are all the other millions of women we don't know about whose work was not read or heard. That's grass-roots too.

We were talking about evangelism earlier and I said that I was interested in evangelization to women who are alienated from the church. David Watson said that he thought they amounted to only a tiny bit of the audience, that they didn't constitute a majority. I understood what you're saying about what you get out of whichever grass-roots group you're studying. There are other sectors of grass-roots groups in North America that have already provided that kind of liberation theology. But unfortunately so many of these people haven't been listened to. This is not as much of a problem in the black church as it is with women in particular. We are atomized, and often attached to the leadership of some man. Because we're separated like that, our voices get separated too. I think the black church has been able to move as they have because they've been together.

Watson: I wasn't dismissing the alienation of women from the church as something that did not merit attention. Rather, I was saying that a more immediate priority was to evangelize all the women who are in the church but who don't grasp their grass-roots affliction.

Mercadante: I'm concerned that many women are leaving the church.

Gutiérrez-Cortés: We have two basic problems with criteria. One criterion is need and the other is relation. Hermeneutics has been done on the basis of need or necessity. That's why we think of liberation or blackness or feminism, or family in the case of my church: we've been thinking in terms of need. But it seems to me that in the Bible, especially in the Old Testament, we find the criteron of shalom—a *relation* criterion, involving your relation with God and with your neighbor. And in the New Testament we find the criterion of reconciliation, which is again a relation criterion. And I think that both of these can be joined into a single criterion, a pastoral criterion, concerned with restoration in all aspects. Such a criterion, I think, could mediate between need and relation.

Gil: It seems to me from the discussion that we are in danger of absolutizing certain contexts. In the papers presented, the question of the role of Jesus Christ and of the very nature of the God he reveals has, as a hermeneutical center, been somewhat obscure. I think this is especially a danger in the Brevard Childs school, which ends up giving us an almost flat Bible. We cannot overlook the way in which the crucified and resurrected Jesus stands over against our context endorsing and judging it. And that judging and saving comes in different ways in different contexts. If we absolutize the Bible, or even speak of it in terms of either the North American or the Latin American context—and I am speaking as one who comes from outside both contexts—it seems to me that we flatten the Bible. We simply omit the endless problem of judgment and salvation. For example, concerning Samuel's paper, I would want to question whether it is true that all theology begins in praise. It may also begin in lament. Lament is as legitimate a theological context as praise and doxology. 1 Peter is written from a persecuted church. Revelation, which has most of the worship material of the New Testament, was written within a peresecuted church. The gospel of Luke probably comes out of a persecuted church. And if we look at a book written from the other side, from within a successful church, such as the gospel of Mark, it certainly does not do theology within the context of praise. Quite the contrary. Therefore, I think, Scripture itself gives pointers to the hermeneutics we should be proceeding with. The role of Jesus Christ as crucified and risen Lord, especially for evangelicals, is something we ignore or take for granted at our peril.

Hays: I have a concern of a different kind regarding Clark's comment, which was simply allowed to fall like a brick and was then ignored. It seems to me that, if I understood him, he felt personally offended and assaulted by some things that were said here. I'd like to know whether it was soley Jerry Sheppard's paper that did that. Jerry isn't here, so we cannot deal with reconciliation at the moment, if that's what is needed. If there are other things, we've got to clear the air among ourselves before we can talk about hermeneutics. Could you respond to that?

Pinnock: Yes, it was Jerry's remark. I know Jerry and I've heard him, before. I have found Christian reality within the evangelical groups he's talking about. I know its easy to assault such groups and make fun of them, to present shallow criticisms that suggest that all their problems are painfully obvious. But there is genuine Christianity there, too. I try to serve my Christ. I love my God. I don't read theology for entertainment. Critics must be careful. I think there's a kind of racism in assuming that nothing clearly supportive needs to be said about certain people, in the fact that the deadliest accusations can be made and there will be applause all around. I know we're guilty of other things, so maybe I should say nothing. But I would encourage caution. Yes, I was responding to Jerry's paper.

Cummings: One question, Clark. Did you feel that he misunderstood you in the summary he made? Was that a quotation from you—the quotation to the effect that the Bible contains errors, but teaches none?

Pinnock: No, I confess to saying that. I'm not referring to his comments about me. I'm troubled by the way he handled the whole topic, suggesting that inerrancy is just politics. I think he trivializes much and puts the issues in the worst possible light. These concerns deserve more sympathy.

Cummings: I'm sorry. I know Jerry too, and I don't think he hates who he is. He was trying to point to some important issues that have been obscured for a long time in the history of theology. We are all Christians here. This is not a personal issue. I am not here to make racist comments. For me, the issue is the gospel of Jesus Christ, and I think that's the issue for all of us. I think Jerry was trying to get at the political status of evangelical religion in North America and the fact that evangelicals have ignored this issue for an awfully long time.

Costas: Which is how Samuel concludes. I just wish he would have said more on that. That's part of our context. The questions we are asking concern evangelicalism, context, hermeneutics, and politics. I think that is also a part of our reality here at this conference. Clark's statement on racism was politically charged. I want to be able to deal with it. And I want him to have the freedom to say it. I want to have the freedom to be able to confront it, but not in a personal way. We want to deal with it in relationship to the fundamental issue we're dealing with: context and hermeneutics. I think this is very important, because we have a very pluralistic evangelical group here, even among the individuals from North America. Some of us are minority evangelicals, and we need to have the opportunity to say, "Hey, you're not speaking for me." That also has to be brought in from the Latin American side. It is very important also to say that Latin Americans are not a homogeneous unit. We are talking about hermeneutics and context *in the Americas,* and believe me there are other Americans than those who carry a blue passport. If we can focus discussion in that direction, I think we will find an exceptional richness.

Branson: In closing this evening, I would like to pick it up on another thing Clark said that we should have taken up earlier—worship. We have some English hymnbooks, and Spanish hymnals arrive tomorrow. In the morning, before we start our small groups, let's have some time of praise and singing. May I also suggest now that we have a few prayers offered and then have the Lord's Prayer together as a way to close our day and request that the work of the kingdom be done among us.

[*Editor's note:* The following discussion took place later in the week. It is included here because it takes up issues covered in the first day's discussion.]

Sheppard: The biblical scholar cannot avoid church history, even contemporary church history, because he or she must understand the sociology of the various denominations and the ecumenical challenge. There's no escape; there's no sanctuary for the sort of antiquarian discipline that allows some people to shut themselves away in closets and miraculously work out a whole mature theology and church. There has been a breakdown of this old definition of biblical theology. Within the last couple of decades the situation in biblical and theological studies has seemed to become quite chaotic. The heritage of that old compartmentalized system has ensured that in many cases there has been very little conversation between church historians, theologians, and biblical scholars in the U.S. Many of us wish to encourage a new sense of the interdisciplinary task. We also wish to recover some of what was present in the sort of seminaries that used to meet in pastors' homes. The task of biblical studies must be tied to the ministry of real people, to the need of those who are in pain, who need to hear a word of hope and liberation from the Scripture.

Universities frequently dictate the criteria of excellence for the seminaries. You may have a different situation here, but there are some rough similarities in ways the universities govern accreditation and a young scholar has to meet those criteria. How long do you postpone the whole task of theological exegesis in order to get credentials from the departments that govern your future as a young scholar? This is not to say that there are no good points to the process. Theology in the old rich sense is not opposed to the university but somehow wants to master the university disciplines and stand with a larger claim upon the whole body of truth. So we continue to look for ways to do that with some integrity.

It is fascinating to me that the situation in the U.S. is in such chaos and foment. The old modernist distinctions between fundamentalist and liberal have severely eroded. The labels do not work very well anymore. I don't know what to call myself any longer. When I went to Union to teach, I had a whole string of modified adjectives. I called myself a noncharismatic, neo-Pentecostal, young evangelical, erstwhile neo-orthodox postmodern biblical scholar. How do you choose a correct title to locate yourself? There are lots of surprises now. George Cummings, a black evangelical theologian who studied at Gordon-Conwell and at Union, is here at these meetings. James Forbes, a black Pentecostal preacher of the highest caliber in the U.S., is at Union. It's just unpredictable who you'll find doing what in many institutions in the U.S. I think that's a hopeful sign. It might challenge some of the unhealthful connections within the Americas between the more conservative evangelical groups and many mission groups. Here I am venturing into issues that many of you can articulate far better concerning the long history of the benefits and liabilities of the mission enterprises from the U.S.

I should note that my sister and her husband have been independent Pentecostal missionaries here in Mexico for about fifteen years. Her husband is what I call a "John Wayne missionary." He loves being in the mission field with his own donkey. I am aware of the anti-intellectualism in such groups. He once told me, "Jerry, I have no use for commentaries." That did disappoint me. So I tried to explain. "Sometimes you must preach some pretty good sermons," I said. "Have you ever thought about taking all the sermons on a given book and putting them into a collection to share with others? That would make a fine commentary!" So I am aware of the anti-intellectualism and anti-education dimensions of many of the Pentecostal groups. I have a kind of love-hate relationship with my own tradition.

In the U.S. I have had to struggle in studying what I am calling now the politics of exegesis. I want to know what creates the poverty of imagination in certain communities that allows certain hermeneutical proposals to be acceptable and others not, or certain political postures to be acceptable while others are not. The Assemblies of God, a white Pentecostal group, was condemned by evangelicals in 1929 along with all modern Pentecostalism. Then it was invited to become a member denomination of the National Association of Evangelicals in 1942. The Assemblies had been protesting for years that it was really orthodox in hopes of convincing the fundamentalists to become Pentecostal. Of course, it turned out that the liberal mainstream was more inclined to join via the charismatic movement in the sixties. The Pentecostals chose the wrong crowd. But after joining the NAE, the Assemblies then formed the Pentecostal Fellowship of North America (PFNA) along with other Pentecostal groups, and that organization turned out to be lily white. A black denomination applied for membership and was turned down.

I am saddened by the history of these relationships. Pentecostal groups were first condemned by the fundamentalist-evangelical groups. As a young student out of Bible college, I could not have attended such schools as Talbot or Dallas Theological Seminary, because these conservative evangelical seminaries would not receive Pentecostals. Now things have changed. Pentecostal students are the second or third largest group present at Fuller Theological Seminary. However, when I look at the background of my own Pentecostal heritage, I believe there has been a kind of selling out. We are losing the connection with the black church, the shared fellowship with a much more multiracial, multiclass reality. And now the Assemblies of God have become "orthodox." They're more fundamentalist than the fundamentalists. Their politics are as far to the right as anyone's, and as white too. I am fascinated by this whole situation, and much of it I lament.

One last historical example. The Assemblies of God, like most Pentecostal groups, did not originally adopt dispensational eschatology. Later, however, in order "to get righteous" with the fundamentalists, they became dispensationalists and condemned all teachings that didn't advocate dispensational interpretation. This led to the current dispensationalist excuse for building up nuclear arms. The United States is a special angel to Israel, and the final battle of history will be fought in Armageddon, not here. So we've been told by Pat Robertson of The 700 Club that we should contribute to their buildings in Virginia because they'll still be standing in the millennium, thanks in part to the nuclear buildup in the U.S. The politics of the Assemblies, their perception of the world, and their sense of the future for the U.S. are governed by the poverty of imagination they inherited from the rigid dispensationalism of fundamentalism.

When I look at the situation in the Americas, it is easy to understand why we need a clearer sociological understanding of these denominations. I find it painful to realize that there's so little conversation in Latin America between Baptists and Pentecostals. How unecumenical evangelicalism is here! And I suspect that some of that is an inheritance from the U.S. missions system. Through money, through the public relations needed to hold the trophy up high in the U.S., these boards encourage the isolation and fragmentation of the Christian community. I speak here only as an amateur looking over the fence.

I will end on this note: I am delighted to talk here with Steve Reid, because many of us have been wrestling with the current situation in biblical hermeneutics in the U.S. We are trying to find the greater signs of hope. In the United States, we have a reaction against modernism, against a kind of historicism that tries to control the text with a high-powered antiquarian method of analysis. If the fundamentalists erred in elevating the words of Jesus by printing them in red, we biblical scholars have erred just as excessively by putting every doublet in italics and letting it promptly disappear from the commentary, creating an alternative text purified from late redactional hands. When Hugo Gressmann, the protege of Herman Gunkel, sat down to write his commentaries on 1 and 2 Kings, he placed before him not the canonical 1 and 2 Kings but rather the latest oral level of the reconstructed narrative. We have not only dismissed history of interpretation, but in some ways we've dismissed the biblical text itself. The challenges for many of us come not only from the postmodern critique of that kind of commentary, but also from the churches that have the Bible. They stand in need of interpretation of a text they already have, not a better text than the one they have. One of the new challenges facing all of us in biblical studies is the question of what is going to replace these high-powered antiquarian methods in the postmodern period.

I believe we need what we might call a "canon-textual approach"—that is, an approach that tries to honor the context of a scripture within a faith. On one level it can be understood simply. On another level, it is a tremendous challenge intellectually to the disciplines that we now have in our seminaries. It rejects the proposition that a scholar has to create an alternative text every time he or she begins with the Bible. And it entails more than simply responding to a postmodern critique—something that's important to those like me who come from a Pentecostal background. It's a matter of having a common text that one shares with the poor. We don't want to enter this new phase in a way that is precritical or that denies the gifts that God has given us within this modern period, with all its great advances in medicine, literature, and hermeneutics. But at the same time, we don't want to turn the Bible into some kind of icon or deity. That sort of move would put an end to the conversation with the very churches that led us into this whole thing in the first place.

Pinnock: Jerry, I felt that you treated my evangelical community unfairly in your paper, but I like what you said here; it was more helpful. I think a reading of the Gordon-Conwell situation in the best way shows that we're concerned with this text too, this canonical text—concerned that it not be lost sight of or compromised. You read the Gordon-Conwell affair in the worst possible light—that's all.

Sheppard: Well, I purposely, self-consciously, did that, partly because I'm troubled by the price the Assemblies of God has paid in their attempt to "get orthodox." I see that as evidence of a kind of right-wing modernism that I can't help but reject. I don't see it as hopeful or helpful for the future. I am frankly suspicious of much evangelical talk about hermeneutics and theology. Again, I am generalizing too much in my use of the term *evangelical*. I am not including, in fact, people around this table in much of what I am saying. But when many evangelicals talk about hermeneutics or a theology of culture that involves talk about evaluating the demonic or the propitious in culture, they often don't recognize that the commitment to infallibility limits how well they can do the job. If our highest affirmation of Scripture is always a double negative, it makes me worry a little. It is politically loaded, and our recognition of those politics is missing in these discussions. It's as if this was just a battle over the issue of how many methods can be applied to what text. It's not that to me at all. It really is a matter of the humanity of Jesus Christ, of the humanity of the Bible, against a docetic view. I am equally frustrated by the National Council of Churches' lectionary, which, by omitting the maleness of Jesus, has created a docetic Christology. To my way of thinking, they're the fundamentalists of the left. I'm bothered and bored by both.

Osborne: That's what I would like to elaborate on, Jerry. I think that every ideology is politically motivated—but politically motivated in terms of exclusivistic answers. It occurs in every field, in every school. Every one of us has come from traditions. And we're in danger of creating a new ideology of purity even in what we're trying to do here.

Sheppard: Sure. I know. We're in danger of creating another kind of right consensus. But if we do that using wisdom and fear of God, aware of the frailness of our human effort rather than blind to it or purposely mystifying it, I believe we can help. We cannot simply continue to pretend that this is merely a hermeneutical issue.

Osborne: Yes, and that's why I wouldn't want to categorize the issue of inerrancy as a major problem—because there are many inerrantists who are trying to do just what you are saying.

Sheppard: Right—Ramsay Michaels is one.

Osborne: Exactly.

Sheppard: And that is the problem. You're certainly right. In that sense I even recognize that at Union I may find my confessional loyalties in different places than some of my colleagues. One's own personal history may make it difficult to cast one's lot with a given group. The PFNA is a good example. I would argue they inherited from the NAE both their faith statements (to which they simply added a spirit-baptism statement) and their inclination to reject black Pentecostals.

Hubbard: I wonder, Jerry, if you could comment on what you mean specifically by the politics of the Gordon-Conwell situation. It seems to me that you used the term "politics" in a different way.

Sheppard: In the letters from both Bob Cooley and Roger Nicole there is a rather striking appeal to this "evangelical constituency." Let's define that constituency. Who is this vague constituency? And then we must ask a hard Christian question. That constituency deserves our pastoral care, love, and ministry. But where do we draw the line between diplomacy and hypocrisy? We must raise the question in order to prevent it from becoming any more clouded than it already is. I want to know where the constituency is and put that on the table. Is Harold Lindsell behind it? The Board of Trustees? We can talk about some concrete things. Talk about politics! Nothing could be more political than Harold Lindsell's books. This affects all of the Americas. Nothing could be more political than the impact of these forces on Latin American Mission. When LAM pulls away from seminaries and they collapse, is that for the glory of God? How does one evaluate that political decision to withdraw support? Here in Mexico City, it is easy to learn about the politics behind the influence and the manipulation from the evangelical side. But you may not fare much better if you let Union Theological Seminary tell you how to run the seminaries here! We don't do all that well with the Hispanics in New York City. And one of the problems that Pentecostal churches face is that when the students finish Union Seminary, it is likely that they won't be any good in the Pentecostal churches anymore. So the relation of the seminary to the churches is a political one—*politia*. I want to raise those connections to a greater consciousness to keep that present, because the gospel is political in this sense.

Scholer: Two things may help explain the political situation at Gordon-Conwell. You didn't mention earlier that there is nothing in the book for which Ramsey Michael was censured that he had not publicly taught and publicly debated, nothing that was not well known to every faculty member and administrator and member of the Board of Trustees. It was only the publication of the book that changed the situation by introducing this political constituency issue. The second thing is not as widely known—that President Cooley's mail in the first four months of public airing ran nine-to-one in favor of Ramsey.

Sheppard: Roger Nicole says that there was no doubt that Ramsey had in good faith signed their entire statement of faith. This should be a warning to the Americas. You can sign the statement of faith, but other things can still happen to make everything blow up in your face. That's the politics of exegesis.

Stam: Clark, I'd like to make an observation about your comment concerning the best possible light and the worst possible light. There are some who see liberation theology in the worst possible light and see evangelical theology in the best possible light. Others reverse that. I think there's a need to value the importance of empathy. In one sense, I think we have to look at everything in the best possible light, the fairest. Of course I would also have to concede that in some instances the reality—the situation under Hitler, for instance, and in some parts of Central America today—can be worse than the worst possible interpretation.

Sheppard: As we continue this discussion, I need to make a confession. It's often those whom one loves most that one criticizes most severely. If I didn't believe so much in the purpose and power and significance of the evangelical movement, I wouldn't waste my time examining it. I don't mean to just vilify evangelicals per se. The term is so broad. Is the black church evangelical? I want to know what this "evangelical constituency" is and how much it will tolerate.

Watson: As I listen to what you say about politics in evangelical seminaries, it occurs to me that the same could certainly be said about the politics of the mainline seminaries. The tenure system has become a self-perpetuating oligarchy, and it's apparently allowed to go on without any question of accountability to the church. Are you suggesting a way to outflank this? I would certainly agree with you that the scholar-pastor is a vanishing breed. In the past three years we've seen three scholar-pastors retire at Perkins, and not one of them will be replaced with a person with similar qualifications. The politics that control these seminaries, whether they be of the evangelical establishment or otherwise, really seem to have a lock on this. Are you suggesting some way of getting around that?

Sheppard: I just have some ideas. First of all I want to learn their language and try to out-talk them. Working within the language of the academy, I'd like to demystify as much as possible. I know that's not a big solution but I'd like to be one of those who works at the demystification of these games regarding this vague constituency. At least we can respond, "You're saying this, but look at what you're really saying when you're using this language." I think evangelicals have always worked to demystify liberals. It's time for us to do the same thing with evangelicals. And I say the same thing to Pentecostals.

1.2.1

Our Audience: Atheist or Alienated?

CLARK H. PINNOCK

It may sound like an easy task to determine the nature of the audience to which we hope to put the claim of the gospel of Jesus Christ, but it is not. True, the Bible itself tells us who our human audience is in a global sense, independent of context. The Word of God speaks about humankind fallen and under God's righteous anger yet nonetheless claimed by God in love, and as classical Christians who believe the Bible, we are confident that this book understands the audience we face better than it understands itself and better than we can hope to understand it. Furthermore, we are confident that the Spirit of God is able to bring light where there is darkness and enable people to see themselves as God sees them. Grateful for these realities, we must still take into account what our audience is like in the specific historical sense, and this the Bible cannot do for us. If we want to be able to frame the Christian message effectively for people today, we will have to understand what excites them, what moves them, what ails them, what deceives them. We need the sort of discernment Paul had regarding the spirit of the Athenians, which enabled him to preach the message he did there. My task is to try to discern the character of the contemporary audience.

Before setting forth a thesis in this regard, let me acknowledge three things that make the venture difficult. First, the contemporary world is a buzzing confusion, full of contradictions; it does not add up to just one uniform audience at all. Even in just that portion of the audience in the Americas there are scores of communities and subcommunities with distinctive characteristics of their own. How then can I hope to be on target for a majority of the people here at the conference? Second, there is a spirit at work in the children of disobedience and a mystery of iniquity that make the precise nature of any audience apparent only to God and only partially visible to any human observer or even participant. Third, and most difficult, is the problem of cultural bias on the part of the interpreter. We are part of the audience we seek to understand, and we have an investment in the situation.

Objectivity is very hard to come by. There is a lot of suspicion these days about such things. Why does Bultmann depict modern man in the peculiar way in which he does? Why does he describe the kerygma in such a strange manner? Why do theologians read the audience and the gospel the way they do? It could be that human beings are afflicted by so many ailments that the different interpreters are simply zeroing in on different ills. But it is also possible that the different analyses might have something to do with biases stemming from the culture, social class, and psychology of the theologian. I admit to being only a little aware of this problem. I hope that as I speak others will weigh what I say and contribute as best they can to helping us all make some progress toward overcoming such biases.

"Atheist or Alienated?"

The committee handed me this catchy title. It was a kind gesture, designed to make my job a good deal easier by narrowing down my options to two. The question then becomes whether the audience we are addressing consists of nonbelievers or nonpersons. These alternatives reflect the positions of two groups of theologians: those who consider the truth question paramount (Does God exist?) and those who press the prior importance of the social question (Is there justice to be hoped for?). Who is on target—Pannenberg or Moltmann, the North Atlantic academic theologians or the "practical" political liberationists? I suppose that in giving me this title, the committee might even have been setting me up to preside over a debate between those who favor the priority of epistemology and those who emphasize praxis theology.

I will state at the outset, then, that I consider both the truth question and the justice question to be important. Which of the two is the more important is situation-relative. I do not agree that the truth question collapses into the justice question, as Miranda would have it. "Love God" and "love your neighbor" are are two great commandments, not one. I resent it when I hear anyone suggest that the theologian devoted to truth questions is morally inferior to the theologian who concentrates on justice issues.

In view of the pluralism of our audience, it is not likely that *atheist* or *alienated* or any other adjective is going to adequately characterize it. Instead of setting out to find the ideal adjective, I think we should set ourselves to the more promising task of trying to determine the spirit of our age, which seems to be putting its imprint on every individual in the audience to some degree.

Secularist Humanism

I would like to suggest that the key determinant of the modern situation, an attitude that is affecting enormous numbers of people often catastrophically, is simply *godlessness*. Humankind is engaged in the suicidal pursuit of radical autonomy—freedom from God—and Christians ought to be saying that such a course is doomed. Dorothy Sayers once attributed the creed "I believe in Man" to St. Euthanasia. This is a humanism that believes in man *rather than* God and advocates living in a godless way. It seeks to interpret all reality in materialistic terms and reserves the right to determine values to man alone. It came to expression in the Enlightenment and has been working as a powerful leaven in Western society ever since. It was formally defined in the Humanist Manifesto of 1973, which a large number of influential people signed (e.g., A. J. Ayer, Anthony Flew, S. H. Hook, Francis Crick, Andrei Sakharov, Isaac Asimov, B. F. Skinner, Betty Friedan, Jacques-Lucien Monod, and Gunnar Myrdal).

Sometimes when Christians attack secularism they fail to distinguish between true and false humanism, and between secularity and secularism. There is a difference. Modernity is characterized by a turning to the world as opposed to turning to an otherworldly standpoint, but that emphasis is not in itself necessarily unbiblical or anti-Christian. After all, God made the world good and gave life within it dignity and worth. Otherworldliness becomes unscriptural when it ignores God's serious decision to create a material world and to redeem it. But we can properly speak of a Christian humanism and secularity that is far from godless, that affirms the goodness of life in the creation. C. S. Lewis was surely a humanist in this sense. Though second to none in attacking the pretensions of secularism, he appreciated the powers of reason, valued the moral dimension in human experience, and cultivated the creative instinct in himself. We evangelicals must not surrender such great words as *humanist,* or *liberal* for that matter, because they denote important features in our own faith stance, which strives to be both life-affirming and open-minded. Indeed, I would even argue that the term *humanist* does a better job describing our Christian beliefs than it does secularist beliefs, which are deeply antihuman when the logical implications get worked out.[1]

Positive humanism values a number of things for which I am grateful as well: the powers of reason, liberty of conscience, unfettered science, a concern for moral issues, human freedom, political and economic liberalism, the freedom of the church from the state, the importance of the temporal, the right to be wrong, and so forth. What could be more humanizing than God's decision to create and then to elect unto salvation the human race in Christ?

But because positive and negative humanism have become so tangled in modern experience, we have to develop skills of discernment and integration to deal with them. As with prophecy, we have to test all things, holding fast to what is good, and abstaining from every form of evil (1 Thess. 5:21-22).

1. For more on this issue, see Robert E. Webber, *Secular Humanism: Threat and Challenge* (Grand Rapids: Zondervan, 1982); Norman L. Geisler, *Is Man the Measure? An Evaluation of Contemporary Humanism* (Grand Rapids: Baker, 1983); and James Hitchcock, *What is Secular Humanism?* (Ann Arbor: Servant Books, 1982.)

Paul gives us the basis for a suitable appreciation of secularity when he exhorts us to think on all those things that are honorable, just, pure, lovely, and gracious. "If there is any excellence, if there is anything worthy of praise, think about these things" (Phil. 4:8). We must obviously take care to avoid the evils lurking in godlessness, but in doing so we must take care not to reject secularity because we disapprove of secularism.[2]

When we attempt to realize a beneficial secularity in our lives, we may find that we will also need to rework some topics in classical theology. The church never gets its theological thinking perfectly right; there is always room for reformation and change. It may well be, for example, that the way we have spoken of God has been too wedded to a historical thinking associated with Greek thought and that we will have to speak of God in more dynamic terms.[3] One need not embrace process theism to respond to this need. Evangelical theology ought to be "revisionist" too, within biblically permissible limits.

Promethean Humanism

We should not, of course, let our enthusiasm about positive humanism blind us to darkness of negative humanism. In the French "Enlightenment" this sort of humanism came to expression in a virulent attack upon all forms of Christian belief and a parallel assertion of the unlimited freedom and rights of sovereign man. It was a rebirth, as Peter Gay says, of ancient paganism, the worship and glorification of humankind.[4] In part reacting to the bloody wars of religion and to the splintering of the church by the Reformation, such individuals as Voltaire ridiculed the churches and their ancient creeds and urged intellectuals to turn their attention away from God and religious superstitions to focus exclusively on humanity and its potential. From that point on it became commonplace for the elite in Europe to think in secularist and materialistic ways. Although this radical mode of thinking never touched anything like a majority of the population (such a thing was not possible before the recent advent of general literacy and the development of mass communications media), it was a major development in human thinking, ominous in its implications for Christianity and, indeed, for the human race.

I am not claiming that this "enlightenment" was universally acclaimed as such from the beginning. It was not. From the first, in the terror of the

2. On the need for discerning theological integration, see Richard C. Lovelace, *Dynamics of Spiritual Life* (Downers Grove, Ill.: InterVarsity Press, 1979), pp. 172-84.

3. Hans Küng makes this point in connection with the challenge of Hegel in his book *Does God Exist?* (Garden City, N.Y.: Doubleday, 1980).

4. Gay, *The Enlightenment: An Interpretation*, 2 vols. (New York: Knopf, 1975).

French revolution, the dark side of secularism was apparent, and the lesson has been repeated with increasingly horrific intensity in the concentration camps and gulags of the twentieth century. How ironic that the secularists should rail against the Christian inquisitions when their own crusades for humanity have spilled so much blood, unleashed so many unthinkable horrors. The rise of Romanticism and the religious revivals of the nineteenth century constitute evidence that large numbers of people came to realize how sterile a creed materialism is, that it cannot begin to do justice to the full dimensions of human existence. Nevertheless, the infection was well advanced, and the implications of secularist humanism surfaced in ever more radical ways. Feuerbach declared God to be a projection of man's own divinity. Marx built atheism into the heart of his social speculations, dismissing religion as the opiate of the people and God as a distraction in the struggle for revolution. The Darwinians championed the animality of man. Freud declared religious belief to be a neurotic illusion. Nietzsche drew out the nihilistic implications of man-worship: declaring itself sovereign, humankind must deny all constraints on its freedom, and proceed to invent its own morality—which entails forsaking all the gentility associated with the infamous Christian outlook. Altogether, humankind lurched a long step in the direction of antihuman humanism.

Aleksandr Solzhenitsyn has been speaking out of late about this crisis. In his Harvard address he cited anthropocentricity and in his Templeton address godlessness as the cause of the modern breakdown.[5] Humankind's worship of itself and its material needs to the exclusion of the religious dimension has impoverished the twentieth century and left us weak, says Solzhenitsyn—in fact, we are near death. In particular he indicts Marxist humanism, with its boundless materialism, its hatred of religion, and its pseudoscience as the deadly consequence of man-worship. He speaks of "the calamity of an autonomous, irreligious humanistic consciousness" and suggests that we are now paying for the mistakes of secularism we did not recognize early enough, mistakes that are now becoming horribly visible. Referring to the slaughter of innocents in the Soviet Union, he says, "Men have forgotten God; that's why all this has happened." We are witnessing nothing less than the devastation of the world, he says: "the entire twentieth century is being sucked into the vortex of atheism and self-destruction." He maintains that only atheists could have planned the ultimate brutality of the gulag and the vicious persecution of faithful believers. At the same time, he sees a ray of hope: "for no matter how formidably Communism bristles with

5. For the Harvard address, see *Solzhenitsyn at Harvard: The Address, Twelve Early Responses, and Six Later Reflections* (Washington: Ethics & Public Policy Center, 1980). His London address, which he delivered as winner of the Templeton Prize for Progress in Religion in 1983, was entitled "Men Have Forgotten God" and was published in the *National Review*, 22 July 1983.

tanks and rockets, no matter what successes it attains in seizing the planet, it is doomed never to vanquish Christianity."

Nor does Solzhenitsyn spare the West in his critique. Here too he sees the drying up of vital religious faith and an incoming tide of commercial materialism and secularism. We are prey to a sapping of strength from within that is more dangerous than violent opposition from without. After decades of erosion, the meaning of life in the West now amounts to little more than the pursuit of personal happiness. We have gradually fallen into moral relativism and convenience. "Judging by the continuing landslide of concessions made before the eyes of our own generation alone, the West is ineluctably slipping toward the abyss. Western societies are losing more and more of their religious essence as they thoughtlessly yield up their younger generation to atheism." Thus, Solzhenitsyn sees the West, too, traveling down the dead-end street of humanism toward the threat that may destroy the whole world. The noose grows tighter around the neck of mankind with every passing decade, he maintains, and there seems to be no way out for anyone. "All attempts to find a way out of the plight of today's world are fruitless unless we redirect our consciousness in repentance to the Creator of all; without this, no exit will be illumined, and we shall seek it in vain." In the London address he sums up his point this way:

> To the ill-considered hopes of the last two centuries, which have reduced us to insignificance and brought us to the brink of nuclear and non-nuclear death, we can propose only a determined quest for the warm hand of God, which we have so rashly and self-confidently spurned. Only in this way can our eyes be opened to the errors of this unfortunate twentieth century and our hands be directed to setting them right. There is nothing else to cling to in the landslide: the combined vision of all the thinkers of the Enlightenment amounts to nothing. Our five continents are caught in a whirlwind. But it is during trials such as these that the highest gifts of the human spirit are manifested. If we perish and lose this world, the fault will be ours alone.

The communist East and the capitalist West are both ripe for judgment because each has forsaken God in its own way.

In the Western world, secularist humanism takes many intellectual forms. There is the evolutionary humanism of Julian Huxley, which goes so far as to project a universal religion without God to help preserve human values. There is the behaviorist humanism of B. F. Skinner, which replaces all religion with science and offers a technique for changing human behavior in ways deemed desirable by experts like himself. There is also the existential humanism of Jean-Paul Sartre, which places its emphasis upon individual freedom and denies God as an unwanted limit upon human autonomy. Dewey's humanism is pragmatic, accepting the use of the word *god* so long as it is understood to denote humanist values rather than a supreme being. The humanism of Ayn Rand, in stark contrast to Marxist collectivist humanism, focuses on the individual ego and affirms the virtue of selfishness. These different forms of humanist thinking are not united or consistent with one another, but listing them gives some indication of the pervasive global reach of the atheistic spirit in the contemporary world.[6]

On the level of popular culture, there was and is the cult of self-worship in North America that began in the sixties. In those days, John F. Kennedy epitomized a spirit of pragmatic confidence, the assumption that we could solve any problem if we wanted to. There was not much room for God in such a mentality, but that did not stop Harvey Cox from adopting it in *The Secular City,* in which he advised Christians to live like humanists themselves. While it was true in the Viet Nam years that the young people protested against the presumptions of omnicompetence and other pretended virtues of the system, they too were a pretty self-indulgent lot, and the human rights they sought most persistently were the rights to use drugs and practice free sex. Their hostility to society was in part an expression of their rejection of anything that might restrict unlimited freedom. Some young people did try to live more simply, but for the most part it was just the form of materialism that changed—from cars to motorcycles, from dish washers to stereos, from liquor to LSD. The affluence of the parents became the self-indulgence of the youth. The freedom the Me Generation wanted was basically a freedom from responsibility, from moral rules; they hated the past and were indifferent to the future. "Me" and this moment matter; the rest can go to hell. Families broke up in record numbers since commitment wasn't cool. Experimenting with gay lifestyles became the rage and was gaining social respectability until the AIDS disaster. Thousands turned to psychology to find out who they were and how to get people to do what they wanted. The human potential movement offered to put people in touch with their real selves and promised fulfillment of all they were meant to be. Anything that gave pain or struggle or frustration was frowned upon. It was the culture of narcissism, celebrating an obsessive, unhealthful preoccupation with the self and feeling good. Sin was out; all impulses were regarded as good. Evil was the failure to grow, and morality was something one chose for oneself. "If it feels good, do it."

Although not everyone by any means adopted such a philosophy, its spirit is very widespread in North America and constitutes as serious a threat to Christianity as communism does with its open hostility to religion. The individual becomes the test of everything, and even religion is subject to the authority of the almighty self seeking infinite gratification. It destroys the

---

6. Geisler does a particularly good job of analyzing and critiquing secularist humanism in its intellectual forms in *Is Man the Measure?* Webber in *Secular Humanism* and Hitchcock in *What Is Secular Humanism?* concentrate more upon its popular cultural expressions.

soul of religion without bothering to attack the body. Its gospel is spread to everybody through television, rock music, films, the print media, and advertising. It is codified into law through secularist court decisions and indoctrinated by way of the statist school system. But there are suitable Christian responses to the challenge of godlessness in its modern forms.

Religious Liberalism

In the nineteenth century, theologians made a bad mistake in their attempt to come to grips with secularism. They abandoned the infallible authority of biblical revelation and accommodated the gospel to secularist thinking. The idea was to reach modern man with a fresh interpretation of the message, but the result was a serious perversion of the truth and a tragic weakening of the Christian movement. This blunder we call *religious liberalism*. It was meant to serve as a halfway house for people coming into the church, but it actually served as a halfway house for people leaving it. It had no appreciable effect upon the secularists except to make them feel that it was only a matter of time until the liberals came all the way over to the secularist side. Religious liberalism failed as evangelism but succeeded famously as the instrument for the secularizing of the churches. It watered down every major tenet of the creed and made of theology a religiously tinged form of secularism. What could possibly attract a secularist to it? It is no wonder that the secularists who did convert—Muggeridge, Maritain, Eliot, and Lewis, for example—became orthodox Christians, not liberals. Orthodoxy offers something really different; religious liberalism does not. From the latter, the content has drained away, the vitality has waned, and the only dogmas left are political opinions indistinguishable from those of other secularists. We evangelicals must take care not to imitate the liberals in responding to secularism. They tried to make Christianity "relevant" and only succeeded in emptying out the churches. Liberalism is self-destructive; the future belongs to biblical and classical Christians almost certainly.[7]

Is There Then Nothing We Can Learn?

There is much we can learn even from our fiercest enemies without in any way accommodating to their unbelieving ways. Such great modern heresiarchs as Feuerbach have produced trenchant criticisms of our faith that can

7. Thomas C. Oden describes himself as having been a liberal theologian for many years before rediscovering the classical theology of his Methodist tradition. He tells the story of his pilgrimage in *Agenda for Theology* (New York: Harper & Row, 1979).

serve to purify and deepen our understanding and commitment if we let them. Has it not been the case very often, as Feuerbach alleges, that theology has defended God at the expense of man? Has not a dualism that we adopted from the Greeks devalued earthly life and set Christianity up for precisely this kind of critique? Was Marx not onto something when he noted that religion in Europe displayed a distinctly bourgeois character and supported the interests of the ruling classes? Isn't the effect of Freud's criticism really to demand that we be more honest in dealing with religion and stop putting theological names on psychological disorders? And did not even poor old mad Nietzsche have hold of some insight when he called attention to the great contrast that often exists between Jesus and the churches, and when he ridiculed the God of popular belief—God the Santa Claus, God the postman? Of course all these atheists were hopelessly one-sided in what they condemned and unconvincing in what they proposed to put in its place, but it remains the case that there was something to what they said, something we need to take heed of and can learn from.

The Passing of Modernity

But might it not be that in the twentieth century the assumptions of secularism have been so badly shaken by events that the most appropriate Christian approach is just to watch this kind of man-centered modernity fade away? Voltaire may have announced the demise of religion, but is it not the humanist creed that is now in danger of disappearing? Perhaps all we have to do is to live out our biblical faith in the presence of decaying materialism. Why seek to land a fatal blow when death is already at work in its members?

To some extent I think that modernity is a sick, dying giant. There are signs that we are at the end of an era. Certainly secularism is not as attractive as it once seemed. But I would be very careful not to underestimate the harm that it can and is still perpetrating in our world. We cannot afford to let our guard down. Even if the wheat may in this instance show promise of outlasting the tares, let us not underestimate the harm the tares can still do. Recall the picture in the Revelation of Satan, who, knowing his time is short, redoubles his efforts and intensifies his destructive activities. In North America, for example, the different forms of the mass media continue to disseminate secularist viewpoints to practically everyone. Pornography is a dramatic example: increasingly outrageous attempts are being made to debase and exploit human sexuality in the name of healthy freedom of expression. In the realm of the law and the courts, too, a concerted effort has been made to construe moral obligations in secularist ways that contradict historical traditions and popular sentiment.

Evangelicals have long talked about such things, but it took fundamentalists to *do* something. If nothing is done to prevent it, the secularists will lead us into irreparable moral chaos and manipulation. In the East, communism may be dying as a faith to lift the human heart, but the death of this tyrannical system could take a hundred years and sweep away the human race with it. Even if we are living in the dying phases of Enlightenment humanism, we dare not stand idly by waiting for it to collapse. Too many people would be swept away or crushed in the fall of such a structure. We face a real and present danger.

The Critique of Presuppositions

One type of Christian response to godlessness involves exposing its deadly implications. Secularism is based upon the myth of human wisdom and competence and leads inexorably to emptiness and destruction. It must be exposed as the great lie it is. A little more education and scientific achievement is not going to make a utopia on earth. Godlessness leads to nihilism and terrorism. All such values as truth, morality, and religion that make life human are reduced to nothing more than whims and inventions. Radical automomy leads to the abyss. We must add our voices to those of Muggeridge, Schaeffer, Maritain, Solzhenitsyn, and others who like the child in the ancient tale have had the forthrightness to declare before all present that the emperor has no clothes. Human beings who submit to the temptation to think of themselves as gods and endeavor to frame good and evil according to the dictates only of their own desires are doomed. This is an important factor in the drama that is being played out in contemporary history. Belief in the ultimacy of chance and the divinity of man destroys all meaning and morality. It produces various philosophies of pessimism and programs of terror as the fanatical secularists strive to wrench the world into shapes agreeable to their own visions. Secularism, as Peter said of something like it, promises us freedom but actually delivers us over to bondage (2 Pet. 2:19).

Rational Refutation

Not all Christians will agree with me here, but I believe part of our response must be to point to the irrational character of secularist humanism. At the simplest level there is its "ecumenical" problem. One cannot reconcile the attitude toward religion expressed by Huxley or Dewey with that of Marx or Rand. Some humanists are radically egocentric, while others retain a social orientation akin to that of Christian ethics. Some see hope in science, while others look to the existential self for salvation. But more important than internal inconsistencies are the scientific and philosophical difficulties they all run into. Again, it took the fundamentalists to call them on this.

Why is that? It is generally conceded that substantial enigmas remain in theories of naturalistic evolution. If there is no God, the universe must be everlasting, but there is evidence to suggest that it is not. Scientists such as Robert Jastrow have concluded that the world had a beginning in time. Then there is the matter of life springing into being spontaneously and evolving into forms of unbelievable complexity, like a ball bouncing up a flight of stairs without anyone's having thrown it. One can detect a problem here without consulting any of the scientific details that make it unlikely. It is a credit to the enormous influence of modern science that so many Christians have been docile for so long in the face of this really astonishing theory.

The same sort of problem can be expressed philosophically: how is it that we insist on finding causes for everything in the world but do not consider it relevant to ask about the cause of the whole? Bertrand Russell's answer—"It's just there, that's all"—doesn't say much for the quality of his rational powers. Imagine looking for rationality behind every detail in the world and not looking for it in relation to reality itself! There is a problem too in the area of the status of the mind and thinking in a world that is supposed to be only material. Are thoughts reducible to atoms in motion? If so, what status do they have as rational truths? If reality is not mental as well as material, what are we to think of secularist arguments themselves? But how can it be mental as well as material if there is no God? If everything in the universe can be reduced to physical and chemical events, thoughts and theories cannot have the status humanists give them. In the moral realm too there are deep inconsistencies in the way secularists speak about the relativity of all values and then hold to their own set of values as if they were eternal and universally obligatory. Secularism is a house without a sound foundation, and it is important for Christians to work at showing this is so.

The Power of Pentecost

Although the current vogue with political theology encourages us to forget it, the gospel in fact speaks to the religious needs of people in a way that surpasses anything secularism can offer. Many secularists are aware of their problem of course. They feel they ought to be able to engage the whole person more effectively and retain a mystical dimension in humanism if they can. Since Comte many have suggested such things as a humanist hymnbook, humanist testimonies, and humanist prayer. But it has proved difficult to make the substitution convincing when there is no personal God out there to fellowship with. Worshiping that speck of cosmic dust called man falls short of providing religious fulfillment. Yet Sartre and Walter Kaufmann show that they are well aware of man's need to transcend himself and somehow incorporate the category of God into their atheism. Saying we are the product of chance is easier than feeling it and living it out. Freud can say that religion panders to human wishes and neuroses, but is something so profound in relation to basic human needs so easily dismissed?

All Christians, and not merely philosophers and intellectuals, can participate in this mode of refutation. It is a matter of record that state-imposed godlessness over six decades has not succeeded in stamping out religion in the Soviet empire. Indeed, brief encounters with Walesa and the Christians of Russia seem to suggest that religious faith is one of the few flames of vitality and hope still burning in that bleak universe. It is a wonderful irony that communism should have turned out to be the opiate of the people and religion the source of hope. In the West too we are seeing the empowering of the churches. Worthy of note is the Pentecostal resurgence in South and Central America and the charismatic leavening of much church life in North America as believers are newly opened to the fresh breath of God's Spirit. The rediscovery of the Spirit will change the face of the church. Having enlivened the church, it will doubtless go on to challenge secularism at its weakest point—its inability to satisfy the deepest urges of the human heart.

The Cost of Discipleship

One of the things that has turned many away from religion to the faith of secularism is the failure of the churches to be obedient to their own gospel in relation to the historical situation we find ourselves in. We pray that God's will be done on earth as in heaven, but we ourselves do little to bring that to pass. Obviously one way for Christians to respond to humanism is to live out of the gospel ethic and conform their lives to biblical law—to take the cause of man in the name of God, as Küng expresses it so well in *On Being a Christian*. To act in this way would be both to obey our Lord Jesus and to counter the overt and subtle forms of materialism in the world.

In this connection, there are some unresolved differences that go far back in Christian history. Should we proceed in a neo-Puritan manner, dedicated to the reform of the morals of the whole society, or should we proceed in an Anabaptist way, placing the emphasis on the witness of the intentional community in the midst of a dying world? Both approaches are being tried by different groups with histories that go back at least to the Reformation. To some extent the setting will favor one or the other. In Russia for example, the church has little choice but to act like a sect; in Canada the possibilities are somewhat larger.

Added to this are serious differences of analysis as well as interpretation of the Bible. How should we pursue peace in our world? Sakharov and Djilas tell us it is not safe for the West to be weak, but others tell us that the problem is American imperialism. Whose economic principles do we adopt as we pursue justice in the international order—Reagan's or Galbraith's? Is the United States part of the problem or part of the solution to the suffering of the less developed countries?

However we stand on these differences and approaches, I hope that the whole Christian community can agree to work on behalf of the needy neighbor and work as well to ensure that uncertainties will not nullify the powerful witness that can be made in the service of love.

Conclusion

Mankind has been living out the experiment of human autonomy and godlessness since the fall of Adam, but we have been summoned to live in an age when really radical versions of the experiment are in progress. That age is probably nearing its close now that its fragile assumptions are becoming so evident. We can be sure that if the parousia does not intervene, secularist humanism will be replaced by something else. It is my hope that a restored and rejuvenated Christian church will replace it, that our faith will act as a leaven to affect the whole lump, that it will grow like the mustard seed to become the largest of trees.

* * *

Additional Comments by Pinnock

This was not an easy paper to write. I make reference to the main difficulty I faced in the introduction: the cultural bias of the interpreter. I'm sure the critiques will help me focus on that further. How we perceive the audience depends significantly on where we are standing and looking from. The conference has already helped me to get a better perspective on this, and I'm sure it will continue to do so.

As I suggest in the paper, the committee handed me two possibilities for characterizing the audience—as atheist or alienated. I chose the former, but my sense of the spirit of the gathering tells me that I may have made the wrong choice. The interest here in political theology tells me that many of you would have made the other choice, and that may well be the big question about the paper. I could have easily made that choice. Atheism and alienation, secularism and oppression, are both very important problems, and I don't think the issue is all that polarized. In fact, the two problems are clearly related. I think of 1 John 4—how can we say we know God if we don't love our neighbor? Godlessness has an ethical side. Nevertheless, I hope you will be able to understand something of my reasons for deciding as I did. The twentieth century reveals in a strong way the truth of Romans 1:25—that men and women love the creature more than the Creator—more radically than ever before. Not being content merely with false gods, they actually seek to rid the universe of God. The causes and effects of this attitude are far-reaching. The issues are not simply academic; they're shaping the face of our world today.

Now, I would like to provoke the discussion further by sharing with you three opinions that relate to political theology and my general thesis. Maybe all they will do is create a target for you to shoot at. If so, that's fine—at least the target will be clearly in view. I would like to raise some points about the connection between Marxism and liberation theology.

First of all, the record of Marxism in relation to justice is so bad that it's hard for me to understand why so many consider it to be such an excellent resource. Perhaps they are working on the assumption that the tool can be separated from the whole system. But, as Solzhenitsyn stresses, Marxism is an atheistic utopianism that spares no persons who stand in its way. And of course the Marxist utopia is never realized.

Second, it seems to me that what Marxism has offered us has failed in terms of allocating resources. However appealing radical politics may be to intellectuals, it is irrelevant to the poor because it results in failed economies. It may be very dangerous for me to mention this, but we might as well be very concrete. I'll comment on an impression I have with regard to Mexico itself. I stand to be corrected, of course. Mexico owes $80 billion on loans it has received. It has oil, and yet it is insolvent. Why is that? There may be a good answer, but my suspicion is that it is the result of having adopted a disastrous approach to economic allocation, and that it should be changed as rapidly as possible. A revolution, in fact, is needed—but not a socialist revolution.

My third opinion is that there are very definite positive values in democratic capitalism, even though I hear almost nothing except condemnation of it in this group. Democratic capitalism has produced a great deal of liberty, justice, and prosperity. The system looks bad because it has made many mistakes. It's easy to condemn because it doesn't even pretend to offer a utopia. It doesn't have that advantage. It just offers a practical approach to things that has resulted in a good deal of impressive liberty, justice, and prosperity. It is in fact another kind of revolution, though not a kind that is normally given that name today.

I object to the way in which North American Christians simply collapse in a paroxysm of guilt at the first criticism they received from political theologians. We must have the courage to say what we actually think. I've tried to do that here.

Toward the end of the paper I mention ideology, by which I simply mean looking at the world in a certain way. I just outlined a way of looking at it

myself. I agree with Segundo that we have to make some choices here—
between socialism and capitalism, for instance. My choice in this matter is
the opposite of his, precisely because I think it is better for the poor. I am
disturbed by the ways in which our ideologies can distort the way we
approach particular evils in the world. It troubles me that the World Council
of Churches could not condemn Afghanistan, that it could find injustices
only in the West and never in the Soviet bloc. Of course this has to do not
only ideology but also with constituencies—the orthodox in particular. But
Sojourners was right in saying that this is inexcusable. Victims are victims are
victims, and ideology ought not to blind us to the fact that there are victims
in all existing systems. That is, of course, a message for neoconservatives,
too—for people such as Novak in the United States who praise the virtues of
democratic capitalism but conveniently ignore its victims. That does not
improve their case, and I want to make it clear that I won't have any part of
it. If victims have been created as a result of democratic capitalism, then that
is the case we have to confront with repentance and change.

1.2.2

Response to Pinnock by John Stam

I'd like to read a bit from Clark's paper so that we have it before us, and then begin my comments.

> The question [is] whether the audience we are addressing consists of nonbelievers or nonpersons. These alternatives reflect the positions of two groups of theologians: those who consider the truth question paramount (Does God exist?) and those who press the prior importance of the social question (Is there justice to be hoped for?). Who is on target—Pannenberg or Moltmann, the North Atlantic academic theologians or the "practical" political liberationists? . . . I will state at the outset . . . that I consider both the truth question and the justice question to be important. Which of the two is the more important is situation-relative. I do not agree that the truth question collapses into the justice question, as Miranda would have it.

Now among a number of things I've liked about this paper, and some in the paragraph I read, is the fact that Clark begins with the truth question. For a long time I have felt that the truth question, the *Wahrheitsfrage,* is of pressing importance in evangelical theology. And I'd like to do two things this afternoon. First, I'd like to come at the truth question from a different starting point. And second, I'd like to suggest that the truth question is a two-edged sword, that it ought not to be handled casually.

The starting point here, the place where my questions and problems begin, is with the little parentheses: some theologians "consider the truth question paramount (Does God exist?)." Truth-question theologians are existence-of-God theologians. Social-justice theologians are not truth-question theologians. These categories are counterposed.

I have difficulty equating the existence-of-God question with the truth question. A more fruitful rendering of the truth question about God than "Does God exist?" might be "Who is God as revealed in Scripture?" This entails questions of how God is known and what faith in God amounts to, what God requires of us. I don't mean to suggest that "Does God exist?"

isn't an important question, but I would insist on the greater importance of answering a question like that in the context of the larger perspective I just mentioned. When the question is formulated in this way, a new possibility emerges: it is possible that "Does God exist?" theologians have focused the truth question in an imperfect way or perhaps even evaded the real truth question—and the possibility then arises that the so-called justice theologians are not evading the truth question but in some cases framing the question in a more biblical and compelling way. That's the essential response I have to Clark's paper.

Now because that I feel that the truth question is so important for evangelical theology, because we are passionately committed to evangelical theology, and because our theme is hermeneutics, I would like to go on to a second point. However we understand it, the truth question has very challenging implications for evangelical theology with regard to exegetical and methodological problems. We have much to learn about our own exegesis of Scripture and theological tradition on the one hand and about our exegesis of contemporary theologians on the other—especially those with whom we disagree. Here, too, we must start with the truth question.

First, the priority of the truth question will obviously require of us the most relentless honesty and accuracy in investigation and humility and respect for our theological opponents. Here's where the truth question becomes a two-edged sword. Glib characterizations and unfair caricatures will hardly stand the test of the truth questions, whether they come from the right or the left, as we noted last night. Yet many evangelical theologians, including some Clark mentions favorably in his paper, seem to me to be more theological propagandists than real theological investigators, earnest and humble seekers after the truth. Some seem to think they already possess truth, that they have little or nothing more to learn, that they need only protect their package of truth against its many enemies and threats. They then go on, it seems to me, to assume that they can be quite careless about their accuracy in interpreting others—and sometimes in interpreting Scripture. Too often they take a flippant and distorting approach to the thought of their theological victims.

Personal experience with some evangelical theologians in both North America and Latin America has led me to a second related conclusion. I believe that much of evangelicalism faces a desperate crisis precisely in the face of the truth question at two levels: a hermeneutical, exegetical crisis in how we interpret not only the biblical text but also in how we interpret other theologians, and an ethical crisis in how we carry on the theological discourse and in the honesty with which we interpret others. On close analysis, some evangelical leaders seem to me to be theological and ideological absolutists but ethical and epistemological relativists. Here I want to mention with no apology a friend and professor of mine named last night, Harold Lindsell. *Christianity Today* published an article on Latin American theology by

Rene V. Williamson that was so bad, so irresponsible that I would not have accepted it in an undergraduate course as a term paper. For example, Williamson accuses one Latin American theologian of atheism on the basis of an article this theologian had written. In this article, the theologian had explained the thought of Nietzsche in an extended section, using several quotes; he ended by refuting this thought in a devastating way. But Williamson picked out the quotes from Nietzsche and attributed them to the Latin American theologian, accusing him of atheism on that basis. I wrote to Harold Lindsell and pointed this out, and in a series of about seven letters, Lindsell went around and around on one theme: "My friend Rene Williamson would not intentionally deceive the public." I think that's relativism. He said, "Everybody has a right to his opinion. Professor Williamson thinks that way, and he has a right to say so." But I didn't have the right to point out a few little details about the truth question, and I think we can call that theological and ideological absolutism. There's something sacred, untouchable there, but in the ethics of theological discourse it's relativistic.

I had exactly the same experience with a foreign missionary in our country, in the country of which I am a citizen, Costa Rica. This missionary consistently says things that simply are not true about Nicaragua. I present him with documented evidence to the contrary, but he will not acknowledge it. The truth question doesn't seem to press on him. Sometimes he will deny that he said what he said—even in cases where he wrote it down, where the record is still available. If I press him on it, he says, "Well, I have a right to my opinion; you ought to respect my opinion." I respect *reasons,* but I'm a bit reluctant to respect opinion just because it's opinion. I think there's a lot of this sort of attitude—we might call it "opinionism"—shot through evangelicalism. It seems as though people feel they can serve God by suppressing the truth question.

Now, another facet of this problem among evangelicals is the ethical and aesthetic issue of theological courtesy. Here again, the truth question too often gets left behind in the smoke of the explosive *ad hominem* arguments that are frequently used in polemical attacks on theologians whom we do not consider evangelical. Such tactics don't really confront the serious issues and challenges posed by these individuals. Earlier this week, I spoke with a Mexican theologian who is quite upset by the fact that an evangelical had criticized one of his books as a sort of "theological burp." I radically disagree with the assessment of this critic, although I know him to be a very serious biblical scholar; the point is that I think he stepped outside the bounds of the aesthetics of theological discourse by characterizing an entire piece of work as a burp. The ethical question (involving humility, honesty, and respect) and the aesthetic question (involving style and good taste) are both very important in theological debate. Certainly evangelicals, the theologians of the superabounding grace of God, ought to be the most grace-full and courteous of participants in such debate.

I have some other comments I'd like to make. They break the rhythm of the general analysis of the truth question by getting into some specifics, but there are a number of statements in Clark's paper that I want to look at more closely. I agree much more with the starting point and with the main thrust of the paper than with a number of the details that come up along the way. And I would like to follow Clark's exhortation to expose ourselves to the relentless thrust of the truth question.

First, there is the question I alluded to earlier of whether one group of theologians takes the truth question seriously and the other group not. I think Clark's statement about Miranda ("the truth question collapses into the justice question") is an unfair caricature. I've read his book three times and grappled with its involved exegetical argument. I think that before his whole argument is reduced in this fashion, the exegetical evidence ought to be handled very cautiouly.

Second, I have questions about Clark's classification of a number of recent converts as orthodox. What kind of orthodoxy is being referred to here? What kind of Christian theologian is Solzhenitsyn himself? There's a tendency to grab on to these people because they're heroes and then to dismiss much that is ambiguous about their thought, especially concerning whether there's anything remotely evangelical about it.

Third, regarding the truth question in ideology and politics, Clark has very honestly admitted that he has written a very political paper. I simply want to observe that he presents a strictly East-West perspective and a corresponding theology; the issue in this paper is godlessness vis-à-vis an East-West God. I live in a country where day after day civilians are being killed by mercenary troops totally financed by the U.S. They couldn't possibly function without the U.S. money. These troops have probably killed three or four times as many civilians as the Spanish Inquisition killed in three centuries. Very good friends of mine—Christians, civilians, and some voluntary military personnel—have been killed. Where's the truth question in relation to that? This killing is being covered over by such a network of lies that we'd have to talk hours to begin to get at the truth of the matter.

Perhaps it would help the discussion if we introduced the concept of idolatry. What sort of god do we have in the U.S. who would tell us how bad the Soviet Union is and have us continue to kill in these Latin nations in the name of Western Christianity? We can so easily use this authoritative viewpoint as an escape mechanism to avoid facing the murderous, criminal truth prophetically. And so, here is the truth question again, along with the ethical, political truth question. I appreciate Clark's challenge, and I think we have an obligation to go beyond just quoting Solzhenitsyn (it seems to me that there are even better hermeneutical keys to the Soviet reality) in light of all the terror he says is being committed in that state. But, it remains the case that Solzhenitsyn and Russia are far away from us, and murder is going on in our backyard.

From the 10th to the 17th of December 1981, a military operation in which U.S. officials were present took the lives of well over a thousand Salvadoran civilians, thirty percent of whom were under nine years of age and thirty percent of whom were over sixty years of age. Well over a thousand people! Everybody was talking about Poland. Remember that these are tiny countries. If an equivalent percentage of the populations of the U.S. or the U.S.S.R. were killed in this way, I think it would outdo any of the terrors presently being attributed to communism. And the godly Western Christian United States of America is actively and aggressively and criminally involved in this. So, I cannot suppress this truth question, which I know first-hand. When I arrived at this conference, I was greeted with the news that a dear friend had been killed, a civilian, a saint in my estimation. He had been shot down by a bullet that originated in the Pentagon of the U.S.A.

1.2.3

Response to Pinnock by Linda Mercadante

Clark is a apologist of proven ability, and I think he's demonstrated that again in what he's done here. I think he's right to be concerned that we could collapse in a paroxysm of guilt and fail to address and support what we rightly hold dear. We do have a tendency to knee-jerk guilt reactions. But that doesn't mean that we have to deny the problems and sins that remain, that we don't have to repent of them. I'm grateful to John Stam for pointing that out.

Clark has raised three key hermeneutical points in his paper: (1) the rootedness of the interpreter, which was Clark's starting point; (2) the pluralism of the audience, which we are all well aware of here as well as in our homes; and (3) the multiplicity of interpretations, which is the human character of the tradition. If you recall, Clark said that far from being able to claim objectivity, we must realize that our different interpretations may be as much the result of our biases as any legitimate differences in focus. In saying this, he has pointed to this third key hermeneutical point, the history of multiple, often widely variant interpretations. This multiplicity has led many to question whether there really is any single meaning in a passage of Scripture that is more truthful than the rest. Clark also touches briefly on the fact that theology is far from perfect, that it may well need reformation and change periodically. In saying this, he's being true to the Reformation principle of *ecclesia reformatis semper reformanda*. And I can only support that. Of course, he stresses that all such reform must take place within biblically permissable limits.

There are, however, other equally crucial elements in the hermeneutical discussion that we ought to raise in connection with this paper's general theme. For example, even those who hold to a high view of the Bible's inspiration and authority must view it *within* rather than outside of the traditioning process; we must all acknowledge the considerable extent to which it is rooted in its own milieu. I do not hear this concern expressed often in evangelical circles. While historical criticism has dealt at length with this factor, there has been no real effort to take the next step of bridging this huge historical time gap. Sometimes the proponents of historical criticism claim that it is scientifically objective, but despite the fact that it was developed in an effort to free the text from literalistic dogmatism, it has ironically served in many instances to make Scripture accessible only through the mediation of experts, and thus even more remote to the average person.

It is we, the current generation, who are faced with the problem of interpreting the Bible's fundamental message in a way that is both true to the text—cognizant of the immense historical distance between those Christians who wrote it and ourselves—and yet also true to Scripture's always new, always relevant message. Later I would like to take a closer look at Clark's use of the word *relevant* and the way he shows that it has been tainted because of the contact with liberalism, but before that I want to raise another issue concerning our understanding of that word.

Christians in every age have tried to be responsive to Scripture's always new, always relevant message. In the Middle Ages, for instance, the allegorical method was used in a genuine attempt to make Scripture come alive for the people. We ought not to dismiss it as just spinning dreams; it was in some instances a very profitable approach. In our own age, the Kantian and Heidegerrian revolution in thought has brought us to a staggering awareness of the problems of historical distance and the ways in which the interpreter is deeply rooted in his or her own world. This awareness provoked some strong reactions. Some individuals despair that definite meaning can be derived from anything in Scripture; others are arrogantly confident that they can dispense with all these problems simply because they are Christians with the Spirit and therefore entitled to claim infallible interpretive powers. Neither of these reactions acknowledges our responsibility to listen to God speaking through the Scripture to our own situation.

We have to take account of the immense interpretive problems that have been disclosed through the philosophical, historical, and critical biblical studies, as well as through work in the fields of psychology and sociology. Clark has focused on the desire and yet the failure of liberals to make the Scriptures and Christian faith relevant. And he has warned us to take a lesson from this failure. But what should this lesson be? Is it that we are relieved of our responsibility to help our contemporaries hear the Scripture? I'm sure Clark doesn't mean that. Or is it that we should courageously proclaim the gospel to a godless world whether or not it is listening, whether or not it can understand what we are saying? If this is part of the lesson, then I think it has a decidedly Barthian ring.

As you know, Barth saw the gospel distorted horribly by Nazism, and this led him to reject all forms of natural theology, to condemn all efforts to seek a point of contact in human nature through which people could learn of God by unaided reason. He held apologetics as a separate discipline to be out of the question. This raises a real problem for an apologist: Barth clearly says that we should proclaim the gospel, but he denies that there is anything in human nature that could give a glimmer of God.

The contemporary hermeneutical debate has made it evident that sometimes the lack of understanding on the part of nonbelievers is as much due to the obscurity of the packaging as to the offense of the message itself. I suspect that some of you may have objections to that point, but I really want to stress it because my experience and studies tell me that this historical gap, this distance, has to be taken seriously. Many people find the gospel message obscure, and a lot depends on how we proclaim it—which means making it relevant. The point of apologetics is to deal with this very problem: translating the gospel message so that the audience can actually be at once the audience of Scripture and the audience of the Word of God.

Using the word *audience* to describe solely the nonbelievers seems to me to put us, who are mostly trained professionals, in an us-them situation. What happens then is that *we* approach the Scripture, *we* interpret it, *we* analyze *their* problems, and then *we* tell them what *we* feel they need to hear. But, is anybody out there listening? We do not have a captive audience. The most captive sort of audience we encounter is an audience of other Christians, the sort we get when we teach or speak to one another like this, or when we preach to established congregations. In such contexts, the "us" and "them" are one, the Body of Christ, and an us-them attitude is not appropriate at all. But I believe that it is equally inappropriate when we move into the world of nonbelievers.

Unbelievers can detect an us-them mentality in a minute, and they are turned off by it. If we approach them with that attitude, we will produce precisely the opposite of the effect we want to achieve. Our witness to nonbelievers will be genuine only if we first approach God in the Scriptures with an attitude of openness—as Gadamer puts it, "with an effort to be 'sensitive to the text's quality of newness.'" This newness in the text challenges our preconceptions, but it also shows us what is indeed relevant to the situation in question. This newness challenges us to go beyond our own small world and achieve the fusion of horizons that Gadamer so ably speaks about. To reject as anthropocentric the fact that we inevitably start from our own perspective on the matter does not, as Anthony Thiselton demonstrates, do away with the problem. Instead, when we take an us-them approach, we unwittingly give the appearance of throwing the gospel "like stones" at the heads of nonbelievers. (By borrowing this metaphor of Paul Tillich's, I'm not implying that I advocate a full Tillichian position. I disagree with his contention that it is *only* from the culture that questions should be allowed to arise and that it is *only* there that we are permitted to give answers. But we might do well to pick up some of that emphasis—maybe much of it— because it is only when we grapple with our own culture that we realize how imbedded we are in it, and realize also that God speaking through the Scriptures may be challenging us to change.)

If relevancy is part of what we should strive for—is, in fact, the only way we can approach the Scriptures, then why did the liberals fail? Weren't their motives praiseworthy? Didn't they have the same concern to communicate the gospel to their culture in understandable terms? In his paper, Clark insists that "they abandoned the infallible authority of biblical relevation and accommodated the gospel to secularist thinking," that they "watered down every major tenet" and tragically weakened the faith. In many ways this is a fair indictment. Thomas Merton has put it well in *Conjectures of a Guilty Bystander,* where, speaking about witnessing to nonebelievers, he says,

> I think . . . in our eagerness to go out to modern man and meet him on his own ground, accepting him as he is, we must also be truly what *we* are. If we come to him as Christians, we can certainly understand and have compassion for his unbelief—his apparent incapacity to believe. But it would seem a bit absurd for us, precisely as Christians, to pat him on the arm and say: "As a matter of fact, I don't find the Incarnation credible myself. Let's just consider that Christ was a nice man who devoted his life to helping others."

I also think we ought to add several things to Clark's characterization of the liberals. We should give them credit for fully realizing the challenge that modern philosophy and science were making to Christianity and for trying to translate the gospel so that the age could hear it. On the negative side, I think we should grant that liberals failed not because they were too relevant but because they were paternalistic. They had that us-them attitude. While on one hand it was "we the liberals" in solidarity with the modern world against "them," the stiff-necked conservatives, it was a paternalistic sort of "we"—"we the liberals" giving "them the worldly" what they needed. It was not always clear that these scholars let themselves be addressed by Scripture first.

Schleiermacher, for instance, had to deal with the difficult combination of a Pietist upbringing and a full appreciation of the Kantian revolution in thought, and yet he still felt he could save his contemporaries from their seemingly inevitable rejection of religion. Because neither he nor they could talk confidently about objective truth anymore, he shifted the discourse to religious feeling, which he thought was firmer ground and which also fit in with the latent romanticism of the time.

While Schleiermacher's efforts were quite successful at the time, his approach was very different from that of Martin Luther, whose rootedness in and personal struggle with the Roman Catholic system prompted a break-through in his reading of Scripture and resulted in an answer to his own dilemma as well as that of his age. In Luther's case, personal openness to Scripture combined with a genuine identification with the age to bring startling, powerful results without any paternalism, without an "us-them" attitude. As an aside, let me add that to deny Luther's solidarity with the people because he later reacted against the peasant uprisings is, I believe, a failure to understand the fundamental identification he quite unself-consciously had with the common plight.

In many ways, Luther represents an ideal, something we can aspire to. Contemporary evangelicals are very much guilty of this us-them mentality. It would not be the least out of the ordinary for a male North American evangelical minister to tell a group of independent-minded career women that if they would accept the authority of Scripture, their concerns for equal treatment at work and at home would be solved. Similarly, it would not be extraordinary for the same minister to tell a battered wife at a crisis center that if only she were a Christian, none of this would have happened. Such answers simply do not fit the questions these women are implicitly asking. The minister assumes he understands these two situations and is giving the answers these women "need," but the natural response of the women—and I've seen this many times—is to express complete puzzlement, or simply to dismiss him as irrelevant, or to express outright hostility at his presumption and lack of understanding. If the minister had genuinely understood his own complicity in the oppression imposed on women by his cultural system, he would have been freed to approach their problems in an entirely different manner—indeed, they might all have had the opportunity to be freed by the gospel together.

To be sure, even if we understand another person's situation well and really do give a response that is both gospel-oriented and appropriate, that other person may still reject both us and the gospel—but at least it would not happen because we failed to understand and address the real questions—that is, because we failed to be relevant.

To summarize, I am contending that relevancy—or whatever word we might use to mean "really addressing the situation in all its particularity"—is an essential element for any Christian witness. We can achieve this kind of relevance only when we have been challenged by the Scriptures to go beyond our own preconceptions, have allowed ourselves to be questioned by God speaking through the text. At that point we *must* move forward, although cautiously, to proclaim the gospel in terms our age can hear. We can do nothing else: if we do not do this, *we* will not hear the gospel either, because we are part of the age. The subject-object or us-them mentality presents serious problems; it can lead to paternalism and a failure to communicate.

There are other significant issues that I would like to raise in connection with the agenda of the paper, but I only have time to mention them briefly here. Two that come to mind immediately are the problems of dead metaphor and of theological terms that no longer communicate. How, for instance do we communicate a gospel of love and justice to women—as well as to men—when much of the metaphors and language communicate a strong male dominance? How do we speak of sin as fundamentally an assertion of pride when pride is one thing that some people have never been able or been permitted to experience? These issues, along with the problems of relevancy and the us-them attitude, are crucial factors in any discussion of our task to communicate the gospel. I hope that we can grapple with these issues together in a spirit of love and unity.

1.2.4

Response to Pinnock by George Cummings

First, I want to affirm Dr. Pinnock's assertion that the truth question and the justice question are both important. The title assigned to him, as he rightly indicates, points to the fact that some theologians consider the truth question paramount and others press the importance of the social question. Perhaps the conference was designed, as he suggests, to encourage a debate between those who favor the priority of epistemology and those who emphasize praxis theology. Since neither of us was a member of the conference planning committee, perhaps we will never know. In any case, the point is clear: this compartmentalization is unnecessary with respect to the gospel.

Having established this point, however, the paper goes on to reduce the central contradiction in modern life to atheism. I want to challenge this notion as I see it emerging in the paper and to argue that godlessness is a reference point, relevant only insofar as the term *atheism* is demystified of its ideological implications in the American context and reinterpreted as the historicization of idolatry in the values, structures, and sensibilities of modernity. It is within this context that the problem of alienated humanity must be understood and given priority.

The title "Our Audience: Atheist or Alienated?" also seems to reflect the perspective that assumes that Christians, by virtue of their faith commitment, have privileged access to the objective truth concerning God. With regard to the epistemological question, allow me to quote my friend, teacher and, colleague Dr. Cornel West:

> Since we can neither reduce truth to the spheres of science, art, and religion nor view the world *sub species aeternitatis* [from the standpoint of eternity], we must acknowledge our finitude and fallenness. This acknowledgment entails that when we say we "know" that a particular scientific theory, art object, or religious description is true, we are actually identifying ourselves with a specific tradition of social practices, group of persons, or community of believers. There indeed may be good reasons why we identify ourselves with particular traditions, groups, or commu-

63

nities. But there are, ultimately, no reasons with the force of logical necessity or universal obligation that justify, confirm, or validate our preferred theories, art objects, and descriptions. In fact, for Christians, Jesus is the truth, a reality which can only be existentially appropriated, not intellectually grasped by fallen humans caught in ever-changing and finite descriptions.[1]

Dr. West goes on to assert that if there is any test for the truth of particular Christian descriptions, it is their capacity to facilitate the existential appropriation of Jesus Christ. This means that any true Christian description makes the reality of Jesus Christ available, that it encourages putting one's self on the line in the negation and transformation of prevailing realities. It encourages going to the edge of life's abyss and finding out whether the reality of Jesus Christ, as understood through one's finite Christian description, yields life, sustenance, the means to development and maturation, and societal amelioration. I would simply call your attention to Matthew 11:4-5. When John the Baptist heard about Jesus, he sent his disciples asking him, "Are you the one who was to come, or should we expect someone else?" And Jesus replied, "Go and tell John what you hear and see: the blind receive their sight and the lame walk, lepers are cleansed and the deaf hear, and the dead are raised up and the poor have good news preached to them." Go tell what you *hear* and *see*.

The second point upon which I would like to comment affirmatively is Dr. Pinnock's recognition that the pluralism of cultures and communal interpretations presents immense problems for hermeneutics and Christian theology. However, it is significant that he does not acknowledge his own particularity. Is it enough to make references to "classical Christianity"? The question in the modern world is not simply about the gospel but about *interpretations* of the gospel. Theological language, it has been pointed out many times, is not neutral or nonideological.

A third and final point I would like to make in this section of my response is that I appreciate Dr. Pinnock's description of modernity as having its roots in ancient paganism, the fruits of which we now experience as we live in the postmodern world.

On the other hand, I also have some problems with the paper. For example, Pinnock states that "if we are going to be able to frame the Christian message effectively for people today we must try to grasp what excites them, what moves them, what ails them, what deceives them." It seems to me that this statement trivializes the modern world struggle for life in the face of the deathly character of the world's present reality. The struggle ought not simply be to *frame* the gospel but to *enact* it in order to affirm and give life in the face of evil and death. I think it was Irenaeus who

---

1. West, *Prophesy Deliverance!* (Philadelphia: Westminster Press, 1982), p. 97.

said *"Gloria Dei, viven hominis"*—"A living people is the glory of God." In his book *The Beginnings of Christian Dogma*, Martin Werner has argued that the early Christian theology arose in order to confront the contradictions that were central to the lives of the early Christians. The return of Jesus, once thought to be imminent, did not occur. The Christians were confronted with the realities of the Greco-Roman world and they needed to theologize in order to make sense of these expectations. Werner's perspective encourages us to be aware of the fundamental contradictions intrinsic in modernity. It is proper and appropriate to recognize these issues, events, and concerns that move people to speak of God. The obvious question is "What is the mission of the gospel in modernity?"

Again, in the paper, Pinnock criticizes José Miranda for collapsing the "truth question" into the "justice question" and then asserts that "'love God' and 'love your neighbor' are two great commandments, not one." I agree with John Stam that he misrepresents Miranda here. Miranda's perspective is informed by the biblical notion, grounded in the Old and New Testaments, that the love of neighbor is the concrete expression of one's love of God. This historicization of one's faith is so critical that in 1 John 2:3-6 we read that those who are disobedient are *liars*. Later on, we are provided with the helpful distinction between secularity and secularism, while the determining factor in secular humanism is identified as godlessness. Solzhenitsyn is cited to substantiate Pinnock's thesis that the character of modern secularism is atheistic, that "the entire twentieth century is being sucked into the vortex of atheism and self-destruction." On the other hand, he applauds the values of positive humanism: the powers of reason, liberty of conscience, unfettered science, a concern for moral issues, human freedom, and so on. This is that point at which Pinnock's own social position manifests itself most explicitly in the paper.

I have already made clear my own position on the character of this understanding of modernity: it is characterized by the enthronement of the authority of science and the return to pagan neoclassicism and the subjectivist turn in philosophy characterized by Descartes. I would further note that the postmodern era is characterized by a crisis in the authority of science itself. Science has been demythologized, much as religion was in the period we call the modern era. And modern paganism has degenerated into cynicism, fatalism, hedonism, and narcissism. Bourgeois Christianity in the modern and postmodern period in North America and Europe appears precisely the way it was described by Marx, Freud, Feuerbach, Nietzsche, and Barth. Pinnock's biases as a North American male are manifested at this point: he overemphasizes the social ills of the Communist East without making equally explicit references to the sordid history of the "Christian West." Indeed, in the modern and postmodern world, the Christianity of Europe and North America as much as the secularity provided the idolatrous ideological backbone of the most oppressive forces in the world—the imperialist, racist, sexist, and classist forces of Europe and North America that have perpetrated the most devasting dehumanization on particular segments of humanity. John Hope Franklin, the noted black historian, estimates that ninety to one hundred million Africans were killed in the Middle Passage.

One of the most important features of the postmodern era is the emergence of the voices of the marginalized segments of humanity, the victims of the godlessness of the post-Enlightenment world: black people, yellow people, red people, women, peasants, the poor, and others. These groups, which Jerry Sheppard calls "submodern groups," have been absent from the modern discourse, or at best at the periphery of it. In many cases these groups have transcended the parameters of the modern discourse and have forcefully articulated a contextual perspective radically different from that of the theologians who represent the mainstream of modern theology. For these victims in South Africa and the Philippines, in the United States and in El Salvador, the central contradiction of their lives is the historical reality of poverty and oppression perpetrated upon them by socio-economic systems supported by Catholics and Protestants among others—religious bodies whose religion and politics can be equated with the ideology of the status quo, the dominant classes.

Religious and secular ideologies have both been instrumental on behalf of the economic interests of the dominant class. Both the humanist ideology of communism and the liberal democratic ideology of the United States have been theologized as tools of imperialism. Christian institutions, evangelical included, have often served the interests of the ruling class, so it is not surprising that in the Third World exported Protestant evangelicalism has been defining the parameters of theology and the mission of the church. Protestantism and Catholicism are simply two representatives of Euro-American colonizing interests in the Third World. Even the political reduction of the debate to the East-West tension fails to comprehend the idolatry or godlessness of the situation. And this is the point: it is not just a question of godlessness; it's a question of idolatry, as John Stam has pointed out. It's the idolatry of those institutions, values, and sensibilities that shape human life in the modern era. The ideology and idolatry of national security, of "vital interests," is itself an aspect of the theologization of American ideology. It functions in a religious way in the United States to justify certain imperialist activities that the government of the United States engages in.

In this concluding section, I would like to raise a few points for our consideration regarding our discussion of "context and hermeneutics in the Americas." The masters of suspicion—Freud, Feuerbach, Nietzsche, Marx, and so on—do indeed have much to teach us. Like Christianity, Marxism has progressive traditions as well as dogmatic traditions. It has traditions that are far from what the reality of the ideology is intending to speak about. If we could get beyond the rhetoric about Marxism and Christianity, we might see some values, some sensibilities, that shape our actions in the world, that we hold in common. Surely Marxist philosophy, Marxist dialectical materialism, is atheistic. No question about that. But that's not the issue. There are things that we need to learn. If we can be sensitive as we engage in that discussion, it might lead us into another vast area of exploration.

Marx did not define religion as merely the "opiate of the people." In that same context he wrote that "religion is the sigh of the oppressed creature, the sentiment of a heartless world, the soul of soulless conditions."[2] These words are positively interpreted by many liberation theologians concerning theological perspectives of the oppressed. Their religion, their interpretation, is enacted from the condition of powerlessness. This was the gospel that the slaves found in the text, despite the distortions given to them by their Christian masters. We must acknowledge the problem of the mystification and distortion of the gospel and its message if we are to be clear on the precise definition of the gospel to which we refer. Indeed, the mystification and theologization of Americanism, politics, and religion is a central theme in the lives of many in the Caribbean and in Latin America. The redefinition of the gospel from the underside must be allowed to shape our presuppositions about text and context in the creative ways that Gerald Sheppard has suggested.

A methodology for approaching the hermeneutical task from the perspective of the oppressed could be a dialectical methodology that recognizes the need for demystification and proceeds in three ways. First comes negation—the *unmasking* of the socio-political and ideological realities underlying the interpretation. We should take a look at whether Clark Pinnock calls our attention to the location of United States evangelicalism vis-à-vis religion and politics in the United States, for instance, and at whether Samuel Escobar tells us anything regarding the social location of evangelicalism in Peru. Second comes *preserving* the central essence of the prophetic gospel as it is found in the text, without all of these ideological trappings. Third comes *transforming* our interpretation of the gospel in a way that is more consistent with the text itself and with the perspective of those who speak from below. This methodology implicitly recognizes that the partnership that included only philosophy and theology must now be expanded to include disciplines such as economics, sociology, and critical analysis. Further, it acknowledges that the interpreter of the text must be more self-conscious about indicating the limitations of his or her own particularity and about analyzing the interpreter for his or her ideological presuppositions and commitments.

2. Marx, "Contribution to the Critique of Hegel's Philosophy of Right: Introduction," in *The Marx-Engels Reader,* ed. R. C. Tucker (W. W. Norton, 1978), p. 54.

1.2.5

Reply to Comments by Pinnock

Thank you very much for the response. These issues are very difficult and terribly important, especially the ones George Cummings is raising. And I thank him for presenting them in the way he did. This is a Christian discussion, and I appreciate that. First, responding to John Stam, the committee gave me this topic, this antithesis. I made a choice, so some of my development had to do with that need for a choice. It actually helped me, but I concede that it probably needed better formulation, which is what John said.

I liked what he was getting at about the need for honesty in evangelical theology. The point applies to any number of people. Norm Geisler came to my mind before you mentioned Lindsell. The interesting combination of absolutism and relativism in ethics turns up in Geisler's system of hierarchy. It's ironic that he has called others on that issue in the Evangelical Philosophical Society. It was suggested that Geisler was compromising inerrancy, which is a beautiful joke. Perhaps that is also a good way to address the relativism issue.

On this matter of the problem of ideological distortion that I raised at the end of the paper, my point was that you have to have an ideology—I was agreeing here with Segundo. Everyone looks at things in certain ways. I don't think ideology has to have a tainted meaning, but whatever one's ideology, it will create distortion. The reports on Nicaragua make this clear to me. It does seem clearly the case that America is viewing this situation in the light of fixed understanding of the implications of Marxist dogma. They hear "Marxist" and they automatically connect it with past examples in which Marxism meant the imposition of terrible, awful terror. But that cannot automatically be read into this situation. If that is a distortion, we, as Christians, must reject that ideology. We must then oppose, I must oppose, any such threatened intervention. I used the provocative term *gangsterism,* and that turned on me. There are, of course, other kinds of gangsters in the world than those I cited. The U.S. does practice a kind of imperialism. And it often fails to act according to its more praiseworthy ideals. In fact the U.S.

and the Soviet Union are very similar in the extent to which they act as imperial powers. I don't want to compare body counts, measure what happens in the gulags and Phnom Penh against something on the other side. But of course George was right to bring up the most devastating example— slavery. Slavery was also an Arab problem, but that doesn't deny the Euro-American tragedy. What I admire about democratic capitalism as a theoretical system, then, too often is not put into practice.

Linda Mercadante raised some very profound issues. First, there is the matter of how we approach the topic of relevancy. William Hordern has spoken of theologians who *translate* and theologians who *transform*. Translating takes place when theologians try to recover what the Bible says in new words, when they rephrase the original in creative new ways so that it can be understood by their contemporaries. Using the old words can keep it from getting heard. Using new words may make it understandable. So we strive for a fidelity to the Bible's message, a creative translation. This is what Tillich and Bultmann sought to do, but in my judgment they crossed the line into a transformation that did not take the biblical content seriously enough. I think this is more true of Tillich than Bultmann. Bultmann rejects the idea that he is a transforming theologian, insisting that he has a high view of Scripture; in fact, he sees it as very unique and crucial, as the decisive Word of God. As John Stam and Linda Mercadante pointed out, we should not distort the views of these people. They are terrifically capable, and they deserve our open-minded consideration.

Linda's other point was very interesting: *we* are the audience, so we should listen first if we're going to be relevant to people. We have to do as Tillich says in his *Introduction to Systematics:* listen for the situation so that we can speak to it. I even like Tillich's suggestion that we should take the content of revelation and relate it to the questions that are raised. I don't think he did that, but the idea is right. I think Francis Schaeffer tried to do that; I know there are weaknesses in his work, but I appreciate his attempt to answer the modern questions as Tillich said we should.

George has a tremendously informed understanding of the world. He indicated his view of the world just as I did in my paper, and I grant that his expertise surpasses mine. These two views stand over and against each other with no clear way to mediate between them. I cannot deny many of the things he said, and in fairness to his position I must grant that what he points to as evils really are evils. But that doesn't resolve the difference between the two views, the two understandings of revolution—the kind connected with what the U.S. was originally meant to be and the kind that many now wish to have here in Latin America. Maybe George is right in saying that these views are tied to commitments you make, but I cannot agree with his assertion that the views cannot be judged except by the test of practice. I think there are other tests. That's not to say I'm afraid of the praxis test— indeed, I think history provides evidence that is quite favorable to my view in terms of what produces justice and peace. There's not much more I can say in response to his critique. It's so broad that it doesn't permit a middle ground, and I don't feel I can concede the major points. Perhaps for the time being we can agree to disagree. And, of course, to continue to discuss our differences. I want to remain open to the views of all of the participants here.

1.2.6

General Discussion of the Pinnock Paper and Responses

Roberts: First, it seems to me that there's another question that could be raised concerning the dichotomy between truth and justice, a question that intrigued me years ago when I started writing black theology. It came from a student who wanted to work with people who were suffering. The question is "Does God care?" I found in responding to that question that I was able to deal with problems of both truth and justice. I think it's a question that oppressed communities are asking from the depths of despair around the world. Second, we haven't said very much about oppression within the United States, except for Linda Mercadante's comments about women. In recent years, since the Reagan administration began, there has been great suffering in the United States on a grand scale as a result of economic pressures on old people, poor people, women, blacks, and so forth. In this sense, the United States and other Western nations in the postcolonial period are rapidly becoming Third World nations. I don't see how our theology or our theological institutions or our churches are addressing that reality, which will only become more problematic in the decades to come.

Pinnock: Thomas Sowell's view is that black people were just beginning to make it at the very time when the Great Society decided to help them and that approach to the problem locked them into a terrible situation. He claims that the best thing to do is to get rid of that system, which is what Reagan is doing.

Cummings: That's one of the reasons why we need to be very precise about our social analysis. Certainly there are different ways of analyzing society. There's a tendency in the United States to talk about the problems of El Salvador and Nicaragua or of blacks or Hispanics or whoever as if these problems have just appeared in history and have not been systematically perpetrated upon them. I would encourage some serious analysis of those conditions with respect to their effects on the lives of people. Obviously, I would disagree with Thomas Sowell.

71

Costas: I think Clark used some terms that need very precise defining. For example, "democratic capitalism." Just what is it that we're talking about when we use that concept? You seem to be contrasting Marxism on the one hand with democratic capitalism on the other. But of course there are various traditions that are, in fact, a mixture of the two—the socialist-democratic tradition, for example. It is critical that we acknowledge that tradition, because it is working—socialism within the framework of a pluralistic democracy. Now I know that in North America it is frequently the target of cheap shots from such places as the Institute on Religion and Democracy and the American Enterprises Institute. Yet they have not really dealt in depth with that option. We need to start looking at the various systems.

Second, I think it's very important for us to bear in mind that the question we've met to deal with was not, at least intentionally, given an apologetic bent. Rather, it was cast in terms of how one gives shape to the nature of the theological discourse. Whose questions are we answering in the development of our theology? Some of us—some of us here—find ourselves completely excluded from the theological discourse that has emerged out of evangelical circles. We constitute a significant number of evangelicals. I'm talking here specifically of American blacks, Hispanic Americans, native Americans, Latin Americans, and I would venture to say a large number of women. We have yet to hear an intelligent systematic evangelical discourse from within establishment evangelicalism that answers the questions posed by these "nonpersons." This evangelicalism, which has controlled access to all the institutions in the evangelical world, access to the publishing houses, access to evangelical culture and subcultures, has focused on theological discourses that are geared to answer the questions of the Enlightenment. These are questions associated with a white, male-dominated society. Clark has pointed this out as a critical issue. I heard George responding to it. But then I heard Clark say, "Well there's your point of view, and here's my point of view. What can we say about it?" Does that represent the sort of attitude we have to expect from white Anglo-Saxon evangelical Protestantism? That's the answer I've been given for a long time, as long as I've been an evangelical. That's the answer I was given in seminary. That's the answer I was given in my own local church, and I was one of those kids who went to a white church. That's the answer I hear from these other institutions. Liberation theologies, which make no claim to be evangelical, have been trying to cope with the question of the nonperson. Feminist theology is trying to cope with the question of nonpersons. Black theology is addressing that issue. And the theology of Bartholomew de las Casas here in Mexico is addressing that issue. So, I pose the issue to see if somehow evangelicalism can take this challenge seriously.

Pinnock: What I was trying to say earlier is that the dilemma can't be resolved easily, that I can't reconcile our positions in just a few minutes. That was the No. As for the character of the evangelical community in North

America, yes, it's mostly white. The community came together because certain people decided to take a stand for their biblical convictions over and against religious liberalism. They called themselves evangelicals. They developed a network that was mostly white because they were mostly white. The people began working on their own projects, starting colleges, establishing publishing houses. But now, of course, there is a definite need for the opening up that Orlando is asking for. The community needs to be much better and fuller.

Gutiérrez-Cortés: It was said that ideologies distort knowledge. We also know that each of us comes with an ideological background, assumptions. We subjectivize our knowledge, and the more we do so, the more difficult it is to comprehend the object of knowledge. As theologians, we must not forget the center of our point of view, the knowledge of God: he is the object of our knowledge. So, we have a huge task before us with regard to our ideologies. We have to examine our prejudices and deal with them before we can transmit the gospel of Christ.

Watson: What Clark has done for us is to present a position against which we can bounce a great deal of criticism. I have a feeling that if he had not presented the position as strongly as he did, we would to some extent be beating the air now. He's helped us to get the issue of ideology out into the open. Now that we've done that, now that we've agreed that it's important for us to prevent ideology from getting in the way of presenting the gospel, it seems to me that the question remains how we should go about removing that ideological prejudice. I want in particular to ask our brothers and sisters in Latin America how they would suggest that those of us who are trying to teach and to pastor in the North American context should go about it.

Stam: Paul says in Romans, "Be not conformed to this world." Both in Latin America and North America, we need a Christian prophetic consciousness of the evil around us, so that rather than rationalizing it and theologizing it, assimilating it theologically, we will be able to develop a critical distance and awareness. This must begin very slowly, maybe in Latin America as much as in North America among a given sector of the Christian community. But the idolatry we have spoken of is associated with what Paul refers to as being "conformed to the world."

Padilla: It seems to me that this is not just an intellectual problem. If it were just an intellectual problem, perhaps it would be easier. I just made a tour of evangelical colleges in the U.S. and had a chance to speak to a large number of students and professors. It is a shocking experience. It seems terribly, terribly difficult to help people who are caught in this situation, totally dominated by a given ideology—Reaganism right now—just to realize what the issues are. Time after time the same questions come up, and the same assumptions are there: "We are a wonderful nation. We are working for freedom and justice." So I keep saying, "Freedom and justice? For whom?" Quite frankly, I was a bit depressed after this experience. I can tell that there is a social captivity of the church, which I'm sure is true not only of the church in the U.S., of course.

This is where I see that a meeting like this fulfills a function. Somehow, we have to begin with our own situation, with ourselves. I met a number of college professors who had visited Nicaragua, and several of them said to me that they had had a second conversion. No matter how much you argue about Nicaragua, you will never be able to help people to an existential experience like those people had. They had to come to Nicaragua and talk to all kinds of people—those who were against the government, those who were for the government, evangelicals, Roman Catholics, every kind of person they could find in that context. It seems to me that there is a tremendous need for this sort of personal, first-hand experience. Though, as I've I said many times, you don't have to go to Nicaragua; just go into the slums of the cities of the U.S. Heilbroner tells us that there are thirty-six million people living under the poverty line in the U.S. So it's not a question of having to pay your fare to come to Nicaragua. In fact, people would do better to look into their own cities to find out about what is going on in the world. When they talk about freedom and justice in the U.S., they are talking about a very small segment of society— especially in relation to the population of the whole world.

Cummings: A comment about your criterion, Rolando. It demonstrates the loaded ideological character of these terms themselves. If all the people in the world want peace and can't have it, what does this mean? We, that is to say the United States, say we want peace, and we can't understand why the Soviets are destabilizing the Western Hemisphere. Nicaraguans say they want peace, and the only reason they are militarizing is because the United States is destabilizing their country. The West Germans say they want peace because they don't want to get caught in between. Everybody wants peace. Well, what are we talking about precisely when we say Jesus brings peace? Peace! This language itself is so loaded and problematic.

The second comment I wanted to make is about this "democratic capitalism." What do we mean when we say this? Our assumption has something to do with our definition of "democratic" and our definition of "capitalism." We know that only twenty-five percent of the people in the United States choose the president anyway, and most of them have been dominated by the hegemony of the media all of their lives. "We hold these truths to be self-evident, that all men are created equal"—but not black men, and of course not women. Which men are we talking about? These assumptions are rife throughout our culture, and we need to unpack them and look at them. I don't mean to be divisive, I just want to say that it's time to unpack these prejudices, acknowledge them, and then go on. We say we are committed to Jesus Christ—then let's be serious about it.

Gutiérrez-Cortés: Ideology hides things. I hide myself from myself with my ideology, and my ideology hides me when I'm using it. Theology should do the opposite; it should clarify not only the terms we use but everything that can prevent the understanding of love of God and love of neighbor. And peace offers a way to begin reaching beyond ideology. I'm certain of the love of George Cummings. He trembles when he speaks and I tremble also— because for us it's a spiritual burden. We're from different backgrounds, but we sing with the same intensity "what a friend we have in Jesus." He bore our pain. Pain is important. Peace is radical health. This health we talk about Jesus giving is what we need. We are not talking about some kind of peace that tries through political agreements to reach a solution. Thank you for reminding me that even in theological circles we need to rediscover our terms. As Linda pointed out, if we can no longer use the words to communicate to others, then it's time to look again at the words and find out why.

Hays: I have a response related to David Watson's request for guidance from those of you who do represent Third World perspectives: what then should we do? That question I suppose reflects the speech in Acts when Peter, on the day of Pentecost, preaches that great speech and people are so convicted and cut to the heart that they say, "What then should we do?" And Peter has an easy answer—he says, "Repent, and be baptized and you'll receive the Holy Spirit." But, I've already repented and been baptized and received the Holy Spirit, and I would like to hear something addressed to the situation of the North American evangelicals. I think there are many of us who essentially accept the critique that we have heard, offered here by representatives of the Third World who feel alienated from the power structures of our culture. I was talking with Pablo about how I as an educated white North American am appalled, ashamed, and dismayed at the things the government of the United States is doing in the world. I feel powerless to change it or to have any real impact on the current public opinion in the United States, even among my Christian brothers and sisters. So my question to all of you is "What then should we do?" What is an appropriate response for the church, the evangelical church in North America, to make?

Stam: I would like to make a suggestion along the lines that George has been pursuing. We must rediscover the gospel in Scripture, try to break our minds free from identifications of the gospel in Scripture with all ideological positions, and seek out the vitality of the gospel that can itself orient us regarding our ideological options. What about the movement of "radical evangelicals"? Is it creating a place where evangelicals can get together in this kind of a commitment?

Hays: Not on any very large scale in my experience.

Osborne: The problem, too, is the baggage, an entire ideological stance that goes far beyond the complex aspect of the oppression of minorities. It is difficult to try to fight your way through all the baggage. I think one of the large problems for evangelicals in the university and seminary settings, which we represent, is that the students by and large do not even want to hear. They just want to become a part of the establishment and get the goodies. We're in a very difficult time; it's pragmatism we're facing. I attended a seminar on "Theologians and Politics" in Washington a year ago where we heard from an expert on polls and trends. In a later discussion, he said that the polls indicate that theologians are to the left of center, and graduating students are to the right. So the theologians are speaking, and nobody's listening. We've got to bridge this gap created by the overpowering pragmatism of the American student. I don't know how to do that.

Mercadante: It's been my experience that ideologizing works the other way too. I'm at Princeton Seminary, where I see many students arrive as evangelicals, but within two days they no longer use the term. If you'd wake them up in the middle of the night and ask them if they're evangelical, they'd probably say No. It doesn't take long to get the message that this is not a good thing to say around there. Of course Princeton is the birthplace of the fundamentalist-modernist controversy, and the feelings are still present. To indicate that such things are relative, I remember when I said at Berkeley that I was going to Princeton, they said, "You're going to go to that arch-conservative school? How could you possibly leave the halls of freedom for that?"

An "evangelical" is now understood to be either somebody who doesn't know the issues or somebody who knows the issues but refuses to deal with them. Earlier, at Regent College, I had many colleagues who were very enthusiastic and excited about their faith and would gladly say that they were evangelicals. Later, though, I found that the majority of them refused to call themselves evangelical; they had become embarrassed about that title and its associations. Had they been ideologized by the culture? I think evangelicalism is in a troubled time right now. Some people are giving up their evangelicalism while others are clinging to it.

Gil: I'd like to address the questions concerning what we in the First World can do. I hear what I would call excuses for doing nothing. I don't think it matters one iota what the polls say about whether we will be popular or unpopular. It's true that the issue is complex. But we don't have to come up with a completely new economic order and a completely new worldview before we do anything. Too often our words say one thing and our actions say another, especially those of us who teach in seminaries where the manner of life is not all that liberating. It is not surprising that students opt for conservatism. Most of us are leading very conservative lives. Students read *us* rather than listening to our lectures.

As Peter suggests in Acts, repentance might not be a bad place to start. By repentance, I do not mean the normal evangelical response of getting off to the next guilt trip, because all that does is strip us of any motivation, any possibility of moving forward. Repentance should be a change of direction, a new style of living—a motivating force rather than a debilitating factor. But, as with the Exodus, you don't get a map before you leave Egypt. You're told to go and that God will be with you. When we ask for the map, even if we ask the Hispanics for a map, the blacks for a map, I think we're asking the wrong question. No one is going to provide us with a map. If we were prepared to take the first steps, we might be surprised. The God of the Exodus will reveal the next step to us. If we aren't ready to listen to that voice, we are going to remain in Egypt forever. I think that the only way we can break out is by beginning in this way, even if the first step might be wrong.

Sánchez-Centina: In trying to answer this question how to break away from our ideologies, we must not approach the issue just on the academic and theoretical level. We need to grapple with the issues of real life. There is no other way to start understanding and communicating unless we start by saying that we are not *the* theologians, we are not those who are giving the answers, we are not those who are going to change the lives and minds of people. Rather, we are struggling and deciding today how to take in our hands the solutions for these problems of oppression. And to understand the ministry of Christian leaders and theologians in Latin America, we have to keep our ears and eyes open to where the struggle of the Christian faith is going on today in Latin America and the world.

Watson: I think that's the very point which demands our focus. I think that if any group of evangelical Christians in North America could have heard the singing of that psalm two hours ago, they would have a very different impression of Latin American theology. What tends to happen is that the analysis of the way in which the gospel is related to the reality of the Latin America context gets put first. But of course it is the gospel that gave rise to that analysis, and it is the gospel that should come first. It is this point that leads to so much miscommunication. I think it is in this regard that Clark's strong points have not been given enough attention. Regardless of what one might think about his analysis, he is correct in insisting that we in North America must get back to the gospel and let the gospel do the work of analysis for us. I often conclude that we ought to be following your lead, but we have no sense of the empowerment that it has given you.

Costas: I wish I could believe that. And I sincerely say that: I wish I could. I do believe with you that there is a one-sidedness to Latin America that is typically portrayed in the North American scene. Class struggles and revolutions come through. The other side—basic communities, worship, praise—doesn't always come through, and sometimes that is the side that provides the energy. For example, we brand Latin American liberation theology as systematics and as ethics, when in fact it is pastoral theology. It emerges out of pastoral concerns. On the other side, the black church in North America and the Hispanic church have been very energetic, very spiritual. That's the source of power. Preaching is central. But the moment you hear even the style of that preaching, it is bracketed, it is characterized as esoteric. The media, the culture is so powerful, and has worked within the premise of power, that the nonwhite is easily incorporated in a stereotype and put into a little bracket. When I was in Costa Rica, I believed that I was at the very heart and nerve of history. But then I came to Philadelphia, and I discovered that we were just a little speck over there.

Our spirituality is also bracketed. I have a black colleague who teaches worship. Within the very first semester, five white students came to complain about him. They could not stand the fact that here was a black person teaching whites and blacks and others how to worship. It's okay for blacks to worship, but our white brothers don't want to learn from them. My colleagues here know that I praise the Lord. I'll sing in class, I'll preach, I'll let myself go. But for three years I was imprisoned in those classes. I could not let go because of the context. And then all of a sudden the Lord began to liberate me. I can't do mission studies in any other context but the context of praise and prayer—hallelujah and amen! The key was how to get my white brothers and sisters in those classes not to feel threatened. Not to feel threatened! See, the problem is that it is very difficult for a dominant society to function in an environment in which they cannot call the shots, they cannot have the power, where they will have to feel vulnerable like the rest of us.

There lies the big problem concerning ideology: ideologies are always related to power. The power of the American dream, the power of the melting pot, the power of the American mainstream project had to be confronted with the power of the minorities. There is an ideological problem, but America did not know this for a long time. Often this kind of reorientation involves a very painful experience. A woman colleague had to help me in that way last year. She took me on. I could not understand what I was saying that was humiliating her. Finally I called another colleague, and I said, "Please tell me, what was it I said?" He said, "You simply trivialize her." It was a shock. I cannot explain how deeply shocked I was. I spent an entire weekend praying about it, thinking about it, talking about it. I was intimidating a colleague, and she had to face me head on to help me realize that something had to change—that I had to change. Finally, I was able to say, "You know, it all started with my doctoral defense. You humiliated me." We got it out! Confrontations, ideological confrontations, are essential for us to become aware of some very subtle facts concerning power and vulnerability. I would like to think that evangelicals have something to say about vulnerability—about what it means to be converted, what it means to be broken and to be restored again. Rather, we have bought lock, stock, and barrel into the power, and those necessary items are pushed aside.

Watson: I agree with Orlando concerning his analysis of how pastoral theology is at the base of any good theologizing. But you have not clarified why you believe that putting the gospel first, rather than putting the analysis first, would not work in the North American context.

Costas: Because "the gospel" has been ideologized, used as a power factor. And you must have the ideological views of that "gospel" challenged.

Watson: My question is, why not let the gospel do that?

Cummings: Why not let the gospel do it? Because evangelicals use the term *gospel* in reference to a particular stand vis-à-vis the world. You said earlier that you wished others could have heard our singing of the psalm prior to our analysis, because what often gets projected in the United States is an analysis without the witness. You suggested that the witness points to the gospel, and that it is the gospel that allows Latin Americans to approach the text and their lives in such a way. But the American definition of the gospel is connected to certain ideological presuppositions that evangelicals bring to the table. When I say *evangelicals,* I mean what most of us mean when we use the term, as Orlando has pointed out many times: white evangelicals. When the black church or the Hispanic communities come to the evangelical table, they must come on the terms already determined by white evangelicals. I have very concrete examples. I was offered ordination in a white evangelical church. When I said that I was in a black community and I wanted to have black pastors participate, the white minister told me that those pastors would have to sign the Statement of Faith of the National Association of Evangelicals. But the faith of the black church does not have to be validated by anybody in the white evangelical world. Our faith has been there for hundreds of years. So, on whose grounds are we talking about this "gospel"? That's the issue. On whose grounds are the parameters of the dialogue or discussion being defined?

Why won't "getting back to the gospel" work? I have spent years studying the civil rights movement and Martin Luther King. There is no more saintly a person in the Christian world than Martin Luther King. His assumption was that if we can just demonstrate to America its apostasy with respect to black people, the people would change. And then it didn't happen. We demonstrated it, clarified it, articulated it, stated it out straight. We turned to the gospel, used the Scriptures, and it still didn't happen. So there are people who have a history of saying, "Okay, let's go back to the gospel," and everybody agrees, but almost nobody changes their lifestyle.

Alton: I want to respond to René's comments about his tour of American colleges and to the questions raised by Richard about responding.

As we studied the Exodus theme in our group this morning, God's words were "I have seen their affliction and I have heard their cry." Yet what church people, what seminary and college students, have not had is an opportunity to see the affliction and hear the cry? If what comes first is the theology or the institutional power and not the experience, then the teaching is going to fall on deaf ears. So you're going to be producing those left-of-center professors and right-of-center students who are graduating and filling right-of-center churches. Perhaps it would help if the seminary professors would take the small step of taking their students with them into the problem areas of our own cities or to Third World countries in order to do theological reflection in that context. This is partly by way of personal testimony. I wouldn't be sitting around this table, having grown up in those kinds of institutions, currently serving that kind of institution, if I hadn't had that kind of an experience in the midst of my theological reflection.

Hubbard: When we talk in terms of starting points, we can proceed in two ways. We can think in terms of the large, global arena, where we push the political buttons to achieve certain goals. Or we can start locally, right where we are. In other words, we need to talk about seminary professors modeling the gospel in very practical, down-to-earth ways—in the ways we live, in our lifestyles, in our community involvement. My wife, for example, got involved with disabled people, people with cerebral palsy, developed some friendships through a volunteer organization. This led me into new friendships and new perspectives. I suppose the principle is what Jesus taught in the parable of the Good Samaritan: Whoever you happen upon down the road, that's your brother; that is the person that God wants you to deal with. Without setting aside the larger issues, we can repent by turning in a different direction in our own contexts and prayerfully looking for opportunities, whether in the area of race relations or political justice or with disabled or elderly people. Find people who are hurting and who are in need, and you will probably find a systemic problem that you will have to address.

Gil: I would suspect, Robert, that you see the gospel differently now through identification. That's the liberating potential of the question David asked. There are leads of this sort in the gospel that are so obvious. For the most part these things have just passed us by for so long. We ought not to be surprised, as evangelicals, that we wrestle not with flesh and blood or that our blindness isn't just on a very superficial level. Principalities and powers are at work blinding us in the way we read our Scripture.

1.3.1

Toward a Contextual Christology from Latin America

C. RENÉ PADILLA

The great difficulty that Christians generally have in relating theology to social, economic, and political issues is closely connected with their lack of an adequate Christological foundation for Christian thought and action. Quite early in the history of the church, the Christian message was cast into philosophical categories, and the historical dimension of revelation was completely overshadowed by dogma. The classic Christological formulas—the Nicene Creed and the Chalcedonian definition—systematized in metaphysical language the biblical data concerning Christ as fully God and fully man and as indivisibly one, but they lost sight of Jesus' concrete actions in history reported by the evangelists.[1] The Christ of dogma replaced Jesus of Nazareth, who identified himself with the poor and the oppressed.

The problems of dogmatic Christology were compounded with those related to the role that Christianity played within Christendom beginning with Emperor Constantine, which was similar to the role that the old state religion had played in the Roman Empire. The heavenly Lord was seen as possessing the functions and powers of an earthly king and standing behind the Christian emperor who ruled in his name. Jesus' historical mission was blurred by this image of a "political" Christ forged by the Christian ideology of empire.[2] Even after the "Christian West" had ceased to be reality, Chris-

---

1. See A. N. S. Lane, "Christology beyond Chalcedon," in *Christ and Lord*, ed. Harold H. Rowdon (London: Inter-Varsity Press, 1982), pp. 257ff. Lane is undoubtedly correct in his claim that "the starting point for Christology should be the historical Christ, as portrayed in the New Testament, not the eternal Trinity" (p. 276).
2. See Hans Schmidt, "Politics and Christology: The Historical Background," *Concilium*, 6 (June 1968): 39ff.

tianity in the West continued to serve as a civil religion in which political overtones derived from a misconstructed image of the glorified Christ were retained while the political relevance of the historical Jesus continued to be ignored.

By contrast, the Christ of popular religiosity was the dead Jesus, defeated and helpless, eloquently portrayed by Velásquez in his Spanish Christ. It was, again, a Christ unable to respond to the cries of the poor, a symbol of their passivity in the face of their oppressors. Of this Christ wrote Miguel de Unamuno,

> El Cristo de mi tierra es sólo tierra, tierra, tierra, tierra . . . carne que no palipita, tierra, tierra, tierra, tierra . . . cuajarones de sangre que no fluye, tierra, tierra, tierra, tierra . . .[3]

The Christ of traditional Western Christianity failed to provide an adequate basis for Christian social and political responsibility. The traditional images of Christ have made it very clear that a Christianity that disregards the historical Jesus may be useful for personal piety or civil religion, but it is neither faithful to the witness of Scripture concerning Jesus Christ nor historically relevant.

Needless to say, these are the images of Christ that have generally defined Christian thought and action in Latin America for almost five centuries. They can be traced back to the christ brought by the conquerors in the sixteenth century—a christ that, as is widely recognized within the Roman Catholic Church today, was at best a weak representation and at worst a caricature of the New Testament Christ.

In light of this situation, one can hardly exaggerate the importance of the "discovery" of the historical Jesus that has taken place in Roman Catholic circles in Latin America since the early 1970s. Already in 1947, during a visit to thirteen Latin American countries, John A. Mackay noticed the emergence of a new image of Christ in this region.

> The hour has arrived in Latin America in which Jesus Christ is considered in general terms as having some kind of meaning for the secular order. Up to now he has been an invalid, a misrepresented and misunderstood prisoner within an ecclesiastical order which, having ceased to be his mouthpiece and servant, has become his patron and promoter.[4]

A quarter-century later, the new image of Christ would attain the shape of one who, far from hiding in the luxurious temples of the rich and the

3. Unamuno, "El Cristo Yacente de Santa Clara (Inglesia de la Cruz) de Palencia," in *El concepto contemporáneo de España,* ed. Angel del Rio and M. J. Benardete (Buenos Aires: Editorial Losada, 1946), p. 130.

4. Mackay, *El otro Cristo español,* (Mexico: Casa Unida de Pulicaciones, 1952), p. 279.

powerful, brings good news to the poor, proclaims liberty to the captives and recovery of sight to the blind, sets free the oppressed, and announces the good year of the Lord.[5] One need not agree with this Christology in every detail to recognize that this return to the historical Jesus is beyond doubt the most significant theological development that has taken place within the Roman Catholic Church since it was established in Latin America. In 1947 Mackay said that the attempt to "reinterpret Jesus Christ to peoples who have never in any way regarded him as relevant to thought or life" was "the supreme religious task to be accomplished in Latin America."[6] This Christology has certainly made big strides in that direction.

On the other hand, it must be recognized that the most common images of Christ in evangelical circles in this region very often fail to do justice to New Testament Christology.[7] Despite its theoretical acknowledgment of Christ's full humanity, evangelical Christianity in Latin America, as in the rest of the world, is deeply affected by docetism. It affirms Christ's transforming power in relation to the individual, but is totally unable to relate the gospel to social ethics and social life. In our case, Mackay's challenge remains unmet.

This paper is a modest attempt to outline a Christology that juxtaposes the historical Jesus with the Latin American situation for the sake of "the obedience of faith." In the first section I will underline the importance of history in relation to Christology. I will then address myself to the most basic Christological question: Who was Jesus of Nazareth? Finally, I will discuss the relevance of this Christology, rooted in the canonical Gospels, to thought and life in Latin America.

1. Christology and History

A fundamental premise of contemporary Latin American Christology is that the Gospels are essentially reliable historical records and that the portrait of Jesus that emerges from them provides an adequate basis for the life and mission of the church today. Hugo Echegaray, for instance, reasons that "if in the Gospels the element of confession had prevailed and been developed in detriment of history, distorting it beyond recognition, the task of

5. On this, see especially *Jesús: Ni vencido ne monarca celestial,* ed. José Míguez Bonino (Buenos Aires: Tierra Nueva, 1977); Leonardo Boff, *Jesucristo y la liberación del hombre,* (Madrid: Ediciones Cristian dad, 1981); José P. Miranda, *El ser y el Mesí* (Salamanca: Ediciones Sigueme, 1973); Jon Sobrino, *Christology at the Crossroads: A Latin American Approach,* (Maryknoll, N.Y.: Orbis Books, 1978); and Hugo Echegaray, *La práctica de Jesús,* (Lima: CEP, 1980).

6. Mackay, *El otro Cristo español,* p. 278.

7. See "El Cristo de la predicación evangélica en América Latina," in *Jesús: Ni vencido ni monarca celestial,* pp. 77ff.

describing Jesus' praxis would be impossible."[8] This does not mean, of course, that the Gospels are to be regarded as "biographies" of Jesus in the modern sense or that the methods of scientific exegesis are to be rejected. It does mean that the historicity of the gospels can be safely assumed and theologians are therefore free to concentrate on defining the meaning of Christian discipleship today.

Quite clearly, this approach allows no disjunction between the Jesus of history and the Christ of faith. Instead, it sees Christology as inseparable from Jesus of Nazareth. In Jon Sobrino's words, "There can be no Christology of Christ apart from the history of Jesus of Nazareth."[9] Such an affirmation implies a recognition not only of the historical validity of the Gospel records but also of the historical basis of the Christian faith. Faith in Christ is never to be identified with wishful thinking or pious feelings. It is faith rooted in history, and consequently it constantly seeks to become historically relevant. "If Christology disregards the historical Jesus," warns Sobrino, "it turns into an abstract Christology that is historically alienating and open to manipulation."[10]

Emphasis on the humanity of Jesus is in complete harmony with the biblical view of Christ as true God and true Man. Jesus of Nazareth *is* Christ, the Son of the living God, the historical nucleus of the revelation of the Father. It is in the totality of his humanity and his historical career that God has uniquely manifested himself. The Word who was in the beginning, who was with God and who was God is inseparable from the Word who became "flesh" and lived in Palestine in the first century. No Christology can claim biblical support if it does not take into account not only the New Testament passages related to the preexistent and cosmic Christ but also the evidence that the Gospels provide concerning his life and ministry.

Unless the humanity of Jesus is given full weight, no real link can be established between his mission and that of his followers. In what sense can one say that "whoever claims to live in him must walk as Jesus did" (1 John 1:6) if the historical existence of Jesus of Nazareth is overshadowed or even ignored in the name of a "high Christology"? And what is the value of a Christianity in which Jesus is worshiped as Lord, but Christian discipleship—"the way of Jesus"—is regarded as largely irrelevant to life in the modern world?

2. Who Was Jesus of Nazareth?

Most Christians would theoretically agree that Jesus was not God in disguise, walking several inches above the ground. They would affirm his

8. Echegaray, *La práctica de Jesús,* p. 60.
9. Sobrino, *Christology at the Crossroads,* p. xxii.
10. Sobrino, *Christology at the Crossroads,* p. 353.

humanity with the same force as his deity. More often than not, however, their descriptions of him show that they fail to conceive him as fully human, as one who was tempted "in every way, just as we are," yet "without sin" (Heb. 4:15). As a result, his life and mission are generally assumed to be irrelevant to their own lives and mission here and now.

If the relevance of Jesus' example and teaching is to be seen, a new reading of the Gospels is needed. The question that Jesus posed to his disciples at a crucial time in his career is still to the point: "Who do you say I am?" (Matt. 16:15). To be sure, a full answer to that question cannot be given outside the context of a personal relationship with him. If the incarnation is taken seriously, however, it is also the case that no answer will be complete unless it gives full weight to the historicity of Jesus. Faith in Christ the Lord involves faith in Jesus of Nazareth; it therefore calls for some kind of understanding of the historical context in which he lived and carried out his ministry. [11]

Assuming that the Gospels are reliable historical sources, what is the image of Jesus that historical studies derive from them?

In *Jesus and His Contemporaries,* Etienne Trocmé claims that from the texts going back to witnesses of the life of Jesus it is possible to reconstruct several portraits of him. According to his inventory, the Jesus of the "dominical sayings," as perceived by his disciples, was a prophet of the kingdom of God mysteriously present in history; the Jesus of the "apophthegms" was a skillful debater who placed himself on the same level as his adversaries, the Jewish intellectuals of the time; the Jesus of the biographical narratives was a political-religious figure, acclaimed as Messiah by the mass of Jewish people after he had expelled the merchants from the Temple; the Jesus of the parables was an ingenious moralist who appealed to the lower-middle and the middle class; and the Jesus of the miracle stories was a semidivine magician who impressed the multitudes of Galilee. Jesus took the initiative to present all these images, says Trocmé, and all were accepted without any attempt to integrate them into a coherent whole. "By not proposing any synthesis between these portraits," claims the French scholar, "he suggested that none of them, and none of those which could be superimposed upon them, could do full justice to his person and his mission." [12]

The study of the Gospels does indeed suggest that there was a wide variety of views concerning Jesus among his contemporaries. This fact is clearly exemplified in John 7, where Jesus is shown to have been perceived as a man driven by the desire to become a public figure (vv. 3-4), a troublemaker (v. 11), a good man (v. 12a), a deceiver (v. 12b), a self-taught man (v. 15), a demon-possessed man (v. 20), a daring man (vv. 25-27), an amazing miracle worker (v. 31), the Prophet (v. 40), the Christ (v. 41), and

11. Of special importance for the study of the historical background of Jesus' life is Joachim Jeremias's *Jerusalem in the Time of Jesus* (Philadelphia: Fortress Press, 1975).
12. Trocmé, *Jesus and His Contemporaries* (London: SCM Press, 1973), p. 125.

the greatest speaker ever heard (v. 46). Does that mean, then, that no coherent picture of Jesus of Nazareth is possible on the basis of the evidence? Are we simply to think that Jesus accepted a wide variety of portraits of himself in the interest of bringing to the kingdom of God groups that were as different from each other as they could be?

No detailed analysis of the evidence brought forward by Trocmé in support of his theory can here be attempted. Given the limitations of time, much of what I say will have to be taken as a preliminary statement of a thesis that needs further elaboration. My claim here is that Jesus of Nazareth did intend to present to his contemporaries a coherent picture of himself—namely, that of God's Messiah who, in fulfillment of Old Testament prophecies, had còme to inaugurate a new order in which God's rule of love and justice would be established in anticipation of the end. This new order would be made visible in the community of his own disciples, the firstfruits of a new humanity marked by love to God and neighbor as well as by renunciation of personal prestige, material wealth, and earthly power. His messianic role would be fulfilled in terms of the Isaianic Servant of the Lord who would take his people's sins in death upon himself and would win for them a favorable verdict from the Father and a righteous status before him. His mission would find its continuation in the mission of the church by the power of the Holy Spirit.

The fact that the heart of Jesus' proclamation was the kingdom of God has been recognized by scholars representing a wide theological spectrum.[13] Mark sums up this proclamation by saying, "the time has come. The kingdom of God is near. Repent and believe the good news" (Mark 1:15). Jesus' proclamation, however, was made not only in words but also in terms of his entire life and mission. Behind all the portraits of Jesus that Trocmé finds in the Gospels stood Jesus of Nazareth, a messianic prophet, "powerful in words and deed before God and all the people" (Luke 24:19), in whom and through whom God was acting in a definite way to establish his kingdom. All of his teaching and action was structured around the kingdom of God, from which they derived their meaning and significance. The dominical sayings, the "apophthegms," the biographical narratives, the parables and the miracle stories recorded in the Gospels all point in the same direction: Jesus was the bearer of the kingdom, the *autobasileia*, the kingdom in person.

According to Jon Sobrino, there were two distinct stages in Jesus' ministry. In the first stage, before the Galilean crisis, Jesus proclaimed the kingdom as an eschatological reality embodied in his own person and work.

13. Rudolf Bultmann, for instance, states that "the heart of the preaching of Jesus Christ is the Kingdom of God" (*Jesus Christ and Mythology* [New York: Scribner's, 1958], p. 11); Joachim Jeremias states that "our starting point is the fact that the central theme of the public proclamation of Jesus is the kingly reign of God" (*New Testament Theology*, vol. 1: *The Proclamation of Jesus* [London: SCM Press, 1971], p. 96).

After the Galilean crisis, says Sobrino, Jesus lost the favor of the masses and ran into conflict and suffering, as a result of which "the kingdom took on the features of the work attributed to the suffering Servant of Yahweh."[14] That break between the first and the second stage of his ministry, however, involved for Jesus a break within himself, "a rupture in his faith," a disjuncture between a concept of the Christian life as a journey toward God and a concept of it as a journey toward a God not really known.[15] Jesus moved from the role of a herald of an eschatological kingdom calling people to trust in God, to the role of a suffering visioner summoning people to radical discipleship in the service of the kingdom.

This argument carries little conviction. The evidence does suggest that in the latter phase of his ministry Jesus told his disciples with increasing emphasis that he was to suffer and be rejected and killed (Mark 8:31, 9:31, 10:33). There is no compelling reason to believe, however, that there was a time in his career when he expected to fulfill his mission without having to suffer. Whether or not Jesus understood the words with which he was commissioned at his baptism ("You are my Son, whom I love; with you I am will pleased," Luke 3:22) as an explicit reference to kingly enthronement (Ps. 2) and suffering servanthood (Isa. 42), the fact remains that from its very beginning his ministry was marked by these two themes. It was as the suffering Servant of the Lord that he would fulfill his messiahship.

The way Jesus went about his ministry was such that it could not but puzzle people in general, provoke suspicion in many, and infuriate those who held positions of privilege in the religious-political establishment. A brief listing of some of the features of his work will make that clear:

> He spoke with authority despite his lack of theological study, which was regarded as the essential requirement for the profession of a scribe. He saw himself as a prophet and claimed the authority of a prophet.[16]
>
> He claimed to be related to God in a unique way and addressed him as 'abbā, "my Father."[17]
>
> He was "a friend of publicans and sinners" and ate with them. As a result, he surrounded himself with people who, according to the common convictions of the time, were rejected by God and had no hope of salvation.[18]
>
> He affirmed that the kingdom of God was present in history and being manifest in the healing of the sick, the raising of the dead,

14. Sobrino, *Christology at the Crossroads,* p. 58.

15. Sobrino, *Christology at the Crossroads,* pp. 94, 362.

16. See Jeremias, *New Testament Theology,* pp. 76ff.

17. See Jeremias, *New Testament Theology,* pp. 61ff., and *The Central Message of the New Testament* (London: SCM Press, 1965), p. 30.

18. See Jeremias, *New Testament Theology,* p. 112.

and the preaching of the gospel to the poor. It was obvious to him that the kingdom of God does not come by the power of the sword, was not intended to satisfy nationalistic Jewish aspirations, and was not associated with success or wealth. It is the kingdom of *God*, and it brings a total inversion of values. Its blessings belong to the poor, to the hungry, to those who weep, and to those who are hated. By contrast, those who are rich, those who are fed, those who laugh, and those who are socially accepted lack its blessings. All of Jesus' ministry throws into relief his special concern for the poor and the oppressed. He saw himself as a prophet who had been anointed to preach good news to the poor, to bring freedom to the prisoners, sight to the blind, and liberation to the oppressed—to proclaim "the year of the Lord's favor." He interpreted his mission in light of God's purpose to establish justice on the earth. [19]

He concentrated his ministry on the uneducated, the ignorant, and the disreputable. He spent much of his time going through all the towns and villages of the underdeveloped province of Galilee, preaching, teaching, and healing. He looked at the crowds with compassionate eyes, for they lacked leaders and therefore had no sense of direction or peoplehood. [20]

He attacked religious oppression and rejected empty religious ceremonies, self-assured piety, and the idea that one's relationship with God is dependent on merit. He was critical of the priests, the scribes, and the Pharisees, and he vividly expressed God's judgment on the religious establishment of his day by the cleansing of the Temple. He claimed that justice and mercy are the great objectives of the law. [21]

He condemned wealth and regarded greed as idolatry. He himself was poor and lived simply, but his poverty was freely chosen, not imposed on him by social conditions. He could therefore eat with the rich while at the same time regarding wealth as dishonest and opposed to God. Taking into account the jubilee prescriptions, he called his disciples to practice kingdom economics by redistributing their capital, and he ordered a wealthy man to sell his possessions and give to the poor. [22]

19. See Washington Padilla, "La vocación detrás de la vocación," CERTEZA, April 1982, pp. 160ff.

20. See my essay "Mission Is Compassion," *Missiology,* 10 (1982): 323ff.

21. Trocmé's argument that Jesus instantly became a public figure by driving the merchants out of the Temple is, however, unconvincing.

22. See Jose I. González Faus, "Jesús de Nazareth y los ricos de su tiempo," *Encuentro,* May 1982, pp. 145ff.; and Ignacio Ellacurria, in *Jesús: Ni vencido mi monarca celestial,* pp. 129ff.

He defined power in terms of sacrificial service and affirmed non-violent resistance as a social stance in full harmony with the kingdom.[23]

He summoned his disciples to social nonconformity patterned on his own and to a community of love and justice, forgiveness and sharing.[24]

The total impression derived from these facts is that Jesus of Nazareth took upon himself a prophetic role in the tradition of the old prophets of Israel. It is not surprising that the most common verdict on him on the part of his contemporaries was that he was a prophet, as suggested by the apostles' answer to his question regarding who people said he was: "Some say John the Baptist; others say Elijah; and still others, Jeremiah or one of the prophets" (Matt. 16:14; cf. Mark 6:15; 8:28; Matt. 21:11, 46; Luke 7:16; John 4:19; 6:14; 7:40, 52; 9:17). Nor is it surprising that when the conflict with the Jewish religious-political establishment came to a head, he was arrested and brought to Pilate under the charge of stirring up the people and inciting them to rebellion (Luke 23:2, 5, 13). Quite clearly, he had become a public figure, and his words and action were interpreted as a real political threat that had to be countered.

No justice is done to the evidence provided by the Gospels in any reconstruction of Jesus' death that disregards the political charge implied in the *titulus* written on the cross: "This is the king of the Jews." He did not die as a religious teacher who had become an unbearable annoyance to the members of the Sanhedrin but as a political rebel whose messianic claims and public activity could be interpreted as a subversion deserving the penalty that the Romans reserved for seditious provincials at that time: crucifixion.

3. Christology and Social Ethics

If the Christ of faith is the Jesus of history, then it is possible to speak of social ethics for Christian disciples who seek to fashion their lives on God's purpose of love and justice concretely revealed. If the risen and exalted Lord is Jesus of Nazareth, then it is possible to speak of a community that seeks to manifest the kingdom of God in history.

To be sure, Jesus' example cannot simply be transposed to the modern world. The incarnation took place in a particular situation, and we live in another situation. The point here, however, is that because of the life and teaching of Jesus of Nazareth we are not free to understand Christian ethical

23. See John Howard Yoder, *The Politics of Jesus* (Grand Rapids: Eerdmans, 1972), pp. 90ff.
24. See Yoder, *The Politics of Jesus,* pp. 115.

conduct today as if his lifestyle were not an alternative—indeed, the only alternative—for us. In Echegaray's words, "Jesus does not create a rigid model of action, but he does impel his disciples to creatively prolong the logic of his praxis in the different historical circumstances in which they are to proclaim, in word and deed, the gospel of the kingdom.[25]

The starting point for *Christian* social ethics is the fact that God has revealed his purpose for human life in a unique man: Jesus of Nazareth. The basic question for Christians in Latin America, therefore, relates to the way in which faith in Jesus is to be lived out in their concrete situation. Because the Word became flesh, they cannot but affirm history as the context in which God is fulfilling his redemptive will. The historicity of Jesus leaves no room for a dualism in which the soul is separated from the body, or for a message exclusively concerned with salvation beyond death, or for a church that isolates itself from society to become a ghetto.

Jesus' prophetic ministry had a shape and color that corresponded to the historical circumstances in which he lived. The church in Latin America today cannot claim to be rooted and built up in Christ unless it both takes due account of Jesus' role and is itself prophetic in its life, teaching, and action. One can hardly exaggerate the urgency that questions related to religious oppression and legalism, injustice and poverty, wealth and power have for the mission of the church in this context.

If our brief analysis of Jesus' concern for the poor is correct, then the basis for "a preferential option for the poor" is clearly established.[26] Those who confess Jesus Christ as Lord cannot close their eyes to the impoverished masses in the cities and the poor peasants in the rural areas of Latin America.

The cross was the most eloquent expression of Jesus' solidarity with sinners. The giving of himself in death is at the very center of the gospel and defines God's method to accomplish his redemptive purpose. Jesus left no doubt as to his intention for his followers: if he chose the way of the cross, they are to follow him to the cross also. That means in concrete terms that for the Christian there is no other ethic than the ethic of love and sacrificial service. As George Casalis has put it, "Passover means that the world has finally passed from the slavery to power to the freedom of service."[27] Jesus' death was not only God's atonement for sin but also his act of liberation from selfishness and his norm for a lifestyle that asserts love and justice.

The church in Latin America urgently needs to experience the cross as far more than the cultic symbol of a privatized faith. It needs to experience it as God's victory over the powers of darkness and therefore as the basis to challenge every dehumanizing power, be it militarism or consumerism,

25. Echegaray, *La práctica de Jesús,* p. 198.

26. This "preferential option" has become one of the most basic stances in the Roman Catholic Church in Latin America in the last decade.

27. Casalis, "Jesús: Ni vencido ni monarca celestial," in *Jesús: Ni vencido ni monarca celestial,* p. 124.

statism or materialism, legalism or hedonism. It needs to experience it as God's call to affirm servanthood over against coercion, love over against violence. It will then be better able to proclaim it as the means to freedom for the oppressed and the oppressors, the rich and the poor.

The resurrection marks the culmination of a Christology rooted in the history of Jesus of Nazareth. Through it God has released in history the powers of the New Era. A new order has definitely arrived, and its resources are available to men and women through the Holy Spirit. God has once for all confirmed that the way of Jesus is the way of victory—the victory not of worldly dominion and arrogance but of sacrificial love and service, not *over* the cross but *of* the cross.

The power of the resurrection is the power for a new lifestyle patterned on Jesus. The same power that raised him from the dead is the power that transforms sinners into neighbors willing to act in love for others. Impelled by it, Christians are able to act in response to human need—not in order to bring in the kingdom but because the kingdom has already come in Jesus of Nazareth and is yet to come in all its fullness.

1.3.2

Response to Padilla by Douglas Webster

René, what I see you offering in this paper is a kind of hermeneutical key which has been alluded to a number of times: the historical Jesus of the Gospels. Elsewhere you have written that "the basic problem of biblical hermeneutics is to transpose the biblical message from its original context into the context of the modern readers or hearers so as to produce in them the same kind of impact that the message was meant to produce in the original readers or hearers." You go on in that context to talk about the hermeneutical circle and the importance of the interpreter's own situation. I think we see in light of your paper that Jesus, the historical Jesus, is normative. I appreciate your stress on the coherent picture of the historical Jesus that the Gospels give us. I think that goes back to what Samuel Escobar said in his paper, affirming the belief in the unity and continuity of Gospels and epistles and the Old Testament. I appreciate as well your unified and holistic understanding of salvation. I could go on picking up your theme and stressing how important it is that we focus on the faithfulness of Jesus as an example for our faithfulness, his identification with the marginalized people as a model for our identification, the growth and development of his own self-awareness as a model for our discipleship and our self-awareness, his antagonism to the religious establishment as a model for our antagonism to the establishment, his sacrificial death and his victorious resurrection as our hope and also as a call to suffering.

You say something very interesting in your first paragraph—that the great difficulty Christians generally have in relating theology to social, economic, and political issues is closely connected with their lack of an adequate Christological foundation. I know what you mean. I think I would say that we get a new difficulty when we begin to relate the historical Jesus to economic-social-political issues. Maybe that's a difficulty with joy, but it is nevertheless a difficulty that we may be experiencing.

Now, with that said, I can go on to report on my reaction to the paper. You present us with a challenge to stress the historical Jesus in the Latin

American context—a context in which the historical Jesus is already very familiar because of the way he has been presented by liberation theologians. As a North American theologian, I then look to people like you to clarify what it means for evangelicals to stress the historical Jesus in this context. On another occasion you wrote that "no interpreter regardless of his culture is free to make the text say whatever he wants it to say; his task is to let the text speak for itself and to that end he inevitably has to engage with the horizons of the text via literary context, grammar, history, and so on. The effort to let scripture speak without imposing upon it a ready-made interpretation is a hermeneutical task binding for every interpreter, whatever his culture." So you challenge us to understand the historical Jesus as the hermeneutical key, but you raise the question in my mind of how it is you understand the evangelical, historical Jesus to be truer to Scripture than the Latin American liberationist historical Jesus.

In your paper you bring up the Chalcedonian definition. I have read Leonardo Boff's assertion that Jesus did not in fact possess what the Council of Chalcedon said he did—hypostasis—that he was completely empty of himself and completely full of the reality of the other, of God the Father. Now, I also want to keep in mind what John Stam said earlier about doing justice to our theological colleagues who may disagree with us. However, to follow the liberationists (Boff, I think, being somewhat representative) is to believe that relationalism subsumes ontology. The metaphysical, ontological reality of the incarnation is no longer stressed as much as the relational, historical, horizontal dimension. So I need clarification in order to understand just what the Latin American evangelical, my colleague, is saying. You widely criticize traditional images of Christ and docetic images of Christ, and I want to say "Amen" to that. I feel I am already trying to say that in the North American context. I also want to say we do not want innovative or speculative Christologies that are more the creation of a post-Enlightenment modern theology than they are of the biblical text. Again I want act and interpretation to come together as Escobar suggested they should in his paper.

I also have a question. If the Roman Catholic Church has authentically stressed the historical Jesus, why don't we see some telling fruits of their work? Why isn't there criticism, even redemptive criticism, of folk religions? Why isn't there a dismissal or disavowal of anti-Protestantism? Why don't you have this kind of conference with your Roman Catholic theologian brothers? You both seem to be saying the same thing on the surface. Is Gutiérrez's concern for the nonhuman, the nonperson the same as your concern? Jesus, as he looked at the masses, saw them as harassed and helpless, as sheep without a shepherd. Do you understand this in the same way the Latin American liberationists do? As I see it, when Jesus says "as sheep without a shepherd," he is referring to himself as that shepherd. The harassment and helplessness is not merely a matter of economics or politics but of his lordship. I think you underplay something of the dynamic of the context. I would like to see some clarification here.

Two other points, and I will close. I would like to understand better the significant place that the poor do play in our Christology. I do not think we believe that Jesus was evangelized by the poor; I think we believe that Jesus evangelized the poor. I do not think we are comfortable with Assman's "epistemological privilege of the poor" or with Jon Sobrino's nonexplanatory Christology or with seeing the cross as the crucifixion of all logic, with Sobrino's disavowal of the Christological hymns, which he sees as playing into the same kind of abstract Christology that Chalcedon does. The evangelical needs to speak to these issues on this continent. Nor am I comfortable seeing Jesus' death totally in political terms—and on that, North American evangelicals and Latin Americans might agree. There is too much ambiguity in that historical context. In one sense Jesus could have walked away from Pilate a free man. I don't think that Pilate was worried about Jesus' civil disobedience, peaceful as it was. I think it was more a question of a kind of political power play that was more easily resolved and expedited by killing Jesus. There's something in the ambiguity of that which parallels the situation of Christian brothers who die with guerrilla groups without leading or fighting along with them. In some ways it wasn't a design on Jesus' part. There are two emphases in Scripture. In one sense you find Jesus as a victim, almost by chance. On the other side you have Scripture telling us that from eternity this is how it was to be. Those two things need to be heard. We need to understand his politicized death (and I believe it was a very real political reality), but we also need to see how that exists alongside this other emphasis in Scripture.

Thank you, René, for your paper.

1.3.3

Response to Padilla by Emilio Antonio Nuñez

I would say that René and I are basically of one mind on Christology. First, I will provide further reflection on René's historical references. He has made reference to the history of Christology, including the political Christ of medieval times or the Christ brought by the Spanish conquerors to our subcontinent. We are indebted to the Roman Catholic Church, because Catholic monks and priests were the first missionaries to proclaim the name of Christ in our lands. Of course, from our evangelical point of view, their Christology suffered distortion. Even Catholic theologians admit at the present time that there were shortcomings in the Christianization of Latin America. It is interesting to remember that the same year Columbus rediscovered America, the Spaniards reconquered the Spanish city of Granada, a conquest that meant the end of Arab domination in Spain. The Muslims used the sword to impose their religion, but the Spaniards also used the sword to impose their Christianity on the people in what is now called Latin America. The Christ that they introduced in Latin America was, as René has suggested, a political Christ, and the conquest was also a missionary enterprise in the name of the pope and in the name of the king and queen of Spain.

It is paradoxical that in popular religiosity in Latin America, the Christ emphasized by the Roman Catholic Church was the human Christ—or, more precisely, the suffering Christ, the Christ on the cross, the dead Christ. The most important day during the Holy Week is not Easter Sunday, as in North America, but Good Friday, the day when Jesus dies. This is the emphasis. There is also emphasis on the baby Jesus in his mother's arms. This Jesus, of course, was not able to speak, was not able to defend the slaves under the Spanish domination. So in traditional Roman Catholicism, Christ is on the Cross or he is in heaven or he is sacrificed again on the altar, in the eucharistic celebration. But he is not Jesus the liberator, walking, living among us.

As René has mentioned, there are now Roman Catholic theologians who are recovering the New Testament relevation of the historical Jesus. However, as I mentioned last night, we have to remember that there is a variety of Roman Catholic systems in Latin America now. Some people in the United States have the impression that liberation theology is being accepted by all Roman Catholics in Latin America; that is not true. You see a difference, for instance, between Bishop Romero in El Salvador, who was killed because he took sides with the people, and Monsignor Casaruego, the archbishop in Guatemala, who was strongly conservative. Of course liberation theology is exercising some influence on the Catholic people in Latin America, but a strong conservative branch of the Roman Catholic Church remains.

I appreciate René's emphasis on building his Christology on the Scriptures. This emphasis is not new. I know that this is the way in which he wants to theologize from within our social context in Latin America. We evangelicals do not hold with the contrast between the historical Jesus and the Jesus of faith, but I believe that we have to work more in regard to the progress of revelation in the Christology of the New Testament. The Lord Jesus Christ told his disciples that the Holy Spirit would come to remind them of the things he had taught and that the Holy Spirit would also come to preach about him. This indicates that the Lord Jesus Christ did not reveal everything to his disciples about his person. So, within the framework of the New Testament revelation, we have progress in Christology. We evangelicals in Latin America have to work on our understanding of this progress.

Regarding René's thesis that the Jesus of the New Testament is God's Messiah, we need to take into consideration not only the synoptics but the whole New Testament. At the beginning of Jesus' ministry the disciples did not seem to understand his mission; they were discouraged when he died. To say that Jesus is the Messiah we have to go not only to the synoptics but also to the epistles. The postresurrection testimony is essential, I think, to demonstrate that Jesus is the Messiah.

Now, my biggest question as a Latin American preacher and teacher is how to recover in my own theological thinking and teaching the humanity of Christ without falling into the trap of another ideology. One of the reasons we inherited a Christology that understands only the deity of Christ is that many of the missionaries who came to Latin America came out of the liberal-conservative controversy in North America. In their apologetics, they were trying to defend the deity of Christ, to answer the liberal challenge. The apologetics I was taught in a Bible school forty years ago emphasized Christ's deity. Now we have come to realize that that Christology and apologetics are under the influence of a particular ideology. But it is too easy to leave one extreme only to move into another. Now I am supposed to preach the historical Jesus, the Jesus who took sides with the poor.

After the Second World War there was a strong anticommunist sentiment in evangelical circles in North America and Latin America. To be a real evangelical, a genuine evangelical, one was supposed to be faithful to the policies of the U.S. State Department and the Pentagon. Evangelicals were supposed to defend capitalism. But now we are confronted by another challenge. To be a genuine, an authentic evangelical, we are supposed to defend a particular form of socialism. In earlier days, I was asked to wear Uncle Sam's hat. Now I am asked to wear Che Guevara's beret.

We need to underscore the teaching of the suffering Christ and minister to a suffering people. But it is also imperative that we announce the resurrected Christ, who has the power of the new life. He is the mediator between God and man, because he is the God-man. We do not yet have a Christology written by a Latin American evangelical on the basis of the Scriptures in response to the questions, suffering, and hope of our own people.

1.3.4

Response to Padilla by John Howard Yoder

I don't think that what I have to say will be quite as original or interesting or provocative, because I mostly agree with what the paper says. So what I'll find myself doing is saying not so much "Yes, but" and "No" but "If this is true, then what?" or "What would we need to go still further in the same direction?" So, I think I am only asking questions about whether René finished doing what he set out to do or whether we have more work in the same direction.

René starts with the way in which a dogma, a corpus of dogmatic definitions, took over the scene and replaced the concrete humanity of Jesus as a person in Palestine. If that was a mistake, we ought to ask why it happened, and there is not much of that sort of analysis going on. One set of people would say they bought into Hellenistic ontology. But why did they do it, and why was that wrong? Very often, the longer-range critique says that a mistake was made, symbolized by Constantine, when state power was tied to the Christian value system, but that points back to the fourth century, and the problem René is talking about can be traced back farther than that. Another set of people would say that it has to do with the breach of fellowship with the synagogue. I am just saying we have to work to do. The more this observation matters, fundamentally, with respect to where we locate our own Christological discourse, the more accountable we are to explain how it went wrong.

The other part of the explanation that we owe to ourselves and to others is what the alternative would have been. Would it have been no dogma? As Emilio was just telling us, there is already a beginning of a high Christology in the New Testament epistles. Or would it have meant exactly the same dogma, but with an added reminder not to forget the historical Jesus? How would that have preserved the balance that historically wasn't preserved? Or might it have been that there should have been different dogma, that there is actually something wrong with the formulations? If your formulations of how this Second Person of the Trinity (Nicea) was both divine and human (Chalcedon) actually lead you to deny what they formally say regarding such things as the real humanity of that Man, then maybe we need a different dogma. Maybe we shouldn't assume the adequacy of the ecumenical creeds. One of the odd things about Western evangelicalism is that although it is very critical about everything else Catholic since the fourth century, it is utterly uncritical of the credal functions of an imperial institution. In the case of Nicea, it was an unbaptized German general who formulated the crucial passage of *homoousios*. A century and a half later at Chalcedon, a considerable number of the results were the product of riots. I think we need a demythologizing of the credal process in the early medieval church, one that would fit with ongoing Protestantism. That is not my agenda here, but we have to start thinking about that.

Regarding "Christology and History," specifically Sobrino's affirmation that we have to start with the history of Jesus: here again it is "Yes, but." I don't think it is going to be sufficient in the contemporary debate to say—as René says and as several of of us have affirmed—that the basic image of who Jesus was, historically, is reliable. It is not nearly as fuzzy as certain fads in higher criticism have sometimes made it seem, but that doesn't mean that it has become solid. There are new fads, or perhaps new abidingly valid developments in hermeneutics, that in other ways make it clear that it is not as simple as we thought to say that we know who the Jesus of that story was. I intentionally bypassed them in my Jesus book ten years ago by specifically narrowing my focus to the canonical report, but that is of course a simplification of the total exegetical task. There was tradition, evolution. There were trajectories in the developments of what words mean before they got written down, and there continue to be trajectories of what they mean since they were written down. So we have named a confessional stance if we say it is the Jesus of history, but we haven't finished figuring out who he was or how we can use the text to talk about him. The best example of that continuing debatability is one that I'll come to a little farther down the line.

René develops nine different traits that define who Jesus was, what he was like. I think they are all correct, they are all there, they are all important. But there is one omission, which I don't think was intentional but which I do think is significant. Jesus is verbally explicit about the privileged place of the enemy in his discussion of whether we love the way God loves. It is not just the outsider and the oppressed and the poor; they have their place, and that often hasn't been said adequately, though it is beginning to be said adequately. But the gospel story itself is stronger than that. Beyond the outsider who is now treated without discrimination there is the enemy, who is the touchstone of whether our love is like God's love. This has a special weight on textual grounds, for it is the only place in the New Testament where we are told to be like the Father. We are often told to be like Jesus, who loves the enemy. Sometimes we are told to be like Paul, who gets his nerve up to think he's a model for us. But this is the only place we are told to be like the Father, in the way he loves his enemies. In both the Lukan and

Matthean versions of the Sermon on the Mount we receive this teaching. That particular attitude toward enemies is the subject of three of the six oppositions between the old way and the new way in Matthew 5. It is, of the various components of the moral teaching of Jesus, the one that is realized most dramatically in his own life career decisions. Jesus was tempted to become a righteous, violent liberator, and he chose not to.

We don't know about his struggles with all the other temptations, of gluttony and fornication and the other sins that we all commit and he didn't, but we are told about the temptation to be a zealot. I should say that my conviction about the story is not universally accepted. It is an example of the difficulty, the ambiguity of knowing who the historic Jesus was. Luke tells us that the historic Jesus decided not to be a zealot leader because he believed in loving the enemy. That has something to do with liberation. It has more to do with domination as a standard pattern of Christendom's history for fifteen hundred years. It therefore becomes something of a test case for whether the historic Jesus can actually tell us something about our lifestyle that stands in judgment on us and renews us with the promise of a very different way. I think René wouldn't be opposed to adding this to his list of nine points. I think it is at least one tenth of the novelty of the New Testament. Jesus said this and did this and died for it. We don't know that he died because he didn't want to commit adultery. We don't know that he died because he honored father and mother. We do know that he died because he didn't lead the zealots the way that they wanted to be led. We know that even the title on the document on the cross located that element of conflict as a part of a definitional (not an exclusive or exhaustive) part of the meaning of the cross. So that is a filling out and a deepening and a radicalizing of the newness of the claim to the career of Jesus as a model.

There is another issue that I will simply call a problem. If we say that the humanity of Jesus is the base, then we have to explain things that are not based *immediately* on the humanity of Jesus but are based there in some derivative way. Jesus said some forward-pointing things about the Gentiles coming into the messianic age, but he also said some non-forward-pointing things. He spoke as if he were accepting the Palestinian and Jewish limits of the current definition of God's peoplehood. By the time we get through Acts in the Lukan account, or as we study the Pauline corpus (especially Ephesians), we come to understand that a crucial component of having arrived at the messianic age is that the Gentiles are all in, or invited in, that the wall is broken down and that it is broken down by the cross. We need some understanding, beyond this specific case, of the fact that God's mission goes beyond Jesus' mission. We see the sweeping in of the Gentiles being part of the purpose of Jesus' mission, but it is something that Jesus did not do but which the Holy Spirit did through the apostles right away. How many more things are there like that, that are based on his humanity derivatively, but not immediately? What does that do to notions of continuing revelation or even notions of closing the canon? There are places where the human Jesus was insufficient. He didn't finish the job, and he said he didn't. That's why we need the Holy Spirit.

That points me to a last category with several subheadings within it. Christology means more than human life, than resurrection. The high Christologies of John 1 and Hebrews 1 and Colossians 1 tell us that the one who became incarnate was already a participant in creation; the themes of preexistence and creation are prominent. Now, both high mainstream theologies, Catholic and Reformed, and some modern theologies, like that of Richard Neibuhr, try to decrease the centrality of Jesus by surrounding him with Father and Spirit in a distributive way. We need a trinitarian ethic in order to have three different strands. The New Testament does it the other way around, putting Christ above—even above creation. That means we need a Christology that is bigger than the human Jesus and that takes creation, providential meaning in the course of human history, ultimate hope, ultimate kingdom into Christology. Divine activity is not distributed so that the Father does certain things and the Son does other things and the Spirit does still other things. It is rather that Christ does these things as the preincarnate Logos and these things in the flesh and these things by sending the Spirit. So it is all Christological, and that raises a number of issues we must pursue.

Very often our debate about social ethics brings us back to how we relate what is given us in the human Christ concerning our human discipleship to what we know about God as providence running the nations. God is the Spirit of giving new guidance. A lot of people would agree that Jesus was who the Gospels say he was and then go on to say that we need not follow his example because we have other leading or because we are called to help God with the providential task of running the world through the state or liberating the poor through a new state. At that point the relation of the Christ that is Jesus incarnate and the other manifestations of divine power and authority will have to be thrashed through. The New Testament does it more adequately than Richard Niebuhr. Ascension, lordship, place in the kosmos, place in creation—all these are involved.

Likewise, the meaning of Pentecost, guidance, and gifts, have to do obviously, immediately, with the Third Person of the Trinity. But it is the Spirit of Christ, it is the Body of Christ, that is thereby brought to life. It is the members of Christ that became active. There are many components of discipleship that we ordinarily talk about in our lay language in terms not of the Son but of the Spirit but that actually belong in Christology. We need to talk about Jesus in such a way that it is in the light of Jesus that we know what the gifts are, or that it is in the light of Jesus that we know what we are empowered to do. The power of the Spirit of Joy and the other dimensions of charisma do not become autonomous but subordinate to the incarnate meaning of what kind of person that particular Man turned out to be when he was the Man who did what God wanted him to do as the guide for what the Spirit is supposed to do.

1.3.5

Padilla Replies

I think that Webster assumes that the figure of the historical Jesus, because of the influence of liberation theology, has become *the* figure of Christ in Latin America. That is not so, not at all. The portraits of Christ in Latin America continue to be mainly, almost exclusively, the ones that I present here: the Christ of dogma, the political Christ, and mainly *el Cristo de mi tierra*, just the dead Jesus. That must be kept clear: liberation theology has had some influence, such as encouraging people to study the Gospels and the rest of the New Testament, but that is not a general phenomenon.

I am trying to begin with the historical Jesus, and therefore I do not introduce the language of ontology here. Precisely. My claim is that because we are so concerned with ontology, we have not given enough attention to the historical Jesus. The first section of my paper, "Christology and History," provides an answer to your question. Why speak of Jesus' relation to the Father instead of talking about the nature of Christ as the Second Person of the Trinity? Because I believe that he who was with God and who was God is inseparable from the Word who became flesh. I would insist that that is where we have to begin—with the historical Jesus. I do not deny the possiblity of framing a Christology in another language. But my argument here is that too much of that has been done already, and because of that the church has often failed to take into account the whole question of the life of Jesus as a real basis for thinking and acting here and now. I am accepting some of the insights that come from liberation theology. I do not agree with some of the emphases that you find in Sobrino, for instance, but it seems to me that we have to see the value of his work and the work of other Roman Catholic exegetes. There is valid exegetical work there even though at some points we may disagree with their exegesis.

Now, on the question of the death of Jesus, I do not present it only in terms of a political event. I do accept the other aspect presented in the New Testament. But it is one thing to talk about the why and the intent of God's eternal purpose, and it is something else to talk about the dynamics of history. It is very clear in the Gospels that there was a political accusation and it was a political event. We must not play that down because it points to something that relates to our own life here and now. I appreciate the comments made by my colleague in the fraternity, Emilio Antonio Nuñez. I would accept that we must do more work on the whole question of progress and development of Christology within the New Testament itself. In fact, this is a part of my answer to you: in the New Testament, the whole canon presents the historical Jesus who is the resurrected Christ, and also the preexistent Christ and the Cosmic Christ. But Christ is never unrelated to Jesus. It is Jesus who is the Cosmic Christ, who is the preexistent Christ.

How do we recover the humanity of Jesus without falling into the trap of another ideology? I honestly believe that we can try to gain some "objectivity" with regard to the meaning of the gospel by going back to the historical Jesus—at least making the attempt to do so. It seems to me that that is one of the main instruments we can use to deideologize our theology, to take the figure of Jesus Christ seriously, including the announcement of the resurrection. I am impressed by the way Paul expresses the whole thrust of his message. He is talking about the resurrected Jesus when he says that he announces the crucified Messiah. You cannot separate the resurrected Lord from the crucified Messiah.

Some of John Yoder's comments are prickly, especially the whole question of dogma and how it developed and why. I don't regard myself as a dogmatician, and I must admit that I have not worked extensively in the area of dogmatics. It seems to me that in the Nicene and the Chalcedonian formulations you do find the assertion of the humanity of Jesus. The problem is that it is stated and then that is it. The affirmation is named, but it appears to be insignificant. What does that mean in practical terms? That is where we get lost. The dogma becomes the one thing we have. We talk about Christology, yet we fail to relate the historical Jesus to that Christological dogma. It is not enough to say that the image of Jesus that we extract from the Gospels is reliable. There are conflicting, or sometimes complementary images of Christ in the New Testament. No single image of Jesus Christ says everything about him; therefore we have the wealth of statements and images concerning him. To that extent I would agree with Trocmé, who says that no one can get hold of Jesus of Nazareth, not completely. But I do believe that there is a coherent picture that is presented in terms of what I have argued here: the Messiah who brings in the kingdom of God and the prophet.

Finally, Jesus is explicit about the place of the enemy—I would agree with that. This is one aspect of Jesus' ethical teaching that must be taken seriously. I am not sure about the connection between the statement about love for the enemy and his own death. In the end John Yoder seems to think that perhaps the whole of theology should be placed under Christology, or am I misunderstanding that? That is a possibility. I was thinking in terms of a Christology that takes into account mainly the historical Jesus, although I accept that Christology is more than that. We have an exalted Lord, but I would still emphasize that fact that the exalted Lord who is presented in the epistles is still the crucified Messiah, none other.

1.3.6

Discussion

Mercadante: I'd like to take issue with something right at the outset in the strongest possible terms. I think you've gone too far, René, in your objections to the development of dogma. I think you have set up a false dichotomy between dogma and the Jesus of history, which you believe was covered over by dogma. You stated that they did recognize the historical nature of Christ, and thus the historical Jesus, but that they just left it at that. This has been a criticism of Chalcedonian and other early Christologies. But those people were well aware that they said it and left it. They did that as a recognition of the character of mystery. I think we should be grateful that they said it and left it for us to ponder as a mystery also. If they had tried to work it out exhaustively, it would have been even more philosophical than what you don't like now.

What you are trying to do and what they were trying to do is in a sense exactly the same thing. I think you are contextualizing Christology, and so were they. They were forced into explaining who Christ was and is in terms that their culture could hear. It was a very philosophically oriented culture, and in some ways we can be thankful for that, because Christianity was forced to come to terms with a lot of difficult issues. Of course theology is always being reformed, and we have a right to go back and correct this now. But setting up a false dichotomy poses the utmost dangers for the church. It's almost like saying we can skip all those centuries. I find this to be a real problem in evangelical, Protestant Christianity. It is believed that we can skip all those centuries and go back and get to the real Jesus. But the way we have gotten the message from Jesus is through our brothers and sisters who have transmitted it to us, as well as through meeting Christ in person. The only way you have been able to come to this is through the work they did then. I know that the decision to make the distinction between *homoousios* and *homoiousios* was political. Even now the orthodox and ourselves are split just because we lack understanding. Nevertheless, Latin American churches are involved in similar political struggles. I would hesitate to critique so strongly the early church.

106

Padilla: I would begin by asserting that I can do without the dogmatic formulations of the church. In fact, many people in Latin America do without them. They do not even know what the Chalcedonian affirmation says. I doubt very much that even one percent of evangelicals in Latin America would know what the Chalcedonian affirmation or the Nicene creed says. They simply don't. They do without it. What they cannot do without is the Bible. So, it is a question of perspective.

Mercadante: I think that is a false split.

McAlpine: That may be why the church is so unhealthy both in North America and in Latin America. We do without Chalcedon and Nicea. We believe in the divinity without the humanity or vice versa, thinking they are unimportant.

Mercadante: Gadamer says the only way we even know who we are today is because we are in a stream of tradition. The only way we preach the gospel is through that stream; we are part of it and there is no way to get out of it.

Padilla: But listen to me! In Latin America we have a struggle with the church that says "Scripture and tradition," and we always say, "No, Scripture, Scripture, Scripture, Scripture." And when we sign a statement, like the Wheaton statement or the NAE statement, we say "Scripture is the authority for all matters of faith." We never say that the dogmas are.

Mercadante: Even the Reformers didn't reject that aspect of tradition. They have been misread. It is naive to say that you would separate the two.

Padilla: But you can. It is done all over Latin America.

Scholer: Perhaps in North America there are very few people who could tell you what the Chalcedon creed is, and that is partly a problem of ignorance in the Christian tradition. Ignorance doesn't validate itself. However one relates to those creeds, they deal with genuine issues that had integrity in their own context. In studying patristics as a New Testament person, I am impressed with the genuineness of their agenda in trying to resolve certain Christological problems. They saw serious implications concerning the validity of the whole program of redemption and salvation. I don't think that should be undercut. Some of those creeds are abstract to us only because we live in a different context. If we want to get into context, if we want to get into each other's context, we have just as much obligation to get in the context of our forerunners who also struggled with the faith.

One of the major themes in patristic research right now concerns a restructuring of the Arian controversy. At the International Conference on Patristics last September in England, there were more papers given on Arianism than on anything else. There have been some discoveries of new sources. When we look at the anti-Arians, the people who were following these creeds, they generally suggest that the only intent of the Arians was to devalue the deity of Christ. Now we know, from Arian commentaries that have been recovered, that the Arians were motivated by a pastoral concern to guarantee the humanity of Christ. This arose out of a desire to identify with people in their churches who had problems. So, René, you have a very good point at that level. There was real struggle over the humanity of Jesus in the Arian-Athanasian controversy, and we do need to reconstruct it and understand it better as part of the history of Christology.

Nuñez: As I read the first page of René's paper, I find that the issue is not whether or not we are supposed to use the Chalcedon creed or the Nicene creed. He is just saying that those creeds or dogmas replaced—the Christ of dogma replaced—Jesus of Nazareth, who identified with the poor and the oppressed. All we have to do is to relate those dogmas to Scripture to see whether this is true or not. Those dogmas left out the emphasis on Jesus of Nazareth, who identified himself with the poor and the oppressed.

Cummings: I agree. The paper merely emphasizes, as David also said, that we have to look at Christology again with respect to what has up to now been known as the deviate tradition, Arianism. It is not a question of rejecting the tradition. It is a question of how you go through the tradition and how you acknowledge which tradition you go through. It is not just a question of Athanasius; it is also Arius. Arians weren't just idiots or people looking for a deviation. They were people concerned about the salvation of human beings.

Stam: I appreciate, Linda, your observations, although I agree with René. I think it is very important that we have this historical consciousness of how Scripture has come to us. But we must also see that context critically. It is very interesting in light of David's comments about Arianism with a pastoral concern. I see this metaphysical category coming to the apologist in the Alexandria school. But I don't agree with you that the whole world was so philosophical. It was a class option to put the gospel into the language and thought of an elite. The mass movements were pretty well bumped out. The same metaphysical language in the nineteenth century is questioned. Kierkegaard wants to go back to Socrates and beyond Socrates. I don't think we are eternally married to the metaphysical language with which Chalcedonia said some very vital things for a certain strata of its society.

Costas: I would agree with what Emilio said in reference to René. He is trying to emphasize the humanity of Christ. On the other side, however, René is coming out too much on the side of not recognizing the dogmatic importance of Chalcedon—namely, the attempt to keep together the unity of the God-man who is Christ. That is critical for the very faith that we confess as evangelicals. I see Sobrino and Boff attempting to do that within the Catholic context of Latin America. They have to respond to a series of philosophical arguments and see the validity of Chalcedonia for the Catholic confession. That is why I have problems with what you say, Doug. You give the impression that the only way we can make use of Chalcedon is by keeping a certain fixed metaphysics that binds us to the categories that were used in the fourth century. In many ways we cannot be bound to it. In order to maintain our own evangelical integrity, we do not have to buy into the philosophical framework that evangelicalism developed during the nineteenth century, but we must understand it. Most positions of defining, rejecting, or accepting people as evangelicals are not made on the basis of Scripture but on philosophical criteria. René is defending here the argument that Scripture stands over the tradition. Also, we must realize that there are different philosophical categories that Latin Americans are working with, such as the question of phenomenology and the category of mystery that is very present in many of the Catholics, such as Enrique Dussel. Are you asking us, Doug, to buy into that fixed metaphysical framework in order to keep our evangelical integrity?

Webster: Not at all. What I am suggesting is that you are giving a selective reading to liberationists. You are not seeing their desire to do away with the ontic and the noetic categories, and the evangelical must speak to that. I do not know how best to formulate that as long as you come up with an essentialism in terms of the very being of Jesus, God himself, and do not sacrifice to relationalism or historicism. I want the ontic and noetic categories saved with the praxis that I see you emphasizing. Just as we should not condemn liberationists from our selective reading, you should not commend them with a selective reading.

Costas: But the selective reading is our right. We have never bought lock, stock, and barrel the framework with which liberation theologians work. We have occasionally had to struggle with them precisely because of that. We have reserved the right to interpret Marxism from our own perspective and to question some of the epistemological categories with which they work.

Webster: I mean the selective reading that comes to us in terms of commendation. I mean you must deal with them in their totality.

Costas: Are you not judging us therefore? Do you not presume we omit something?

Webster: I do not see it written. I do not hear it said. Where does the criticism come?

Costas: I think René has provided a very serious criticism in the issue that matters for us. Sobrino has not taken the full account of the historical Jesus.

Webster: The critique of a two-stage division in Sobrino is a good point; but where is Sobrino's theism? You have to deal with Sobrino's theism.

Costas: No, no, no. You have to judge René on the basis of his claim, which is a defense of the resurrection. That is unfair criticism. You are judging René on the basis of Sobrino. You have to judge him on the basis of what he says or does not say.

Padilla: I do have a paper on Sobrino, where I deal with that question; I am not dealing with Sobrino here. My question is New Testament Christology.

Webster: The statement you make in your second paragraph—that statement really does not express the totality of your perspective at all, does it?

Padilla: No, but it does say what I want to say. The Christ of dogma replaced Jesus of Nazareth.

Webster: Give us more credit. We have heard the message of the historical

Jesus in a context. We have heard you say that. But we want to also hear evangelicals in Latin America say that something is wrong with the liberationists.

Padilla: I have said enough.

Yoder: Could we ask the two partners to come back to the place where Orlando was pushing Doug? Doug wants to make sure we hear that he doesn't recognize anything as evangelical he can't call essentialist and ontic. It seems to me that Orlando is saying that that is not an automatic criterion of being an evangelical.

Webster: John, that is not the issue here. The issue is Christology.

Yoder: But I wonder what your reasons are for believing *essentialism* to be a good word. And I want to know whether René agrees with them or not. I can't tell whether you're just in different worlds, talking past each other. I don't know why essentialism is essential to you, Doug; I don't know what is at stake. Why do you imply that René has to denounce nonessentialism before you'll trust him?

Webster: I trust René completely. René has satisified me in the other readings totally; it is a point of emphasis here. I want my confession that Jesus is the Christ to be understood in the most profound terms and not allowed to be compromised by some kind of humanizing by degree, by relational categories. Now, whatever you come up with to preserve that integrity of the confession, which is what I see Chalcedon doing and Scripture doing, is fine.

Hays: Maybe part of the difference lies in the distinction between the historical Jesus and the canonical Jesus. Traditionally, people who have used the category of the historical Jesus have used it precisely as a way of trying to circumnavigate Christological doctrine. I think the thing that has Doug's hair standing up is that you start in as if that is exactly what you are trying to do. He wonders if you are not trying to do a historical-critical reconstruction of Jesus that is then going to be normative and that can critique any kind of metaphysical claims about Christ, perhaps even including those found elsewhere in the New Testament, such as in the Gospel of John.

It seems to me there is a certain danger there, in the way that you are using the category "historical." For those of us with theological training out of the European–North American tradition, we hear something very different when you start talking that way. When you affirm the historical Jesus you say, "I want to talk about a Jesus who is a real person and lived in the midst of the real struggle of people in history." But when the European biblical scholar hears "historical Jesus," that means the critically reconstructed Jesus, which has to be sharply distinguished from the canonical Jesus of the churches' confession. I think there is a real ambiguity that runs right through your whole paper on that issue.

Cummings: Neither Sobrino nor René is talking about the Jesus who can be recovered by historical criticism.

Hays: He most certainly is.

Watson: This was precisely the point I was going to raise. There are two statements, René, that you made which I think we need to look at quite closely. First you say "Christianity that disregards the historical Jesus may be useful for personal piety or civil religion, but it is neither faithful to the witness of Scripture . . . nor historically relevant." Then you go on to say, at the end of the first paragraph of your first section, "It does mean that the historicity of the Gospels can be safely assumed and theologians are therefore free to concentrate on defining the meaning of Christian discipleship." Perhaps the point that Linda was pressing was not so much the question of dogma here but the fact that even the historical Jesus as a person is a statement of faith. Your statement is certainly a statement of faith, because the historical evidence, as all of the struggles of the nineteenth century and the "new quest" have shown, essentially points to the fact that when you do try to reconstruct this Jewish carpenter you run up against so many brick walls of history that you can't do it. If we affirm that the historical Jesus is in fact a person, we do so out of faith. And the point I want to make, which perhaps takes us in a slightly different direction, is that evangelicals North and South do in fact affirm this historicity as a point of faith. Many Christians in the North do not accept this, so we have a very real point of dialogue here. The sort of historical Jesus you want to give us—by stripping away all these layers of history and getting back to a Jewish carpenter who lived and breathed and identified with the poor—may find receptivity among evangelicals in the North more so than among a great many other Christians who don't even affirm the historical Jesus but who look for other ways of affirming their Christianity. Perhaps I can put it best by quoting the title of a paper that appeared in the *Journal of the American Academy of Religion:* "The So-called Resurrection of Jesus." We must start by seeing that the historical Jesus is an evangelical affirmation of faith.

Scholer: I think there is a kind of methodological or procedural issue at stake. I don't think anyone has to be expected to deliver his or her whole load at any one time. In other words, I think it's very defensible for René or anyone else to speak to a particular issue. But there is pressure that says that every time you speak on any theological issue you have to run by all your confessions or what you say won't be accepted. That's part of the evangelical pressure that's very wrong. One ought to have the authenticity and the integrity to speak to one issue and to speak to it forcefully and not have to fly every flag every time.

Webster: We really didn't need to extend the conversation on this issue. It's merely a qualifying challenge to the evangelicals in Latin America to say something to that side. Period. You accept it or you don't. I'm getting feedback that's excusing it. I'd rather hear someone saying "Yes, that's a problem. I see that. We need to address ourselves to that in our Christology."

Padilla: Do please notice that I have a footnote there, and to me it's very important because as far as I'm concerned, my approach to Christology on a dogmatic level would very much coincide with Lane's.

Gil: To some extent my concern is that René's paper is not contextual enough. He has done historical work but has not given enough attention to the way that the different Gospel writers have to reinterpret Christology in their different situations. I would raise a very serious question, the one that is raised when someone says very simply "Jesus is the Christ." The name "Jesus" interprets "the Christ" as much as "the Christ" interprets "Jesus." We must remember that in the first century the dominant idea of messiahship is exactly the view of Jesus that you're trying to get rid of. In the Gospels themselves this battle is being fought. I think it's not by chance that in the triumphal entry in Matthew when he quotes Zechariah 9, the prize text on contemporary messiahship, he leaves out "triumphant and victorious is he." But we've called it the "Triumphal Entry." The very thing that he knocks out we make the title. He is battling with exactly this problem, that if we just say "Jesus is the Christ," we must go through the process of contextual reinterpretation before we can affirm that, otherwise that's a meaningless statement.

Padilla: I think I do that. I think I have taken into account at least what it seems to me is very clear in the three synoptic Gospels—that messiahship is interpreted in terms of servanthood. I think that is one point of agreement in the Gospels.

Gil: It is my point, you see, that you're not allowing each one to stand within its own context. If we're not careful, the historical Jesus will become another ideological Jesus. That is, in the same way the creeds cause difficulties. We face the danger of getting this all worked out for this part of the twentieth century and for this place, only to find that two generations from now it will have become the new dogma people are going to fight against. We're going to put Jesus in our pocket again, although that's exactly what you said we must not do. Unless there's a little bit of relativism—a harsh word—at this point, the opposite, this ideological dogmatism, is a danger.

Costas: The category of history is already well-defined by René at the very beginning. The Latin American emphasis is normally on the historical Jesus. We're not bound by European scholarship at this point, because we begin from a much greater grasp of the fact that Christ, that Jesus, are historical facts of Latin American culture. They are historical facts of the Latin American reality. Jesus is not strange to us. You have to begin to grope with that problem: we have the presence of the Christ of the Andes and the beaten Christ of the West Indies all the way back into the sixteenth century in Bartolomé de Las Casas. There is a challenge in here that we have made over and over. Jon Sobrino makes it quite clear at the outset of his Christology. Europeans cannot write the total agenda. We simply have to plead for a critique on the basis of what is in there. We have very specific references to the reality of Christ in Latin American history.

Second, I do want to emphasize the importance of Chalcedon, because it is an important safeguard that may not come through sufficiently, René. There is a movement (perhaps Emilio was pointing in that direction), a progression that biblical scholars follow for understanding this Jesus of Nazareth in the light of history that is given to us in the Gospels. It is a movement from below. Here we have the humanity and the focus on the cross, and then the resurrection as a confirmation. There is another movement within the New Testament itself that is being safeguarded by Chalcedon—that this man of God, who is declared by the resurrection "the Christ," is also the revelation of the eternal Word. This revelation of the eternal Word, the revelation of the Son of God, comes to us in faith as a revealed fact, a posteriori to be sure, but nevertheless in a fashion that marks another movement—Christology from above. Now that element, that Jesus, may be what Doug is wanting us to clarify. Perhaps this is not explicit enough, because the resurrection here comes at the end in one or two paragraphs, when in fact the New Testament presents itself on the basis of resurrection faith. We not only have to say "Jesus is the Christ"; we also have to say "the Christ is Jesus." That is the essential point that Chalcedon is trying to keep.

Gil: But I think you'll have to acknowledge that the Europeans have made these points. Volume one of Jeremias's *Jesus* contains all these points.

Costas: Yes, but wait a minute. It is in the context of Latin America that that has to be said. We were given two images. John MacKay (I'm critical of MacKay; some of my colleagues are not) gave us two pictures. The Christ that Spain gave us was a dead Christ, an agonizing Christ, a suffering Christ, a struggling Christ, though not necessarily an impotent Christ. Spain also gave us a baby Jesus. But it isn't a baby that dies. The Spanish vision is a vision of life, of the purity of life, of the importance of children, of the emergence of a culture that has yet to be defined and that is growing. John MacKay, from his Scottish perspective, with his Protestant bias, says that these symbols, which are part and parcel of our culture, are not really good symbols. European Protestantism, especially British Protestantism, works with an overpowering doctrine of the resurrection of Christ; it has no place for a cross. Nor does it have a place for an incarnation or for the growth of this baby that is going to be part of this emerging continent. We have to rethink that. The reason I consider "Jesus is Christ" to be as important as "Christ is Jesus" in the context of Latin America is that it is important that our Christology be neither impotent nor triumphalistic. We need an affirmation that insists on the solidarity of humans with God—as obedience—and the solidarity of God with us. Only this can save us from triumphalism on the one hand and impotence on the other. In Latin America we desparately need both. If you challenge us, if you challenge us to work more, then I am prepared to accept that. I think this is the agenda that's before us.

1.4.1

Salt to the World: An Ecclesiology of Liberation

DAVID LOWES WATSON

A word needs to be said at the outset about theological method. We are met in a country that reminds us that First and Third Worlds are more than geographical concepts. Our discussions will hopefully embrace the *praxis* that this affords and reflect the immediacy of our context. At the same time, for our deliberations to have integrity, we must accept that each of us brings to the conference something of our own context. *Praxis* begins with the concreteness of present reality, and the starting point of this gathering is perforce a pluralism of precontextualized theologies seeking further clarity through a particular and intentional reflective process. Perhaps *pluralism* is too broad a word at this juncture; we shall have to see. But at least it is probable that we shall begin with a twofold precontextualization. On the one hand, some of us come from the context of Western theology, with its particular method of critical reflection on the gospel as traditioned in the Scriptures and teachings of the church. On the other hand, the method of much Third World theology, and especially that which comes out of the Latin American context, is critical reflection on the reality of human history in the light of the gospel.

The theological creativity engendered by this contrast of methods has been with us for some time, and by no means least in the interface between liberationism and evangelicalism. Indeed, the similarity of perspective on Christianity and culture in these two theologies is potentially the most significant cutting edge of contemporary Christian witness. Both are critical of mainstream Western theology, arguing that it has been more accountable to its Enlightenment criteria of critical reflection than to the gospel. Evangelicals object that this has resulted in an enervation of the Christian witness

114

in order to meet the criteria of philosophical systems.[1] Liberationists argue that Western theology has in essence become an intellectual abstraction of a faith that can be properly understood only if it is practiced in the world.[2] Rather than being principally concerned with interpreting the gospel as illumination of human understanding or elucidation of human culture, evangelical and liberation theologians alike seek to investigate the impact of the gospel on the human race. They regard the essentials of the Christian message as efficacious in the lives of human beings in human society, and although they begin from very different hermeneutical starting points (the one of scriptural authority and the other of historical praxis), there is a common objective: to convince the world that the gospel of Jesus Christ is nothing less than the saving power of God over human sin, personal and social, cultural and systemic. Between the concern of evangelicalism to communicate the initiatives of God's salvation in Christ and the insights of liberationism, which point to the significance of those initiatives for human society, lies the potential for a creative synthesis that could provide a truly evangelistic theology for our time.[3]

Before such a synthesis can be forged, however, much work remains to be done in the area of mutual response between evangelical and liberation theologies, respecting the integrity of the methods of each. In this dialogue, evangelical theologians from the West must accept two contextual premises. First, evangelical theology has a thoroughly Western pedigree. Like mainstream Western theology, evangelical theology employs the method of abstract critical reflection, even though it has a particular hermeneutical focus. Second, Western theology has for the most part adopted this method of abstract critical reflection because that is how Westerners happen to function in the context of their culture. To maintain the integrity of this dialogue, therefore, evangelical theologians, while not conceding the validity of their Western method of abstract critical reflection, must grant that the theological insights of liberating praxis are equally valid. Put differently, if the context of Western theology is a culture in which critical reflection motivates and precedes active Christian witness, whereas the context of liberation theology is a culture in which active Christian witness is the source and the occasion of theological reflection, then Western evangelical theologians

1. See, for instance, Carl F. Henry, "The Undoing of the Modern Mind," in *Evangelical Roots: A Tribute to Wilbur Smith* (Nashville: Nelson, 1978), pp. 101-20. Cf. Van Harvey, *The Historian and the Believer* (New York: Macmillan, 1969), pp. 3-37.

2. José Míguez Bonino takes even Jürgen Moltmann to task (see *Doing Theology in a Revolutionary Situation* [Philadelphia: Fortress Press, 1975], pp. 149ff.; cf. Gustavo Gutiérrez, *A Theology of Liberation* [Maryknoll: Orbis Books, 1973], pp. 217-18).

3. On this, see Richard G. Hutcheson, Jr., *Mainline Churches and the Evangelicals: A Challenging Crisis?* (Atlanta: John Knox, 1981), p. 96.

must be open to questions of critical reflection posed by liberation theology that would otherwise not be raised.[4]

The mistake often made in this dialogue is what can best be described as hermeneutical impatience. Instead of asking to what extent the questions of liberating praxis provide an opportunity for theological self-correction in Western theology through its own method of critical reflection, the urge to realize a creative synthesis fosters the propounding of liberation hermeneutics as an imposed corrective—an imposition that is of course resisted. By the same token, instead of accepting the methodological safeguards implicit in liberation theology and thereby allowing for an appropriate response to questions raised by the critical reflection of Western theology, liberating praxis is viewed as mere Marxian analysis, and Western hermeneutics is imposed as a corrective. This imposition is resisted too, not least when the Western theology is evangelical, in which hermeneutics is not always adequately distinguished from evangelistic zeal.

All of this amounts to a weighty error in cross-cultural theological communication. On the one hand, theologians of Latin America find it incomprehensible that North American theologians can remain so abstract, arguably seeking refuge in a critical reflection that conveniently avoids the particularities of costly witness.[5] On the other hand, North American theologians find a hermeneutic of historical immediacy to be potentially fallacious in the sweep of a tradition that has been tested by many oppressions and persecutions.[6] One result of this cultural miscommunication is that insights of liberation theology have yet to have an impact on the average North American congregation, which feels confronted rather than challenged or stimulated by the whole concept of historical praxis. The issue is not that liberation theology makes affluent and comfortable Christians defensive, though of course this does happen; such people have long since become immune to injections of the gospel and have no difficulty in resisting it. The issue is rather that theologies that have been forged in contexts of oppression cannot be *transferred* to contexts of affluence and comfort. They

4. This is not to suggest that theologies of liberating praxis have not been written in the Western world. The signal contribution of black and feminist theologians precludes any such assumption, as does the pioneering work of Frederick Herzog, whose *Liberation Theology* (New York: Seabury Press, 1973) stands as a hermeneutical breakthrough for North American theology. But the point remains that mainstream Western theology works from theory to practice, from reflection to action, and the potential for dialogue with liberation theology from that vantage point has not yet been realized.

5. On this, see Orlando E. Costas, *Christ outside the Gate: Mission beyond Christendom* (Maryknoll: Orbis Books, 1982), pp. 119, 126, 131-32.

6. So suggests Jacques Ellul in *False Presence of the Kingdom* (New York: Seabury Press, 1972), pp. 91ff.

must be *transplanted.* And to be transplanted from Latin America to North America, a theological method of liberating praxis must be contextualized, not only as a timely challenge to affluence and comfort but also with full regard to a theological method that moves from reflection to action. When this is not taken into account—and it rarely is—there is genuine frustration on the part of the North American Christians with the shout of liberation from the South. They very much wish to be more collegial in the faith, but they feel that whatever they do will inevitably, inexorably, fall short of the costly discipleship demanded by the liberating praxis of the Latin American context. And little wonder. For the oppressions that have engendered liberation theology are, with the pivotal exception of minority groups, unknown to most North Americans. What they need is motivation for discipleship from within their own theological tradition, albeit stimulated by another tradition and another method.

It would seem that the way to avoid such an enervating stalemate is to withdraw from premature attempts to forge a creative synthesis and to invest time and energy in the pressing task of theological dialogue between North and South, with mutual integrity of method. Such at least is my intent in this paper. I argue for an ecclesiological perspective within the criteria of Western theology—critical reflection on the Scriptures and teachings of the church—but in light of questions raised for those criteria by Latin American liberation theology.

Christian Identity: Election for the World

The perennial problem for the Christian is one of identity. This is because Christians live in the tension of particular faith and global humanity, neither of which can be sacrificed to the other, and both of which constantly threaten the integrity of the church. As José Míguez Bonino has put it, there is a "split of consciousness" intrinsic to Christian existence in which memory, hope, and identity are confessed as one in faith but are empirically experienced as an irreducible duality.[7] The Christ event, grounded in the Judaic tradition, is historical and specific.[8] Yet its significance is to be found only in its universal reality. For Christians, therefore, the necessary task is that of discerning the particularity of the gospel without denying responsibility to

7. Míguez Bonino, *Doing Theology in a Revolutionary Situation,* pp. 154-55.

8. Mircea Eliade has written that "Judaism presents an innovation of the first importance. For Judaism, time has a beginning and will have an end. The idea of cyclic time is left behind. . . . When a Christian of our day participates in liturgical time, he recovers the *illud tempus* in which Christ lived, suffered and rose again—but it is no longer mythical time, it is the time when Pontius Pilate governed Judea" (*The Sacred and the Profane* [New York: Harcourt, Brace & World, 1959], pp. 110-11).

human existence or the future—what has been termed the practical dimension of hermeneutical theory.[9]

When the tension of Christian identity becomes problematic, it is usually because Christian hermeneutics has attempted to circumvent the polarity of the particular and the universal, resulting either in a Christian tradition that has lost its significance or in a Christian message that is less than relevant to human existence. Likewise, any concept of Christian identity that avoids the "split of consciousness" will either view salvation selectively or fail to provide a distinctive Christian witness to the world. This last has been a persistent tendency in North America, where a civil religion propounded by the Protestant churches and the state blurs the focus of Christian proclamation. Unwilling to enter into a relationship with God that is distinct from American covenant history, the church attempts to impose a sacred interpretation on the secular, refusing to accept the fact that the secular is also God's sphere and therefore inherently valid. In so doing, it loses its authority, because the secular, while accepting a certain degree of sacralization, does not regard the church as having more or less significance than any other social structure.[10]

Writing in the context of the 1976 bicentennial of the United States, Richard John Neuhaus discerned the immediacy of the problem:

> The church needs rather an imaginative re-appropriation of its own tradition, a theological recovery of nerve, a new confidence to live in dialectic with the larger culture, an unembarrassed readiness to affirm the scandal of its particularity. Only such a church can "save its own soul."[11]

It is when the church truly appropriates this tradition that the significance of the dialectic becomes clear, for Christian identity and hermeneutics both: the particular Christ-event reveals the universality of God's saving righteousness, in which there is neither Jew nor Greek, neither slave nor free, neither male nor female, neither Northern nor Southern hemisphere, but only a oneness in Christ Jesus (Gal. 3:28). If the church addresses the questions of human existence at the expense of its particular historical tradition, concern for relevance will domesticate the living Word—as, for example, in the preoccupation of the Western church with ecclesiastical self-

9. See James M. Robinson, "Hermeneutic since Barth," in *New Frontiers in Theology, 2: The New Hermeneutic,* ed. James M. Robinson and John B. Cobb, Jr. (New York: Harper & Row, 1964), pp. 8-9.

10. On this, see, for example, *White House Sermons,* ed. Ben Hibbs (New York: Harper & Row, 1972). "Gosh-awful nice words," wrote Hiley H. Ward, reviewing the book in *The Christian Century,* 1 November 1972, "but long ago, the Lord spoke to a prophet, and the king invited the prophet in. And the chief of state trembled."

11. Neuhaus, *Time toward Home: The American Experiment as Revelation* (New York: Seabury Press, 1975), p. 209.

preservation, reflecting the narcissism of contemporary Western culture. [12] By the same token, a church that regards itself as historically absolute becomes invulnerable, unalterable, and aggressive. [13] The Christian *evangel* cannot be an exclusive concept, nor yet can Christian discipleship. Indeed, when the scriptural foundations for Christian self-understanding are properly investigated, it becomes clear that the distinctiveness of the people of God has never been at the expense of the rest of the world. Their proper identity has always been that of being called into a particular relationship with God for the purposes of proclaiming a universal message.

As Paul reminds us in Galatians 3:29, Christian identity is grounded in the spiritual history of Israel and rooted in the concept of election. Their calling as the chosen people of Yahweh led the Israelites into real and severe conflicts, not only exposing the struggles and enigmas of human existence but also posing the fundamental question of the truth or falsity of the divine message. [14] The idea behind election was important from the beginning of the nation's existence, and even though it came into use theologically at a comparatively late date, the belief that they were Yahweh's special people goes back much farther in the Hebrew tradition. This is not to antedate its development but to recognize that Abraham's response in obedience to God was a significant moment in the history of Israel's election, by which Israel was called to be a blessing to all nations (Gen. 12:1-3). [15]

While the concept of election is implicit in the earliest documents of the Pentateuch, it is in the J presentation that the stories of the traditions are first taken and fashioned into a saving history through which God, after the human attempt to construct a history has been shattered, chooses Abraham so that through Israel salvation might come to the whole world. [16] The achievement of the Yahwist is not only to place each event in the larger context of God's saving action but also to portray the relationship between Yahweh and the Israelites as intensely personal. Yahweh thinks out loud (Gen. 8:21-22), identifies very closely with the earth (Gen. 9:6-7), and engages in genuine dialogue (Gen. 18:22ff.). There is a sense of fearless,

12. See Alfred C. Krass, *Evangelizing Neo-Pagan North America* (Scottdale, Pa.: Herald Press, 1982).

13. So says Jürgen Moltmann in *The Church in the Power of the Spirit* (New York: Harper & Row, 1977), p. 153. Cf. Krass, *Five Lanterns at Sundown: Evangelism in a Chastened Mood* (Grand Rapids: Eerdmans, 1978), p. 77.

14. See G. Quell, s.v. *eklégomai* in *Theological Dictionary of the New Testament,* 10 vols. (Grand Rapids: Eerdmans, 1967), 4: 161. This work will be cited subsequently as *TDNT*.

15. See Gerhard von Rad, *Old Testament Theology,* 2 vols. (New York: Harper & Row, 1962-65), pp. 178ff.

16. See Johannes Blauw, *The Missionary Nature of the Church: A Survey of the Biblical Theology of Mission* (Grand Rapids: Eerdmans, 1974), p. 5.

direct encounter with the deity, a deity so accessible as to seem almost vulnerable. [17]

The Yahwist strand also gives the Israelites a universalistic concept of history. God's grace to Israel is something that concerns the whole human race. In the eighth-century prophets, culminating in Deutero-Isaiah, we find that the will of the God who has called a particular people to know him distinctively is nothing less than that their special knowledge must be shared with all peoples:

Thus says God, the Lord,
    who created the heavens and stretched them out,
who spread forth the earth and what comes from it,
    who gives breath to the people upon it
and spirit to those who walk in it:
    "I am the Lord, I have called you in righteousness,
I have taken you by the hand and kept you;
    I have given you as a covenant to the people, a light to the nations,
to open the eyes that are blind,
    to bring out the prisoners from the dungeon,
from the prison those who sit in darkness." (Isa. 42:5-7)

As the prophet suggests, only in and through this mission to the world could Israel fulfill the purpose of God's election, an election not of particular privilege but of universal responsibility. It had profound implications for the identity of the Israelites as the people of God both as messengers and as servants, and it proved to be a source of deep enrichment for their inheritance. [18] The election of God was to be interpreted in terms of purpose and service, a call for discipline and accountability. The Israelites could expect to be singled out by God primarily as those from whom more was expected. It was by no means a call to superiority:

"You only have I known of all the families of the earth;
    therefore I will punish you for all your iniquities." (Amos 3:2)

"Are you not like the Ethiopians to me, O people of Israel?' says the Lord.
"Did I not bring up Israel from the land of Egypt and the Philistines from Caphtor and the Syrians from Kir?" (Amos 9:7)

When we find election definitively expressed as a statement of faith in the Deuteronomic writings, therefore, it is important to note that the concept takes its radical form only in the context of this universal perspective of

17. See Norman Habel, *Literary Criticism of the Old Testament* (Philadelphia: Fortress Press, 1971), pp. 48, 51.
18. See H. H. Rowley, *The Biblical Doctrine of Election* (London: Lutterworth, 1950), p. 68.

history.[19] And in this radical form, election emerges with a twofold nature. On the one hand, the status of the elect is clearly that of being called to a task, a calling emphasized as a wholly divine initiative. On the other hand, the scope of God's sovereignty is understood to extend over all nations. The particular choice of Israel thus becomes a mystery. No discernible reason can be found for God's choice of a people of little account.

> For you are a people holy to the Lord your God; the Lord your God has chosen you to be a people for his own possession, out of all the people that are on the face of the earth. It was not because you were more in number than any other people that the Lord set his love upon you and chose you, for you were the fewest of all peoples; but it is because the Lord loves you, and is keeping the oath which he swore to your fathers, that the Lord has brought you out with a mighty hand, and redeemed you from the house of bondage, from the hand of Pharaoh, king of Egypt. Know, therefore, that the Lord your God is God, the faithful God who keeps covenant and steadfast love with those who love him and keep his commandments, to a thousand generations. (Deut. 7:6-9)[20]

The continuing basis of Israel's relationship with Yahweh was the Sinai covenant (Deut. 5:2ff.). It was entered into freely, a response to God's gracious acts towards the Israelites, and it had to be renewed voluntarily by each generation. Yet it was not unconditional. Even though the predominant nature of the covenant was God's grace, and the initiative remained with God, commandments from God were subsequently revealed. It was in the appropriation of Yahweh's will that Israel's identity was established, and although obedience was not a prerequisite for entering the covenant, it was a requirement for remaining in it. When Israel failed to accept this obligation, it was made clear that it was also God's election that was being repudiated (Isa. 1:2, 4; Jer. 18:1ff.; Hos. 6:7, 8:1).[21]

This need for obedient response to God's initiative gave the covenant a worldly quality, grounded in the historical realities of God's actions. This is indicated by the honesty with which the relationship is recounted in the Old Testament. It was what Yahweh had done for the Israelites that constituted the graciousness of the covenant and at the same time manifested the directness of the election call. Nor was this the God of polytheistic tolerance whose aim had always been to preserve the established order and to integrate

19. Sellin Fohrer states, "It was only the Israel which had learned to look at herself from the outside, and for whom her own existence among the nations had become a problem, that was in a position to talk about election" (*Introduction to the Old Testament* [Nashville: Abingdon Press, 1968], p. 178).

20. See Alan Richardson, "Instrument of God: The Unity of the Biblical Doctrine of Salvation," *Interpretation* 3 (July 1949): 276. See also von Rad, *Old Testament Theology*, 1: 170; and Blauw, *The Missionary Nature of the Church*, pp. 29ff.

21. See von Rad, *Old Testament Theology*, 1: 192, 194, 229ff.

religion with the world. This was the God whose redemptive work judged the sin of humankind. Moreover, while the election of Israel was corporate, the covenant was addressed to each member of the nation, demanding an individual response together with that of the people as a whole. And, among other responses from the Israelites, this directness could incur their rage. So vital was their covenant relationship with Yahweh that they sometimes dared to believe protest was more fitting than submission.[22]

Paradoxically, the directness of Israel's relationship with Yahweh was weakened when the universal implications of their covenant with him were subsumed by its religious and theological dimensions. It is in the E tradition that this first becomes evident—as, for example, when the blessing of Abraham transferred to Isaac is interpreted in such a way as to emphasize the religious aspect of election more strongly (Gen. 22:17-18). The concept begins to lose its significance for other peoples as Israel is set over against the other nations rather than being a means of blessing for them. God's dominion and fellowship become something restricted to Israel, a tendency further developed by the D and P traditions; as a result, the calling of Israel becomes not one of election for other peoples but selection from them (Num. 23:9b). The world of the nations becomes the world of paganism, and foreign gods are censured as apostasy from Yahweh (Exod. 32). Instead of the election of Israel being part of God's salvation history for the human race, we find specific acts of election by God primarily for cultic and kingly purposes. In the struggle against the Canaanite nature religions, election takes on an axiomatic and exclusive connotation.

Perhaps this was a necessary defense against erosion by other religions, but the crucial question is posed by von Rad, who asks whether a theology that saw Israel's existence in the eyes of Yahweh so strongly conditioned by praise could have strayed this far from the proper road.[23] Put differently, the people of God in active and positive relationship with their God were truly free to proclaim salvation for the nations. But a people turning away from God began to cling to an exclusive identity as a form of defense, unaware that in so doing they were weakening their covenant relationship. The further consequence of this religious exclusiveness was a failure to sense God's judgment. Regarding themselves as God's people over against the nations of the world, they looked for a "Day of Yahweh" when their foes would be vanquished. They did not heed the prophets, who warned them of their own approaching day of reckoning. "Yahweh kept knocking at their door, but they paid no heed."[24]

Yet even when the nation as a whole seemed to have repudiated the covenant—and therefore their election—there remained an element that

22. Walter A. Brueggemann, "Covenanting as Human Vocation: A Discussion of the Relation of the Biblical and Pastoral Care," *Interpretation* 33 (April 1979): 123.

23. Von Rad, *Old Testament Theology*, 1: 354.

24. Von Rad, *Old Testament Theology*, 2: 137.

accepted the obligations implied by their election and thus conveyed the heritage to those who followed:

> And the surviving remnant of the house of Judah shall again take root downward, and bear fruit upward; for out of Jerusalem shall go forth a remnant, and out of Mount Zion a band of survivors. The zeal of the Lord of hosts will accomplish this. (Isa. 37:31-2)[25]

This is why it is important to note that reprobation does not appear in the Old Testament as a corollary of election.[26] Indeed, if there is a dialectic operative in God's election, it is judgment and mercy, in which the God who makes demands also supplies the grace to fulfill those demands—a righteousness which is also a salvation.[27] The definitive dimension of election is not God's choice between peoples but the manifestation of saving grace—a grace that does not undermine responsible human behavior. The human choice is whether or not to be involved in God's saving activity, which continues in spite of human response.[28] The awesomeness of God's sovereignty is that human beings are free to resist the grace of saving righteousness, and it is in the particular election of Israel that the dynamics of this grace and resistance are representatively brought into focus.[29]

Recent biblical scholarship indicates that the Rabbinic religion of the intertestamental period manifests the same emphases. The postexilic period of Israel's history might have engendered an element of isolationism and even exclusiveness in order to preserve Judaism through perilous times, and it may have deprived the Jews of motivation to proclaim their revelation from God to the world, but this by no means transformed the concept of covenant into a legalistic works righteousness.[30] Election to covenant with Yahweh remained a gracious concept, with a focus on God's love.[31] This understanding is also to be found in the Qumran literature, and in the Apocryphal and Pseudepigraphal writings.[32]

When we turn to the New Testament, therefore, the difference in the

25. Cf. Jeremiah 31:31-4 and Ezekiel 11:19-20.

26. See Quell, *TDNT*, 4: 175.

27. See Norman H. Snaith, *The Distinctive Ideas of the Old Testament* (New York: Schocken Books, 1964), pp. 79ff.

28. See Paul Lehmann, "Deliverance and Fulfillment: The Biblical View of Salvation," *Interpretation* 5 (October 1951): 397.

29. Robert E. Cushman provides a lucid statement of these issues in the context of Western thought in his essay "A Study of Freedom and Grace," *The Journal of Religion* 25 (July 1954): 197-211.

30. See E. P. Sanders, *Paul and Palestinian Judaism: A Comparison* (Philadelphia: Fortress Press, 1977), p. 233.

31. Says Sanders, "The intention and effort to be obedient constitute the condition for remaining in the covenant, but they do not earn it" (*Paul and Palestinian Judaism*, p. 180; see also pp. 85, 95, 119, 124).

32. See Sanders, *Paul and Palestinian Judaism*, pp. 320, 420-23, 428.

Pauline pattern of religion is not one of grace as opposed to works. It is rather that instead of a righteousness that comes from obedient response to God's covenant initiative, there is now a total dependence on Christ. Obedience is still the condition of the covenant relationship, but it is Christ who brings the people of God into a new covenant. It is Christ who sustains them in their righteousness, and it is being one with Christ that affords death to sin and gives the promise of resurrection. The new covenant is nothing more or less than participation in the transformation of the human race, accomplished by Jesus Christ and to be fulfilled at his return (Eph. 1:9-10, 20-23; Col. 1:19-10; 2 Pet. 3:13).[33]

As with the covenant election of Israel, the new covenant is a special relationship with God that carries responsibility for the world. Throughout the New Testament, the church is described as the elect of God, an election that developed out of Israel, and as such it appropriates the same principles of grace and service (Gal. 6:16; Eph. 1:13-14; 1 Pet. 2:9).[34] In the Pauline account of the Last Supper, for example, and in the lengthy discussion of election in Romans, it is clear that God's grace is extended to all peoples (1 Cor. 11:23ff.; Rom. 9:27, 29; 11:4ff.). The church is the new Israel of God, called and chosen by God—but chosen to receive, by particular grace, the commission to proclaim a message of universal hope.[35]

That the universality of this commission was not at first understood by the church is evident in the biblical records of the Apostolic Conference (Acts 15; Gal. 2).[36] Paul was primarily concerned with the task of proclaiming the gospel to all people without distinction, willing to become "all things to all men" (1 Cor. 9:22). The church in Jerusalem was concerned more with the distinctive identity of the people of God (Gal. 2:12). The Conference drew these concerns into a dialectic, Paul the missionary showing concern for the mother church, and Peter and the Jerusalem leaders acknowledging the necessity of preaching a gospel for the whole world. The concept of the servant church that emerged from this tension appropriated the dynamic of the Israelite covenant: the people of God elected for the nations of the world. The power of the new covenant lay in the awareness of the resurrection believers that God's saving grace is universal.

33. See Sanders, *Paul and Palestinian Judaism,* p. 549. See also Russell Shedd, *Man in Community: A Study of St. Paul's Application of Old Testament and Early Jewish Conceptions of Human Solidarity* (London: Epworth Press, 1958), pp. 172-73.

34. See Shedd, *Man in Community,* pp. 129ff.

35. So says Cushman, "Biblical Election as Sacred History," in *Our Common History as Christians: Essays in Honor of Albert C. Outler,* ed. John Deschner, Leroy T. Howe, and Klaus Penzel (New York: Oxford University Press, 1975), pp. 197-216. There is no better treatment available of the relevant scriptural texts on this theme, made all the more pertinent by Cushman's driving concern for the Oikoumene as the sphere of God's salvation.

36. See Gunther Bornkamm's account in *Paul* (New York: Harper & Row, 1971), pp. 56ff.

This is brought to its most eloquent expression in Paul's letter to the Romans, where the full scope of God's salvation is declared. The whole of the world is in the birthpangs of a new creation, and the elect of God are privileged to share in its firstfruits (Rom. 8:18-25, 28-30). The true purpose of election within global redemption is brought to its ultimate crisis as Paul, with deep anguish and joy, places his own people in their proper salvific context. Even the hardness of the Jews toward the new covenant has a purpose (9:10-24), because God's plan is for all to be called to forgiveness through the present rejection of a few (11:13-16, 28-32).

Wolfhart Pannenberg has brought these scriptural concepts into a historical perspective of the church demonstrating convincingly that the contemporary church faces a very real crisis of identity.[37] If the mission to which Christians are called is that of proclaiming the universal acts of God, then the church must look beyond itself to the will of God for the world, avoiding the dualism of defining itself as a particular institution over against human culture. Christian self-understanding must be that of election to a particular relationship with God *for* the world, not *from* it. For most of its history, argues Pannenberg, the church has failed to fulfill this worldly role, being dominated by the Augustinian identity of a spiritual rather than a worldly manifestation of God's elective grace. This has left a religious vacuum in Western political life that has been filled across the centuries by a wide range of civil religions, many of them Christian in their character, but none of them theocentric as was the early church. Indeed, the nationalisms spawned by these civil religions have often appropriated the very sense of election that the church has surrendered. The ecclesiological task is therefore quite urgent:

> It may be considered high time for the Christian churches and their theology to recognize the elements of corporate election and mission as well as of judgment in the political history of Christianity. It is urgent that they be redeemed from the ambiguities and perversions of their alienated persistence in the form of civil religions of particular nations. A re-appropriation of the subject of historical corporate election of the people of God may also relieve the churches themselves of a narrowly ecclesiocentric perspective focusing exclusively on the church as an insititution.[38]

The irony leaps from the page. The people of God, called to particular covenant in order to proclaim the salvation of God to the peoples of the world, surrender their birthright to the nation state. And having surrendered their true identity, they resort to a false one: the church rather than the world as the *locus* of their faith.

37. See Pannenberg, *Human Nature, Election and History* (Philadelphia: Westminster Press, 1977), pp. 69ff., 81ff.
38. Pannenberg, *Human Nature, Election and History*, p. 82.

The ecclesiological task is indeed urgent, and it is not altogether surprising to find that the most creative work in this area should be coming from a liberated Roman Catholicism, stimulating and stimulated by Vatican II.[39] Ecclesiology has always been the blind spot of Protestantism, and while this has provided some fundamental intellectual freedoms for the gospel—biblical interpretation, for example—it has also fostered the personalizing of the gospel as a *cultus privatus*.[40] Schleiermacher's brilliant systematization of this has led to the development of a progressively insular soteriology in much of Protestant theology as well as a doctrine of the church that is for the most part incidental to personal religion.[41]

Even more significant for this liberated ecclesiology is the fact that one of its major sources is Latin America, where the church is confronted by oppressions that make its proclamation of the gospel a very real point of identity. We can agree with Pannenberg that a recovery of identity for the Western church lies in the reappropriation of biblical election, understood in the Judeo-Christian tradition as chosenness for the purpose of proclaiming the universal acts of God's saving righteousness. But the liberating praxis of Latin American theology presses us to look more closely at this identity in the present reality of worldly witness, asking what it is we are to proclaim, and why.

Heroic Minorities: The Challenge of Latin America

One of the most important American scholars to address this issue is Juan Luis Segundo, whose role as a practical theologian in developing post–Vatican II Roman Catholic thought has been substantial. His ecclesiological study *The Community Called Church* is definitive; his contextual application of its insights, *The Hidden Motives of Pastoral Action,* is incisive.[42] We shall follow his argument in some detail.

39. And in turn stimulating and stimulated by Medellin.

40. See Moltmann, *Hope and Planning* (New York: Harper & Row, 1971), pp. 131ff.

41. It is salutary to refer to the exact wording of Schleiermacher's concept of the church, and to be reminded of how Protestantism still labors under the weight of his terminology: "That a Church is nothing but a communion or association relating to religion or piety, is beyond all doubt for us Evangelical (Protestant) Christians, since we regard it as equivalent to degeneration in a Church when it begins to occupy itself with other matters as well, whether the affairs of science or of outward organizations; just as we also always oppose any attempt on the part of the leaders of State or of science, as such, to order the affairs of religion . . . it is only the maintenance, regulation, and advancement of piety which they can regard as the essential business of the Church" (*The Christian Faith,* 2 vols. [New York: Harper & Row, 1963], 1: 5-6).

42. Segundo, *The Community Called Church* (Maryknoll, N.Y.: Orbis Books, 1973); *The Hidden Motives of Pastoral Action* (Maryknoll, N.Y.: Orbis Books, 1978).

Segundo affirms at the outset that precisely because the church is historically limited, being born at a specific moment, it confirms the nature of the
Christ-event as universal. The message of the Christian revelation is therefore based not on the supramundane and the transcendent but rather on the
particularity of an incarnational happening. It is this very particularity,
suggests Segundo, that prevents the human race from projecting its own
limitations onto God, and the church from projecting its limitations onto
God's saving righteousness: "revelation is not a formula entrusted to the
Church for safekeeping. It is rather a living Word which calls out to human
existence in every age. And man's understanding of it advances as humanity
itself grows and deepens through its own questioning."[43] The universalism
of God's salvation plan is clear not only in the man Jesus but also in his
teachings. The key factor in God's judgment on humanity will be "What
did you do for me when I was hungry, thirsty, alone, and mistreated?" These
are actions that are particularly incumbent upon Christians but that are in
fact required of all people, and can be found in them. The church often
pictures humanity traveling down a road that does not of itself lead to
salvation; this must be corrected with a vision of a common humanity.[44]

The question thus becomes "What distinguishes the Christian in this
common journey?" If the particular revelation in Christ has such universal
implications, is there any validity for a particular community of faith? For
Segundo, the answer is a qualified affirmative. The particularity is that some
people on this common road know, through revelation, something that
relates to all. They know the mystery of the journey. And what they know
they know in order to make a contribution to the common quest.[45] The
church is the community of those who, within the divine plan that is
common to all humanity, are entrusted with an understanding of what is
happening through the revelation of the Christ-event.[46]

The function of this particular community among a pluralism of God's
saving activities is that of a sign, "a visible community with its formulas of
faith and its sacraments, ready to meet and dialogue with those who are
moving towards the gospel and confronting the questions raised by love."[47]
It is a function that carries a responsibility toward the world, because the

43. Segundo, *The Community Called Church,* p. 19. Cf. Karl Rahner, *Foundations
of Christian Faith: An Introduction to the Idea of Christianity* (New York: Seabury Press,
1978), p. 161.

44. See Segundo, *The Community Called Church,* p. 9.

45. See Segundo, *The Community Called Church,* p. 32. See also pp. 40-41: "The
contemporary expression of Christian thought as reflected in the writings of the New
Testament did not see any special importance in distinguishing between the thanks
they owed God for reasons relating particularly to their status as Christians and the
thanks owed by all men to him if they only knew what Christians knew. . . . Only on
rare occasions do the early Christians give thanks to God specifically for what relates
to them as Christians."

46. Segundo, *The Community Called Church,* p. 76.

47. Segundo, *The Community Called Church,* p. 60.

first law of revelation for the Christian is incarnation. "The world will believe in a faith that is fleshed out in today, not in a faith tied up with other conceptions of man."[48] The very nature of this revelation impels the church to live out its sign knowledge in the world, for the Christ-event reveals that the whole of the world is God's creation, and the whole of history belongs to God. There is no dichotomy between sacred and secular, for the sacred is "in the entire edifice, in the big temple we are to construct in history, and not just in the cement that is the little temple." The construction of this big temple requires the momentary segregation of the little temple, just as our existence of love requires a moment of setting ourselves apart from others. But this momentary segregation of the little temple must be done in such a way "that it truly forms a cement and a leaven, rather than turning into a conventional formalism wherein the would-be salt loses its savor."[49]

It follows, therefore, that membership of the church must be elective. Segundo is sensitive to the charge of elitism implicit in this, but feels that he answers it adequately by defining the election as that of risk. "The only aristocracy [the Christian] will get, if he really wants it, is an aristocracy of self-giving and love that may even entail death."[50] The true ecclesial community consists of "heroic minorities," and the sign work of the church is that of selective and costly discipleship.[51] Indeed, it is the failure of the church to be selective in terms of costly discipleship that deprives it of its identity. "To put it more plainly, the church today must ask herself if all her so-called members truly belong to her, and if some non-members might not truly belong to her. This was a question which even the primitive Church had to ask herself."[52] The reason for the church's lack of selectivity is the mistaken wish to be the community of all peoples instead of a sign to the world community—a wish to be the kingdom of Jesus Christ rather than to proclaim it. "If the community called Church wanted to be the community of all mankind, or at least of the majority of mankind, it would have to take the line of least resistance and make it as easy as possible for people. In reality, however, the Church will always be selective. The line of least resistance is an egotistical tack."[53]

The progression of Segundo's argument seems to question the very substance of the Christian message, but he does not hesitate to press it. If the church is a sign community within a pluralism of God's saving activities accepting the aristocratic role of self-giving love, it follows not only that the membership of the church is elective but also that

48. Segundo, *The Community Called Church*, p. 37.
49. Segundo, *The Community Called Church*, p. 75.
50. Segundo, *The Community Called Church*, p. 84.
51. Segundo, *Hidden Motives of Pastoral Action*, pp. 18, 33, 71, and passim.
52. Segundo, *The Community Called Church*, p. 79.
53. Segundo, *The Community Called Church*, p. 83.

at least in some cases the Church (i.e. visible membership in the Christian community) is not always and everywhere the ideal situation with respect to salvation for all men. . . . Only by recognizing the fact of a pluralistic society will the Christian realize once again that he is to function as a sign. Only by meeting the non-Christians of his day will he be able to undertake a mature consideration of the objective formulation of his faith so that he may make the authentic Good News accessible to his contemporaries.[54]

This is at once salutary and liberating for the church. It is salutary in its implication that the church cannot regard itself as the community of the saved; it must battle the desire to *be* the kingdom of God rather than to accept the responsibility of announcing it.[55] It is highly instructive for the Christian to look into the world for the hope of God's salvation and to accept the relevance and necessity of such discoveries for the nature and content of the evangel itself—an evangelization of the church *by* as well as *for* the world. On the other hand, it is liberating for the Christian to find God's salvation operative beyond the Christian community: liberating in that it can free it from the ecclesiocentricity that too often degenerates into the pragmatism of self-maintenance, liberating in that it can free it for the fuller vision of the elective commission of God that lies beyond the parochialism of privatized salvation, liberating in that it absolves the Christian from the two-kingdoms riddle of being in and yet not of the world. There is offered instead the reality of being totally in and of the world yet knowing that a new age is already present and imminently to be fulfilled.[56]

What clearly gives this ecclesiology its cutting edge is Segundo's conviction that the role of the church in the world is qualitative, not quantitative. The very scope and panorama of God's salvation means that the church does not and cannot exist merely for the benefit of those who belong to it. On the contrary, it exists in the world to benefit the rest of humankind, and even a cursory overview of human history shows the absurdity of an ecclesial self-perception as the *locus* of God's salvation. Not only is there the question of why God took so long to establish the church—some two million years after humankind had existed on earth.[57] There is also the enigma of why there is

54. Segundo, *The Community Called Church*, pp. 83, 93.

55. This of course is of special concern for the role of the ordained ministry, as I have tried to demonstrate in "Professing the Call to Serve," *Quarterly Review* 2 (Spring 1982).

56. Herzog puts it well: "Some do acknowledge God. Their unusual stance is a new beginning in the history of mankind. They are directly related to God, like children to parents. They acknowledge unconcealment. That is, they are directly involved in hammering out their destiny. All who acknowledge the incarnate Word find a new direction of life. True acknowledgment of God is possible only through trust in the one who first acknowledged God's unconcealment fully" (*Liberation Theology*, p. 34).

57. See Segundo, *Hidden Motives of Pastoral Action*, pp. 136-37.

such a long delay in the universal acceptance of its offer—if indeed it can ensure its members of some privileged status with regard to salvation.[58]

And if proof of this were needed, it can be found in what happens when the gospel is preached only to win adherents to the church: its message is disempowered. It becomes nothing more than a means of security for church members. The result is an ever-diminishing concept of discipleship, in which the church requires the absolute minimum in obligations in order to keep the maximum number of people—what Segundo describes as the "general rule of pastoral prudence."[59] If the church is to be free from this institutional enslavement, free to be the church, it must be able to trust the gospel as a message for the world; and in taking it to the world, it must find its true power. For the gospel is the hope of God's salvation, and those who proclaim it are the salt to the world, the sign of the New Age that is to come (Matt. 5:13-14; Mark 4:21, 9:50; Luke 14:34-35).[60]

All of this has profound implications for the Western church in general and its ecclesiology in particular. In the first place, it makes inexorably clear the fact that the message to be proclaimed by the church must be the universality of God's saving righteousness. God's elective activity in the world never isolates particular communities or individuals but rather exemplifies his love for all nations and persons.[61] Yet the identity crisis of the Western church in its own culture is persistently exported to the rest of the world, mistakenly articulated as the soteriological problem of universalism. The manifold divisions this has occasioned in world evangelism are with us yet, and while great strides have been made toward a collegial acceptance of the issue,[62] it remains fundamentally a question of unattended Western theological homework.

Take, for example, the following comment from John Stott's response to the now famous Nairobi address of Mortimer Arias:

58. See Segundo, *Hidden Motives of Pastoral Action*, pp. 136-37.
59. Segundo, *Hidden Motives of Pastoral Action*, pp. 32, 72ff.
60. At this point a word should be said about the omission from this essay of the *communidades de base*, an ecclesiological factor that would seem to be unavoidable in the discussion. While in no way denying the crucial role of these basic ecclesial groupings in Latin America or their affirmation of a liberated church at the grass roots, I am in this essay primarily concerned with the potential for ecclesiological dialogue between north and south in the Americas. And for Christians in the north, the first step, it seems to me, must be an ecclesiological reformulation. Attempts to foster basic ecclesial communities in the United States meet with limited success in the mainline church for precisely this reason. See articles by Rosemary Ruether and Kate Pravera in *Christianity and Crisis*, 21 September 1981.
61. See Pannenberg, *Human Nature, Election and History*, p. 108.
62. As, for example, in the very fine evangelical statement at the Seventh WCC Assembly at Vancouver in the summer of 1983. See *TSF Bulletin*, September/October 1983, pp. 18-19.

Universalism, fashionable as it is today, is incompatible with the teachings of Christ and his apostles, and is a deadly enemy of evangelism. The
true universalism of the Bible is the call to universal evangelism in obedience to Christ's universal commission. It is the conviction, not that all
men will be saved in the end, but that all men must hear the gospel [of
salvation] before the end, as Jesus said (Matt. 24:24), in order that they
may have a chance to believe and to be saved (Rom. 10:13-15).[63]

What this fails to take into account is that God's salvation is operative within
the world as well as through the church. Indeed, if we accept Segundo's
argument, it is difficult to avoid the inference that the universality of the
evangel is as much as an issue in our own time as it was at the Apostolic
Conference of the early church. It is a question not only of the Christian
taking into the world the message of what God has accomplished for the
human race in Jesus Christ but also of expecting to find God at work in the
power of the Holy Spirit beyond the church. The purpose of God's election of
the church should never be viewed as a source of separation or favor—what
Robert Cushman has aptly described as the centripetal inertia endemic
among the historic branches of Christendom.[64] God's love is universally
present, and the task of the church is to discern this presence and proclaim
it—evangelism "from below" rather than "from above."[65]

Western theologians have not taken fully into account the significance of
this insight that has come, poignantly and powerfully, from the Latin
American context of suffering and oppression. As never before, the message
of salvation that comes to the individual in Christ is robbed of its meaning if
it stops short of universal hope. The love of God abroad in the world is
experienced by these Christians because the gospel assures them of the
presence of Christ in their suffering. And because Christ suffers with them as
well as for them, they know that the gospel is not only only a message from
the church to the world but also a message from the world to the church. The
soteriological question is not whether all will be saved in response to the
proclamation of the gospel; that is a matter for speculation in a church that
witnesses in freedom and affluence and whose theologians continue to wrestle with the theodicy of resistance and apathy among their people. But for a

63. Stott, "Response to Addresss by Bishop Arias," *International Review of Mission*
65 (January 1976): 31.

64. See Cushman, "Biblical Election as Sacred History," p. 210.

65. This is to adapt the ecclesiological formula advanced by Cornelius Ernst in
"The Necessity of the Church in the Context of Non-Christian Religions," in *Documenta Missionalia 5: Evangelization, Dialogue and Development,* ed. M. Dhavamony
(Roma: Universita Gregoriana Editrice, 1972), pp. 224ff. In the context of liberation
theology, the concept has recently been given very particular and trenchant treatment
by Bishop James Armstrong, *From the Underside: Evangelism from a Third World
Vantage Point* (Maryknoll, N.Y.: Orbis Books, 1981).

church that knows the cost of witnessing in the midst of oppression, the saving righteousness of a God whose credentials are presented from a cross is inextricably bound up with human history. The question of salvation is thus placed firmly where it belongs: within the sovereignty of a divine grace that will prevail until all eyes are opened and all tears dried (Rev. 21:1-4)

It is at this point that Segundo's ecclesiology presses us to the hermeneutical question. For when the church takes the gospel into the world and finds that God is already there at work, the universality of God's saving righteousness becomes particular and incarnational—not only in Jesus of Nazareth but also in the stuff of human history. The hermeneutic then becomes startlingly clear, what Segundo has described as a circle of continuing change in our interpretation of the Bible, dictated by the continuing changes in our present-day reality, both individual and societal.[66] And of special significance for our present investigation is the segment of that circle concerning the proclamation of the gospel. If the church finds its identity as the herald of God's salvation by seeking that salvation in the world as well as in its own Scripture and tradition, then God's gracious initiatives in the reality of human history are as much a part of the evangel as the scriptural witness to the Christ-event. The challenge of Latin America is to let the world evangelize the church, and the argument implicit in Segundo's ecclesiology becomes explicit as a hermeneutic of evangelism.

The advantage of a circle, of course, is that it can be entered at any point. The hermeneutic of evangelism is perhaps best approached by entering the circle at our starting point of Christian identity. For when the people of God appropriate the universality of God's salvation in the context of elective privilege, they are liberated for a freshly empowered proclamation of the gospel. If Christians are chosen to be the people of God in order to proclaim God's salvation to the world, a failure to do this constitutes a repudiation of their covenant relationship. Evangelism is thereby rendered a necessary dimension of their faith as well as an obligation of their discipleship—a far more authentic basis for their identity than the self-imposed burden that the salvation of another person depends on the extent and the efficacy of their evangelistic skill or commitment. At the very least, such a burden requires that millions of Western Christians now living side by side with neighborly pagans either assume a posture that struggles with the hope of one day being able to win them for Christ, or it calls for an attitude of profound gratitude that grace has prevailed in their own lives while it has not in the lives of others. In either instance, the result is an alienation from the world and an evangelistic and ecclesial self-centeredness that inures the church to the presence of Christ among the poor, the blind, the naked, the starving, the captive, and the oppressed of the world.

Those who have learned from the Bible how salvation operates, notes Paul

66. Segundo, *The Liberation of Theology* (Maryknoll: Orbis Books, 1979), pp. 5ff.

Lehmann, know that conversion is a matter of election. Their energies are therefore directed toward the apostolic mission to make all people "see what is the plan of the mystery hidden for ages in God who created all things; that through the church the manifold wisdom of God might be made known to the principalities and powers in the heavenly places (Eph. 3:9-10)." With such a mission, the Christian life acquires a "cosmic point and global social passion," and the church joins in the travail of the whole creation.[67] It is a passion and an empathy that compels the church to evangelize, whether or not there is response.[68]

The notion that must be restored to the center of the church's evangelistic activity, therefore, is the vision that affirms the missionary vocation of covenant.[69] It was this that gave the early church its missionary impulse and differentiated it from other sectarian movements of the time.[70] Just as the message that the Israelites were commissioned to proclaim was predicated on God's sovereignty over all the nations of the world, so the evangel of the church presumes a unity of history in which God is active in the fullest range of human affairs.[71] The identity question for the Christian is ultimately that of vocation, since faithful Christian living is a response to the divine initiative with a sure and certain trust that God's promises and purposes will not fail. As the sign community, as salt to the world, Christians represent the dynamic of humanness as the interaction between the God who calls and those who are called.[72] It is a calling that takes the Christian into the world, where the universality of God's grace is evident in human history. But above all, it is a call to evangelize and proclaim.[73]

And herein lies the hermeneutic of evangelism. The church finds the gospel by proclaiming it, by handing over to the world the message that has been traditioned in its scriptures and teachings and by announcing to the world the saving works of God perceived in human history. This at once affirms the actions of God by acknowledging the historical reality of a

67. Lehmann, "Deliverance and Fulfillment: The Biblical View of Salvation," *Interpretation* 5 (October 1951): 398, 400.

68. See Rowley, *The Biblical Doctrine of Election*, p. 169. Cf. Stott, *Christian Mission in the Modern World* (Wheaton: Tyndale House, 1975), pp. 38-34.

69. So contends Josef Amstutz, "Toward a Legitimation of the Missions," in *Evangelization in the World Today*, ed. Norbert Greinacher and Alois Muller (New York: Seabury Press, 1979), pp. 33-34.

70. See Ernst, "The Necessity of the Church in the Context of Non-Christian Religions," pp. 226-27.

71. See Pannenberg, *Human Nature, Election and History*, p. 89.

72. Brueggemann, "Covenanting as Human Vocation," pp. 121, 125.

73. See K. Luke, "The Biblical Idea of *Marturia* (Witness)," in *Documenta Missionalia 5*, pp. 55ff. See also René Latourelle, "Evangelisation et Temoignage," in *Documenta Missionalia 9: Evangelisation*, ed. M. Khavamony (Roma: Universita Gregoriana Editrice, 1975), pp. 79, 87.

particular and representative election and also ensures the faithful traditioning of a gospel message that is *of* as well as *for* the world.[74]

There remains, however, one further question to be considered—a question raised by the critical reflection of the Western part of this dialogue. In a
word, it concerns the scope of human sin. We are pointed in this direction by
an astute observation of Orlando Costas, who questions whether liberation
theology deals adequately with the issue of nature and grace. If we accept
Segundo's argument that God's saving grace has been extended to all human
beings as a result of the Christ-event, then we must assume that men and
women have the moral capability to cooperate with God in the construction
of the kingdom by shaking off the bondage of oppression. This is to take a
very optimistic view of human nature, suggests Costas, and it is questionable whether such a view can be reconciled with the biblical witness. For the
Bible understands alienation "not only as a rupture of human relations
(injustice) but also a rebellion against God (ungodliness)."[75]

In the exhilaration of a liberated Roman Catholic ecclesiology, this is a
timely reminder that the Reformation was not merely a religious peculiarity
of the Renaissance but a fundamental course correction for the church. The
theological method of the Reformation tradition has much to contribute to
the dialogue that, as we have tried to demonstrate, must precede a synthesis
of First and Third World theologies. And in considering the hermeneutic of
evangelism, the point at issue is the content of the evangel. Given that the
identity of the church is election to proclaim God's universal salvation, and
given also that the gospel to be proclaimed must be honed in the historical
reality of the world to which it is proclaimed, the scriptural witness of the
church remains no less a part of the hermeneutic circle. The proclamation of
the gospel must be responsive to the historical reality of God's saving activity
in the world, but it must also be accountable to the scriptures and teachings
of the church. The present reality of God's salvation must not subsume the
particularity of the Christ-event.

The question thus becomes how a gospel that is universal can be histor-
icized in a hermeneutic of evangelism without becoming syncretized in the
immediacy of world history. If the hermeneutic of evangelism is not to
become part of a circle locked into an eternal present, albeit a historical
present of God's salvation, this question must be faced very directly.

Human Sin: The Challenge of Evangelicalism

It will be helpful to approach the question initially through the work of
Karl Rahner, who has been the taproot for much of Segundo's theology. It is
Rahner's presupposition that there is a universal and supernatural salvific

74. See Robert Bilheimer, "Confessing Faith in God in the United States Today," *International Review of Mission* 67 (April 1978): 151.

will of God really operative in the world. The goal of the world is God's self-communication to it, a self-communication that is universal in the Holy Spirit, coexistent with the spiritual history of the human race and world. Since this is necessarily addressed to a free history—for it can take place "only in a free acceptance by free subjects, and indeed in a common history"—it exists either in the mode of acceptance (justification) or rejection (disbelief and sin). There is, however, a climactic moment, a beginning

> which indicates that this self-communication for everyone has taken place irrevocably and has been victoriously inaugurated, . . . [a point at which it] reaches its real breakthrough and the real essence of what it is . . . [when] the victory and the irreversibility of this process has become manifest in and in spite of this ongoing dialogue of freedom.[76]

Inasmuch as the universal self-communication of God, the Holy Spirit, is historically tangible in the eschatological triumph of the incarnation, the Spirit communicated to the world is in reality the Spirit of Christ. And to "that historical person who appears in time and space" Rahner ascribes the title of *absolute savior*.[77] It is toward Christ as absolute savior that the "memory" of all faith is directed—memory, that is, in the Platonic sense of *anamnesis*, or the Augustinian concept of *memoria*, relating not only to things past but to things still to be found—toward that salvific outcome of history made by God's freedom and man's freedom together. "The absolute savior is what memory anticipates, and this anticipation is present in all faith."[78]

This is a powerful affirmation of the absolute salvation of God. Yet there is a sense in which Rahner's concern to be open to God's salvific will in a common human history can lose the precise focus of Christian election and the distinctive hope of the Christian message. As Alexandre Ganoczy has observed, Christianity appears in Rahner as "the quintessence of true humanity and even human nature itself in so far as it has been redeemed and set free by Christ."[79] Everything depends on the reality of God's salvation being "grasped, understood, and accepted as an act of faith that is in each case subjective and personal." And the weakness of this Christological approach, suggests Ganoczy, is that the risen Christ, the absolute Savior, is the basic datum in such a way as to render the message of the historical Jesus less than important for the knowledge of the Christian faith.[80]

75. Costas, *Christ outside the Gate*, p. 129.

76. Rahner, *Foundations of Christian Faith*, pp. 193-94.

77. For a thorough examination of this theory in Rahner's work, see Robert J. Schreiter, "The Anonymous Christian and Christology," in *Interreligious Dialogue*, ed. Richard W. Rousseau (Scranton: Ridge Row Press, 1981), pp. 175ff.

78. Rahner, *Foundations of Christian Faith*, pp. 31ff., 320.

79. Ganoczy, "The Absolute Claim of Christianity: The Justification of Evangelization or an Obstacle to It?" in *Evangelization Today*, p. 22.

80. Ganoczy, "The Absolute Claim of Christianity," p. 22. Cf. Schreiter, "Anonymous Christian," pp. 194, 197.

The point is well taken. It is one thing to share in the universal hope of
the human race, anticipating the future of God's absolute salvation. It is
another to be commissioned with a message to take to the world. And in
defining a hermeneutic of evangelism for the church, it is of paramount
importance not to confuse the message with its theological implications.
God's absolute salvation is the hope to which the gospel points, but the
evangel itself is historically quite specific. The evangelistic issue for a hermeneutic of evangelism, therefore, as opposed to the theological issue, is
that the content of the evangel must not be subjected to or limited by the
present reality of human history or experience.

While affirming the fullness of the salvific outcome of history, for example, Rahner does not pursue his eschatology beyond an existential present:

> What we know about Christian eschatology is what we know about man's
> present situation in the history of salvation. We do not project something
> from the future into the present, but rather in man's experience of himself
> and of God in grace and in Christ we project our Christian present into its
> future.[81]

To the extent that God's salvation is not yet fulfilled in the world, the
Christian message must have this anticipatory openness. Without a grounding in the historical particularity of the gospel, however, an openness to the
absolute future of God can too readily become a preoccupation with present
existence, albeit Christ-centered. And entrapment in the present is precisely
what is challenged by the announcement "He has come!" The New Age, the
kingdom of God, the *basileia*, God's absolute salvation is in our midst.[82] The
man of Nazareth, who walked the roads of Palestine, who sweated Jewish
sweat, who ate with sinners, who was crucified, who died and was buried
when Pontius Pilate was governor of Judea, and who was raised from the
dead when Pilate still governed, proclaimed a message and articulated a
hope. He gave definitive shape to God's salvation as well as providing its
climactic inauguration, and we are to anticipate its fulfillment in his return.
We do not project something from the future into the present. God does.

It is for this reason that Christian proclamation cannot be the projection
of future hope on the basis of past or present experiences of God. The tension
of God's salvific history, which is to say human history, is not a dialectic
progression but an expectancy.[83] Evangelism is the communication of a
message entrusted to an elect people by a God who breaks into the present
with the wholly new. God's *novum*, moreover, has a definitive shape in that

81. Rahner, *Foundations of Christian Faith*, p. 432.

82. See Moltmann, *Theology of Hope* (New York: Harper & Row, 1967), pp.
227ff. See also Krass, *Five Lanterns at Sundown*, pp. 66-87.

83. See Krass, *Five Lanterns at Sundown*, pp. 143ff. See also Blauw, *The Missionary
Nature of the Church*, pp. 72ff., 104ff.

the risen Christ, whose Spirit is abroad in human existence, was also the crucified Jew.[84] It was this man who announced the New Age, who is now its firstfruits, and who challenges human existence persistently, inconveniently, disconcertingly, shatteringly. As the covenant people of God, Christians are the constant irritants of a world in which Christ is not yet fully Lord. Their distinctive message is predicated not on their experience of God's eschatological triumph but on the historical fact of its happening and the historical promise of its fulfillment. John Deschner presses the point to its ultimate historical particularity. The vision of a common humanity, he suggests, can only be realized by a Christianity that is humbled by its own encounter with the particular community of Israel, in which Christians have been mysteriously granted a place.[85]

And it is here that Reformation theology, notwithstanding its vantage point of freedom and affluence in the Western world, must press the hermeneutic circle of liberation theology at the point of evangelism. For even as the common road on which humanity is embarked leads to the fullness of God's salvation—a road given as clear a direction historically by Segundo as existentially by Rahner—the Christian has a very specific message to announce. It is not merely that God's universal salvation has come to this planet in Jesus Christ. This salvation was also given its definitive interpretation by the Jewish community that first responded to his ministry. In a word, the Christian tradition is the Judeo-Christian tradition, and the Christ-event is historically particular not only because it originated with a carpenter from Nazareth but also because it was nurtured by a nation that already understood itself to be elect.

For the content of the evangel this means that we have to take the Old Testament seriously. And to take the Old Testament seriously means that we must take Paul seriously and therefore sin seriously.[86] The flaming center of the gospel tradition is Jesus Christ, crucified and risen, present in power, and soon to be our judge (2 Tim. 4:1; 1 Pet. 4:5). But the gospel message is traditioned in Scripture, the originative witness to Christ, in which Paul stands as principal theologian of the Jewish faith in the light of the revealed Messiah. His unfolding of the nature of sin and the reconciling work of

84. See Moltmann, *Theology of Hope,* pp. 299ff.; and *The Crucified God: The Cross of Christ as the Foundation and Criticism of Christian Theology* (New York: Harper & Row, 1974), pp. 160ff., 178ff.

85. Deschner, "Aspects of 'Community' as Christians Could Understand It in Dialogue with People of Other Faiths and Ideologies," in *Faith in the Midst of Faiths: Reflections on Dialogue in Community* (Geneva: World Council of Churches, 1977), p. 43.

86. See Snaith, *Distinctive Ideas of the Old Testament,* pp. 60ff. In light of our comments about Schleiermacher (see note 41), it is noteworthy that he pays scant attention to the Old Testament in his work, maintaining that it is not sufficiently relevant to the Christian faith.

Christ is as much a part of the evangel as the call of the Old Testament prophets for justice and the announcement by Jesus of the New Age.

The conscientization of Christians to the immediacy of world history and the breadth of world religion engenders, of course, an increasing awareness of the need to contextualize the Scriptures both in their first-century setting and for the contemporary church. The insights afforded by the *comunidades de base* as they engage in this exercise have already become legendary, and the power with which the biblical images emerge in the hands of a scholar whose roots are with the oppressed leave the Western mind reeling.[87] Yet alongside the common history and the hope of a New Age, there must be the challenge of the gospel to human sin—social and systemic, but also deeply personal—and it is this that evangelical theology has traditioned most faithfully since the Reformation.

In the final analysis, it is sin that confirms the graciousness of the covenant vocation of Christians, that precludes both the church and human history from being the subject of God's saving activity.[88] The particularity of the gospel is Christ and Christ alone. As long as Christ is the focus of the evangel, the universality of the message is assured—the New Age of Jesus Christ, the only absolute for those of the sign community.[89] Their privilege is to know it as an incipient reality through forgiveness of sin and reconciliation with God. Their commission is to announce it as the sure salvation of their planet.

87. See Elsa Tamez, *Bible of the Oppressed* (Maryknoll, N.Y.: Orbis Books, 1982).

88. Such is the contention of Hans Küng in *On Being a Christian* (New York: Doubleday, 1976), pp. 540-41: "In these days the Church must never make itself the content of the proclamation, may never publicize itself. It must point away from itself to the presence of God which has already dawned in the living Jesus, which it also awaits as the critical consummation of its mission. Thus it is still only moving towards the universal and definitive revelation of God in the world. It may not therefore claim to be an end in itself."

Moltmann concurs: "A Church which forgets that it is something temporary, provisional, interim, celebrating victories which are really defeats, is overtaxed, and must retire, since it has no genuine future. A Church, however, which remembers that it will find its end, not in itself but in God's kingdom, can hold out through all historical upheavals" (*The Church in the Power of the Spirit*, p. 153).

89. See Ganoczy, "The Absolute Claim of Christianity," pp. 26ff.

1.4.2

Response to Watson by Orlando Costas

This paper is a bold attempt to walk the narrow road between evangelical and liberation theologies and between academic and praxiologically critical reflection. I believe it works with what can be called a "biblical dialectic methodology." It claims to be "a creative synthesis" that will provide "a truly evangelistic theology for our times." The author looks for such a synthesis in what might be called a liberating theory of the church. The paper is, in my opinion, important for several reasons.

First, it is a serious attempt to find a common ground for a substantive dialogue between two different ways of doing theology from two different contexts. In making the attempt, David Watson offers a rich ecclesiological agenda for this consultation. Indeed, he brings the question of context and hermeneutics to bear on the church and its evangelizing mission.

Second, David makes a reverential and yet critical use of the canonical Scriptures as source for the theological understanding of the church. He brings together on the one hand the evangelical concern for the priority of the Bible in the theological task, and on the other, the Western—we must put this in quotes—"the Western liberal insistence" on studying the Scriptures critically and historically. And yet he does so bearing in mind that both emphases are mediated by the interpreter's social reality. I think this alone makes the paper unique, because often people do not want to recognize that.

Third, the paper reflects an astute awareness of the Latin American critique shared by others in all Christendom projects of an ecclesiology rooted in a Christendom framework which is neither theologically sound nor missiologically motivated. Such an ecclesiology lacks evangelical identity, historical relevance, and, above all, eschatological vision. It is an ecclesiology which is neither open to outsiders nor committed to an ethic of transformation. In short, it is an ecclesiology rooted in a Christendom project which is protective and defensive, static and hopeless.

Fourth, the author makes an admirably courageous effort to bring together the Latin American liberation perspective of a single unified human history (understood as salvation history) and the evangelical critique of a

139

universalist soteriology that does not sufficiently take into account the fact that the gospel challenges the reality of human sin. Thus the paper values that evangelical suspicion of all anthropologies that overestimate human nature and all soteriologies that posit an unqualified universalist view of saving grace. David keeps these two perspectives in balance by focusing on Christ in the conclusion of his paper. He says as long as Christ is the focus of the evangel, the universality of the message is assured. The reality of sin reminds us, on the other hand, that only in Christ do we find "forgiveness of sin and reconciliation with God," a fact that "precludes church and human history both from being the subject of God's saving activity."

Despite the value of David's paper, however, there are certain issues I want to raise with regard to its content and sources.

First, I find the universe of his discourse lacking in both scope and concreteness. David works with a double geocultural referent, as he plainly states—namely, Latin America and "Western" theologies. Likewise, he focuses his reflection on a church-world dialectic. The former is, in my opinion, not sufficiently global or complex, and the latter is not sufficiently concrete. The categories of Western and Latin American are not necessarily mutually exclusive. Interestingly enough, David's Latin American conversational partners are very Western theologians, including Segundo and Míguez Bonino. They not only come from European societies but they have been trained and they think in Western patterns. On the other hand, the Western world is, like Latin America, a very complex social cultural mosaic. It is no longer possible therefore to speak of North America as a Western continent without bearing in mind the fact that it has become a complex multicultural society. This is, I think, especially true in the realm of religion. Granted that the dominant theological discourse in North America is Western, David nevertheless needs to give greater visibility to the fact that there are minorities, alternatives, that are challenging the hegemony of traditional Western thought in both academic and practical ecclesio-theological thought. And since this is a consultation on context and hermeneutics in the Americas, we need to bear in mind the various contexts and hermeneutical theories being used in the Americas.

Second, while I appreciate David's focus on salvation for service, I question the way in which he locates the church's identity in its election for the world. Indeed, he himself points to Galatians 3:29 as a point of departure. To be sure, this text does speak of the church's Abrahamic heritage, but it also speaks of Christ as the one in whom the church finds its identity. It is because Jesus is the Messiah that the church is connected to Israel. It seems to me that Israel's identity is found not in its election as such but in the one who elects—the great I AM, Yahweh. God calls Israel to become a special treasure, his very own people. And if this is the case, it is no less true that God finds historical identity in Israel, a poor fragile nation, the most insignificant of all nations.

Israel finds its identity in God and thereby becomes significant for the nations, for those who dwell outside the covenant. God appears as "the God of Israel and the nations" insofar as the nations have no identity apart from him. And we find that "Israel and the nations" give God historical identity in the extent to which they stand in need of his grace. Israel is directed to make special provision for its poor, its widows, its orphans, and for foreigners. God is identified as their God; they have no one else.

God is thus revealed through the voiceless, the outsiders, the least. God's historical referent is the neighbor—especially the poor neighbor, the people from the under side of history. Consequently, such people profoundly affect the identity of the people of God. In the words of Jeremiah, "to know God is to care for them." God identifies himself with them. God takes their side. I believe this explains, by the way, why Matthew's Gospel insists that Christ's historical identity is mediated by the sick, the prisoner, the hungry, the foreigner. Jesus hides behind them. He is the good Samaritan. As the early Christians taught, wherever Jesus is found, there is the church. The church's identity is thus affected by the outsider. If the church is to find Jesus, it will have to go where Jesus is. To be the church, to be God's people, is to be in a constant pilgrimage toward the insignificant outcast people, for therein lies the true source of its being. Or in the words of Leonardo Boff, "it is in the other that we encounter the Great Other."

With this in mind, it is very difficult for me to appreciate two of the sources of Watson's argument—Wolfhart Pannenberg and the ecclesiology of Vatican II—for both represent a dangerous transition from a church-centered ecclesiology, which is the basis of Augustinian Christendom, to a neo-Christendom ecclesiology of a neo-Thomistic inspiration. The Vatican II ecclesiology can be traced to the integral humanism of Jacques Maritain, whose perspective was baptized by the Catholic Action movement of the Vatican in the thirties as the new mission strategy of the Roman Catholic Church. The focus of this perspective lies in the development of politics, education, and labor institutions, wherein a new leadership is trained to serve in the world and thus permeate—assault—the various structures of the world. Now, we know the consequences of this in Latin America. It simply failed in every aspect, and the church finally had to recognize this as they organized the episcopal conference of 1955, and especially in the Medellin conference and its aftermath.

With Pannenberg the links are not as clearly demonstrable, because he does not provide any practical political models, except possibly in connection with the link between his ethics and political theology and the ideological position of the Christian Democratic Party in West Germany. I submit that that is something worth looking into, in that the connection may be very significant. I know that we can trace that sort of thing in the case of Neo-Calvinism in Amsterdam and the interesting connection between the Protestant Christian Democratic Party and the Catholic Christian Democratic Party. Perhaps we ought to pursue these issues.

My last point pertains to the extensive discussion of Segundo's ecclesiology. I can appreciate the emphasis on the committed minority and its value for a critique of the visible structures of the church. There can be a significant correspondence for those of us who are inside mainline Protestant churches. It is a very useful reference. But I have serious questions concerning the way Segundo formulates his minority ecclesiology. He puts it in the framework of an unqualified soteriological universalism. Of course this helps him solve the quantitative problem, the problem of the many, what we call in evangelical piety "the lost." But it also makes him vulnerable to the problem of tampering with the mystery of grace and judgment. Segundo with his Teilhardian and Rahnerian categories appears to know far too much. This is a criticism that Jon Sobrino makes of traditional Christologies. We may legitimately say he knows too much when he presumes to know the end. That settles everything. It eliminates the quantitative problem. It suggests that we are now free to move on to the qualitative issue.

By proceeding in this way, Segundo opens himself up to the criticism that he is in effect establishing a new type of Christendom. One who assumes that everybody is a believer can then begin to construct a new kind of minority church. Evangelicals have to take care to overcome the temptation of ecclesial triumphalism, of assuming that the gathered community of believers is the only one in need of salvation. That is a legitimate problem we have to deal with. On the other hand, we must insist that the quantitative question of the lost is still a major issue to be grappled with theologically and missiologically. Otherwise, we are faced with a major problem of biblical integrity. If we have the high view of the Bible that we say we have, then the question is not closed. It cannot be closed for us. We must continue to wrestle with it. The lost are still lost.

1.4.3

Response to Watson by J. Deotis Roberts

I feel Watson has given us an extremely high-quality paper, thoughtfully researched and very provocative. He has worked to bring the best insights of two traditions together in dialogue to present a hermeneutic of evangelism. I'm greatly edified by his attempt to provide a meaningful bridge between the particular and the universal, which has been a nagging problem for me for some time. His constructive interpretation of election and covenant, biblical faith and theology is extremely helpful. I'm very grateful for the number of issues and perspectives which the paper brings out for us to deal with, and I think this is a good context in which to engage these issues. But I'd like to raise some points on which I would like further enlightenment.

I find very helpful the suggestion that one is elected to service, not to privilege. In the very beginnings of black theology, we were enchanted by the idea of being a chosen people, but in my reflections I became aware that there are perils as well as promises in taking on the burden of being a chosen people. We have to grapple with these concepts seriously, and I think Watson has done so. But his position challenges us, and I think we will want to pursue it further.

I would like to know more about how we get together on the two approaches to relating the church and the world. We have the church evangelizing the world on the one hand, and the world evangelizing the church on the other. What about the gospel that exists, as it were, beyond the church? How do we remain anchored in Scripture and tradition and so forth if we take these assertions to their logical conclusion? We have already talked about the centrality of Christ. That helps me to see where the anchor might be, but I still would like to know a little more about the nature of this Christology. It seems to me that the broad scope of the paper would indicate that there has to be an adequate Christological position to cover the broad front that is being set forth.

The paper raises questions of authority, of norms for faith, about the place to stand as a Christian in the challenge that election places before us and before the church.

Since I have been concerned about a theology of the church, I really am concerned about the ethical, social, and political implications of all this. Paul Tillich says that inasmuch as evil has a structure, a *gestalt,* it has to be opposed by a structure. I have been concerned about the role of the church as a gestalt opposing evil in the world. Is there something further to be said about the church not only in terms of its evangelizing ministry but also in terms of the transformative mission in the world?

While I celebrate the exploratory and open stance of the paper, I do wonder about how Christianity will maintain its integrity in the world of pluralism that Orlando and I have already spoken about—especially as the Third World invades the First World. How will we fare as Christians? Where do we take our position? How do we become effective in our evangelizing process in a world that is fraught with the confluence of cultures and religions? And what about the fate of the missionary movement if the theology of the paper is taken seriously? How can the theology of missions and evangelism be used to slow down if not turn around the thrust of the church growth movement which is being propagated not only in parishes in North America but also in missionary programs and theological education programs in many parts of the world? How will we deal with world religions that also proselytize and evangelize in our territory? What about the theological initiatives of non-Western churches and theologies?

My impression is that the cutting edge of theology today is not in Europe, as it may have been at one time, but in Africa, Japan, and many other parts of the so-called Third World, the non-Western world. I believe that the theology of the church is extremely central, and as Watson indicates, it is not exalted very much or taken very seriously by many Protestants. We do learn a great deal by looking at the way in which the Roman Catholic Church has taken ecclesiology with deadly seriousness. I think there are some areas that need further exploration and development in the outline we have: the nature and mission of the Holy Spirit and the question of what sort of doctrine of revelation would be sufficiently inclusive to be viable for the evangelism that we pursue here.

The North American situation, as we have been told by both David and Orlando, is not monolithic. It's not homogeneous, not all white. The Third World, the Two Thirds World, is invading the metropolitan centers of our country. I have looked at this close up, and this is probably where I can make my best contribution—by recounting some of my own engagements.

I've been very close to the Black Mayors' Conference. There are more than 225 black mayors in the U.S. Their recent successes are beginning to turn the political scene around in major metropolitan areas, cities like Washington, Philadelphia, Los Angeles, Atlanta, Chicago, Detroit. Now what does this mean? Have we really come to grips with the complex situation that has led to this change in the political climate of the U.S.? How do we relate this political breakthrough with the ongoing economic plight of the

masses of black people? As Jesse Jackson has put it, what we have are black
mayors presiding over white plantations. And as long as this is so, the more
things change, the more they will remain the same.

Have the churches—black churches, white churches, any churches—
begun to unpack the significance of this socio-economic and political situation and how this has to be addressed by an understanding of the gospel?
There's a need for critical and careful sociological, political, and economic
analysis before we can begin to think biblically and theologically about
engaging these issues. I don't see seminaries addressing these issues. As a
matter of fact, these issues are at the periphery of the curriculum of our
~~minaries~~. We are simply not preparing church leadership to engage this
Watson's paper is challenging us to
~~g~~ood outline and it must be engaged

1.4.4

Discussion

Pinnock: Dr. Watson, could you illustrate more how the world evangelizes us? That's not a familiar notion to me.

Watson: If we take the gospel into the world intentionally, then we find God at work there, particularly among those people who are most responsive to the gospel in the midst of the sort of oppression and suffering that we perhaps would not have traditionally regarded to be a context for the gospel. It's not that this evangelization comes to us as an articulation of the gospel as we tradition it, but it most certainly comes as an affirmation that the Spirit of God is at work in the world beyond the church, at work leading us to the New Age that Christ promised. I think what I'm trying to get at with my phrase "being evangelized by the world" is that we've got to break through the idea that we have a monopoly on God's saving work.

Pinnock: Exactly what does "evangelized" mean there? Being led into the meaning of the good news?

Watson: Yes, evangelism as I understand it is first of all the good news that in Jesus Christ this planet has been brought God's conclusive word of salvation. We now have to join in the task of bringing this to its fulfillment. It's not that we make this salvation happen but rather that we're privileged to join in what is happening to bring it to fulfillment. Now if, in fact, it is not the church but the planet that is the locus of this salvation, then what we see as we take the gospel into the world is corroborating evidence that we do have the message of salvation and that the word we bring not only evokes a response but brings us new insights into what it is that God is doing. On the other hand, if we make the church the locus, then we cannot really be open to that two-way traffic.

Reid: How would you define the church?

Watson: I would define the church first as those who are called by grace to be the ones commissioned to take to the world the message of salvation in Jesus Christ, and second the ones who are supremely privileged to know, as they do this, that it is indeed the message of salvation. We are the ones, among a pluralism of God's saving instruments, who have the knowledge of

146

what is happening. To come back to Orlando's point, I would certainly concur with his reminder that all of this is in Christ. In fact, I state this in my overview of the Old and New Testament passages. We find our identity in Christ, but we only appropriate the gospel to the extent that we are doing what we've been called to do with it—which is take it to the world.

Costas: Doesn't this presuppose your Christology? Christ is the evangelist par excellence, and the church, insofar as it is in the mission of Jesus, so evangelizes. Likewise, it is the same Christ who hides, as it were, in the world and who comes to us. There is that dual movement, but the focus of course is Christ.

Watson: Certainly. And that's why in the conclusion, I introduce this rather grandiose idea that "we are open to God's future." The particularly Christian function in that future is to speak of the Jewish carpenter as the One who has brought us that salvation. And when I refer to the gospel and proclaiming the gospel, I always mean that—that it is in fact the gospel we have received and we hand over to the world. So it must, by definition, be Christ-centered.

Osborne: David, I think your definition of evangelism, saving work, salvation is still a little nebulous. I'd like you to clarify a little more, in terms of this continuum that includes evangelical and liberation views of salvation as either spiritual or praxis or a combination of both. What do you mean by it?

Watson: Are you asking me what I mean by "salvation"?

Osborne: Yes, and "message of salvation" and "saving work."

Watson: Well, I think the message of salvation is the answer to the prayer we pray regularly—"Thy kingdom come, thy will be done on earth as in heaven." It is the announcement that the new age inaugurated in Jesus Christ is to come to fulfillment on earth as in heaven.

Osborne: Moltmann? Pannenberg?

Watson: Well, Moltmann; not so much Pannenberg. I would affirm Pannenberg's proleptic eschatology, even though I do not agree with him that it has not happened fully yet in Christ: I think it *has* happened fully in Christ. What we have to do now is to announce its imminent fulfillment. If you are trying to get at whether I am trying to say that the person who responds to this gospel and makes a commitment to Christ is therefore something less than saved in traditional language, I would have to say Yes, because that person is also saved only in hope (Rom. 8).

Osborne: I'd like you to respond to Orlando's last statement: the lost are still lost.

Watson: Well, the word I respond to in Orlando's statement is that it's still a *mystery*. We have no way of superimposing any human scenario onto what remains an ultimate mystery. The point is that by having an ecclesially centered soteriology we've tried to resolve the mystery prematurely. We've tried to do it by saying, "well at least we know this, that those who have

come into the body of the church are OK, never mind those who have not."
What I want to do is make the whole thing a mystery and say that until such
time as all things are revealed, our particular task is to proclaim a universal
salvation for all who will hear. As to the mystery of those who do not
respond, we must leave that with God. The real thrust of trying to bring this
into a North American context, as I said in the paper, is that the
soteriological question is not whether all will be saved in response to the
proclamation of the gospel. That is the speculation of a church that witnesses
in freedom and affluence and whose theologians continue to wrestle with the
theodicy of resistance and apathy among their people. Get into a context of
oppression and suffering, and that is a wholly moot question. In fact it's
completely peripheral.

Webster: You seem to develop the idea of election on the basis that the
church couldn't handle the idea that it had a message of salvation for the
unevangelized. I'll ask the question of you another way. What is the distinctive problem of the unevangelized? What do I say about the unevangelized? Do they have a problem, and what is it?

Watson: Well the unevangelized obviously need to hear the gospel.

Webster: Why?

Watson: Because first of all that is the commission that has been given to
us, to take this good news to them.

Webster: So the reason is that we've been told to do it, rather than that they
need it.

Watson: It's both, but the reason *we* do it is that we have been called to do
it. The point I was making here was that if we do not do it, we are
repudiating our covenant with God. So the motivation to evangelize is not
that we hope by our good work to bring people to something that is going to
be a matter of eternal difference for them. Rather, the reason we evangelize is
that we have been called by God to do so. We must therefore reach as many as
possible as often as possible with the message we've been given, regardless of
their response.

Now, if we focus on the response as the purpose of evangelizing, then of
course we're going to become selective, we're going to direct our energies
where we will evoke the most response. More importantly, we are going to
dichotomize between those who do and those who don't. But it should be our
purpose to reach everybody as often as possible.

Webster: That concerns evangelistic strategy. But what is the distinctive
result? Isn't there a kind of dichotomy between those who receive and those
who reject? Or is the gospel there in the presence of both, one consciously,
the other anonymously?

Watson: Well, I think the purpose behind that question concerns the
potential alienation between the church and the world. If that is the focus,
we start to look at the extent to which we think people have responded rather
than at the message, which is that the New Age will one day prevail.

Webster: It seems to be something different than Linda's comments about the we/they dichotomy, which creates problematic attitudes. You seem to be saying something in a theological way that jeopardizes the sense that those who have not been evangelized are lost. I think biblically I need to see them as lost.

Watson: Oh yes, but biblically we also need to see ourselves as lost with them until the fulfillment of the New Age. That's my point. We are to see the global scope of God's salvation to the point that we will choose to identify with the lost, our own knowledge of God's impending salvation notwithstanding. If we take the position that God's salvation is for those who have responded to evangelism as opposed to those who have not, we thereby presume to have plumbed what is in fact still an eschatological mystery. That is what I thought Orlando was suggesting. I am saying that we have to identify with the lost by saying that this is what God is bringing in, and we have to keep saying this over and over and over again. We have to put our lives where our words are so that we bring the message with integrity. We cannot say that we choose not to identify with those who still refuse to respond.

Webster: I can understand that. Paul said he would willingly be damned if that would help his people find Christ. I can understand the mentality, the empathy.

Costas: I think that the issue is again, like the criticism of Segundo for knowing too much, that we evangelicals need to criticize ourselves for claiming to know too much. "Are you saved?" "Yes, I'm saved. I thank the Lord that I'm saved." Then we turn around and act as if we are not saved. The point is subtle, and we evangelicals tend to lose sight of it: the church needs equally to be evangelized. The primary motivation for evangelism cannot be negative—that people are damned in hell unless they hear the word. That is the fearful reality; that is part of the mystery. But the other side, the more positive one, is that this is good news. There is forgiveness; there is a new world which is coming into being. Now are we going to stress the positive side of it, or are we going to stress the negative side? I don't see too much warrant in the New Testament for stressing the negative. I do see a lot of warrant for stressing the positive, which is what I hear in David's presentation.

Yoder: I'm with several of the others in wondering if we have posed the issue adequately in our discussion. I have an impression that the Watson presentation of Segundo gets us a little off track, because I think Segundo is saying something else. I don't think he would say the things you've just said about lostness. He has a rather deeper argument from the Rahnerian tradition for saying that the world is in fact saved but just doesn't know it. That is different from saying that we have a proclamation we owe to everybody, that is for them all *if* they hear it. My problem with Segundo is that he doesn't adequately specify the nature of the salvation that we know everybody has.

And then there is also the point—and here I agree with Orlando—that he seems to know that with more certainty than I think we have reason for.

In the classical vision of medieval Catholicism, to be saved meant that when you died you didn't go to hell but to heaven—maybe by way of Purgatory, but at least you know you'll make it because of what you did on earth. Then Protestantism came along and changed that by saying that the thing on earth that determines whether you go to heaven when you die is whether you believe the gospel rather than the other things that the church wanted you to do. But salvation is still located in another world in such a way that it is meaningful to talk about it, meaningful to affirm that some people are destined for it while other people are not. Now, as far as I can tell, people like Segundo are first of all denying that there is that other world, and then affirming that everybody's going there. It's a process of correction with regard to tradition that hits the tradition at two different places and then negates itself. But that isn't original to them, because that's been Protestant universalism for some time. There are liberal Protestant universalists who say "There is no such place as heaven, but everybody's going there." Until we have specified more clearly what we actually mean by salvation, I'm not sure that it's a real question. If we say "fullness of life on this earth to which God has destined the planet," then most people aren't going to get there. They're lost in human terms, and even if they hear a Catholic or a Weselyan message of salvation and believe that their souls are saved for another world, they're still in a mess for this world. I don't think we have our categories clear enough to go on with an argument about the Yes or No of *who* until we know *what* is being offered to everybody.

Moderator: At this point, we only have time for a response from David.

Watson: I think the emphases on salvation as future and on the mystery are very valuable. Paul, in some ways, is perhaps the most significant theologian of the New Testament concerning those emphases on salvation and hope. But he is also the one who said, "I wish I could be damned for the sake of my people." I don't know how to make sense of some of that New Testament language. Coupled with that future fulfillment of salvation and the mystery aspect of salvation is also what one might call the experiential appropriation or the realization of salvation.

I think the last few exchanges indicate the extent to which those of us in the Western tradition are still grappling with a very personalized form of salvation. It is always very difficult for us to look at God's salvation in terms of any sort of global eschatology. It seems to me that God's salvation is very clear. It is eternal light for all in Christ. Now, to the extent that this happens in terms of resurrection, we are clearly involved in the birth pangs of this new creation. Incidentally, since the resurrection is so integral to the gospel, I assume that we all affirm its reality. These birth pangs persist as such a deep mystery that all we can do is affirm our participation in this in Christ. But I do regard our salvation to be eternal life with God through Christ, whether that comes as something which is beginning here and now or something that we must await at the resurrection.

There is a difference between looking at this point from a context of oppression and looking at it from a point of freedom and affluence. The whole concept of what God's salvation is in a context of oppression becomes very clear. It has to be a New Age. But for those of us who have so many luxuries here and now, it certainly does become a point of intellectual wrestling. And that's what I was trying to break out of in terms of presenting an ecclesiology which from a context of oppression brings the real issue down to the hope of the New Age.

This also affects how we understand and how we work with the evangelistic message. We have to look first of all to a gospel which is continually honed not only as we turn time and again to the Scriptures but also as we take the message into the world. This evangelistic process of taking the message to the world is a very, very important sharpener. If it is the gospel that we take to the world, then the hearing it receives and the response it evokes are part of the evangelization *we* receive. Furthermore, this process also makes certain that we are evangelizing with the *gospel*. It provides a check.

John, concerning your further point about Segundo's argument for universal salvation and the extent to which some of us are privileged to know—I thought I dealt with that by quoting the Amstutz article in which he takes Rahner (and, by implication, Segundo) to task. He does this by pointing out that such an argument avoids the specificity of the crucified Christ. In fact, it is in this Jewish carpenter that we have the paradigm for salvation, but it is not a universal knowledge that some of us have the privilege to know about. Such an approach fails to ground salvation in the historical Jesus.

II

Study Groups

Exodus

Frank Alton
Virgil Cruz
Thomas McAlpine
✦ Stephen Reid
Edesio Sánchez-Centina (in absentia)
John Stam

2.1.1

The Book of Exodus: A Laboratory for Hermeneutics

STEPHEN REID

An Autobiographical Comment

I come to this task with some hesitancy. Not only for all the scholarly reasons that one can immediately think of, but also for another more personal reason. As a child and teenager I enjoyed the stories in the book of Exodus, but as a seminarian my relationship with this book was tarnished. I remember telling a white person in my denomination that I was continuing my education to study Hebrew Scriptures.

He replied, "That's great. You probably want to study Exodus." The basis for his comment was that the black people who had an interest in Hebrew Scriptures are Exodus specialists. From that point on I specialized in Judaism of the Persian and Hellenistic period. It was only when my teaching assignments demanded that I return to the book of Exodus that I was able to do so without the sense that white folks thought that, of course, all black folks loved Exodus and hence played yet another racist game on black people.

Our temptation as people of color is to play the white folks' game and make the book of Exodus part of our canon within the canon and let it become our proof text for liberation. What are some ways around this? How can we get out of the maze?

I will begin with a discussion of the things that I think are erudite and insightful about the book of Exodus. However, you will find that as this paper proceeds, it will be an invitation to Bible study. I share with you the questions prompted in me by the spirit and letter of the text. I have no brilliant insight concerning most of these questions, but I think they represent questions that Third World theologians must address. I can only hope that my questions, with the help of the Holy Spirit, might prompt something in you.

Methodological Alternatives

It is no longer fashionable to do tradition history analysis, source criticism, or form criticism as the only methodological alternatives. These methods have now become in some sense a staple. They are now presuppositions of most exegetical work. The same could be said of the straight structuralist material. As Rolf Knierim has said in retrospect on form criticism, "structuralism has forced form critics to take a more careful look at the structural dimensions of texts but will probably not itself find a large following in the U.S."[1] There are three alternatives available presently to scholars in the U.S.: holistic analysis, canon/canonical criticism, and sociological exegesis.

The first alternative is rhetorical criticism. Under this broad topic come a number of different practitioners. In fact, some have labored to put in this category those who would try to use modern literature as a conversation partner in the explication of texts using the categories of literary/rhetorical criticism. The recent commentary on Ezekiel 1-20 by Moshe Greenburg is an example of rhetorical criticism par excellence, although he calls it "holistic criticism."[2]

Another alternative is the method of "canon criticism" or "canonical criticism," of which Brevard Childs has made use.[3] He prefers the term "canon criticism" because he perceives it not as a technique in the reconstruction of the semantic range of a particular ancient text but rather as a stance toward the material and the way in which we approach the material. "Canonical criticism" as presented by James A. Sanders has a somewhat different agenda. His concern is to appreciate the pluralism of the text, a pluralism that he holds to be part of the adaptability of Scripture for our life.

1. Knierim, "Old Testament Form Criticism Reconsidered," *Interpretation* 27 (1973): 459.

2. Greenburg, *Ezekiel 1-20,* Anchor Bible (Garden City, N.Y.: Doubleday, 1983), p. 18.

3. See Childs, *Biblical Theology in Crisis* (Philadelphia: Westminster Press, 1970), pp. 13-147; *The Book of Exodus,* Old Testament Library (Philadelphia: Westminster Press, 1974), pp. ix-xvi; and *Introduction to the Old Testament as Scripture* (Philadelphia: Fortress Press, 1979), pp. 71-83.

His goal is to make the exegetical task "true" to the style in which Scripture was produced in a community of faith.[4]

There are several facts that must be kept in mind as one ruminates on the debate of "canon" and "canonical" criticism. First of all, in 1969, when Childs wrote *Biblical Theology in Crisis,* the assumptions about biblical exegesis were somewhat different than they are today. His students as well as some of the arguments in that book made part of the agenda of "canon" criticism commonplace before we knew what it was. For instance, his strong appreciation of the final form of the text rather than a myopic preoccupation with the oral stage of the text has become a given in many circles of biblical scholarship, and that was not the case in 1969. Similarly, his understanding of the need for a synchronic rather than a completely diachronic reading of the text has also became a part of the mindset of biblical scholars in the U.S. Finally, his strong emphasis on the affective side of the Bible—his insistence that the Bible should be interpreted as Scripture, as normative in the lives of those who take it to be set apart—has likewise became a major force in the way biblical studies take place in the U.S.

Another thing to keep in mind is that Childs and Sanders are not the only people working in the vineyard of the canon and canonical critical interpretation of Scripture. There are scholars such as Ronald Clements, Joseph Blenkinsopp, and Gerald Sheppard.[5] As Walter Brueggemann has noted, these scholars have accented the method in terms of its redaction critical aspects.[6] For our purpose this is a major breakthrough, inasmuch as it makes clear from a methodological standpoint something that was all too hazy in previous writings from this perspective—namely, that the sociological context of the material provides a hermeneutical key for the reinterpretation of Scripture.

From the perspective of the black church there is something missing in the canon/canonical critical methods: the function of the Holy Spirit is not discussed. The Holy Spirit is mediated in the body of Christ, which is to say that the church must play an active role in coming to an understanding of the

4. See Sanders, *Torah and Canon* (Philadelphia: Fortress Press, 1972), pp. ix-xx; and *Canon and Community: A Guide to Canonical Criticism* (Philadelphia: Fortress Press, 1984).

5. See Clements, "Patterns in Prophetic Canon," in *Canon and Authority,* ed. G. W. Coats and B. O. Long, (Philadelphia: Fortress Press, 1977), pp. 42-55; Blenkinsopp, *Prophecy and Canon* (Notre Dame, Ind.: University of Notre Dame Press, 1977); and two contributions of Sheppard—"Canon Criticism: The Proposal of Brevard Childs and an Assessment for Evangelical Hermeneutics," *Studia Biblica et Theologica* 4 (1974): 3-17; and *Wisdom as a Hermeneutical Construct* (New York: Walter de Gruyter, 1980).

6. Brueggemann, *The Creative Word: Canon as a Model for Biblical Education* (Philadelphia: Fortress Press, 1982), pp. 1-13.

canonical process. However, to the degree that this occurs, the term "canon/canonical" becomes anachronistic. We have to be concerned not merely with the semantic range of a particular passage as found in the Scripture, but also with the treatment that passage has received in the life of the church. Canon must not serve as a limit to cut out the role of the church and its critical traditions or the role of the Holy Spirit, who gives life to the church.

Another alternative is sociological exegesis, a term coined by John Elliot.[7] Sociological exegesis is centrally concerned with the biblical text. The sociological work is done for the purpose not of historical reconstruction for its own sake but rather for the better explication of Scripture. There are three different types of sociological exegesis, produced by the microtheorists, the macrotheorists, and the hermeneutical sociologists.

The microtheorists are those who primarily study a particular phenomenon (e.g., prophecy) but do not take into account the macrosociological issues. These scholars have by and large made use of the findings of anthropologists and ethnographers. Their method is represented in the work of Robert R. Wilson, Thomas W. Overholt, David L. Petersen, Howard C. Kee, Gerd Theisen, and John Gager.[8]

The macrosociologists tend to be much more interested in society types. These scholars draw more on the work of sociological theorists and less on that of ethnographers. While they are interested in phenomena of ancient Israel and early Christianity, they always evaluate these phenomena in the context of society types. The work of Marvin Chaney, Norman Gottwald, and John Elliot would be examples.[9]

The most popular example of the interface of biblical theology and the social sciences can be found in the work of the hermeneutical sociologist/theologian. These scholars have read the work of Victor Turner,

7. See Elliot, *A Home for the Homeless: A Sociological Exegesis of 1 Peter, Its Situation and Strategy* (Philadelphia: Fortress Press, 1981).

8. Wilson, *Prophecy and Society in Ancient Israel* (Philadelphia: Fortress Press, 1980); Overholt, "Seeing Is Believing: The Social Setting of Prophetic Acts of Power," *Journal for the Study of the Old Testament* 23 (1982): 3-31; Peterson, *The Roles of Israel's Prophets,* Journal for the Study of the Old Testament—Supplement Series, no. 17 (Sheffield: Journal for the Study of the Old Testament, 1981); Kee, *Christian Origins in Sociological Perspective* (Philadelphia: Westminster Press, 1980); and Theissen, *The Social Setting of Pauline Christianity* (Philadelphia: Fortress Press, 1982); Gager, *Kingdom and Community: The Social World of Early Christianity* (Englewood Cliffs, N.J.: Prentice Hall, 1975).

9. See Chaney, "Ancient Palestinian Peasant Movements and the Formation of Premonarchic Israel," in *Palestine in Transition: The Emergence of Ancient Israel,* The Social World of Biblical Antiquity Series, no. 2, ed. D. N. Freedman and D. F. Graf (Sheffield: Almond, 1983), pp. 39-72; Gottwald, *The Tribes of Yahweh: A Sociology of the Religion of Liberated Israel, 1250-1050 B.C.E.* (Maryknoll, N.Y.: Orbis Books, 1979); and Elliot, *A Home for the Homeless.*

Clifford Geertz, Mary Douglas, and Peter Berger and have used their ideas as a point of departure for discussing the issues in the biblical texts.[10]

None of these methodological alternatives—holistic criticism, canon/canonical criticism, or sociological exegesis—fits the pastoral needs of my local church. Each represents a part of the theological task. The theology of the praxis of the church is the rhetoric and embodiment of the Word of God in a particular context. These three, however, do address the issue of rhetoric, embodiment, and context if we put them together.

Is there yet an alternative that has been missed? Probably. However, we embrace in these a liberation from the chains of historicism that has bound people of color for too long as we have come to the biblical text.

What do I mean by historicism? I use it here to refer to the use of history as the final revelation on which all other revelation is based. An example from the present research in the area of archeology that might have an impact on the exegesis of the book of Exodus is the historical reconstruction of the Exodus event. The Enlightenment told us that if it did not happen—if we could not *prove* that it happened—then the story could not be true. We in the church have taken over too much of this in our theology.

Why do we believe the Bible? Do we believe because we can prove the historical veracity of the biblical text? Not in my neighborhood we don't! We believe the Bible because the church has affirmed that the Bible is Scripture, set apart as a revelation from God. This is a critique of historicism as well as canon and canonical criticism as we shall see below.

For a number of years we have categorized historians of ancient Israel as "conservative" (e.g., Leon Wood and R. K. Harrison), American "liberal" (e.g., William F. Albright and John Bright), and German "nihilist" (e.g., Albrecht Alt and Martin Noth). For the most part, the "conservatives" were dismissed for being "conservative," the Germans were dismissed for being "nihilists," and the American liberals were left free to determine the shape of biblical theology in the U.S.

The American liberals determined that a number of cities in Palestine were destroyed around 1200 B.C.E., and so they concluded that the conquest by Joshua must be dated to that period. If that is the case, then the exodus event must be dated around 1280 B.C.E. In addition to this reconstruction, the Merneptah stele, which mentions "Israel" (ca. 1236-23 B.C.E.), was also cited as evidence to establish the "accepted" date.

George Ramsey and John J. Bimson have each produced a major work that calls the accepted dating of the exodus event into question.[11] Bimson

10. For an example of this sort of work, see R. L. Choh, *The Shape of Sacred Space: Four Biblical Studies* (Chico, Cal.: Scholars Press, 1981), which is an attempt to bring the work of Victor Turner to bear on exegetical matters.

11. Ramsey, *The Quest for the Historical Israel* (Atlanta: John Knox, 1981); and Bimson, *Redating the Exodus Conquest,* Journal for the Study of the Old Testament—

points out that the argument for the thirteenth-century date for the exodus depends on Exodus 1:11, which mentions the store cities of Pithom and Raamses, and on archeological investigation of the destruction layers of those cities in Palestine. "The locations of Raamses at Tanis and of Pithom at Tell el-Maskhouta have both been claimed to prove a thirteenth-century date for the exodus," notes Bimson, and then he goes on to argue persuasively that Qantir, not Tanis, is the Raamses mentioned in Exodus 1:11, and that Pithom can be located at Tell el er-Retebah.[12]

Bimson also deals with the other pillar of the thirteenth-century date of the exodus, the destruction of the cities in Palestine: "there is no evidence to prove that the cities which fell in the thirteenth-century were Canaanite cities destroyed by the Israelites."[13] In fact, the designation of the postdestruction layer of these cities as "Israelite" has come under severe attack from a number of scholars. Further, these were by and large not the cities mentioned in the conquest stories as those places which were destroyed and burned. All of this evidence leads one to question the thirteenth-century dating of the exodus.

Bimson also points out that other biblical texts, in particular 1 Kings 6:1, suggest another chronology altogether. He concludes that the biblical text is correct, that the conquest took place in the second half of the fifteenth century, and that the exodus occurred before that in the Middle Bronze Age.

Bimson's endeavor is important because it raises new questions about the use of biblical material as well as extrabiblical material to reconstruct biblical history. In addition, Bimson makes us aware of the danger of historicism and the fragility of historical reconstruction. While the coherence of Exodus and the witness of 1 Kings 6:1 may be much appreciated, one is struck with the precarious nature of the argument. In terms of evidence, it is the same style of historical skepticism that Brimson has used in his analysis of Albright and Bright. Methodologically, he has done nothing different from Alt and Noth. And it should be noted before we rush headlong to a baptism of Gottwald's intriguing reconstruction that it too springs not from the positivist approach of Albright and Bright but from the position of Alt and Noth, who describe the conquest as a gradual penetration of a new group. Now, according to Gottwald, the new group was composed of indigenous but clearly marginalized peasants. Each of these alternatives is limited to the degree that it abides by the implicit Enlightenment dictum that only that which can be historically verified as having occurred did in fact occur.

My point is a simple one. From the perspective of sociological exegesis, the exodus material seems to fit into a situation of social upheaval in response

---

Supplement Series, no. 5 (Sheffield: Journal for the Study of the Old Testament, 1978).

12. Bimson, *Redating the Exodus Conquest,* pp. 37, 38-48.
13. Bimson, *Redating the Exodus Conquest,* p. 53.

to an oppressive situation. From the approach that traces the Scripture as an embodiment of the Holy Spirit, the central issue is not historicity but the way that the story has continued to arrest persons of faith in the Jewish and Christian traditions.[14]

Issues in the Interpretation of the Book of Exodus
The Historical Narratives

I have already referred to issues of historicism and authority in general. I would now like to take a closer look at the early narrative material on the personal history of Moses and the story of the plagues and the escape (Exod. 1-14).

I would like to propose tentatively here that the material in Exodus 1-2 is meant to bind the hero Moses sociologically to the Hebrew community that wrote the story. I have noted that it is clearly a mistake to read the material simply as history; I would now like to suggest that it would be just as significant a mistake to take the sociological setting of the event as the measure of the story. I do not believe that we would be justified in proposing that the function of the story in the community is completely dictated by the sociological setting of the particular event even if we were able to reconstruct the event itself—and of course we cannot do so.

I think we could profit by looking at the results of some studies in the areas of ancient Near Eastern cultures and anthropology. Scholars such as D. B. Redford have pointed out that the literary motif of the exposed child occurs with some regularity in the ancient Near East and as well as in Scripture, in such stories as that of the persecution of Jesus.[15] Among anthropological studies, I would cite the work of Victor Turner on the ritual process in social systems in Africa such as the Ndembu, an agrarian society type, which incorporates the typology of Gerhard Lenski.[16] Turner discusses a ritual that demeans the leader of the society, suggesting that it functions to make the community identify with the leadership by making the ruling elite appear to be a member of the "everyday community."

I would like to propose tentatively that we can see both the exposed-child

14. On this, see for instance the statements from the World Council of Churches concerning the authority of Scripture, in *The Bible, Its Authority and Interpretation in the Ecumenical Movement,* ed. E. Flesseman-van Leer (Geneva: World Council of Churches, 1980), pp. 42-57.

15. See Redford, "The Literary Motif of the Exposed Child," *Numen* 14 (1967): 210ff.

16. Turner, *Drama, Fields, and Metaphors: Symbolic Action in Human Society* (Ithaca, N.Y.: Cornell University Press, 1974); and *The Ritual Process: Structure and Anti-Structure* (Ithaca, N.Y.: Cornell University Press, 1969). And see Lenski and Lenski, *Human Societies: An Introduction to Macrosociology,* 4th ed. (New York: McGraw-Hill, 1982).

motif and the ritual demeaning of the leadership in the stories in the first part of the book of Exodus. Moses is portrayed as both the exposed child and a brash and sometimes violent youth. His actions as a youth indicate that he is a member of the Hebrew community despite the fact that he had been "adopted" by the ruling elite.

The miracle stories of the plagues also present some basic problems. I think we should wrestle with these together, so I won't try to provide any concrete answers in this discussion.

Black persons in the United States must reflect on the political implications of the plague narratives. They are more than just miracle stories. They are stories of the unsalvation history perpetrated on one people by another. There are two motifs in this series that we should note in particular. One is the issue of Pharaoh's hardness of heart, and the other is the social function of the miracle stories in the text of the book as we have it.

The suffering of the Hebrew children is similar to the plight of Third World people today. There is oppression. Worse than that, it seems as though God is hardening the heart of the taskmasters in South Africa and their counterparts all over the world. In the material in the book of Exodus, there are two strands of tradition that do not seem to go together. On the one hand is the fact that God hears and is moved by the cries of the Hebrews. On the other hand is the fact that when Pharaoh seemed ready to exercise some compassion simply because it was the expedient thing to do, we read that God hardened his heart, as if to prompt even greater pain and suffering.

What is a pastor or biblical scholar to say when an unemployed black parishioner asks why God would harden the heart of those who work evil upon us so that they might work more ill? It is clear that the work of Niebuhr on the hardness of the heart is completely inadequate for people on the edge of human existence. The connection is made between Pharaoh's hardness of heart and the lordship of God (see Exod. 4:21; 7:13, 14, 22; 8:11, 15, 28; 9:7, 12, 15; 10:1, 20, 27; 11:10). Is it fair for God to use the poor and the oppressed as tools to educate the world?

Brevard Childs asks a related question in his commentary on the despoiling of the Egyptians (Exod. 3:21-22; 11:35-36; cf. Ps. 105:37). What is at stake here is clearly the issue of reparations for the oppressed. The text appears to be trying to deal with the issue of the right of the oppressed to certain recompense from the oppressor for years (possibly centuries) of oppression. These matters are directly related to such pressing contemporary issues as affirmative action in the United States and land reform in Latin America. What does the community of faith do with the tradition of the despoiling of the Egyptians?

The plagues raise other questions concerning their function in the present context beyond the rather tired answer that they are the crescendo for the Passover story. It is not surprising that the commentaries on the whole spend very little time on an investigation of the plague narratives. Childs's commentary on Exodus is an example. And the little material that has been written does not appear to have a major effect on preaching in the United States. What political miracles can we find in the world around us? How are they related to the political miracles related in the plague narratives?

Liberation and Religious Experience

In order to understand Exodus 1-15 fully, one must understand the spirituality of the narrative. Among the narratives in question are the two call narratives (Exod. 3:1–4:17; 6:2–7:7) and also the Passover legend (Exod. 12:1–13:16), in which religious experience, liberation, and ritual all come together in the life of a community of faith. The deliverance at the reed sea is also a story of religious experience and liberation. The cultic symbols of the pillar of cloud and the pillar of fire (Exod. 13:21-22) ought not to be overlooked. Many a scholar has neglected the way these symbols refer to the religious dimension of this very political act (Exod. 13:17–14:31). Finally, the poetry also serves to express the religious experience; it can be said that the poetry is the residue of the religious experience (Exod. 15:1-21). In all these cases it is clear that the liberation is more than a political event in the shallow sense of the term that is put forth by politicians. Rather it is a holistic act that demonstrates faith in a particular historical context—a historical context that then becomes part of the symbol system for the new community. From the beginning of the introduction of liberation theology, Third World theology has been rooted in the spirituality of the community of faith.

Harsh Realities for the Community of Faith

The material that is put under the rubric of the wilderness wandering (Exod. 15:22–18:27) is vital for our study for two reasons. First, it is important because of its content. These stories are concerned with food, water, and the courage to fight a foe that is much more powerful. Second, it is important because it shows quite candidly a community of faith. Metropolitan Paulos Gregarios has suggested that it is the task of the World Council of Churches to determine what type of society we should have in light of the Christian message and then work to realize that type of society as stewards of the Word of God. The wilderness stories relate the attempt of one community of faith to do just that. I should add that I would agree with George Coats that the crossing of the reed sea has elements of the wilderness wandering and murmuring traditions (see Exod. 13:17–14:31) The point of liberation often involves such danger that some will prefer slavery. What are some ways that people in our congregations prefer slavery to liberation?

Another set of material that is often overlooked because it follows the excitement of crossing the reed sea is Exodus 32-34. The story of the golden calf (Exod. 32) is an example of the rebellion/murmuring tradition. It raises the issue of the apostasy of the people as well as the complicity of the religious elite, in this case Aaron (see especially 23:22). What can this say to us about the role of the pastor and biblical scholar? Where does the relationship between spirituality, worship, and liberation come into our lives? What are the "golden calves" in our lives that act as legal stipulations or ethical codes?

This section also presents the concept of the sacred place. The Tabernacle plays an important part in the Exodus story, laying the foundation of the Hebrew children's understanding that there is sacred space. How does this fit into a theology of liberation?

The book of Exodus clearly raises a number of compelling issues. In addition to serving as a laboratory for hermeneutics, it also reminds us of at least part of the agenda for a theology of liberation. The topics of history, moral theology, pastoral leadership, spirituality, and sacred space should be addressed in our deliberations and conversations.

2.1.2

Hermeneutics and Context: The Exodus

EDESIO SÁNCHEZ-CENTINA

I am interested in approaching the topic of hermeneutics from the perspective of the plurality (diversity) of traditions in the Old Testament. In other words, I am interested in pointing out the different crucial historical periods of Israel's life and seeing how the nation used and was fed and challenged by the central event of the exodus.

It is important to point out that in recent years study of the exodus in Latin American theology, and especially in some liberation theologies, has been almost entirely restricted to the stories in Exodus 1-15. The leading authors have developed the topic with strong emphasis on the socio-political aspect, relegating the religious element to a secondary position. Other Old Testament traditions give the topic of the exodus a treatment that is in comparison much more balanced, viewing the event as a struggle on many different levels. In fact, the traditions that view the exodus from the Canaanite milieu show us that oppression and the struggle for liberation reached the character of religious confrontation. Of course, this does not mean that the socio-political struggle remains at the periphery. The biblical witness indicates that both belong to the same reality, and that should clarify a lot of things for us.

In saying these things, I am by no means criticizing standing Latin American theological reflection. Latin American theological practice has not remained static. Studies on different biblical subjects give evidence of a developing understanding of the complexity of realities in Old Testament times as well as in today's. Insightful studies on the poor, the life-death contradiction, the kingdom of God, oppression, and, most recently, idolatry all constitute evidence that although the exodus remains the central focus, it is increasingly coming to be seen in a larger perspective, as belonging to a more complex reality.

It is interesting that the exodus account in the book of Exodus makes no mention of the gods of Egypt as "players" in the exodus drama. It seems that Yahweh does not fight against gods. However, the most ancient poetical traditions about the exodus (traditions older than the prosaic narratives, such as Exodus 15 and the proto-apocalyptic poetry) present the event as a tale of divine power confrontations. Even more striking is the fact that the conflict presented in this older literature is not between Yahweh and the Egyptian gods but against Baal and the religious apparatus of Canaan. As a matter of fact, there are several studies (Soggin, J. T. Barrera, Mendelsohn, et al.) suggesting that several words associated with the semantics of oppression in the book of Exodus have Syro-Palestinian origins and come out of the Canaanite experience, especially from the period of the Solomonic oppression.

As we dip into the *reserva-de-sentido*, the reservoir of meaning associated with the exodus event, it is important that we distinguish between the event itself, as it happened around the thirteenth century B.C., and the many new events and theologies that it inspired and produced. When we look at the testimonies about it, we must remember that they come to us loaded with confessions (theologies), products of new experiences of oppression and struggles of liberation, the most obvious and rich of which are those that come out of the Canaanite context.

We want to keep at the surface of our reflection an awareness of the clear and unquestionable realities of political and economical oppression. We know that in the last analysis those who hold the power want to keep it, to become ever wealthier, to exploit and despoil the largest possible number of people in slavery beneath them. And they will use religion and culture as instruments to maintain the status quo. It is no accident that so many oppressers both inside and outside of Israel were followers of false gods who in many cases strove to remove Yahweh from his position as dynastic or personal god.

I believe that recitations of the exodus experience by the different generations of Israelites throughout the Old Testament period developed slowly into a confession or a creed. I would suggest that we are justified in speaking of an *exodus kerygma*. At least four passages in the Pentateuch are structured following the pattern presented by the kerygma. As Old Testament scholarship has long maintained, they belong to different literary-theological traditions associated with specific historical periods: Exodus 3:7-8 (tenth century B.C.); Exodus 3:9-15 (ninth century B.C.); Deuteronomy 26:5-10 (eighth century B.C.); and Exodus 6:2-8 (sixth century B.C.). All of them have these three elements: (1) the people suffer affliction, (2) Yahweh hears (see and knows) their outcry, and (3) Yahweh comes down to deliver them from Egypt and to bring them up to the land.

We can place each of these versions of the kerygma in the different contexts of Israelite history:

1. Exodus 3:7-8 during the Solomonic oppression (cf. 1 Kings 12; 1 Sam. 8:11-17)

2. Exodus 3:9-15 during the Canaanite oppression, which could be extended from the time of King Achab to that of Jeroboam II (cf. 1 Kings 17-21; Amos; and Hosea)
3. Deuteronomy 26:5-10 during the Assyrian period, involving two opposing models—that of King Manasseh and of King Josiah
4. Exodus 6:2-8 during the Babylonian exile (the last part of the sixth century B.C.) and related to the Ezekiel and Isaiah 40-66 traditions.

Each of these periods had its own liberator, Moses or God. They were not so easily recognized by the people, in part because false leaders and gods also competed for their loyalty. In the contexts of oppression and struggle for liberation, there was always interference of various sorts to the revelation of God's name. The people had to tune their ears to come into harmony with the voice of Yahweh. This is why the literary structure and content of passages throughout the Pentateuch together present the revelation of God's name as a sign of liberation hope: Yahweh! These passages helped the people determine not only the identity of their God but of themselves as well. We can see this most clearly in Exodus 3:9-15 and in Exodus 6:2-8. Exodus 3:9-15 follows a climactic structure: the reality of oppression stands as the base of the climactic structure, and the name of God, Yahweh, stands as the climax. Exodus 6:2-8 follows a chiastic or concentric structure: the experience of oppression and the promise of liberation constitute a core that is encircled by the name *Yahweh*, which is repeated four times.

We should look more closely at the period during which the version of the exodus kerygma in Exodus 3:9-15 made its initial impact—the period between the ministries of the prophets Elijah and Hosea, when Israel experienced the most devastating force of the Canaanite oppression and consequently battled against idolatry most courageously. It was during this period that the exodus was most clearly characterized as an open struggle between the biblical faith and idolatry. And it is by studying this period that we can see most clearly the intimate connection between the exodus event and the Sinai experience. In fact, the exodus event constitutes a framework that defines the Decalogue as a covenant document.

Exodus 3:9-15 is contextually, literarily, and theologically united to Exodus 3:7-8, and the Deuteronomistic tradition is clearly evident in Elijah's battle against idolatry and Hosea's ministry with regard to the so-called "sin of Jeroboam I"—the two golden calves in Bethel and Dan. The Elohistic passage (Exod. 3:9-15) gives the Yahwistic version of the exodus kerygma a new force, a stronger meaning. Soon after their liberation from the Solomonic oppression, Israel fell again under the Canaanite oppression. In an effort to liberate Israel from the Judean shadow, Jeroboam I, the new Moses, gave the people a symbol that soon led to a confusion of gods. Yahweh and his symbol-pedestal, the bull, was changed to Baal and his symbol, the bull. In the new context of Canaan, the symbol of revelation and divine presence over the years became an obstacle to recognizing Yahweh.

The essence of the problem is evident in the desire of the people to limit divine revelation to a single experience and model.

The accounts of the golden calves in Exodus 32, 1 Kings 12, and Hosea 13:1-2 show the people's terrible confusion. The calves are not understood as pedestals or symbols of Yahweh's presence; they are now worshiped as symbols of the lord of Canaan, Baal. The exodus from the Solomonic oppression had served to ensure a new type of oppression. "This is your 'elohim who brought you out from Egypt" (1 Kings 12:28) ceased to be a confession of faith in Yahweh and became instead a creed of faith in Baal. The people had succumbed to a new oppressive structure in which idolatry and injustice joined hands.

We can see the steps that led from an experience of liberation to an experience of oppression in chronological order if we look first at 1 Kings 12, next at 1 Kings 17-21, and finally at the book of Hosea.

1. In 1 Kings 12:25-29 we find a record of the political and religious action of Jeroboam I. It was his desire to provide Israel with something Judah already had: a temple and the symbol of divine presence, the ark. The scholarly studies on this issue suggest that Jeroboam's action was not at all unreasonable or groundless. He was aware of a very old tradition that not only related Yahweh to the bull figure but also to Dan and Bethel. There are a good number of scholars who say that the *pesel-massēkāh* (an image of wood covered with silver) of Judges 17-18 could be a bull symbolizing the presence of Yahweh. It has been also said that Exodus 32:2-6 records a tradition that is neutral with respect the calf of Aaron, presenting it not as an idol but simply as a pedestal or symbol of Yahweh's presence. More clearly, the bull figure in these passages had nothing to do with Baal; the relationship between Yahweh and the bull stems from an earlier relationship between Yahweh and 'el of the Semites.

Having restored to his kingdom a very old and secure tradition, Jeroboam I was certain that he had secured its ancient strength as well. He had, in fact, established his kingdom on Yahwistic grounds, a basis that was maintained for many years. The records of the united monarchy and the first years of the divided monarchy do not contain any references to an open confrontation between those who were faithful to Yahweh and those who worshiped Baal.

2. It is in accounts of Elijah (1 Kings 17-21) that we find the first references to an open confrontation with Baal. The framework of the struggle is the reign of Ahab and Jezebel. By this time the people of Israel had decided that Baal might have some value as a god, filling a role similar to that which Yahweh had filled during the nomadic period and the first years of the settlement time. In turning to Baal, they were not so much rejecting Yahweh as they were reaching out to a new divine power for help in dealing with a more complex reality.

The account shows that a strong effort was made to separate Yahweh from any characterization that might keep him united with Baal. Moreover, all actions that were attributed to the power of Baal were completely put under Yahweh's sovereignty. It was not Baal who gave the rain but Yahweh; in fact, Yahweh was even able to stop it in defiance of the natural cycle of seasons. Wheat and oil were not given by Baal (cf. Hos. 2:5); it was Yahweh who gave them, and he gave them selectively, choosing, for instance, to bless the widow (1 Kings 17).

But it was at Horeb that Yahweh's ties with Baal were really broken. Elijah, the new "Moses," goes to Horeb and there experiences God's revelation. Yahweh did not follow the pattern of revelation shown at Sinai when Moses received the covenant. He did not use the means of revelation he did in Moses' time (cf. Exod. 19:9, 16-18; 20:18). He did not appear in a strong wind or an earthquake or a fire. His presence was proclaimed by a gentle breeze (1 Kings 19:11-12).

The narrative of the vineyard of Naboth closes the episode, showing that the actions of an idolatrous structure end with injustice and wicked actions.

3. Hosea is the one who shows how far the Canaanite oppression could reach. At this time the problem was not that Baal was placed at the same level as Yahweh but that Baal was elevated to the rank of Lord and sovereign of Israel, displacing Yahweh in the life and faith of Israel. Baal was presumed not only to provide the essentials for daily life but also to have attained the historical dimension of Israelite life. According to Hosea, the bulls at Dan and Bethel were no longer considered Yahweh's pedestals but had become idols of Baal. The declaration "This is your God who brought you out from Egypt," directed originally to Yahweh, had changed to "These are your gods who brought you out from Egypt" and was directed to Baal.

This period saw the most devastating oppression of all—an oppression that involved not only the presence of injustice and all manner of social sins but a consequent exclusion of Yahweh from Israel. It was Baal who justified the social pattern developed by Jeroboam II. His kingdom (including the priesthood) was constructed without reference to Yahweh or his covenant demands. Israel stood in real need of a new exodus, a new Moses, and a new divine revelation. It is here that the Exodus 3:9-15 version of the exodus kerygma must have made its strongest impact.

The pattern is familiar. First, there was an outcry of oppression (see Amos and Hosea). Then there came a "Moses," a prophet of God and herald of the divine revelation. The "who am I?" of Hosea (Hos. 1-3) received meaning and force from the "I AM" of Yahweh (Hos. 12:9; 13:4). Finally, in a new context of oppression and suffering, Yahweh let his name be heard anew: "I am Yahweh your God from the land of Egypt. A God besides me you do not know; there is no Savior except me" (Hos. 13:4).

The book of Hosea shows us that the prophet delivered his message with the exodus event in mind. He constantly refers to the exodus and the covenant at Sinai, the two elements of the Decalogue. In fact, we could regard Hosea as a long commentary on the prologue and the two first words of the Decalogue. Several scholars date the initial connection of the prologue with the two first words to the time of Hosea (the self-introduction formula encircles the two first commandments). It is beyond question that the second commandment receives its deepest force in Hosea's ministry.

The "I AM" of the divine revelation stands at the beginning of the book (1:9), linked to the negative *lō'* to indicate what was true of Israel in those days. Israel was *lō' 'ami:* it had rejected Yahweh, and so Yahweh was no longer the God of Israel. The infidelities and injustices of Israel had invalidated "the-being-of-God-for-them." As the Egyptian oppression had served as a framework for the revelation of the name of God, so the sin of Israel and its open rejection (*'zb*) of Yahweh had reversed the fact: Yahweh "disrevealed" himself to Israel: "I am no I-AM for you" (1:9, *'ānōkî lō'-'ehyeh lākem;* cf. Exodus 3:14, *'ehyeh 'ăšer 'ehyeh*).

But the book does not end thus. In the end, the prophet invokes the self-introduction formula not once but twice: "I am Yahweh your God" (12:9; 13:4). And between these two revelations of the divine name and the "no-revelation" of 1:9 there are several references to the experience of the exodus (2:16-17; 9:10; 11:1, 5; 8:13) and the Sinai covenant (3:1; 4:2; 12:10; 13:4). These passages point to the fact that they could recover Yahweh's "being-of-God-for-them" only through a new exodus. Israel had to go back to the "wilderness," had to reject Baal and all divine-political powers (Israel's "lovers"), and commit itself once more to Yahweh. Hosea underscores this last point by using the concept of the "knowledge" of God (Hos. 4:1-2, 6, 14; 5:4; 6:3, 6; 14:9). He stressed the point that God's revelation and knowledge cannot be separated and the people must acknowledge this fact not through lip service to empty doctrines and practice of meaningless rites but through concrete obedience to the terms of the Covenant (4:1-2; 3:1; 13:1-2)—that is, through works of social justice and loyalty to Yahweh.

2.1.3

Report by Thomas McAlpine

We discussed three passages: a portion of Exodus 3, a portion of Deuteronomy 26, and a portion of Exodus 6. I'll summarize the first two.

Exodus 3. Our primary concern was with the pastoral task posed by the early chapters of Exodus. This task arises when one who is oppressed or imprisoned asks why God would harden the hearts of the powerful. It also arises when an executive of comfortable means says "I know about persecution: people at work ridicule me for being a Christian." Examination of the early chapters suggested that for Israel the exodus was not simply a historical experience, but that it was reinterpreted in a variety of contexts and used in various situations as a model for future divine salvation. For instance, this happened at the time of Jereboam II. It is this reuse of Scripture that encouraged us to bring this model to bear today. The use of Exodus imagery in the hymns coming out of the black experience that we call spirituals attests to this powerful way in which God can use Scripture, in particular Exodus. At the same time, aspects of the story, such as the dispossession of other peoples and the hardening motif, suggest that we must be cautious in using this model mechanically, simply drawing lines between biblical figures and contemporary figures. The fact that European settlers in North America and Dutch settlers in South Africa unself-consciously used the conquest and exodus images to justify displacing indigenous peoples also gives one pause in that regard. Obviously there are questions of fact as well as interpretation, but the question may be deeper: in what ways, if any, does Israel's unique status in our common Scripture limit the ways this text can be brought to bear on parallel situations? That question was asked, but—predictably—it was not resolved.

We also noted that Exodus 3 provides us with considerably more than just a collection of pastoral problems. There, in the midst of oppression, Yahweh came and revealed his name. We noted that the divine '*hyh*—"I AM"—was a promise in that situation rather than an invitation to metaphysics (reminding us of the discussion surrounding René's paper on Christology). What does the divine "I AM" promise? Not simply freedom from Pharaoh but also from all the idols of Egypt. In fact, it is precisely *as* Yahweh is present to his people that the idols are revealed as idols. This issue of idolatry is central to life in both Latin and North America.

Deuteronomy 26. Here we encountered an exodus kerygma in a postexodus setting. In the consistently hortatory context of Deuteronomy, it is made clear that the last word has not been spoken even when the land is gained. At the very least the Levite and the sojourner have yet to be provided for. We reflected on the variety of contexts in which such a passage, speaking as it does of partial progress toward the kingdom, can be heard. Certainly it speaks to the context of worship, telling us that we must recover a fresh sense of thanksgiving as a means to the renewal of church life. Again we discussed but did not move close to resolving issues including the patriarchal cast of the language of the text and the possibility of applying the exodus paradigm to other struggles for national liberation.

2.1.4

Final Report from Exodus Group

JOHN STAM

The Exodus study group benefited from two excellent background papers: "The Book of Exodus: A Laboratory for Hermeneutics," by Stephen Reid, and "Hermeneutics and Context: The Exodus," by Edesio Sánchez-Centina. Our group consisted of three Old Testament scholars, a New Testament professor, a theology professor, and an urban pastor. Culturally, our group included four North Americans (including two blacks), a Mexican, and a Costa Rican. We concentrated especially on three key passages: Exodus 3:9-12, Deuteronomy 26:5-10, and Exodus 6:2-8.

Our discussion confirmed the central thesis of our two preparatory papers: the Exodus, for Israel, was not a static historical event in the past but rather a dynamic and growing tradition within the forward-moving flow of the history of the people of God. This exodus tradition produced an exodus kerygma that was progressively reinterpreted in the new historical situations that confronted the nation, serving both as a hermeneutical key to past and present history and as a socio-historical model for future divine salvation. Not only main themes from the Exodus, but even precise terminology and specific details (e.g., "hard service" and "heavy yoke" in 1 Kings 12:4-14 and "golden bulls" in 1 Kings 12:28 and Exod. 32:8) reappear later as decisive keys to new situations. In each new circumstance, the recital of the basic kerygma (the people are oppressed, God hears their cry, and he comes down to deliver them) recontextualizes the exodus tradition in a renewed confession of faith in God.

While recent theological movements (especially liberation theologies) have rightly underscored the central importance of the exodus, they have too often tended to emphasize almost exclusively the narrative of Exodus 1-15 and the socio-political dimension. Within Latin American theology, however, new aspects of the exodus tradition have begun to enrich theological reflection on the exodus without in any way dulling the cutting edge of its socio-ethical demands for justice and liberation. Two themes have assumed special importance: (1) the anti-idolatry polemic, especially in the prophetic refocus on the exodus after Jeroboam introduced the golden calves and Ahab/Jezebel led Israel into unrestrained Baalization of Yahwism, and also (2) emphasis on the struggle between life and anti-life, Yahweh being the God of life and idolatry constituting a force against life (see Deut. 30:19ff.).

Our group found in the passages studied additional insights to enrich and balance interpretations of the exodus. Of special importance is (3) the constant and indispensable correlation of exodus and covenant, of the reed sea and Sinai. The group also emphasized (4) the importance of the narratives of the wilderness wandering for the formation of the community of faith, its temptations, struggles, and renewal through God's grace. Additional dimensions for a broader interpretation of the exodus included the "exposed child" theme, the plagues, God's hardening of Pharaoh's heart, the despoiling of the Egyptians, the de-conscientization of the masses (Exod. 6:9) and their chronic murmuring, dispossession and conquest of the land, spirituality, and sacred space.

We also considered different pastoral aspects of the interpretation of the Exodus narratives. A U.S. urban pastor posed the question of why most North American Christians who read Exodus remain blind to the possibility that they (or their government) might be the oppressors like the Pharaoh of the narrative. Can such parallels actually be clear and valid, derived from the text itself? From another situation came the question of how we should answer a prisoner who asks why God would harden the heart of the powerful. The pastoral problem also arises when an executive of comfortable means claims to know all about persecution because people at work ridicule him or her for being a Christian.

The "I AM" self-presentation formula is linked to the liberation experience in Exodus, Hosea, and Isaiah 7-9. This title expresses above all the availability of Yahweh accompanying the people on their march toward promised freedom and blessing (see Exod. 3:12a). The severe judgment "I will not be 'I AM' for you" in Hosea 1:9 indicates the divine withdrawal of that availability, which Isaiah reaffirms in the Yahwistic terms of *Emmanuel,* "God-with-us" (Isa. 7:14). According to Frank M. Cross, the Yahweh-title may have been a more ancient Canaanite/Semitic El-title ("El who created the hosts") that was only later connected to the pun on the verb "to be." This would suggest that the title should be understood more as historic-salvific than as metaphysical (note the similar Christological thesis in René Padilla's paper for this consultation). The exodus passages present the "I AM" as profoundly relational and yet also transcendentally beyond relationality. Another participant observed that in Exodus 3, Yahweh is first described as sensuous (sees, hears, knows) but then as beyond sensuousness at the end of the passage. In the "I AM" language, as in the synoptic Christology, event seems to have priority over essense, and relationality over metaphysics.

Each exodus passage studied by our group makes significant reference to the covenant as the context and presupposition of the exodus (Exod. 3:6-7, 10, 13, 15; 6:3-5, 7-8; Deut. 26:1, 3, 13, 15-16). The group felt that this covenant theme is inadequately emphasized in much contemporary Old Testament study (e.g., von Rad) and in much liberation theology (e.g., that of Miranda), and that is particularly regrettable because the vital correlation of Exodus and Sinai in the matrix of covenant can contribute important insights to a theology of the exodus. While present at all stages of the exodus accounts, the covenant link seems to have become especially significant in the period between Ahab and Jeroboam II, along with the resounding anti-idolatric polemic. Elijah's struggle against Baalism culminates, significantly, at Horeb, where he encounters anew the God of the Covenant. In the words of one member of our group, "the Horeb encounter excludes every possibility of linking Baal with exodus and Sinai."

The liturgy of Deuteronomy 26, which reinterprets the exodus for the new situation of affluence within the promised land, centers on the worship and offering of the people in obedience to the commandments that structured the life of Israel under God's covenant. Israel's "father" (26:5—Jacob or "our ancestor" in general?) was a "perishing Aramean" ("perishing being a better translation of 'ōbhēdh than "wandering"): weak, vulnerable, threatened, marginalized, and close to death. But divine grace encountered the people and made them a nation, "great, mighty and populous" (26:5c). Those loyal to the covenant, in grateful obedience to the God who had enriched them, would resist tendencies toward the arrogance of success (Deut. 8:17; 9:4; 7:7-8; 9:5) and would nourish the constant renewal of the people of God within the covenant relationship.

This covenant emphasis underscores the continuity of God's saving activity. While the self-designation of God as Yahweh points forcefully to the futuricity of promise (God as future: Moltmann, Pannenberg), its matrix, firmly embedded in the covenant context, points simultaneously to the faithfulness of Yahweh as "the God of the past," the Lord of the ancestors and founders of the nation. God has been at work from the beginning. It is God who has permitted us to survive, and God who has blessed and prospered us. God's mercies, new every morning, accompany the people along the long road to freedom and justice.

The covenant context also highlights the "evangelical" nature of Israel's exodus salvation. The election and liberation of Israel are entirely due to the free grace of God. While Exodus 3:12 recognizes the concursus of Moses along with the divine action ("when you—Moses—have brought forth the people out of Egypt"), the description in Deuteronomy 26 reduces the human participation to an absolute minimum. The "participation" of Israel, according to Deuteronomy 26, was to cry in the midst of oppression (26:7) and later rejoice in the midst of blessing (26:11). In retrospect, Israel recognizes that it was really God who did it all. Our salvation is "all of grace," but the covenant means that this is costly rather than cheap grace.

Hosea also expresses dramatically this purely gracious saving work of

God. It is Yahweh who chooses Israel in love and calls it by grace (Hos. 11:1), despite its unworthiness and rebellion (5:4; 11:7). God found Israel as a child and like a tender father taught it to walk, helping it when it fell and healing its bruises (11:3). God chose Israel as bride, even though it had no betrothal gift (2:19). It was unfaithful, but Yahweh bought it back. Now Israel lacked all strength; only grace could save it. According to Hosea, the story of Israel was grace all the way; grace in the past, grace in the present and in the future.

The theme of land is also central to the exodus accounts, as also in the covenant promises (Gen. 12:1ff, etc.). In some later exodus passages, this emphasis may be related to the Josaianic land reform or to contemporary processes of land acquisition (concentration of productive land). According to Deuteronomy 26, the Israelite is to share the fruit of the land with "the Levite, the sojourner, the fatherless, and the widow"—that is, the non-franchised people who had no legal status based on land. One participant suspected that the terms summarized a kind of "catch-all" category for all nonlandowners.

The group made two observations about the list of nations that Israel would displace when they took Canaan (Exod. 3:8). First, the list roots the Exodus narrative in the geo-political realities of history; to try to spiritualize such a list would be an exercise in ultimate futility. Second, since land is a limited commodity, if some are to gain, others must lose. During the exile, the hope of repossessing land was central to the exodus message, and this too entailed the disenfranchisement of others. This raised many questions in our group about private property, land claims, fishing and hunting rights, and land reform. We also questioned what relationship Abraham's prior presence in Canaan might have had to the land claim of Israel, and how this would compare (for example) to Mayan land rights in Mexico.

Fundamental throughout the discussion was the hermeneutical problem. In each passage studied we found that the interpretation of the exodus was profoundly contextual, directly linked to the realities, experiences, and liberation of the people of God in each new historical situation (e.g., the exodus passages often seem to have a Canaanite background rather than Egyptian). In terms of recent tendencies in hermeneutics, Stephen Reid pointed us to a decisive key to this hermeneutical process: the Holy Spirit in the believing community, which explains "the way that the story has continued to arrest persons of faith" caught up in situations of social upheaval.

While we concluded that the exodus is no mere static datum from the past and that it cannot legitimately be spiritualized out of its historical reality, we also concurred that we ought not to try to apply it mechanically to contemporary political situations as some kind of literalistic "template" that would allow us to equate present-day figures with biblical figures. Within Scripture itself, the exodus accounts are progressively reinterpreted, not just mechanically "applied" as if history constantly repeated itself in identical form. The accounts serve not as a template but as a paradigm, and paradigms have to be conjugated and conjugated correctly.

This discussion was often best sharpened up by some quite probing questions:

> Since Israel was God's specifically chosen people, what hermeneutical grounds do we have to apply the exodus account to any other nation?

> Could not the "exodus paradigm" (template) be best applied in a Zionist hermeneutic of divine right to the land of Palestine?

> How would the exodus paradigm apply to the problem of native Americans (was the U.S. territory divinely "assigned" to the European colonizers?) or to black South Africans (did divine providence transfer their land to the whites who now rule South Africa?)?

> What hermeneutical criteria clarify (endorse or refute) the use of the exodus narratives by anti-Sandinista "contras" in Honduras, who see the Rio Coco as the Jordan they must cross to reoccupy the land given them by God but taken away from them by the Sandinistas? Or the use of the Nehemiah account to describe the Ríos Montt government as a "miracle in motion"?

> Does the exodus account apply to expatriate Cubans now living in the U.S.A.? If so, how?

> Does God take sides? What does it mean to say that God is on the side of the poor?

Hermeneutically, we also confronted repeatedly the question of cultural relativity vis-à-vis the normative authority of Scripture (and its unique irrepeatability, *Einmaligkeit,* as salvation history). We faced this problem, for example, with the strongly patriarchal tone and language of Deuteronomy 26. The appeal to cultural relativism can easily become arbitrary and subjective, applied only when it is to our interest. Yet this factor cannot be left out of account, since it is indeed indispensable to the sound interpretation of many passages. The group saw various guidelines toward a responsible use of the appeal to cultural relativism. First, the problem must be dealt with Christologically (Luther, Barth, Mowinckel). Our concern must be for how our interpretation can be kept faithful to the person and message of Jesus Christ, for how it can most forcefully "urge Christ" upon us. Second, the biblical insistence on justice as an essential attribute of God's kingdom must serve as a guiding criterion for the valid use of the appeal to cultural relativity (see Matt. 6:33 regarding God's defense of the oppressed and defenseless, widows and orphans, etc.). Finally, in rereading Scripture in and for new cultural situations, we must take great care to continue to affirm our common context (covenant) in the community of faith and the demands for "sacrificial reconciliation" such community implies.

Members of the Isaiah Study Group

Orlando E. Costas
Elouise Renich Fraser
Robert Hubbard
Samuel Pagán
Clark H. Pinnock
John Howard Yoder

2.2.1

And Peace Will Be Multiplied unto Your Children: An Introductory Study on Shalom in the Old Testament

SAMUEL PAGÁN

Within biblical testimony and tradition, one writer stands out for his creativity and new theological perspective. Although we do not know his name or background, his poetic and theological qualities identify him as a very important person. The style of his prophetic message is marked by pronounced lyrical and metrical elements, parallelism and assonance.[1] His thinking demonstrates profundity, universality, wisdom, and ingenuity. His theology elaborates themes from the Isaiah of Jerusalem, from Jeremiah, and from Ezekiel. He combines an elaborate and detailed poetic facility with an extensive and intense theological capacity.[2]

We find the message of this great and anonymous poet-prophet, commonly identified as Deutero-Isaiah, in chapters 40 to 55 of the book of Isaiah. Although this section of the book has a certain continuity with the rest of the message in Isaiah, textual analysis has revealed certain features that suggest it was written later.[3] The presumed historical setting, the

1. See James Muilenberg, *The Book of Isaiah*, Interpreter's Bible, vol. 5 (Nashville: Abingdon Press, 1955), pp. 381-83.
2. See my *Resurrección de la Esperanza* (Bayamón: n.p., 1983), pp. 125-26.
3. See C. R. North, *El libro de Isaías 40-55* (Buenos Aires: La Aurora, 1960).

literary style and vocabulary used, and the theological concepts and ideas expounded point to the fact that different authors contributed to this great work. This fine, creative poet Deutero-Isaiah must have prophesied and ministered in Babylon around the years 550-540 B.C.[4] The exiles must have received his message as a revelation of consolation and renewal of hope from Yahweh. In an atmosphere of exile, deportations, military defeats, and captivity, the words of Deutero-Isaiah would have served as a unifying element to keep high the hope of national restoration and return to the homeland of Palestine.

One of the great messages of hope from Deutero-Isaiah is found in Isaiah 54:11-17, in which he speaks of the "New Jerusalem," emphasizing the beauty of the new city and the certainty of its future. The splendor of the city is revealed in the description of its adornments made of precious stones. This passage, which certainly must have influenced the author of the book of Revelation to describe the New Jerusalem as he did (see Rev. 21-22), reveals the gift of the glory and the beauty of the city as an act of divine consolation and mercy. The security of the city, a promise of blessing, is pronounced in military terms, as an act of victory and intervention by Yahweh.[5]

In the midst of the description of beauty, and preceding the promise of security, blessings are pronounced on the citizens and inhabitants of this novel city in a rhythmic parallelism. The text can be translated from the Hebrew as follows:

> All your sons will be disciples of Yahweh,
> and great will by your children's peace.[6]

Deutero-Isaiah indicates that the splendor and strength of the coming city will teach the inhabitants to commit themselves to God and foster peace. To be a disciple of God is to enter into a creative learning process—a process of coming to know in a profound way the values and the will of the One who creates the city. This learning process has as its reward the discovery of a great happiness, a great well-being, a great peace: the discovery of *shalom*. One of the great biblical themes, shalom has a special place in this special city that is home to an enlightening encounter between God and his people. In this process of enlightenment, education and peace go hand in hand. The education involves both a growing awareness and a commitment in response; the peace is the result of serious and liberating pedagogy.

The word *shalom* is often translated as "peace," but it has a breadth and

4. See John L. Mackenzie, *Second Isaiah* (Garden City, N.Y.: Doubleday, 1968).

5. See Claus Westermann, *Isaiah 40-66* (Philadelphia: Westminster Press, 1975), pp. 278-79.

6. Some commentators (e.g., Westermann) translated the text as "your constructors" *(bōnayik)* rather than "your sons" *(bānayik)*. I disagree with this reading, however, on the grounds that verses 11 and 12 emphasize the fact that Yahweh is the constructor.

depth of content that surpasses this narrow meaning.[7] It means peace in the broadest sense, peace that includes well-being, joy, and happiness. The very root of the word, *slm,* contains the idea of general well-being—pointedly *material* well-being.

We can get some indication of the breadth of the concept of shalom by considering the ways it is used in certain other contexts. In Genesis 26:9, for example, when Jacob asks a group from Haran about Laban, son of Nacor, he inquires about Laban's shalom, his well-being: "Is he well [shalom]?" (Jerusalem Bible);[8] "How is he?" (Reina Valera version, 1960); "Is he in good health?" (Good News Bible). The word is also used to describe the well-being of the proud. In the prayer for justice in Psalm 73:3, the prosperity of the wicked is described as shalom—a use that accentuates their physical and material well-being: prosperity, security, and health.

The content of *shalom* is not limited to individuals, however; it is also commonly used in reference to a group or nation enjoying prosperity and stability. Responding to Isaiah's prophecy of judgment, Hezekiah says, "What does it concern me, as long as there is *peace and security* while I live?" (2 Kings 20:19, JB); "At least there will be *peace and security* while I live" (Reina Valera).

In addition to the idea of peace, shalom also connotes a sense of relationship, a dynamic interpersonal or international encounter—a relationship that is not merely static but that actively fosters a common good. In fact, shalom refers not so much to a process that produces universal well-being as to the mutual enjoyment of prosperity, health, security, and happiness. It connotes a relationship of stability among peoples that entails mutual respect and recognition. This aspect of the word's meaning is apparent from its use in contexts of alliances and covenants of friendship between two parties. In addition to promoting the common good, the covenant relationship involves mutual respect—a key aspect of the prophetic use of the concept of covenant to describe the relationship between God and his people. As Deutero-Isaiah expresses it,

> The mountains may go away and the hills may totter,
> but my faithful love will never leave you,
> my covenant of peace will never totter. (Isa. 54:10, JB)

Clearly, then, shalom involves much more than most of our translations of the biblical text capture. The common dictionary definition of *peace* mentions such things as tranquility and calmness, an absence of dissension

---

7. On this, see Gerhard von Rad, "שָׁלוֹם in the Old Testament," in the *Theological Dictionary of the New Testament,* 2: 402-6.

8. This and other references to the Jerusalem Bible are retranslations of the Spanish version of the text rather than citations from the English version.

and disputes, or, in the case of a nation, the absence of war. Thus it is defined principally as the absence of problems, as a state of passive or static tranquility—a tranquility that is not bothered by anything. But shalom connotes a *dynamic* state of exchange, dialogue, mutual respect, well-being, health, happiness, and salvation. Shalom suggests an active and beneficial relationship, not quiet reflection, meditation, or escape.

Shalom is key to our understanding of Yahweh's relationship with Israel. Shalom and the concepts related to it come to Israel as gifts from the Lord. The nation prays to God for shalom, and when they enjoy it, they understand that it has come to them as a result of divine action.

In Psalm 85 we find the exposition of a culmination in the theology of shalom as a salvific act of Yahweh. This psalm, which can be read either as a lamentation of the community or as a prophetic liturgy,[9] reveals a close relationship between shalom and ideas of restoration, salvation, rejoicing, mercy, glory, truth, and justice. It is a song of affirmation that can be divided into three parts: recognition of divine intervention in the past (vv. 1-3), prayer for salvation and restoration (vv. 4-7), and recognition of the goodness of God (vv. 8-13).

The psalm, which is related to Deutero-Isaiah's message of consolation,[10] alludes to the word of the Lord that came to the people—the word *shalom*. The author of Psalm 85 understands that divine revelation will come to the people "if only they renounce their folly" (JB) or "so that they do not return to their folly" (Reina Valera) or "so that they do not return to their foolish ways" (Good News Bible). Shalom is revealed as a divine act that looks to the future. This communication of God is an act of commitment to what will come, to a time when shalom will have real and practical manifestations. The divine message to the people is that they must not return to the anxiety-filled past but must move on to a conquest of the future, to an enjoyment of that which is to come, to the construction of tomorrow.

Psalm 85 is rich in images of this shalom. The themes of the closeness of God, the salvation of the faithful, and the manifestation of glory are all intimate parts of the concept. Mercy, love, truth, justice, and righteousness are all related to the term. The author of this revealing psalm presents shalom not as an abstract metaphysical concept but as a full enjoyment of love, mercy, truth, and justice. The essence of the word is the idea of the extensive well-being produced when truth becomes a reality on earth and justice comes down from heaven. Truth and justice are critical elements of the enjoyment of God-given shalom.

9. See Mitchell Dahood, *Psalms,* vol. 2: *51-100* (Garden City, N.Y.: Doubleday, 1979), pp. 285-90.

10. See W. Steward McCullough, *The Book of Psalms,* Interpreter's Bible, vol. 4 (Nashville: Abingdon Press, 1955), pp. 457-62.

There appears to have been a prophetic circle in which the concept of shalom served as a minor theological theme.[11] Prophets within the tradition, from Micaiah ben Imlah (see 1 Kings 22) to Jeremiah (see Jer. 28), differed in the way they used the term—not so much in the theological connotations they accorded it as in the way they related it to the sin of the people. Because some prophets failed to analyze the national attitude critically, they failed to view the future of the people in terms of the coming judgment. They viewed life and shalom as static, unchanging, continuous, and they resisted relating everyday realities to coming political realities. But, as we have noted, God's shalom is not static, not the external calm of inaction and passivity; rather, it is the product of noble and just activities that translate divine virtues into everyday realities.

It was this broader understanding of shalom that Deutero-Isaiah elaborated in his prophecy. He and his disciples in Babylon (commonly known as Trito-Isaiah, the source of Isa. 56-66) used shalom to describe a special state that announced the salvific and liberating intervention of Yahweh. Deutero-Isaiah expanded and emphasized the relationship between shalom, obedience, and justice. Speaking of the destiny of Israel in Isaiah 48:18, he laments,

> If only you had listened to my commandments!
> Your prosperity [shalom] would have been like a river
> and your victory like the waves of the sea. (JB)

The message relates shalom to God's claims on his people's faithfulness, to the covenant, to the commandments. The oracle juxtaposes unfaithfulness and shalom. Shalom and victory cannot be realized without faithfulness, obedience, and justice.

Already in Isaiah 32:16-17 the idea of this sort of shalom is presented poetically:

> Equity will fix its home in the desert,
> and justice will live in the productive ground,
> and the product of justice will be peace,
> the fruit of equity, quiet and security forever. (JB)

This text points to the relationship between equity, justice, perpetual security, and peace. It conveys a sense of shalom that incorporates virtues necessary for well-being. Security is won not by force but by just treatment. Peace is won not by threats but by equal distribution of goods.

Shalom and justice are similarly related in Isaiah 60:17. In a passage that continues the analysis and description of the Jerusalem to come, the change in everyday realities is accentuated:

11. See A. González, N. Lohfink, and G. von Rad, *Profetas Verdaderos, Profetas Falsos* (Salamanca: Ediciones Sígueme, 1976).

Instead of bronze I will bring you gold,
and silver in place of iron.
Instead of wood I will bring you bronze,
and iron in place of stones.
I will make peace [shalom] your governor
and justice your ruler. (JB)

This understanding of the relationship between shalom and justice was eventually embodied principally in terms of eschatological expectation. When the ideals of shalom were not realized in Israel's immediate sociopolitical context, they were gradually tranferred to hopes for an indeterminate future. The prophets of the exilic and postexilic periods spoke of a time of restoration in which shalom—peace, well-being, health, and enjoyment of life—would reign, a salvific gift from God in response to the earnest prayers of his people.

*   *   *

We have noted some of the important aspects of the concept of shalom. We have seen that education is essential for the enjoyment of shalom. The educational process offers new beginnings, encourages creativity, yields enlightenment, and liberates the conscience. Shalom is the result of the incorporation of the qualities, intentions, and will of God into the everyday life and behavior of his people. Micah describes that will of God in the following terms: "It has been shown you, O man, what is good, what Yahweh requires of you: only to practice equity, love piety, and walk humbly with your God" (Mic. 6:8, JB). According to this great prophet, the divine will that is, in turn, a requirement for the enjoyment of shalom, contains elements of equity, justice, piety, mercy, and humility. Without the sort of education that generates these important virtues, shalom cannot be enjoyed.

Our troubled continent desperately awaits a closer analysis of this key biblical concept. It has been the task of the church to minister in the midst of poverty, injustice, threats, wars, and despair. The people of God in Latin America are living and ministering to a people exhausted by its search for directions and resources with which to meet the future. In this environment of conquest and construction, the revelation of shalom offers incredible possibilities. God's shalom is not the peace of the graveyard, not a contemplative escape from a painful reality, not the calm that comes from refusing to accept bother or dissent. Rather, it is a dynamic and creative response to everyday realities. It comes into being in a context of enlightenment and divine revelation. It results from faithfulness to the covenant, obedience to God.

God's shalom will not be realized in our continent through armed terrorism. Shalom cannot be based on fear of force or a military empire. The shalom we await will come only through the commitment of the people of God to enlightenment and a way of life that reveals and manifests commitment, faithfulness, justice, and equity. When we follow this path, then shalom will be multiplied unto our children.

2.2.2

Jai Alai, Hermeneutics, and Isaianic Peace

ROBERT L. HUBBARD

I

This paper bears a somewhat startling title. The reader may rightly question the relationship between its parts. To the best of my knowledge the prophet Isaiah never played or witnessed jai alai nor was that sport common among the ancient Israelites. Further, *jai alai* has never appeared as a technical term in any book of hermeneutics that I have seen. Nevertheless, I offer jai alai as an analogy for what I conceive to be the purpose of this paper. As you know, the game of jai alai is a form of handball in which two or four players bounce a hard rubber ball off a towering wall. Their tool is the *cesta,* a slender, curved basket that attaches to the player's hand with a glove and is used to fling the ball against the wall in such a way as to prevent an opponent from returning it.

I offer this paper as a kind of wall—something against which to "bounce ideas" and engage the skills of other players. I see myself and my readers as those players, each with his or her own cesta—that is, an approach to Bible study, a reservoir of background knowledge about the Bible, a treasury of past experiences about life in general and Christian life in particular, a cultural frame of reference or way of viewing the world shaped by those experiences—and a sincere, wholehearted desire to play. The paper serves also as a kind of ball, for it represents the first serve in the game—the first move that calls the players to action, to respond, to engage each other, to match their skills with the cesta against those of the other players. There is, however, a limit to my metaphor (Note: I called it an "analogy," not an "allegory"): whereas in jai alai the object is for one player to overcome another in the end, here the goal is to make each player's skills better; in that sense, all players emerge as winners in the game, not from having bested another but from having been made better by others.

Now for some ground rules. The bulk of what follows consists of my interaction with one passage in Isaiah the content of which relates to the general subject of peace—Isaiah 2:1-5. I say "interaction" rather than the weightier word *exegesis* because the former connotes a quest for both—to borrow the well-known phraseology of Krister Stendahl[1]—what Isaiah *meant* (i.e., the descriptive task) and what it *means* (i.e., the prescriptive task); exegesis, by contrast, seeks only the former. I use "interaction" intentionally and in its root sense: I seek action "inter" (that is, "between") Isaiah's message and myself, between his world and my world, between his theological framework and mine, between his ethical stance and mine. Hence, what follows will be more reflective than exhaustive, more concerned with Isaiah's major thrusts than with exegetical minutiae.

Within the interaction, however, will emerge my hermeneutics—that is, my approach to studying the Bible and to applying it to contemporary life. As my readers interact (i.e., repeatedly return the ball to me for response during the course of this paper), differences of approach, cultural perspective, and practical application will likewise appear. That is exciting, for it signals that the dynamics of learning and growth have been set in motion. So, "Service!"

II

Within the book of Isaiah, the words of 2:1-5 tower above the surrounding landscape in majesty, grandeur, and beauty. A breathtaking monument to prophetic poetic skill, they capture the hopes and dreams of every soldier brutalized by the horrors of war, of every mother bereft of a soldier-son, of every child mercilessly robbed of a father. Modern readers—aware of conflicts today in Latin America, Africa, and the Middle East and perhaps even victims of recent combat themselves—find their soul stirred by these powerful lines to exclaim, "Yes, that's exactly what this bloody world needs!" Indeed, there is no question of the relevance of this text for so-called "modern man"!

Several preliminary matters set the scene for us. The question of authorship must be addressed but need not detain us. While absolute certainty eludes us (doesn't it always!), there is every likelihood that verses 2-4 of this passage come from Isaiah, the prophet of late eighth-century Jerusalem.[2] On

---

1. See Stendahl, "Biblical Theology, Contemporary," *Interpreter's Dictionary of the Bible,* 4 vols., ed. G. A. Buttrick et al. (Nashville: Abingdon Press, 1962), 1: 418-20.

2. For a summary and assessment of the options, see Hans Wildberger, *Jesaja 1-12,* Biblischer Kommentar: Altes Testament, 10, vol. 1 (Neukirchen-Vluyn: Neukirchener Verlag, 1972), pp. 78-80. Wildberger personally favors Isaianic authorship. Limitations of space and focus preclude my treating the much-discussed question of the relationship between this text and its parallel in Micah 4:1-5. Instead, I must refer the reader to discussions found in the commentaries cited in note 3.

the other hand, verse 1 is a superscription that introduces a collection of oracles, a collection that may extend as far as 12:6 (the following verse, 13:1, contains another superscription: "The oracle concerning Babylon which Isaiah . . . saw"). Since it refers to Isaiah in the third person, it most likely stems from the hand of the editor responsible for the collection it heads, probably someone other than Isaiah himself. Further, verse 5 is an exhortation, not a declaration (i.e., a jussive verb as opposed to the converted perfects that dominate vv. 2-4), and, addressed specifically to the "house of Jacob," it draws an application of the text for the hearers. Whether it flows from the pen of Isaiah, the editor behind verse 1, or someone else cannot be determined with certainty. Most scholars attribute it to a late hand.

This, of course, raises the question of what is the proper unit of text for study. I have opted for verses 1-5. The inclusion of verse 1 even though it constitutes an introduction not to verses 2-4 but to a larger collection seems justified. It certainly forms the immediate literary context of our text and hence provides the horizon under which it, as well as the rest of the collection, is to be viewed. One may include it, then, because it performs a dual function: it introduces both the collection and our text. On the other hand, the inclusion of verse 5 is more problematic and has divided the scholarly house.[3] The following points favor the retention of verse 5 with 1-4: (1) although the *kî* of verse 6 seems to connect it syntactically with verse 5, the difference in subject ("we" in verse 5, singular "you" in verse 6) makes that connection more abrupt than one between verse 5 and verses 1-4; (2) the exhortation of verse 5 seems more natural as a conclusion to verses 2-4 than an introduction to verses 6ff.; and (3) the verb *hlk* in verse 5 has linguistic and thematic ties to verses 2-4 (*hlk* occurs three times in v. 3). In sum, verses 1-5 may rightly serve as our context.

Consideration of the text's structure, genre, setting, and intention offers a convenient doorway into the text itself.[4] The following is a structural outline of Isaiah 2:1-5:

I. The Superscription   :1
   A. Basic statement: "The word which Isaiah . . . saw"   :1a
   B. Specification: "concerning Judah and Jerusalem"   :1b

---

3. The following favor the inclusion of v. 5: Wildberger, *Jesaja 1-12*, pp. 75, 87; O. Kaiser, *Isaiah 1-12*, Old Testament Library (Philadelphia: Westminster Press, 1972), pp. 24, 29-30; P. Auvray, *Isaïe 1-39*, Sources Bibliques (Paris: J. Gabalda, 1972), pp. 49, 50; J. Scharbert, *Die Propheten Israels bis 700 v. Chr.* (Köln, 1965), p. 257. Those favoring the attachment of verse 5 to verses 6ff. include B. Duhm, *Das Buch Jesaja*, 5th ed., Handkommentar zum Alten Testament (Göttingen: Vandenhoeck & Ruprecht, 1968), p. 39; E. Young, *The Book of Isaiah*, vol. 1: *Isaiah 1-18* (Grand Rapids: Eerdmans, 1965), p. 114.

4. For a discussion of this approach, see Gene M. Tucker, *Form Criticism of the Old Testament*, Guides to Biblical Scholarship (Philadelphia: Fortress Press, 1971).

II. Vision-Report: A Promise   :2-5
  A. Vision-report itself   :2-4
    1. Content   :2-3a
      a. Specification of time: "in the latter days"   :2aα1
      b. Promise of gentile pilgrimages to Zion   :2aα2-3a
        (1) Twofold statement: exaltation of temple
           mount   :2aα2+β
        (2) Promise itself   :2b-3a
          (a) Basic statement   :2b
          (b) Amplification: quotation of nations'
             call to pilgrimage   :3a
             (i) Report formula   :3aα1
             (ii) Quotation itself   :3aα2-γ
               (A) Basic statement (plus twofold
                  destination)   :3aα2+3
               (B) Twofold purpose   :3aβ
    2. Reason   :3b-4
      a. Twofold basic statement   :3b
        (1) "From Zion instruction issues"   :3bα
        (2) "From Jerusalem (issues) the word of
           Yahweh"   :3bβ
      b. Amplification: promise of Yahweh's
        arbitration   :4
        (1) Twofold promise itself   :4a
          (a) "He will arbitrate between nations" :4aα
          (b) "He will mediate for many peoples" :4aβ
        (2) Threefold result   :4b
          (a) They will reforge weapons into tools :4bα
          (b) A nation will not attack another   :4bβ
          (c) They will not learn warfare anymore :4bγ
  B. Closing exhortation to hearers   :5
    1. Addressee: "house of Jacob"   :5a
    2. Exhortation itself: "Come, let's walk in Yahweh's
      light"   :5b

A brief pause to interpret the structure is now in order. Obviously, the text contains two main parts, the superscription (v. 1) and the vision-report (vv. 2-5). The main focus of attention, the vision-report, itself breaks down into two main sections, the vision-report proper (vv. 2-4) and the exhortation to the hearers (v. 5). This observation is not unimportant for our purpose; on the contrary, verse 5 suggests that the vision was understood to have contemporary meaning—that is, to justify a call to action by the hearers *today,* not just to drop clues about the future. In other words, the vision-report about the future logically evokes a response *today*—a point to

which we shall return later. Finally, I note that the vision-report itself
subdivides into two parts, the promise concerning the future pilgrimages of
nations to Zion (vv. 2-3a) and the reason for those pilgrimages (vv. 3b-4).
Behind this structure lies the main point of the vision-report: in the future
nations will visit Zion because only there is to be found arbitration wise
enough to settle international disputes once and for all. Indeed, according to
the text, that arbitration carries such self-evident fairness and effects such
wholehearted acceptance by the parties concerned that warfare, their only
other recourse, becomes totally unnecessary. Further, the permanent availability of that counsel makes all offensive weaponry obsolete.

The question of the genre of the passage must be answered with references
to both the original vision-report in its own right (vv. 2-4) and to the final
text as a whole (vv. 1-5: I am assuming, of course, that v. 5 comes from an
editor other than Isaiah, although I concede that Isaianic authorship of it is
not an impossibility). Now with respect to the former, the verb hzh in verse 1
is the key to defining verses 2-4 as a vision-report (again, I make an assumption—viz., that if v. 1 was written by someone other than Isaiah, it nevertheless accurately reports how Isaiah received the content of vv. 2-4). As
A. Jepsen has pointed out, the term is an Aramaic loan-word that, with
respect to Old Testament prophets, refers to a vision seen by a prophet at
night and accompanied by an audition that he subsequently writes down as
divine revelation.[5] That its direct object here is not "vision" (cf. Isa. 1:1) but
"word" (cf. the same formulation in Amos 1:1; Mic. 1:1) does not negate
this assumption. The genre, then, of verses 2-4 is that of a vision-report. In
passing, I point out that Isaiah, not Yahweh, is the speaker/writer of this
section (cf. v. 1, the omission of the formula "thus says the LORD" and the
total absence of statements in first-person singular).

The genre of the whole text, by contrast, is more difficult to define. That
it concludes with an exhortation to the hearers (v. 5) suggests the possibility
of some sort of underlying cultic form that combined a vision-report with
such an exhortation. Unfortunately, no ready examples come to mind for
comparison (but cf. Mic. 4:5). It is not impossible that some such form was
part of the ritual repertoire of Israel, but we cannot be sure. On the other
hand, if not Isaianic, verse 5 may in fact be simply the homiletical comment
of an editor and may not presuppose any known cultic pattern at all. In light
of these uncertainties, it seems best, at least for the purpose of this paper, to
accept the text as a piece of written literature and avoid describing its
contents in a technical sense. I will settle for tentatively calling it a prophetic
vision-report with exhortation.

The same uncertainties make determination of the text's setting prob-

5. Jepsen, "ḥazah," in *Theological Dictionary of the Old Testament,* ed. G. Johannes
Botterweck and Helmer Ringgren, trans. D. E. Green (Grand Rapids: Eerdmans,
1980), pp. 283-88.

lematic. A further complication is the fact that verses 2-4 also occur almost verbatim in Micah 4:1-3 with an additional verse (v. 4: "but they shall sit every man under his vine and under his fig tree, and none shall make them afraid; for the mouth of the LORD of hosts has spoken") but no superscription (see also the reversal of Isa. 2:4 in Joel 3:10: "Beat your plowshares into swords, and your pruning hooks into spears"). The resulting lengthy debate as to whether the text originally comes from Isaiah, Micah, preexilic cultic worship, or some other source need not detain us. I myself am inclined to view it as Isaiah's work, but even that assumption gives no guarantee of ascertaining its setting. Whether Isaiah wrote it during Hezekiah's reform to renew and confirm the original promise made to Solomon about the temple (Junker), or as a kind of swan song for only his trusted students (Duhm) cannot be determined. Whatever its original setting, two points need to be made. First, the text was passed on for use (perhaps even in worship) by subsequent generations and for inclusion in a collection of Isaiah's oracles, and so at the very least it has a setting in the community of faith that treasured it and handed it down to us. Second, one important observation emerges from the scholarly discussion of the setting—namely, that in composing the vision-report Isaiah drew on the ancient theological traditions about Zion and applied them to the future.

Finally, the intention of the text must be stated. The key, of course, is the exhortation (v. 5) for the vision-report serves to support it. Plainly, the text intends to exhort God's people to live "in the light of Yahweh." This latter expression occurs only in this text, and commentators tend to see "light" as the symbol of Yahweh's salvific, gracious presence, an important idea in Old Testament cultic literature (Ps. 27:1; 37:6; 56:14; 97:11; 112:4). However, I derive its meaning from the present, more immediate context. The spotlight in verses 3-4 falls upon a particular expression of Yahweh's presence—namely, his instruction, the teaching in which nations will voluntarily choose to "walk" (v. 3) and that silences all disputes (v. 4). Hence, "to walk in Yahweh's light" here means to live in accordance with Yahweh's instruction, presumably as mediated in oral or written form by priests, prophets, and sages. In sum, Isaiah 2:1-5 intends to exhort God's people to live in obedience to his word.

This brings us to our "interaction" with Isaiah's word. My discussion will follow the structural outline included earlier. One is tempted to skip over the superscription (v. 1) quickly, but such an omission robs one of important data. Indeed, the verse provides the perspective, the context, the particular "slant" in which the passage is to be understood. First, we are to understand what follows as a vision seen by Isaiah and then reported by him. Behind it stands a real experience of Isaiah about whose details we can only speculate. Probably such details are omitted in order to focus our thinking squarely on the meaning of the experience rather than its external details. It also underscores the fact that it is the *message* that is important, not the messenger. If a vision has occurred, its content is revelation: it conveys information from Yahweh to his people. The addressees are even specified: "Judah and Jerusalem." This detail is important for our understanding of the passage because it short-circuits a potentially disastrous misunderstanding. Without verse 1, we could not know who the message is being sent to—the nations, Isaiah himself, temple priests, wisdom teachers, Israel as a whole, or some other group. No, the text aims at one target: it says something to God's people as a whole.

What does it say? First, Isaiah sees events in the future—literally, events "in the end/latter part of the days." This eschatological phrase also occurs in other, similar preexilic literature (Gen. 49:1-2; Num. 24:14). Evidently Isaiah believed history ("the days") was headed toward some sort of conclusion. He saw the events of verses 2-4 as taking place either just prior to that end or just after it (the phrase can be rendered "in the end of the days" or "in the latter part of the days"). He does not specify how far in the future one must wait for these events but simply points toward the end of history. It is here that Isaiah, primarily a "forthteller" of imminent divine judgment in his day, also serves as a "foreteller" of the future.

During those days, three main things will occur. The first, the catalyst, is the elevation of Mt. Zion, the temple mount (literally, "mountain of the house of Yahweh," v. 2; cf. similar terms in v. 3; 30:29; Mic. 3:12; Jer. 26:18; Ps. 24:3; et al.) as the highest of the mountains (literally, "as the top {beth essentiae} of the mountains"). Anyone familiar with the topography of Jerusalem immediately recognizes this as a radical change in reality, for the city is surrounded by several mountains taller than Mt. Zion; indeed, the latter is a mere molehill compared to Mt. Hermon northeast of the Sea of Galilee. Isaiah does not explain how this incredible elevation is to happen. We are stuck with the question of whether Isaiah intends us to take his statement literally, spiritually, or both. Since texts about Zion often use hyperbole (i.e., Ps. 48:2: "beautiful in elevation, is the joy of all the earth, Mt. Zion, in the far north" for example), I am inclined to see the same device here.[6] In any case, Isaiah indicates that Zion will be exalted in time, that it will be recognized by the world as the earth's premier religious center. Behind this, of course, lies the common ancient Near Eastern idea that sanctuaries—the places where gods and humans meet—are always built on mountaintops, since the latter constitute the borderline between the heavens (the home of the gods) and earth (the home of humanity). Hence, to be a temple on the highest of those peaks implies a superiority and preeminence

6. Kaiser hears echoes here of the ancient idea that Paradise was located atop the mountain of God (Isaiah 1-12, pp. 26-29). He attributes this event to a "new creation"; that is, just as God initiated world history by firmly founding earth above the chaotic, primeval ocean (Ps. 24:2; 93:1; et al.), so one day he will "create" for the Jerusalem temple a place of unshakable prominence. Kaiser is uncertain, however, whether this event takes place inside or outside of history.

over all others, to be the best place in all the earth to contact the gods. It also suggests that the god who lives there is the highest god. Thus, Isaiah foresees unbelievable future greatness for Zion.

Indeed, according to Isaiah, all the world's nations will testify to the greatness of Zion and its God by "streaming" (the verb *nahar*) to it (v. 2b). The verb is a rare one, used only here and in Micah 4:1 and Jeremiah 51:44, in which it is said that nations flow to mighty Babylon; perhaps it originated denominatively from the noun *nahar*, "river." I doubt that Isaiah here alludes to the "river *(nahar)* whose streams make the city of God glad" (Ps. 46:5, cf. 65:10; Isa. 33:21), as Wildberger suggests.[7] Nevertheless, the word paints a picture: roads to Zion from all directions, swamped with a veritable flood of humanity, become riverbeds for streams of pilgrims flowing there as if drawn by the force of some irresistible magnet. Isaiah is untroubled by the inconsistencies in his metaphors (or does he intend thereby to underscore the miraculous, incomprehensible wonder of the event and to highlight the power of Zion's attraction?): how can "rivers" flow *up* to Zion, the new Mt. Everest? He no doubt draws on a prominent theme in Zion theology but gives it a new twist: the psalms glorify Zion's impregnability from invading nations (Ps. 2:4-6; 46:4-7; 48:4-8; et al.), whereas Isaiah praises Zion's desirability and availability to the nations. Is this vision the forerunner of the one that sees the city of God's residence visited by nations without a temple at all (Rev. 21:22-27)? What a marvelous moment of evangelism: God's people need not go to the nations (Matt. 28:19-20; Acts 1:8; Rev. 14:6-7); the nations will come to them!

And they come not (as in Isaiah's day) as swaggering warriors bent on the city's destruction but as humble pilgrims. Isaiah amplifies verse 2b by quoting their "call to pilgrimage": "Come, let's go up to the mountain of Yahweh, to the house of the God of Jacob" (v. 3). The verb `alah, "to go up," is a technical term for a pilgrimage to a holy place (cf. Exod. 34:24; Jer. 31:6; 1 Sam. 9:9; 11:14; Ps. 122:4; and the *Theologisches Handwörterbuch zum Alten Testament*, 2 vols., ed. E. Jenni and C. Westermann [Munich: Kaiser, 1971-76], 2: 275). That their pilgrimages seek the temple of "the God of Jacob" is significant. Isaiah thereby avoids terms that might be misunderstood—terms of Canaanite origin such as "El Elyon" (Gen. 14:18-22; Ps. 46:5; 78:17 et al.), the title of Jerusalem's earlier god, "the Great King" (Ps. 48:3; 95:3)—to stress the fact tht the nations will come not because Jerusalem is a well-known, ancient holy city with a famous god but because they seek an encounter with the God who has declared his lordship in Israel.[8] They will be pursuing the God whom Israel, particularly in Jerusalem, has known over the years (n.b.: this title occurs only in texts that come from

7. Wildberger, "Die Völkerwallfahrt zum Zion: Jes. II.1-5," *Vetus Testamentum* 7 (1958): 68; and *Jesaja 1-12*, p. 83.

8. So contends Wildberger, *Jesaja 1-12*, p. 85.

Jerusalem—Ps. 20:2; 46:8, 12; 75:10; 76:7; 81:2, 5; 84:9; 94:7). This provides a possible clue to the puzzle of why Jerusalem has received this recognition: may not the nations come because they have heard of some recent events involving Israel and Yahweh, events that have caught the attention of the whole world? In passing I would also note that their statement implies that they will recognize Yahweh's preeminence but not that they will begin to worship him exclusively (i.e., "the God of Jacob" really means *their* god," not *our* god").

Certainly, according to Isaiah's vision, they come for one purpose (note the Hebrew syntax of v. 3aβ + γ): "so that he [Yahweh] may teach us out of his ways, so that we may walk in his paths." Israelite pilgrims sought Jerusalem for many reasons—to bring gifts (Isa. 18:7; 60:11; Hag. 2:7-8; Ps. 96:8), to fulfill a vow (Ps. 76:12), to celebrate festivals, or simply to praise God (Ps. 96:7-8; 122:4). Some came to seek a favorable legal verdict (Deut. 17:8ff.; 1 Kings 8:31-32; Ps. 7:9), particularly in cases beyond human resolution. But the nations will seek out Jerusalem for some sort of "teaching" in accordance with which they want to live. What specifically is this teaching?

The answer is found in Isaiah's next statements (v. 3b). First, he says that they will seek the temple for teaching because—and this is my own translation—"from Zion [emphatic: "and from nowhere else!"] arbitration is issued and Yahweh's verdict from Jerusalem." At first glance, my rendering may appear surprising. It draws, however, on Isaiah's second statement (v. 4a), which I take to be a comment that more precisely defines 3b: "He will [converted perfect] arbitrate (disputes) between nations and will act as a mediator for many nations." There can be no doubt that the formula *šāpāt bēn* refers to the issuance of a judgment that arbitrates a dispute between two parties.[9] If this is correct, the parallel formula *hôkîᵃḥ lᵉ* must mean something similar, hence my translation (for a different meaning, see Isa. 11:3-4). This means that *tôrāh* in v. 3b connotes not "law" in a general sense (and the Mosaic law in particular) or general religious teaching but rather "instruction" in the sense of a specific verdict or judgment as in Deuteronomy 17:11, where the word parallels *mišpāt*, "judgment." That the verdict comes in an oracle mediated by a priest or prophet is implied by the parallel expression "word of Yahweh" common in prophetic literature (Isa. 1:10; 28:13, 14; Jer. 1:2; et al.). I am inclined to think that the formula *yāṣāʿ tôrāh* is analogous to the expression *yāṣāʿ mišpāṭ*, which clearly refers to the issuance of legal verdicts (Hab. 1:4; Ps. 17:1; 109:7) and hence might even be a technical legal expression.

9. See G. Liedke, s.v. "špṭ," in *Theologisches Handwörterburch zum Alten Testament,* 2 vols., ed. E. Jenni and C. Westermann (Munich: Kaiser, 1971-76), 2: 1001; and Wildberger, *Jesaja 1-12,* p. 86. Cf. examples of the formula's usage in Genesis 16:5; 31:53; Exodus 18:16; et al.

In sum, Isaiah says that the nations will seek Zion because there Yahweh arbitrates international disputes through oracles via his ministers. Those oracles, however, are "instruction" the correctness of which the nations recognize to such a degree that they obey it long after the pilgrimage to Zion is over. When the court of Judge Yahweh is in session, the school of Professor Yahweh is as well. The nations want both arbitration and education from him. It is, therefore, incorrect to interpret the text as stressing the wise instruction of Yahweh over against his role as judicial arbitrator.[10] To be sure, Yahweh is the wise king, but in this text his judicial mediation constitutes his teaching.

And what incredible results follow international compliance with Yahweh's arbitration! What a stunning climax to this vision! Isaiah sees something unbelievable—nations beating their swords and spears to pieces (Heb. *kittēt,* "to break in pieces, crush," 2 Kings 18:4; Zech. 11:6; 2 Chron. 34:7) and then reforging them into ploughshares and pruning hooks (v. 4b). Obviously, Yahweh's mediation and teaching have rendered international warfare, the other recourse practiced by nations, permanently obsolete—and its weaponry, too. Indeed, the disarmament is not gradual; not even a residual police force or reserve army is left for use in emergencies, not even so much as a list of potential draftees or stockpile of stored weapons. No, Isaiah sees a complete, total, final disarmament, and in so doing again gives a new twist to traditional Zion theology. Psalm 46:10, for example, assured Zion of deliverance from invaders by boldly proclaiming "He [Yahweh] makes wars to cease to the ends of the earth; he breaks the bow, and shatters the spear, he burns the chariots with fire!" But Isaiah foresees no bloody divine Blitzkrieg but a bloodless, peaceful disarmament voluntarily carried out by the nations themselves.

But more than simple disarmament is involved. Ancient warfare required farmers to leave their fields for combat and thus threatened not only their lives but their livelihood. Here military material is reforged from tools of destruction into tools of production. International resources are rechanneled from warfare into agriculture, an enterprise that promotes life, blessing, and happiness. Indeed, for Israel there was no greater symbol of tranquility— indeed, it borders on the proverbial—than that a man be able, without fear at all, "to sit under his vine and under his fig tree" (Mic. 4:4; 1 Kings 4:25; Zech. 3:10). According to Genesis 2, humankind was created to farm, peacefully working fields, sculpting furrows of fruitfulness in the rich earth with ploughshares, lopping off fruitless branches from trees and vines with pruning hooks. For Isaiah that is what life is to be—and what it will be "in the latter days."

10. Contrary to the view J. Jensen expresses in *The Use of tôrâ by Isaiah,* Catholic Biblical Quarterly Monograph Series, no. 3 (Washington: Catholic Biblical Association of America, 1973), pp. 84-95.

In essence, Isaiah foresees a situation similar to that before the catastrophe of Genesis 3 and its resulting disruption of human society (i.e., the murder of Abel by Cain, Gen. 4; the causes of the flood, Gen. 6:5-6, 11-13). Humankind once again returns to farming as in the Garden of Eden. I hesitate, however, to see presupposed here an actual "new creation" situation, although Isaiah may very well have had that in mind.[11] The miraculous elevation of Zion may imply a new created order, but there's little else in the text to confirm that possibility (although see Isa. 11:6-9). The sudden international harmony also seems to imply changes in human nature (i.e., the loss of man's sinfulness which sparks aggression and violence, a new freedom to choose the paths of peace, etc.), but again confirming textual evidence is lacking. The most I can say is that Isaiah assumes both a continuity and a discontinuity with the present historical order—continuity in that he stresses no radical break between then and now, and discontinuity in that at the same time he forsees a great change happening between now and then.

One thing is certain, however. The text concludes with an exhortation to the hearers: "O house of Jacob, let us walk in the light of Yahweh" (v. 5). I have already pointed out that this verse, whether written by Isaiah himself or by someone else, clearly draws an application for the hearers' *present* day from the vision of the latter days. In other words, the vision-report logically implies a response, an application of the vision's meaning in contemporary conduct. The glimpse of the future evokes more than a simple "Wow! that's amazing!" or even a more orthodox "Praise the Lord!" Rather, Israel is to live (i.e., "walk") a certain way after hearing Isaiah's vision-report.

The addressee is the "house of Jacob," no doubt a term corresponding to "God of Jacob" (v. 3). This correspondence hints at a special, close familial relationship between Jacob's clans and his God (one thinks of the idea of the clan and god typical of the patriarchal period). The term is commonly used in Isaiah (which contains nine of its twenty-one total occurrences, Isa. 2:6; 8:17; 10:20; 14:1; 29:22; 46:3; 48:1; 58:1). Isaiah's contemporaries Amos and Micah also knew the term (Amos 3:13; 9:8; Mic. 2:7; 3:9). While in many cases it serves simply as a term for Israel or Judah as a whole, in others it clearly is associated with the events surrounding the entrance to and exodus from Egypt (Gen. 46:27; Exod. 19:3; Isa. 14:1; 46:3; Jer. 2:4; Ezek. 20:5; Ps. 114:1; cf. Isa. 29:22). It was, after all, the "house of Jacob"—then known as the "sons of Israel"—who experienced that great event. All this suggests that this term, perhaps intentionally selected for this context, alludes to that great event in which Israel paradigmatically came to know the marvelous power of its clan God. It implicitly reminds the hearers of Yahweh's past mighty acts on Israel's behalf and, hence, appeals to the nation's feeling of indebtedness to God.

11. Contrary to the view of Kaiser in *Isaiah 1-12*, pp. 26-29.

But the appeal is for Israel to walk in Yahweh's "light." Since this expression occurs only here, one must seek its meaning either in the Old Testament concept of light or in the immediate context. Wildberger opts for the former approach and sees light here as a symbol of Yahweh's salvific, gracious presence, especially as experienced in the Jerusalem cult. [12] In Isaiah 10:17 and 60:1 Yahweh is called "Israel's light." I am, however, inclined to interpret the phrase in terms of the present context. Here one senses Yahweh's presence in a specific way—namely, through his "instruction," the teaching one gains about how to live from the collection of his judicial verdicts concerning nations. The idea of "instruction" may also in this case encompass the other oracles of God known to the hearers—priestly legal traditions, the words of prophets (including Isaiah), and Israelite wisdom. It may include all that one can learn about "Yahweh's ways" at the temple (v. 3a). But there is a particular interest apparent here in those "ways" that enable nations which normally vie militarily to get along with each other peacefully. Those ways are rooted in the perfect justice of Yahweh the Creator, who built the world on a foundation of justice so that all nations might enjoy the blessing and prosperity—the šalôm—that he intended. To practice injustice is to upset the created world order, to unleash the powers of chaos in the world, to introduce disorder into an ordered world. In sum, the "light of Yahweh" here refers at least to his oracles concerning international relations (e.g., that in Amos 1-2) and most likely to all his oracles.

Why, however, should Israel conduct itself along those lines? That is, what is the precise connection between the future pilgrimages of the nations and life in Jerusalem centuries before them? The object of verse 5 seems to be twofold. First, it seeks to shame Israel into facing its obligation to submit to Yahweh's lordship. Simply put, the argument runs along the following lines: "If even the nations who have not, like us, enjoyed the benefits of long years of experience with Yahweh's ways will one day recognize them as right, how much more so we, his own people! If they 'walk' in them (v. 3a), how much more should we!" Second, it confronts Israel with its role as a "light to the nations" in anticipation of those future days. This argument says: "If we are one day to mediate Yahweh's oracles to the world, why not do so *now* by simply following them ourselves?" In short, the exhortation follows the vision with a call to obey what Yahweh has taught them over their years of experience with him, particularly in the area of just relationships. And if one asks where one can learn Yahweh's "instruction" about such things, the obvious immediate answer is to study the teachings of the prophet Isaiah!

Yet one more point must be stressed. If eventually Israel is to be the vehicle (through priests, prophets, and sages) by which Yahweh will teach the nations his ways (v. 3), and if the ultimate result of that future instruc-

---

12. See Wildberger, *Jesaja 1-12*, pp. 85-86; he cites Psalms 37:6; 97:11; and 112:4.

tion is to be international peace (v. 4), and if Israel is called to conduct itself today in light of those two premises, then the implication is clear: Israel must not only obey Yahweh itself today but must also function as a professor of peace among the nations today. That is part of the nation's "walk in Yahweh's ways." It is to teach the nations about the just relationships that promote peace because they conform to the underlying created order of justice.

III

All that I have said to this point has had to do with what the text meant to Isaiah and his earlier hearers. Now I ask a question that is more important to us: What does the text mean today? Here we approach a veritable minefield of difficulties. We must, for example, maneuver from the social context of the theocracy of Israel to our own political and religious context, be it a democracy, monarchy, totalitarian dictatorship, socialistic state, or political hybrid. We must, likewise, steer a course around our own prejudices (we may well be tempted to use the text to reinforce our own preconceptions or to justify our own lifestyles), and those of us who are writers and speakers must also work to avoid catering to the prejudices of our audience (we may well be tempted to "play to the galleries" by reinforcing their biases). Using Anthony Thiselton's metaphor, we might say that it is no easy task to proceed from the horizon of the text to the the horizon of the interpreter. [13]

A summary of my interpretation of Isaiah 2:1-5 is the starting point. Isaiah in a vision sees one aspect of what is to transpire "in the latter days." This era is in the future, either at the end of history as we know it or just after its conclusion. The first event, the catalyst for everything that follows, is the exaltation of Zion—that is, some unspecified event that catches the attention of the world and elevates Zion in its eyes as the holy place par excellence. I make an assumption here that is crucial to the implications I wish to draw: Isaiah understands this event to be an action of Yahweh, not of human beings, and probably some great final future act of salvation. What catches the world's eye in the event is this: it shows Yahweh to be the judge par excellence, the wisest, fairest arbiter of thorny disputes. So impressive is his wisdom that the nations—and this is the next event—humbly come to Jerusalem and voluntarily submit their outstanding conflicts to his arbitration. Indeed, they view their pilgrimage as enrollment in a course in which they may learn his teachings.

Finally, so available and persuasive is Yahweh's arbitration that the

13. Thiselton, *The Two Horizons: New Testament Hermeneutics and Philosophical Description with Special Reference to Heidegger, Bultmann, Gadamer, and Wittgenstein* (Grand Rapids: Eerdmans, 1980).

nations on their own reforge their weapons into agricultural tools, forever foreswear warfare as a solution to conflicts, and no longer learn about combat at all. An era of ideal international peace reigns. That is not the end of the matter, however, for the text backtracks from the future to the present and exhorts hearers to conduct themselves accordingly. To be specific, they are to obey all that Yahweh has taught them, particularly but not exclusively in the area of justice, and to pass on Yahweh's instruction to the nations. The primary content of this teaching is justice that promotes healthy, beneficial relationships.

Now to apply this text, I build a bridge by suggesting a contemporary framework analogous to that of the Isaianic context. I presume, of course, that my readers are Christians who accept the New Testament as the revelatory successor to Isaiah and his Old Testament scriptural colleagues. What follows, then, are the pillars of my bridge. First, today Isaiah's hearers are Christians, the new people of God, the church. The "house of Jesus" is the descendant of the "house of Jacob" and understands itself as the addressee of the exhortation (v. 5). Second, the church is the "new temple" (see 1 Cor. 3:16; 2 Cor. 6:16; Eph. 2:21; cf. 1 Pet. 2:5), the successor to the Jerusalem temple. Any pilgrimages of inquiring nations today must be directed to the church, which is, of course, not centrally located on one specific mountaintop but dispersed throughout the world in countless places and in countless external forms. Third, the church has experienced the exaltation of God through Christ's death and resurrection; that is, it has personally participated in God's decisive, comprehensive, and final (judicial!) act of salvation, that mediated by Jesus. Further, the church has itself experienced the end of war: it has been reconciled with God, and its Jew and Gentile members have been reconciled with each other (2 Cor. 5; Eph. 2). Indeed, "the latter days" are here right now; according to the Gospels they began with the ministry of Jesus. At the same time, however, what Isaiah saw as a single totality—the exaltation of Zion, the recognition of its preeminence by the nations, the arbitration of Yahweh, the ideal era of peace—the church understands to be spread over millennia and made up of further subphases—the first advent of Messiah, the age of the church, the second and final advent of Messiah, the last judgment of all people at the "Great White Throne," the creation of the new heavens and earth.

In addition, as the new temple, the church is the mediator of the oracles of God, the teacher of God's instruction (both Old and New Testaments). Its ministry is itinerant, however, for the Lord has commanded his church to disperse among the nations, spread his teaching, and summon humankind to submit to his Lordship (Matt. 28:19-20; Acts 1:8). The church calls men and women to enjoy "peace with God" (Rom. 5:1) and the "peace of Christ" (Col. 3:15). These are only a foretaste of the final, climactic, unending reign of the "prince of peace" who will return to rule at the end of this present age.

What, then, does it mean for the church to "walk in the light of Yahweh" today? I offer the following reflections. First, the temple must be spruced up, by which I mean that the church must undergo a housecleaning that will restore its power to attract the nations. Jesus taught that the identification card of his followers is their love for each other (John 13:35). Unfortunately, the temple that Jesus reconciled to God now seems to have fallen into disrepair, its walls dirtied by ecclesiastical divisions, its floors unswept of petty doctrinal squabbles. It is hardly the prime example of reconciliation that Jesus intended it to be. Instead, its various factions seem more interested in outdoing their competitors—precisely the way the rest of the world operates—than in offering the world a satisfactory alternative. Worse yet, the temple looks like any other building on the block. It dresses like its neighbors and oppresses like its neighbors. The few repairs that have been done amount to little more than a facade—temporary, token attempts at reconciliation, flashy programs of ecumenism to attract the outsider, slick pronouncements on world problems.

Such things must, like dusty floors and cobwebbed corners, be swept out. The church must reforge its ecclesiastical swords into plowshares of reconciliation, its doctrinal spears into pruning hooks of reunification. It must demonstrate in every corner of the world that men and women can and do live in peace because they know that inner "peace of God which passes all understanding" (Phil. 4:7). The church itself must be the prime example in the way its members care for each other—and thereby recapture the magnetism to attract the attention of a world that yearns desperately for just that kind of peace.

The temple must be spruced up by a spiritual revitalization. By this I mean a recovery of that simple, childlike conviction that God is powerfully at work in the life of the church today— that God's mighty acts of salvation are happening today. The church's testimony to them must be contemporary; it must bear witness to changed lives and healed homes right in its own neighborhoods. There must be a spring in its step, an excitement in its voice, a joy on its face because it is experiencing the reality of God right here and now. The world must see that dynamic life throbs within its breast and that the Christian faith does make a difference. The recovery of this dynamic dimension in the church will cause the world to take notice, to take it seriously, to seek its counsel, to consider its claims thoughtfully, and hopefully to appropriate God's salvation for itself. In my judgment, it is this spiritual vitality that, in part, will draw all nations to the church and thus begin to bring to pass today what Isaiah foresaw.

Second, the temple must be visible to the world. The nations must be able to look up and see it virtually everywhere. It no longer can afford the luxury of isolation from the world—as if it were built in some obscure, inaccessible canyon safely out of view rather than being a "city set on a hill which cannot be hid" (Matt. 5:14). It must be in the thick of things, its members involved in the rough-and-tumble of daily life yet known for their loving devotion to their Lord and their concern for other people. And the temple must not look like any other building. Its architecture—that is, its way of life—must be unique, eye-catching, appealing, showing forth the beauty of a building dedicated not to self-preservation but to self-giving on behalf of the needy, the oppressed, the disenfranchised, the lost. This is the beauty that sets the temple apart from the cold, lifeless tombs around it. That is the beauty that will magnetically draw the nations to it.

But most important, the church's reputation must be that not only of a reconciled community but of a repository of the oracles of God. The rest of the world feels its way through life's darkness guided only by the hunches and opinions of others as blind as themselves. The church, by contrast, must. earn the reputation as the place where God's clear, certain light shines, where his truth illumines the blackness, giving hope to the despairing. It must constantly affirm that the Bible represents the authoritative oracles of God, the only certain basis for daily life and personal belief, the only sure guide through the disastrous cliffs and pitfalls that unenlightened human reason confidently offers—the beguiling "way that seems right to a man" but whose end is "the way of death" (Prov. 14:12). The church's reputation, that magnet that draws the nations to it, must be that of a people of conviction and commitment—a people who know right from wrong, truth from error, reality from illusion, and are unafraid to state their convictions because they are backed by the oracles of God.

At the same time, the church's reputation must be won by practical actions that substantiate its words. Just as it demonstrates the reconciliation offered by the gospel in the loving relationships between its members, so it confirms its possession of the oracles of God when its conforms to its teachings. It not only teaches divine *torah,* it lives it. To borrow from a well-known Spanish proverb, with the church "no hay gran trecho entre el dicho y el hecho" ("There's no great wait between the saying and the doing"). Granting the Bible's complexity of interpretation and application (otherwise conferences such as this one would be unnecessary!), the church seeks a consistency between its doctrinal affirmations and its daily life. The reason is simple: the world is ultimately pragmatic. Long weary and incurably skeptical of elaborate religious claims, the world will not be convinced that the church has the oracles of God unless it sees those oracles applied and working. Its curiosity will not be pricked by anything other than witnessing for itself the truth of God lived out in everyday clothes on the Main Street of life. Only then will the world accept the Bible as God's word and examine its claims.

All this, of course, presupposes a central role for the church in God's plan. That is a central implication of Isaiah's vision. Just as the nations make pilgrimages to the temple because God may be met there, so the church is the means for the nations to meet him today. This bestows on the church an importance that is out of fashion today. As a seminary professor, I frequently

have occasion to discuss with students their experiences in local congregations. Unfortunately, many such experiences are negative. Though I attribute much of their criticism to the inevitable disappointments that
idealistic youth will encounter, I also note a good deal of healthy, valid
criticism. They bemoan, as I do, the institutionalization of the church.
What Jesus gave birth to as a living organism has grown up to be an
organization. The priority of concern for people, whether in the church's
own neighborhood or in the larger world, has lost ground to the priority of
maintaining the organization. Committees steal valuable time from relationships, buildings rob money from charity, programs mortgage meaningful long-term relationships for short-term statistical gains. The church
expends most of its resources, both human and monetary, simply to keep
itself going. Such is the complaint psalm frequently sung in my office—and
I must admit that I have written a few psalms of my own!

Nevertheless, Paul suggests that whatever its faults and blemishes, the
church is still the "bride of Christ"—the organism for which Jesus himself
voluntarily surrendered his own life (Eph. 5:21). Christians today may wish
that Christ would choose another bride—a dynamic, effective para-church
organization, for example—and I admit to frequent embarrassment at the
behavior of Christ's favorite. But my preferences must fall before Christ's.
The desire for a different sort of church grows out of an implicit assumption
that it is only through the church that Jesus has chosen to touch the world.
This implies, further, an indictment of all attempts to find an alternative to
the church. Isaiah's vision calls us not to abandon the church but to beautify
it, to make it as biblical as possible, and thus to make its beauty a clear,
unmistakable reflection of the splendor of God himself.

There is one more major implication to be drawn—indeed, it is the heart
and climax of Isaiah's vision. For the prophet the temple, exalted as the
dwelling place of the wisest monarch available, was the place where nations
found arbitration. That arbitration was the key to international peace. If the
church has succeeded the temple as the focal point of meeting God today,
then Isaiah's vision proposes a surprising yet exciting role for it: it is to be
God's administrator of international justice—in fact, "professor of divine
international justice" as well. Simply put, the church is responsible for
instructing the nations in God's international law.

Behind this stand key biblical assumptions that Isaiah himself held but
that many Christians today seem to have forgotten. First, Isaiah assumes that
God is the master of human history, the one whose hands control the
destinies of nations (Amos. 9:7; Isa. 7:18-20; et al.). As cosmic Lord, he is
also the cosmic Judge who holds nations accountable to his standards of
justice (Amos 2-3). Second, Isaiah assumes that the purpose of God's justice—the justice that all nations are to implement—is to bless God's creation and to promote šalōm within it. This means that justice is not simply a
set of abstract principles scarcely connected to daily life or a long list of

specific rules that stifle daily life with overbearing, burdensome *don'ts*. Neither is it what any given social or political group elects as right or any given elite forcibly imposes upon its subjects. Rather, it is the foundation of the world's underlying cosmic order—as much a part of the warp and woof of creation as the law of gravity or the second law of thermodynamics. Injustice, then, represents a self-destructive, suicidal disruption of that order, for God himself oversees his creation and maintains that order. It is only a matter of time before God, moved by the cry of the oppressed, decisively intervenes to restore order.

Now, of course, the question is how the church can carry out this task of administering/professing justice. The answer depends upon the situation in which the church finds itself. When it has freedom to speak and to participate politically, it may lift its voice in favor of justice before the general populace or governing bodies. Where possible, it may place members in key civil and military positions to wield influence over decisions that touch upon justice. It may even, by virtue of its good reputation, be called upon in reality to mediate between warring factions and instruct both parties in applicable divine truth. On the other hand, in dictatorships the church may have to adopt other methods—sometimes quiet civil disobedience, other times overt public protest. In any case, the Bible itself can be prayerfully consulted regarding the proper method for each situation. With confidence the church may in one situation provide from among its ranks a Joseph or an Esther, in another prayerfully raise its laments to God for a new Moses.

What, then, is the "instruction" to be given to the nations? What topics dominate the syllabus? The following offers only the beginnings of a list of themes drawn principally from Isaiah. First, the church must expose the delusion of national self-sufficiency. Nations are inclined to be intoxicated with their own great achievements. Heady with economic, military, or political success, they soon consider themselves self-sufficient, dependent upon no one, responsible to no one. The church dispels that delusion by reminding them of ancient Assyria. Though a mighty empire, from Isaiah's point of view Assyria was merely a tool in Yahweh's hand (Isa. 10:5), a bee summoned with a whistle (7:18), a razor wielded by the divine barber (7:20). Its greatness is entirely a gift of God; by itself it has no power to provide the air it needs to breathe or the food it needs to survive. These gifts come from God.

The church must also burst all bubbles of national arrogance. To the contrary, it must instruct nations of their accountability before God. Again, Assyria is a case in point. According to Isaiah, when that nation exceeded its divine mandate to punish Israel, when it boasted of its might, when it even blasphemed the name of Yahweh himself (Isa. 10:7-15; 37:4-10, 13-20), it sealed its own doom. The church points to the still visible ruins of Nineveh and Asshur, Assyria's capital cities, and warns nations that they will be held accountable by God for their actions. Arrogance is no match against the fury of divine judgment (Isa. 10:16-19). All abuse of power faces certain punishment.

Finally, by what standard are nations judged? Here the church instructs the world on several points. First, it refutes the belief that might makes right. Mighty nations tend to make their own rules, to define justice on their own terms. What is just becomes what suits their selfish ends—whatever their might can successfully impose on others. Justice is debased into self-centeredness. The church rebuts that God, not human beings however mighty, is the source and definition of justice. Citing the oracles of God, the church condemns nations for their crimes and calls them to restore justice. And it also teaches the ultimate criterion of justice: how well the poor and powerless fare. This is the implication of Isaiah 11:1-9, the well-known "pearl of Hebrew poetry"[14] that promises the advent of a new Davidic ruler whose reign will bring such peace that natural enemies (lions and lambs, children and snakes) will safely eat and play together. Two observations undergird this point. First, the future king's reign specifically aims at bringing justice to the earth's poor and meek (v. 4). Second, the result of that aim is the so-called "Peaceable Kingdom" captured so beautifully by the music of Benjamin Britten and the painting by Quaker Edward Hicks: "The wolf shall dwell with the lamb, and the leopard shall lie down with the kid, and the calf and the lion and the fatling together, and a little child shall lead them" (v. 6).

Now the text presumes a connection between these two observations. The removal of injustices against the poor produces the peace. This means that the reverse is true: the practice of injustice produces war. The implication is that the ideal of justice—its ultimate but perhaps not sole criterion—is its care for the poor. By virtue of their wealth and power, the rich need no care; they can care for themselves. The poor, by contrast, lack the means to do so and must be protected by justice from abuse. By pointing nations to the crux of justice, however, the church puts its finger on a major cause of war and appeals to nations to observe justice. In so doing, it removes the very cause of war and serves as a peacemaker.

Indeed, what Isaiah's vision offers is a strategy for the promotion of world peace. I would call it "world peace through justice." This strategy aims to promote peace by removing the cause of war—injustice. This strategy supercedes all others, for it seeks not merely to ameliorate the evil effects of war or to limit the means by which war is conducted but rather to foster the blessing of peace by seeking to extirpate war's root cause. It offers the only ultimate, lasting solution, particularly when the proclamation of the gospel of peace with God accompanies such efforts.

One should not be too surprised at this unusual role in which Isaiah casts the church. Other biblical texts foresee a similar role for the church. It was

14. The phrase is that of Wildberger, *Jesaja 1-12,* p. 441.

none less than the Lord himself who told his disciples that they would one day sit on thrones judging the twelve tribes of Israel (Matt. 19:28). Likewise, another visionary, the Apostle John, glimpsed God's people reigning (and presumably judging) with Christ during the latter's thousand-year reign (Rev. 20:4, 6), however one interprets that text. Both concur with Isaiah that the church plays a crucial role in the rule of God as the administrator (and, therefore, teacher) of his justice. One could also say that, just as the powers and blessings of the future kingdom of God are present among his people today, so the work of the church in the present world anticipates its role in that future kingdom. Its work for justice, then, is activity on behalf of nothing less than the kingdom of God itself.

IV

I come to the end of my construction project—and what a long project it has been! The wall I have raised before the reader now stands—defective, it is true, in a thousand ways and liable to a myriad of alterations. I have formed it from my own interaction with Isaiah. Its bricks and mortar belong both to Isaiah and me. I hope that my part and his congeal well together. So, with ambivalent feelings of both excitement and fear, having served my humble ball against the wall of my own making, I turn to await the returns of my colleagues. So, *"Ándele! Ál juego!"*

2.2.3

Report by Robert Hubbard

Several things emerged from our discussions with respect to the text of Isaiah 2. There was some initial reaction to the text with regard to the question of Mount Zion, its meaning in the text and its implications for our age. Does the text suggest that sacrifice was still going on at the time it was written? Does it imply kingship in some sense? What is the role of the temple being suggested here? Is it triumphalistic? We wrestled not only with the definition of the temple in the text but also with contemporary misreadings, the dispensationalist view, the Zionist use of the text, and the way it is used by millenarians. From this arose an interesting discussion of the implications of this whole idea for witness to Islam. If this text is linked to Zion, does it not have an ethnocentrist nature that would pose a problem for those who are involved in dialogues with Islam, as at least one of our members has been? We also discussed the contrasting text in Isaiah 19, which refers to the three peoples of God—namely, Egypt, Syria, and Babylon.

We wrestled with the canonical nature of the text, with the presence of both hope and judgment in the same context, which some contemporary analysts consider problematic. I suggested, and there seemed to be some group consensus, that there is an eschatological pattern evident in the text in this regard, that the closely related hope and judgment are two phases of the same process. But reading the text canonically does raise such questions as the meaning of this relationship of judgment and hope and also the significance of the exhortations in the early chapters of Isaiah—"Come, let us reason together, says the Lord." One conclusion that we did draw from the canonical shape of the text is that it seems to assume both the affirmation and the condemnation of Judah—that is, there is an affirmation that Judah will have a special role in the future but also that that special role will constitute a condemnation or at least an exhortation to do what God wants. A further implication is that Israel has a place, but it's not the only place within God's plan. Israel is not the only nation with whom God is dealing.

We did reach tentative conclusions in our discussion of several issues.

First of all, the text of Isaiah 2 pictures the church as a witness or an educator for peace. It was suggested that Matthew 18—where Christ uses the terminology of authority (binding and loosening) concerning the work of the apostles—is relevant in this regard. He is talking about conflict resolution, to use a modern term. Perhaps the Isaiah passage and Christ's teaching are indications of a possible role for the church in peacemaking. Another issue, related to the first, is that the text seems to assume a role of both teaching and arbitration for Judah in the present or in the future. We made the assumption that the church has the same role since the *eschaton* has come, in Christ. This raised the question of what the relationship between the arbitration and teaching functions of the church should be. With respect to arbitration, it was noted that the Christian Legal Society in North America has begun to offer its services for settling disputes. It is more difficult to determine what it means to teach the nations. Someone remarked that some nations would appear to be easier to teach than others. Sometimes it's easier to teach those who are most different from us than it is to teach those who draw from the same religious tradition we do. What does one do about that? But the main question with which we have to deal is what it means for the church today to teach the nations specifically about peace.

2.2.4

Final Report from Isaiah Group

The broad subject "Peace Passages in Isaiah" occupied the attention of this study group. Papers by Robert Hubbard and Samuel Pagán primed the pump for subsequent discussions. Although the latter paper was made available only late in the conference, group members readily concurred with its main thesis that the Hebrew term *shalom* in Isaiah 54:11-17 is a dynamic term of relationship based upon justice.

For the most part, group discussion focused on Robert Hubbard's paper on Isaiah 2:1-5. In general, the group accepted the paper's main thrust but raised questions concerning certain details about the interpretation of the biblical text. For example, does the reference to the temple imply that in the "latter days" sacrifice continues or is presumed to be restored? Does it also suggest the rule of a king, either earthly or messianic? Further, do the nations come to Zion voluntarily, or is some sort of compulsion assumed? What does the word *torah* refer to (i.e., to the whole Pentateuch, to the law of Moses, only to laws touching international relations, to an oracle of Yahweh adjudicating a specific dispute, to a collection of oracles, etc.)? How does this text relate to the picture in Isaiah 19:16-25, which forsees Egypt and Assyria worshiping Yahweh with a status equal to that of Israel? Isaiah 2 obviously assumes a superior status for Israel.

In the course of the discussion, certain issues emerged as central. First, one must set aside certain common and potentially dangerous misconceptions conjured up by the image of Mt. Zion. The interpretation of the image by certain evangelical millennial movements comes readily to mind. From this image, for example, dispensationalists forecast an exclusive role for the political entity Israel in the last days and, hence, applaud the restoration of the modern Jewish state in Palestine and support Israel's territorial claims over against the rights of Palestinian Arabs. Among other evangelicals, the simple equation of Zion with the church has spawned an evangelical triumphalism that has arrogantly assumed that the special status of the church gives it a license to commit all kinds of abuses—allegedly on behalf of the kingdom of God. One glaring, disastrous result of this misunderstanding of

Zion is the wall of ethnocentrism that has alienated the Islamic world from peace with Israel and openness to the gospel. Both Isaiah 2 and 19, however, are indictments against such arrogant triumphalism. Isaiah 19 summons the church to overcome its ethnocentrism, and Isaiah 2 both affirms and condemns Judah, indicating that although it has a place in God's plan, it does not have the only place.

Second, the role of the church as "educator for peace" implied by Isaiah 2 links thematically with several teachings of Jesus. The Great Commission (Matt. 28:19-20) includes the teaching of nations as part of the church's missionary task. When Jesus grants the church the authority to "bind" and "loose" matters (Matt. 16:19), he uses Rabbinic terms that refer to the settlement of disputes. This implies that the settlement of disputes is part of the church's divinely given role in the world. Further, his teaching about the proper way to settle a dispute with a fellow believer (Matt. 18:15-20) portrays a new style of conflict resolution to be practiced by his followers. The question, of course, is how the church is to implement this teaching both in local and international arenas. Certainly the church ought to prod the major nations to pursue better relationships rather than the relentless buildup of arms.

Third, the fact that the biblical canon proclaims both judgment and hope assumes a connection between the two. It describes both a vision of peaceful utopia and the path of repentance that leads to it. Behind this is the dynamic that peace and justice are intimately interrelated. Injustice creates conflicts; justice promotes peace. The question, however, is how the church is to address the issue of injustice in a given context. One approach is to look for some concern shared by the conflicting parties and guide them toward cooperation in resolving the situation. Another is to proclaim the judgment of God on the injustice involved and to call for repentance. In this case, the parables of Jesus serve as a useful bridge to those outside the church. They teach the relevant issues in a pointed yet appealing way. Whatever the case, is it absolutely essential that the church exhibit sensitivity to people even at the risk of rendering itself vulnerable to abuse. It must treat all parties as persons, not things; it must set self-protectiveness aside.

Fourth, effective peacemaking requires an understanding of the relationship between the "old age" (i.e., the secular world system) and the "new age" (i.e., the kingdom of God present in the church). The two coexist today, but how do members of the new age relate to members of the old age? This hermeneutical question has, of course, long confronted the church. How the church defines this relationship, however, determines how it goes about its peacemaking task. Every so-called "peace movement" has worked out its own definition, and all future attempts of the church to work for peace will rest upon similar definitions.

Fifth, another crucial question concerns what it means to "teach the nations." Experience shows that it is easier for the church to teach nations that have different religious traditions than it is to teach those with the same tradition. Christian ministry among Muslims and Jews has been exceedingly difficult compared with, say, that among animists in Africa. One approach to such nations is to urge them to reach beyond the idea of Christianity as a competing "religion" to a larger reality—the reality of the kingdom of God and the shalom it intends to give the world. An appeal to shared concepts (faith in God, obedience, etc.) contributes toward the realization of that shalom in the world.

Sixth, we must work to define the relationship between "teaching" and "arbitration." Are these alternative functions of the church, or do they somehow complement each other? Is adjudication a form of teaching? One contemporary example of adjudication is the arbitration service provided by the Christian Legal Society in the United States, which offers a means for resolving conflicts, particularly among Christians, outside of the courtroom. It offers a model for the church's ministry of reconciliation in other contexts as well and provides a way for the church to make Isaiah's vision of peace a reality.

Finally, the group consensus was that Isaiah's vision excluded the use of modern nuclear arms.

Members of the Magnificat Study Group

George Cummings
Pablo Deiros
David Scholer
David Lowes Watson
Douglas Webster
C. Hugo Zorrilla

2.3.1

The Magnificat (Luke 1:46-55): Reflections on its Hermeneutical History

DAVID M. SCHOLER

I

The purpose of this brief study is (1) to provide a selective, schematized history of the exegesis of the Magnificat (Luke 1:46-55) by North American and British New Testament scholars in the twentieth century and (2) to draw from this particular history of exegesis certain observations about the hermeneutical enterprise for Lukan and New Testament study within the Church.[1]

II

In the first half of the twentieth century (1900-1950) North American and British commentaries on Luke treated the Magnificat with a view to

1. The history of exegesis provided here is indeed selective, but is representative and fair to the history/development of scholarship. Although no attempt has been made to cover the exegetical history of other "Western" communities of scholarship, both Fr. Robert J. Karris, O.F.M., a noted Lukan scholar in our time, and I agree that what is developed in this paper would be true for the pattern of Lukan scholarship in France, Germany, Belgium, Spain, and probably other European countries. This selective history of exegesis has not attempted to include, however, the internal Roman Catholic discussions of the Magnificat related to the person and place of Mary in the history of redemption.

210

particular historical-critical questions and with virtually no attention to issues of its place in Lukan theology or to what could be termed its sociological issues.[2]

The primary questions on the Magnificat treated in this fifty-year period (apart from numerous grammatical, lexical, and historical notes) deal with such matters as the historical value of the Magnificat, the parallels to the Magnificat in the Old Testament (especially Hannah's prayer in 1 Sam. 2:1-10), and the textual problem of Luke 1:46 (whether the original text specifies or implies Mary or Elizabeth). The textual question was widely debated during this period in North Amerian, British, and European scholarship.[3]

W. Manson does make one comment that departs from the agenda I have described:

> redemption is envisaged as a drastic revolution by which the mighty are dethroned, the rich dispossessed, and the proud humiliated. This language, though it is not to be taken literally but in a spiritual sense, shows how intimately in Judaic Christianity the coming of Christ still stirred the chords of national hope.[4]

Note especially the literal/spiritual dichotomy in his comment.

III

In the next quarter century (1951-74) the basic patterns that prevailed from 1900 to 1950 continued to predominate, although some other issues and emphases developed as well. Major commentators began to recognize and discuss social/political issues in their interpretations of the Magnificat.[5]

2. I refer here to the major commentaries of A. Plummer (*The Gospel according to St. Luke,* International Critical Commentary, 5th ed. [Edinburgh: T. & T. Clark, 1922]), B. S. Easton (*The Gospel according to St. Luke: A Critical and Exegetical Commentary* [New York: Scribner's, 1926]), J. M. Creed (*The Gospel according to St. Luke* [London: Macmillan, 1930]), and W. Manson (*The Gospel of Luke,* Moffatt New Testament Commentary [London: Hodder & Stoughton, 1930]). The commentaries of L. Ragg (*St. Luke with Introduction and Notes,* rev. ed., Westminster Commentaries [London: Methuen, 1922]) and R. C. H. Lenski (*The Interpretation of St. Mark's and St. Luke's Gospels {Columbus, Ohio: Lutheran Book Concern, 1934}) were unavailable to me at the time this paper was composed.*

3. *See* S. Benko, "The Magnificat: A History of the Controversy," *Journal of Biblical Literature* 86 (1967): 263-75. Note the terminology "the Controversy."

4. Manson, *The Gospel of Luke,* p. 12.

5. I refer here to the commentaries of N. Geldenhuys (*Commentary on the Gospel of Luke,* New International Commentary on the New Testament [Grand Rapids: Eerdmans, 1951]), W. F. Arndt (*The Gospel according to St. Luke* [St. Louis: Concordia, 1956]), A. R. C. Leaney (*A Commentary on the Gospel according to St. Luke,* Black's

These comments did not, however, indicate a *fundamental* shift in interpretive patterns.

N. Geldenhuys contends that Luke 1:51-53 is the climax of the Magnificat and states that

> in God's choice of two persons of humble life . . . [Mary] sees the powerful revolutionary principle according to which God is going to renew everything through the Messiah. This principle entails a complete reversal. . . . The reversal in human relationships and existence has already begun and will be perfectly completed. (In the course of the past nineteen centuries these words have already been wonderfully fulfilled. But only at the final Consummation will they find their perfect accomplishment.)[6]

G. B. Caird's comment is brief and rather noncommittal:

> If the Magnificat had been preserved as a separate psalm outside of its present context, we might have taken it to be the manifesto of a political and economic revolution.[7]

Caird indicates that the context means, however, that human fortunes are reversed in Jesus' ministry. E. E. Ellis also comments very briefly:

> The last half of the poem describes God's victory in terms of a national deliverance from human oppressors. This is a recurrent note in pre-Christian messianism. The New Testament writers do not deny it, but they redefine it and transfer it to Messiah's *parousia*.[8]

In a context of noting the contrast between rich and poor, L. Morris says only that God "turns human attitudes and orders of society upside down."[9]

W. F. Arndt takes a decidedly polemical tack in his comments:

> Mary uses figurative language. In phraseology literally depicting conditions belonging to this mundane sphere, things are referred to that belong to the realm of the spirit, the invisible world.[10]

New Testament Commentary [London: A. & C. Black, 1958]), G. B. Caird (*The Gospel of St. Luke,* Pelican Gospel Commentary [Baltimore: Penguin, 1963]), E. E. Ellis (*The Gospel of Luke,* 2d ed., Century Bible [London: Oliphants, 1974]), F. W. Danker (*Jesus and the New Age according to St. Luke: A Commentary on the Third Gospel* [St. Louis: Clayton, 1972]), R. Summers (*Commentary on Luke: Jesus, the Universal Savior* [Waco, Tex.: Word Books, 1972]), and L. Morris (*The Gospel according to St. Luke,* Tyndale New Testament Commentary [Grand Rapids: Eerdmans, 1974]). Danker, Leaney, and Summers do not make any significant comments indicating recognition of new areas of interpretation. Danker argues that Elizabeth delivered the Magnificat.

6. Geldenhuys, *Commentary on the Gospel of Luke,* p. 86.
7. Caird, *The Gospel of St. Luke,* p. 55.
8. Ellis, *The Gospel of Luke,* p. 72.
9. Morris, *The Gospel according to St. Luke,* p. 77.
10. Arndt, *The Gospel according to St. Luke,* pp. 60-61.

In a footnote attacking German scholars who believe the Magnificat refers to persons who are literally poor or tyrannical, Arndt states that "in my opinion the meaning of the words of Mary is exclusively spiritual."[11]

During the period from 1951 to 1974, articles by New Testament scholars directed attention primarily to three issues, one of which was genuinely new. Attention continued to be focused on the textual problem of Luke 1:46,[12] and there was renewed interest in the background of the Magnificat including not only the Old Testament but later Jewish literature as well (note especially P. Winter's article regarding a possible Maccabean background for the Magnificat).[13] But the totally new issue—an issue crucial to the integrity of Lukan studies and developments in scholarship following 1974—was the relationship of Luke 1-2 to the rest of Luke (and Acts). Older scholarship may have assumed continuity between the Lukan introduction (Luke 1-2) and the rest of the Gospel, but little if anything was made of this in interpretation. Hans Conzelmann's *Die Mitte der Zeit,* translated in 1960 as *The Theology of St. Luke,* both implicitly and explicitly deals with Lukan theology as if Luke 1-2 did not exist. Conzelmann writes, for example, that

> the introductory chapters of the Gospel present a special problem. It is strange that the characteristic features they contain do not occur again either in the Gospel or in Acts. In certain passages there is a direct contradiction.[14]

This incorrect assessment was soundly challenged by various scholars. It has been clearly and firmly established that Luke 1-2 is integral to the entire work of Luke and that major themes of the whole Gospel are significantly introduced in these chapters.[15] This has important implications for the study of the Magnificat.

IV

The period from 1975 to 1983 has seen the beginning of a new era and a fundamental shift in the interpretation of the Magnificat. Since 1975 three

11. Arndt, *The Gospel according to St. Luke,* p. 62.

12. See Benko, "The Magnificat: A History of the Controversy," and J. G. Davies, "The Ascription of the Magnificat to Mary," *Journal of Theological Studies* 15 (1964): 307-8.

13. Winter, "Magnificat and Benedictus—Maccabean Psalms?" *Bulletin of the John Rylands Library* 37 (1954/55): 328-47.

14. H. Conzelmann, *The Theology of St. Luke,* trans. G. Buswell (New York: Harper, 1960), p. 172.

15. See especially H. H. Oliver, "The Lucan Birth Stories and the Purpose of Luke-Acts," *New Testament Studies* 10 (1963/64): 202-26; P. S. Minear, "Luke's Use of the Birth Stories," in *Studies in Luke-Acts,* ed. L. E. Keck and J. L. Martyn (Nashville: Abingdon Press, 1966), pp. 111-30; W. B. Tatum, "The Epoch of

major, even monumental, commentaries have appeared, along with two briefer commentaries by major Lukan scholars.[16] In addition, partly in the wake of H. Conzelmann's first attempt to deal with Lukan theology, there have continued to appear various studies on the theology of Luke that are particularly relevant to the Magnificat.[17]

All of the authors in this period build explicitly on the observation that Luke 1-2 is integral to the study of the Gospel. The monumental commentaries of R. E. Brown, I. H. Marshall and J. A. Fitzmyer all continue the discussions from the pre-1975 period, including in particular the textual problem of Luke 1:46, the whole issue of Old Testament and Jewish parallels to the Magnificat, and the historical origin of the Magnificat. This interest in its historical origin reflects the new sociological concern evident in these commentators.

The fundamental shift in this period has to do with the inclusion of a genuine sociological question that implies a rejection of the earlier, simplistic literal/spiritual dichotomy and that either significantly complements (or controls) the traditional historical-critical exegesis or transcends it (without necessarily rejecting it).[18]

Israel: Luke I-II and the Theological Plan of Luke-Acts," *New Testament Studies* 13 (1966/67): 184-95; and E. Franklin, *Christ the Lord: A Study in the Purpose and Theology of Luke-Acts* (Philadelphia: Westminster Press, 1975), pp. 80-87, 171.

16. The three major works are R. E. Brown's *The Birth of the Messiah: A Commentary on the Infancy Narratives in Matthew and Luke,* (Garden City, N.Y.: Doubleday, 1977), I. H. Marshall's *Commentary on Luke,* New International Greek Testament Commentary (Grand Rapids: Eerdmans, 1978), and J. A. Fitzmyer's *The Gospel according to Luke (I-IX),* Anchor Bible (Garden City, N.Y.: Doubleday, 1981). The other two works are R. J. Karris's *Invitation to Luke* (Garden City, N.Y.: Doubleday, 1977) and C. H. Talbert's *Reading Luke* (New York: Crossroad, 1982).

17. Among these, I believe the following are particularly important: S. Rostagno, "The Bible: Is an Interclass Reading Legitimate?" in *The Bible and Liberation: Political and Social Hermeneutics,* ed. N. K. Gottwald, 2d ed. (Maryknoll, N.Y.: Orbis Books, 1983), pp. 61-73; R. J. Cassidy, *Jesus, Politics, and Society: A Study of Luke's Gospel* (Maryknoll, N.Y.: Orbis Books, 1978); D. Tiede, *Prophecy and History in Luke-Acts* (Philadelphia: Fortress Press, 1980); W. E. Pilgrim, *Good News to the Poor: Wealth and Poverty in Luke-Acts* (Minneapolis: Augsburg Press, 1981); L. T. Johnson, *Sharing Possessions: Mandate and Symbol of Faith,* Overtures to Biblical Theology, no. 9 (Philadelphia: Fortress Press, 1981); D. Juel, *Luke-Acts: The Promise of History* (Atlanta: John Knox Press, 1983); W. M. Swartley, "Politics or Peace (Eirēnē) in Luke's Gospel," in *Political Issues in Luke-Acts,* ed. R. J. Cassidy and P. J. Scharper (Maryknoll, N.Y.: Orbis books, 1983), pp. 18-37.

18. It should be noted that H. J. Cadbury devotes a chapter of *The Making of Luke-Acts* (New York: Macmillan, 1927) to Luke's social and religious attitudes (pp. 254-73). He discusses Luke's interest in the problems of money, his sympathy with the poor, his concern for women, and the like. Cadbury was clearly ahead of his time, although he shows that texts can be read carefully in other contexts than our own. He gives no mention of the Magnificat in this chapter, however.

Several authors in this period indicate the shift, although briefly. S. Rostagno uses Luke 1:51-53 to state that Jesus came from the circle of the pious poor, that God is on the side of the lowly, and that the Christian message is not neutral but addresses people in their actual situations.[19] R. J. Karris, in his very brief commentary, states that "God's concern for the humble Mary becomes a sign of his concern for the lowly of all ages. . . . God's action . . . presents a dramatic vision of what salvation is all about."[20] R. J. Cassidy begins a chapter entitled "The Social Stance of Jesus" with a discussion of Jesus' concern for the poor, the infirm, women, and pagans, using the Magnificat as his first text from Luke.[21] I. H. Marshall's large commentary actually gives rather little space to this issue, but he does conclude his treatment of the Magnificat by saying that

> it would be easy to over-spiritualize the meaning of these verses and ignore their literal interpretaton. Schürmann . . . rightly notes how the coming of the kingdom of God should bring about a political and social revolution.[22]

A major moment for the Magnificat, however, was the appearance in 1977 of R. E. Brown's commentary on the Matthean and Lukan infancy narratives, The Birth of the Messiah. In this work, Brown gives full treatment to the issues of textual criticism for Luke 1:46 and to the Old Testament and Jewish parallels to the Magnificat (in fact, he provides what is likely the fullest set of parallel texts to date). Brown's creative achievement is his strong and detailed argument that the Magnificat (and other canticles in Luke 1-2) originated in Greek-speaking Jewish-Christian Anawim (Heb., "poor") circles. He notes that although Anawim may originally have referred to the physically poor, it came to mean "those who could not trust in their own strength but had to rely in utter confidence upon God: the lowly, the poor, the sick, the downtrodden, the widows and orphans."[23] After his discussion of the Anawim, Brown concludes by saying,

> the poverty and hunger of the oppressed in the Magnificat are primarily spiritual, but we should not forget the physical realities faced by early Christians. . . . And so vss. 51-53 of the Magnificat would resonate among such groups; for them the Christian good news meant that the ultimately blessed were not the mighty and the rich who tyrannized them.[24]

19. Rostagno, "The Bible: Is an Interclass Reading Legitimate?" p. 65.
20. Karris, Invitation to Luke, p. 40.
21. Cassidy, Jesus, Politics, and Society, p. 21.
22. Marshall, Commentary on Luke, p. 85. In his book Luke: Historian and Theologian (Grand Rapids: Zondervan, 1971), Marshall includes the Magnificat in his discussion of Luke's concern for the poor (p. 141).
23. Brown, The Birth of the Messiah, p. 351.
24. Brown, The Birth of the Messiah, pp. 363-64.

Partly in the wake of Brown's work, subsequent publications continue
this emphasis. J. A. Fitzmyer's monumental commentary also treats the
traditional exegetical questions and is explicitly dependent upon Brown for
the view of the Magnificat's social origins.[25] Fitzmyer has a long introducto-
ry essay on Lukan theology. He discusses material possessions in a section on
"discipleship," and the first text he cites in Luke in connection with the
motif is the Magnificat.[26]

It should be noted as well that both Brown and Fitzmyer deal explicitly
with the role of Mary as a disciple, the connection between Mary and the
Magnificat, and Luke's later remarks about women and discipleship (e.g.,
Luke 8:19-21).[27] Whatever Roman Catholic concern may be indicated here,
it does show the new role of the Magnificat in the discussion of women in the
gospel traditions.

In addition to Fitzmyer's work, the Magnificat received explicit attention
in two 1981 publications on the theme of wealth, poverty, and material
possessions in Luke and in the New Testament. In his treatment of Jesus and
the poor, W. E. Pilgrim notes that Luke 1:51-53 is one of the oldest Gospel
traditions on this motif, and he sees in it the proclamation of God's redemptive, transforming action in history.[28] L. T. Johnson's book opens
with a special focus on the Magnificat under the heading "The Poor Are
Privileged in the Eyes of God, and the Rich Condemned." Johnson writes
that the Magnificat "designates not only those who are without possessions
but those who are oppressed by their fellow human beings and must look to
God for help."[29]

D. Juel's monograph on Lukan theology begins with a chapter on Luke
1-2 and comments on the Magnificat as follows:

> The God who chose Mary and Hannah is a God who has consistently been
> on the side of the lowly and the oppressed. . . . God subverts established
> values in the interest of truth and for the sake of the outcast.[30]

W. M. Swartley's essay appears in a volume that explicitly brings this
fundamental shift of concern to Lukan studies: *Political Issues in Luke-Acts*.
Swartley's essay is the only one in the book that deals with the Magnificat.
He states on the basis of his analysis of the Magnificat and other Lukan texts
that Luke's concept of peace

> stands in the service of making all things new—socially, economically,
> and politically. The variety of Lukan themes associated with his *eirēnē* texts

25. See Fitzmyer, *The Gospel according to Luke (I-IX)*, pp. 356-71.
26. Fitzmyer, *The Gospel according to Luke (I-IX)*, pp. 247-51.
27. See Brown, *The Birth of the Messiah*, pp. 316-19; and Fitzmyer, *The Gospel
according to Luke (I-IX)*, p. 358.
28. Pilgrim, *Good News to the Poor*, pp. 60-61.
29. Johnson, *Sharing Possessions*, p. 13.
30. Juel, *Luke-Acts: The Promise of History*, p. 21.

embraces almost every aspect of life, showing clearly the inadequacy of existing political and religious alternatives.[31]

Perhaps the climactic expression of this post-1975 shift is found in the format of C. H. Talbert's 1982 commentary. Talbert entitles his chapter on Luke 1:39-56 "Mary, Ideal Believer and Social Paradigm," thus combining the concern for women with the concern for the poor and oppressed and giving the latter the explicit title of "social paradigm." Talbert writes that

> the Magnificat . . . clarifies the links between what God has done for one individual and what he will do for the structures of society at large. . . . Stanza two of the Magnificat expands the horizon to speak of God's social revolution through eschatological reversal. . . . To read the Magnificat in terms of Lukan thought, therefore, is to see an individual's (i.e., Mary's) experience of God's grace as prototypical of the way God will ultimately deal with the world at large.[32]

Talbert goes on to argue that Luke does not advocate social reform to change culture, but rather shows that

> Jesus and the disciples fulfill their social responsibility not by being one more power block among others but by being an example, a creative minority, a witness to God's mercy.[33]

V

In the end, I question whether the exegetical-hermeneutical shift reflected in New Testament scholarship after 1974 can be adequately explained, although I can point to four factors that I believe at least contributed to the shift. First, there was an internal critique developing within biblical scholarship itself of the traditional historical-critical method. Such a critique was perhaps symbolized by such widely varying works as those by W. Wink, G. Meier, and P. Stuhlmacher.[34]

Second, biblical scholarship, perhaps especially New Testament scholarship, has been undergoing significant internationalization since 1950 through such things as the establishment of new journals, the convening of international conferences and organizations for New Testament scholars, wide-ranging translation of scholarly works into other languages, improved

31. Swartley, "Politics or Peace (Eirēnē) in Luke's Gospel," p. 32.
32. Talbert, *Reading Luke*, pp. 22, 24, 26.
33. Talbert, *Reading Luke*, p. 25.
34. Wink, *The Bible and Human Transformation: Toward a New Paradigm for Biblical Study* (Philadelphia: Fortress Press, 1973); Meier, *The End of the Historical-Critical Method* (St. Louis: Concordia, 1977); Stuhlmacher, *Historical Criticism and Theological Interpretation of Scripture: Toward a Hermeneutic of Consent* (Philadelphia: Fortress Press, 1977).

travel and communication, ecumenical movements, and so on. Recent biblical scholarship is probably less parochial and isolationist than it has ever
been.

Third, the social revolutions of the last twenty-five years and the remarkable global political events of the same period have certainly made most
educated persons in the United States and Britain aware of new agendas.
Further, such awarenesses are widespread in the ethical and popular literature of the church—mainline, parachurch, and underground or
countercultural.

Fourth, in connection with the other changes and also as a result of the
integration of theological studies with social science disciplines brought on,
at least to some degree, by the growth of doctoral programs in religion and
university departments of religion, we have seen the development of the so-
called new "sociological exegesis," which can be dated in part to the
mid-1970s.[35] This new emphasis has led scholars to bring new questions to
the biblical texts.

VI

In conclusion, I wish to indicate what I see as legitimate and appropriate
concerns in the interpretation of the Magnificat. Without doubt, it should
be a fundamental assumption that Luke 1-2 and the rest of the Gospel of
Luke must be read as one text with basic thematic unity and coherence. The
Magnificat does include and introduce themes crucial for the whole of Lukan
theology.

The larger context of Luke 1-2 puts the stress on the continuity of God's
promise of salvation with its fulfillment in Jesus the Christ. Basic theological categories for understanding revolve around concepts of prom-
ise/fulfillment, the history of salvation/redemption, and Christology
(messianic focus and fulfillment).

The Magnificat itself certainly speaks directly to the theological categories present in all of Luke 1-2 (and in the rest of the Gospel). Specifically, it
includes themes of joy, the pattern of social reversal (with its attendant
concerns for the poor and oppressed), and the inclusion of women among
Jesus' disciples. The aorist verb tenses in Luke 1:51-53 probably indicate
Lukan reflection on the life and work of Jesus Christ, in whom the reversal
took place, and on his continuing community.[36] The social impact of the

35. For a brief history of this period and a partial bibliography, see J. H.
Schültz's introduction to G. Theissen's *The Social Setting of Pauline Christianity: Essays
on Corinth* (Philadelphia: Fortress Press, 1982), pp. 1-23.

36. See the discussions of Brown in *The Birth of the Messiah*, pp. 362-63, and
Fitzmyer in *The Gospel according to Luke (I-IX)*, pp. 360-61.

Magnificat was real in Jesus' ministry and in Luke's church (consider Luke's whole theology of discipleship vis-à-vis material possessions). Yet, Swartley and Talbert, to take but two examples, are undoubtedly correct in maintaining that the Magnificat is not promoting a specific social agenda and/or socio-political "this worldly" program. In the very concreteness of its actuality in Jesus and the church it is also an indication of the transcendence of the values of humility, suffering, and discipleship over riches and oppression; and it stands as an indication of God's eschatological victory in Christ not yet realized.

The traditional historical-critical questions retain their validity even if they are not the only issues—nor, in the case of the Magnificat, the basic ones.[37] The very fact that the Magnificat (presumably) originated somewhere in the first century A.D. and became part of Luke's Gospel means that its parallels to the Old Testament and Jewish literature, the circumstances of its origin and composition history, and even its ascription to Mary vis-à-vis Elizabeth are real and valid issues. The denunciation of historical context and its implications for historical-critical exegesis do little to recognize and benefit from the realities of the historical character of the Christian faith, its traditions, or its Scriptures. What is needed is what I believe is represented in the best of the work surveyed here (Brown, Fitzmyer, Swartley, et al.): the balance of an approach to the text that allows all issues of integrity and reality—from the text, its context, and our context—to be addressed.

37. See my article "Unseasonable Thoughts on the State of Biblical Hermeneutics: Reflections of a New Testament Scholar," American Baptist Quarterly 2 (1983): 134-41.

2.3.2

The Magnificat: Song of Justice

C. HUGO ZORRILLA

Introduction

The number of studies in books and journals that discuss the Magnificat and the theology of Luke-Acts is enormous, and it is even greater for studies of the first two chapters of the Gospel in general and the songs of the nativity in particular.

The critical spectrum ranges from those who classify the Magnificat as a folkloric song without historical credibility to those who argue that the Lukan text is a faithful record of the actual historical words of Mary. I hold to the latter position, assuming the first two chapters of Luke to be a theological unit within the whole work.

I begin this study by addressing problems associated with the textual and theological contexts of the Marian song. Then I approach the text through its structure, observing the relationships and functions of the significant elements in the poem. I conclude by investigating the exalted theological approach that arises from the radically liberating depths of the text, which speaks with directness and sensitivity to the violent experiences and misery in which the poor of the earth live.

Contextual Considerations
1. The Latin American Context

I am able to study the Magnificat only in an awareness of the agonizing reality of millions of men and women who must live deprived of human dignity. I think of those who pass their days in crowded slums, under bridges, in the miserable ghettos of our cities—trapped human beings, tortured, imprisoned for life without being in jail. I think of the poor young woman with a drawn and wrinkled face whose husband returns to their hovel each day in quiet hopelessness, staring blankly, sightlessly, unable to find work. And I think of their half-naked children playing with an empty beer can on the side of the path, under an illuminated sign that refers to a soft drink as "the sparkle of life."

I cannot set aside my existential pretext as a Christian when I come to study the Magnificat. The impoverishment of Latin America has spread beyond its geographic boundaries to the north. I think of the millions of Hispanics in the land of abundance and waste, where they are put to work as a source of cheap labor. And the church is a silent accomplice, trapping men and women in the ideology of "success," "progress," "the good life"—all of which amounts to a Christianized materialism. I cannot help but think of the inhuman injustice of the fact that a mere six percent of the world's population consumes fifty percent of the world's riches, leaving the remaining ninety-four percent of humanity to compete for the other half of the goods that God has given to humankind. And while they complain about the militarism of our countries, such as Nicaragua, El Salvador, and Guatemala, the superpowers continue to spend untold sums of money on military buildups, trying to convince us that they are necessary expenses.

On the other hand, although I cannot escape from an awareness of the Latin American context, I do not mean to suggest that injustice and oppression are limited to this part of the world. The pain and anguish are everywhere, and so the call to service of the living church is rising everywhere. Like Mary, the church serves as a voice for those who are not able to cry out protests of their own. I see in the Magnificat the seeds of a theology that promotes just this sort of service to the oppressed. It gives voice to the viewpoint of the poor in a way that is coherent with the justice of God. Pushing it a little farther, I would say that only the poor can speak on behalf of the poor. And now more than ever they must speak for themselves. Latin Americans have finally discovered that the North American and European theologies do not provide answers to the questions they are asking. With their absolutes and metaphysics, these "white theologies" have contributed to the decontextualization of the churches; they speak of poverty only in the abstract and of the poor only in "spiritual" terms.

The Magnificat is a model of a contextualized hymn giving voice to the experience of the poor. Mary was poor, but she spoke in hope of the greatness of God, secure in the knowledge that the fruit of her womb would be the paradigm of all human dignity.

2. The Textual Context

Before getting into a study of the text itself, I think it would be advantageous to take a look at some of the many critical analyses of Luke 1:46-55. At the outset, we will naturally be interested in the nature of the text, its author, and what sources it draws on. Is the text a literal record of what Mary said, or is it perhaps a composition of Luke? In any case, what was Luke's intent in including the text in his Gospel? I am not suggesting that we are going to uncover the final answers to any of these questions. Indeed, I feel that the most biblical criticism can do is suggest possibilities for better understandings of the text. It is my hope that questions such as these will help us define the socio-religious context of the *Magnalia Dei*.

a. Style

There is of course a general consensus that the text of the Magnificat is poetic in character, but there is less agreement on what type of poetry it is that underlies the final text of Luke.[1] The positions are outlined in Table 1.

Table 1

Critic	Style	Originator
H. Cadbury	Older biblical hymnology	Luke
R. Brown, K. Fitzmyer	Canticle	Existing Jewish collection
H. Troadec	Hymn	Mary
M. Ford	Hymn	Zealot
R. Laurentin	Midrashic hymn	Mary
R. Winter	Psalm	Maccabee
R. Harnack	Canticle	Elizabeth

In light of the fact that the text is generally recognized as a poem, we can assume that it should be interpreted differently than a narrative text. Its style draws on the Semitic poetic heritage, and it is constructed in such a way that it can be sung. Song is the most natural form of praise, a means of expressing joy and worship common enough in Judeo-Christian circles.[2] It is variously used for apologetic, liturgical, and kerygmatic purposes.

If the Magnificat is indeed a hymn—and I believe it is—we have to face the fact that it will be difficult to reconstruct the historical context in which it was composed and even more difficult to speculate with any certainty about who it might have been addressed to before Luke gave it the place he did in his Gospel.

1. See D. R. Jones, "Background and Character of the Lukan Psalms," *Journal of Theological Studies* 19 (1968): 19-50; R. Laurentin, "Traces d'allusion étymologiques en Lc. 1-2," *Biblica* 37 (1956): 435-56; 38 (1957): 1-23; Ralph Martin, "New Testament Hymns: Background and Development," *Expository Times* 94 (1983): 132-36; and Robert Tannehill, "The Magnificat as Poem," *Journal of Biblical Literature* 93 (1974): 263-75.

2. See Martin, "New Testament Hymns," p. 133.

b. Vox Cantanti

It is my belief that the singing voice of Mary can be heard in the Magnificat. I realize that it is difficult to distinguish specifically what can be attributed to tradition from what can be attributed to redaction in Luke 1:46-55—difficult to distinguish, that is, between what belongs to the Jewish setting and what has a Christian character. I am not presuming the ability to clarify once and for all what distinguishes a Jewish hymn from a Christian hymn. I accept the Lukan text as a faithful record of the Marian tradition among the first Christians. H. Troadec suggests that "a direct transmission from Mary to Luke is improbable," but he does not deny that she was the source of this eulogia.[3]

c. Sources

What sources underlie the Magnificat? So many answers to that question have been proposed since the end of the nineteenth century that the overall result has been more confusion than clarification of the issue. This is not to say that the critics have tended to stray beyond the realm of the possible, but it is almost inevitable that their speculations have gone beyond what can be verified with certainty. The categories in which they have speculated include literal dependence on other texts, adaptation of the primary source or origin of this form of exaltation in the traditions of Israel, redaction by the first Christians, and changes in keeping with the general treatment of Judeo-Christian traditions within the theological intentionality of Luke.

It seems obvious to me that Luke 1:46-55 belongs to a special section of the Gospel, that it contains material unique within the larger context. Moreover, despite its Gospel context, it seems to me that the nature of the text itself suggests that it is not a Christian hymn, or at least there is nothing in its configuration that is characteristically Christian.[4] The majority of the students of the Magnificat attribute the hymn to a vital background rooted in the traditions of Palestinian Judaism. Critics such as R. Brown, R. Laurentin, H. Troadec, and I. H. Marshall have found midrashic arrangements that go back to the text of Genesis as well as the prophets and intertestamentary and Qumran literature.[5] With its thematic approach, its characteristic Semitic structure, and its resemblance to a song of victory to Yahweh for the

3. Troadec, *Comentario a los Evangelio Sinópticos* (Madrid: Ediciones Fax, 1972), p. 388.

4. See H. L. MacNeill, "The Sitz-im-Leben of Luke 1:5–2:20," *Journal of Biblical Literature* 65 (1946): 127; and Josef Schmid, *El Evangelio según san Lucas* (Barcelona: Herder, 1967), p. 81.

5. See Brown, *The Birth of the Messiah* (Garden City, N.Y.: Doubleday, 1977), pp. 322ff.; Laurentin, *Structure et théologie de Luc I-II* (Paris: Gabalda, 1957), pp. 4ff; and Marshall, *The Gospel of Luke: A Commentary on the Greek Text*, New International Greek Testament Commentary (Grand Rapids: Eerdmans, 1978), pp. 10ff.

defeat of the enemies of his people, the Magnificat cannot be an *ad vacuum* invention of Luke. As for questions about the degree of Luke's redaction and the extent to which the text exhibits elements of the Marian tradition, Jewish heritage, and Christian tradition, there are no definite answers. The document has come to us in Greek, edited by Luke. I simply assume with Paul Minear that Mary is the central and prime witness in the tradition.[6]

It is difficult, not to say impossible, to avoid the evidence of Old Testament sources for this hymn, of exaltation in a context other than veterotestamentary heritage. In addition to the textual parallels noted by Brown, Troadec, and other scholars in the Old Testament and in interestamentary literature,[7] the associated nativity narrative is reminiscent of stories of other women of Israel. C. T. Ruddick finds not only verbal but also thematic parallels in Genesis birth narratives,[8] and other scholars have suggested that Sara, Leah, Rachel, Hannah, Deborah, Miriam (in Exod. 15), Judith (in Jth. 13), and Elizabeth also served as sources of inspiration for the Magnificat.[9]

In addition to scholarly suggestions concerning textual sources for the Magnificat and the precedents of the experiences of pious women of Israel and the typology of the "daughters of Zion,"[10] there have also been speculations about the influence of the socio-historical context in which it was composed—specifically, the effect of a history of political persecutions inflicted on the people during the time of the Maccabees, Judith, Herod, Agrippa, and the Roman emperors. How are historical elements from the stories of the people of Israel, of Jesus, and of his disciples related to the song?[11] Questions of Lukan redaction aside, there remain issues surrounding the evangelist's treatment of the Magnificat. Assuming that he was aware of the Judeo-Christian tradition of hymnic praise that it draws on, it is fair to ask how the hymn *in its Greek form* fits into the Gospel. Any music associated with it has of course been lost, and it is likely that we have lost part of its semantic base as well. I find it increasingly improbable that the first melodic expression of the song would have been in Greek. Perhaps Mary sang some-

6. Minear, "Luke's Use of the Birth Stories," in *Studies in Luke-Acts,* ed. by Leander E. Keck and Louis Martyn (Nashville: Abingdon Press, 1966), p. 128.

7. Brown, *The Birth of the Messiah,* pp. 358-59; Troadec, *Comentario a los Evangelio Sinópticos,* pp. 410-11.

8. Ruddick, "Birth Narratives in Genesis and Luke," *Novum Testamentum* 12 (1970): 343-48.

9. See John Willis, "The Song of Hannah and Psalm 113," *Catholic Biblical Quarterly* 35 (1973): 139-54; Laurentin, "Traces d'allusion étymologiques en Lc. 1-2," *Biblica* 37 (1956): 435-56.

10. Brown, *The Birth of the Messiah,* p. 323.

11. On this, see Minear, "The Interpreter and the Nativity Stories," *Theology Today* 7 (1950): 365; P. Winter, "Magnificat and Benedictus—Maccabean Psalms?" *Bulletin of the John Rylands Library* 37 (1954-55): 328-47; and M. Ford, "Zealotism and the Lukan Infancy Narratives," *Novum Testamentum* 18 (1972): 280-92.

Table 2

Critic[12]	Source	Style	Language	Role of Luke
A. Harnack	Christian	Hymnic	Greek	Author
I. H. Marshall	Jewish	Midrashic	Aramean	Not author
R. Brown	Jewish-Christian	Midrashic	Aramean	Adaptor
R. Laurentin	Semite	Midrashic	Hebrew	Translator
P. Winter	Semite	Septuagint	Hebrew	Imitator
H. Bojorge	Jewish	Haggadic	Aramean	Transmitter
N. Turner	Jewish	Hebraicized Greek	Hebrew	Adaptor
H. Troadec	Semite	Old Testament	Hebrew-Greek	Compositor

thing similar in Aramean. In Table 2, I summarize the views of scholars concerning the source, style, language, and role of Luke with regard to the Magnificat.

3. *The Context of Lukan Theology*

If we are to understand the text fully, we will have to consider the theological intent of Luke in his Gospel in general and in the nativity accounts in particular. At this level, all manner of difficult questions arise. What was Mary's first intent in the hymn, and to what extent did she participate in its composition? What role did the Christian community play in shaping and preserving the message of exaltation? Who was its first audience? How did the Christ-event affect the way in which Luke, and with him the first Christians, perceived the song? What significance does the text have in the theological configuration of Luke's Gospel? Minear suggests that it stands in the cultic tradition of the first Christians as a testimony of faith, which places it in a seminal prophetic context.[13] On the other hand, we can say that Luke 1:46-55 derives both its Christian resonances and its prophetic-theological overtones from the fact that it stands in both a context of messianic expectation within the popular religiosity of Israel and in a Chris-

12. The views of Marshall, Brown, Laurentin, Winter, and Troadec are present in the works by those authors cited in preceding notes. For the views of A. von Harnack, see "Des Magnificat der Elizabeth (Luk. 1.46-55) nebst einigen Bermerkungen zu Luk. 1 und 2," *Studien des Neuen Testaments und Alten Kirche* 1(1931): 62ff. For the views of Horacio Bojorge, see *The Image of Mary according to the Evangelist* (New York: Alba House, 1977), pp. 7ff. For the views of Nigel Turner, see "The Relation of Luke I and II to Hebraic Sources and to the Rest of Luke-Acts," *New Testament Studies* 2 (1955-56): 100-109.

13. Minear, "The Interpreter and the Nativity Stories," p. 363.

tian document—the Gospel of Luke. In other words, I observe a particular theological context and a global theological context.

Within the particular theological context of Luke 1:4–2:40, apart from the rest of the Gospel, the Magnificat does not appear to have any noticeably Christian characteristics. Outside of its larger Lukan context, it is not all that different from any Israelite psalm of victory or any patriotic hymn in the history of later Judaism. [14] Of course, we can gain any number of valuable insights by studying the Magnificat expressly within the context of these hymns and other songs of messianic exaltation (1:67-79; 2:13-14, 28-32), and within the social context of "the poor," *anawin,* in Palestine. [15]

Within the global context of the whole of the theological thought of Luke throughout Luke-Acts, the messianic expectation of the Magnificat can be seen to gather strength and depth from the surrounding expressions of compassion for the poor, women, the dispossessed, and the despised in Palestine. Luke gives a special emphasis to the place of women and the poor in the kingdom throughout his work, in the accounts of the nativity, in the ministry of Jesus, in the resurrection account, and in reports of the proclamation of the church. He idealizes neither Judea nor the Jewish people. If his gospel focuses on Jerusalem and the extension of the church that began in Jerusalem, he does not limit his message to them but expands his horizon to the continuity in the history of salvation. [16] It is more important for him to dwell on the prospect of messianic fulfillment in the work of Jesus as Savior-liberator among the dispossessed and despised of this world than to be concerned with specifying such details as the hour when the exaltation was sung. It is Luke's intent to emphasize the universal character of the gospel of Jesus, who became flesh among the poor; in this way he gives universal dimensions to the Magnificat, raising it out of its nationalistic particularism. [17] This association of salvation and mercy with the poor is likewise evident in the Benedictus of Zachariah, the Nunc Dimittis of Simeon, and in Luke 4:18-19.

These contextual considerations naturally come through with additional force for the Latin American millions who daily face injustice and dehumanization in the shadows of the abundant wealth and extravagant consumption of a few. It is worth noting here how Luke juxtaposes saving

14. See MacNeil, "The Sitz-im-Leben of Luke 1:5–2:20," p. 127.

15. See Brown, *The Birth of the Messiah,* pp. 346ff.

16. See W. D. Davies, *The Gospel and the Land* (Berkley and Los Angeles: University of California Press, 1974), p. 266.

17. Marshall goes so far as to cite the particularism of Luke 1:46-55 as evidence that Luke is not its author (*The Gospel of Luke,* p. 79). I would argue, however, that it is more a case of nationalism that is being universalized in the Lukan theology through the redactive work of the evangelist (see Troadec, *Comentario a los Evangelio Sinópticos,* pp. 378ff.; and Luke Johnson, *The Literary Function of Possessions in Luke-Acts* [Missoula, Mont.: Scholars Press, 1977], pp. 132ff.).

actions with injustices. God is the principal champion of the needy in these transmutations of unjust realities—a process Edouard Hamel calls "situation inversion."[18] He casts down the powerful, wealthy, and proud and elevates the dispossessed, the poor, and humble. Consider the stories of the Samaritan and the Levite (Luke 10:29-37), Lazarus and the rich man (Luke 16:19-31), the Pharisee and the publican (Luke 18:9-14), and the Gentiles (especially in Acts) facing violent oppression by the Jews: giving, one receives (Acts 2:42-48; 4:32-35; 20:35).

4. The Literary Framework

There is little critical agreement concerning either the genre into which the Magnificat fits or the nature of its stanzaic and metrical composition. To understand the literary framework of the song, we must begin by studying its place in the Lukan context.

The parallelism that Luke establishes between the births of John and of Jesus in Luke 1-2 is very obvious. One can see a transition between the history of Israel and the history of Jesus. In like manner, one can establish a type of transition (or continuity) between the story of Jesus and the story of the church (Acts 1-2). Brown suggests that the Gospel portrays representatives of Israelite piety, and the book of Acts portrays the apostles as representatives of the church.[19] In both cases the Holy Spirit is the key as the gift to the messianic era that brings joy and saving hope. In the first treatise, Luke expresses joy in the poetic and hymnic element; in the second treatise, he announces salvation through the ecclesiastical proclamation.

At the border between the Old and the New Testaments, between the present era and that which is coming, Luke places the diptych of the announcement of John-Jesus (1:5-25, 26-38) in parallelism with the diptych of the birth of John-Jesus (1:57-66; 2:1-7). The Magnificat serves as a song of transition between the two diptychs, just as the song of Zacharias serves as a transitional element between the two births (1:68-79). Charles Talbert also notes that Mary's song is divided into two narrative portions (1:39-44 and 1:56).[20] And, looking more closely at the first chapter of Luke, between the announcement and the birth of John, we find expressions of exaltation and praise to God by Mary and Zacharias concerning the magnitude of God's work to save them from the hand of their enemies. The wording of the announcements and the hymns are organized in a chiastic form, as Paul Minear observes.[21]

18. Hamel, "Le Magnificat et le renversement des situations. Réflexion théologico-biblique," *Gregorianum* 60 (1979): 55-84.

19. Brown, *The Birth of the Messiah*, p. 242.

20. Talbert, *Reading Luke: A Literary and Theological Commentary on the Third Gospel* (New York: Crossroads, 1982), pp. 15ff.

21. Minear, "The Interpreter and the Nativity Stories," p. 116.

It seems fairly incontestable that the text of the Magnificat has a psalmodic character. It remains open to debate whether it is configured in two, three, or four stanzas. Dionisio Mínguez has offered a sophisticated poetic analysis that is helpful in untangling the complex relationship between the elements of association and opposition engendered in the formal expression of the song.[22]

Textual Analysis

In this section my intent is to analyze the text of Luke as it has come to us by way of the evangelist. I will begin with some structural analysis to get at the poetic feeling of Mary as the *vox cantanti* and then proceed to outline in more detail the theological theme supporting the poem.

1. The Narrator

In this section of birth accounts, Luke is interested in letting the characters express their emotions, the intimate part of their theophanic experiences. For this reason he does not describe but rather introduces what happened and lets the characters speak for themselves. In the Magnificat, the evangelist as narrator allows Mary to speak of what she has experienced, and thus he grants her the responsibility and authority for what she sings.

The introduction, 1:46a, is very prosaic and disengaged, very different from what we read in 1:42a or in 1:67. Perhaps the narrator intentionally made it flat in order to give more force, by way of contrast, to Mary's exaltation. The report she gives of her experiences presents the circumstances of salvation-liberation by God as an organically complete whole. The song itself is a unit of feeling that breaks forth with a shout of praise and continues in a prophetic affirmation.

2. Analysis of the Poetic Structure

The poem speaks of two beneficiaries of the mercy of the omnipotent God: Mary (46b-49a) and those who fear him (50-55). The nominal phrase "holy is his name" (49b) serves as a bridge between the two parts of the poem.[23]

22. See Mínguez, "Poética generativa del Magnificat," *Biblica* 61 (1980): 55-77. Cf. Escudero Freire, *Devolver el evangelio a los pobres: A propósito de Lc. 1-2* (Salamanca: Sígueme, 1978), pp. 183-221.

23. Mínguez argues that the adjectives *mighty* (*ho dunantós*) and *savior* (*ho sotér*) modify "his name" (*to ónoma*) ("Poética generativa del Magnificat," pp. 59-77).

a. The First Strophe, 1:46b-49a

(i) *Action of Praise, 46b-47.* The text begins with a parallelism similar to that in the psalms of praise (Ps. 34:13; 35:9; 69:30). This repetitive form confirms the poetic setting of musicality, sustaining and deepening the sense of the global unity of the song, an effect also evident in other verses.

Megalúnei appears five times in Luke in a continual sense, in this case in the present tense—"I continue exalting" or "I magnify." This exaltation is an expression of complete gladness in which *egallísen* (past tense) reflects the joy of salvation as a gift already obtained, but the term has something of a continuing sense in the "magnification" of God. It does not appear that Mary is quoting any particular psalm, although echoes of psalmody are very clear. [24] The cause for this happiness—God's salvation of the poor—is also reflected in the psalms of praise.

If this Marian happiness reflects Habakkuk 3:18 or Exodus 34:9, then this song of entrance has nationalistic connotations in addition to personal connotations. [26] The phrase "in God my Savior" is translated in the same literal fashion in the LXX, and not as "in the God of my salvation" (Hab. 3:18). The same is true of the phrase "God is Lord": *Kúrios ho Theós* (Hab. 3:19).

Such is the force of this thanksgiving, such is the saving power of God as Mary describes it in her song, that the rest of the poem appears to depend on this first parallelism. Some scholars could be correct in showing that the first two lines form an expression of praise as an introduction and that the rest of the poem establishes the reasons for this praise. [25] But all can agree that verses 46b-47 present a robust affirmation in a simple syntactic form:

Verb	Subject	Possessive Pronoun	Complement
megalúnei	he psyché	mu	tónkúrion
egallíasen	tó pneumá	mu	epí tó Theó

The second sentence defines the character of God more by means of the predicate *tó soterí mu.*

```
Magnifies → life   → my → the Lord
and make glad → spirit → my → in God
                       └→my Savior
```

This very clear parallelism contributes to the feeling of the entire poem and suggests a salvation that is not exhausted in Mary. I believe Mínguez is

24. Mínguez, "Poética generativa del Magnificat," p. 21.
25. See Troadec, *Comentario a los Evangelio Sinópticos,* p. 409.
26. Mínguez, "Poética generativa del Magnificat," p. 63.

correct in stating that the meaning of the verbs here is unified through the category of "public proclamation."[27] I would simply add that the meaning is twofold: looking back to Israel and looking forward to the church.

(ii) *Reasons for Praise, 48-49a.* The rest of the poem is tied in by the causal conjunction *hóti,* "because." Verses 48-49a establish the reason for the praise by underscoring the theme of the rest of the hymn. The material not only extends the praise Mary is offering but also serves Luke's intent by introducing the subject of the birth of her son.

The verses have a generally similar syntactic makeup: conjunction, verb in past tense, and complement. The two sentences are separated by a subordinate sentence with an explicative conjunction. With *idoú gár,* the reason for the public praise is increased, the verb being in the future tense: "Henceforth all generations will call me blessed" (cf. the statement of Leah in Gen. 30:13). The more "humble" and "affected" that Mary feels as a "servant," the more reason for her "blessedness" (cf. 1 Sam. 1:11).

The immediate context shows that the blessing of the "slave" *(dúle)* is part of the great event of salvation and a great contrast with the works of the All-powerful. God is the subject of the verbs "look" and "make." Mary goes from the first-person singular to the third-person singular. In both cases God uses Mary to provide the gift of his son. There are a series of opposites that stand out here: greatness/lowliness, powerful/slave, looked-did/say-blessed. From the beginning of the song the protagonist is not the one who exalts but the exalted one, following the tradition of Zephaniah 3:17.

The rhythm in the first stanza is joined as follows:

> Lord
> God Savior ↔ ⌈ because he looked ⌉
> ⌊ because he did ⌋ ← the Mighty One

In an elegant, solemn manner and with all the seriousness of a hymnic proclamation, 49b serves as a transition to the second stanza. The holiness of God resounds in what is before and what follows: his powerful acts of salvation recall the Exodus and his just way of handling his people (see Pss. 111:9 and 103:1; cf. the song of Moses in Exod. 15).

b. The Second Strophe, 50-55

In this second part, no explicit subject is observed. The implied subject, the protagonist of the event experienced by Mary, remains God, *Sotér* and powerful. This is reaffirmed by the four possessive pronouns *autó* and the use of the pronoun as direct object *(autón).*

The connection with the first stanza is deliberate. Following verse 49b, verse 50 begins to expand the reason for so much joy. In his mercy *(éleos),*

---

27. Mínguez, "Poética generativa del Magnificat," p. 63.

God maintains his tradition of justice with those who fear him (Ps. 103:17, 18). Already in verse 48b we found evidence that Mary's experience extends beyond herself, and here we find again that the event she celebrates is the arrival of the Savior-liberator of all humankind. The generations will experience the mercy she describes in verses 50-55.

The bridge in verse 49b is reinforced with verse 50. How is holiness related to mercy? The poem looks toward the great things of the Mighty One and begins to answer in the verses that follow. Verses 49b and 50 begin with the conjunction "and" (kaí).

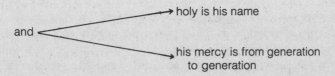

The phrase "those who fear him, those subject to the mercies of God," is a general, inclusive expression denoting individuals like Mary—the humble, the poor, people in need of God. The poem goes from the personal to the collective as paradigm of the liberating acts of God. This is expressed in the poem in an imperfect chiastic form:

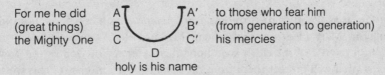

(i) *The Participation of God in the World, 51-53.* The echo of the verb in the present tense—"magnifies" in verse 46b—continues the theme of the first stanza in this section of the second stanza. All the wealth of mercy (vv. 50, 55) and the mighty acts of God (v. 49) flow from the past to the eschatological present. From here on all the verbs are in the past, are linked to God as the sole protagonist, and begin the lines of this strophe, as is the case in the first stanza. The elimination of articles and conjunctions makes the message of the poem more graphic and powerful.

Here the poem takes up the idea raised in verse 49a of strengthening the power of God (as in Ps. 89:10), redeveloping the experiences of the "humility of Mary" in terms more nationalistic than those in verse 48a. God is presented in all his power as the liberator and the justifier of the poor. The opposition between the verbs and their complements is very clear. It is worth noting that the verbs that allude to the poor and humble have a positive connotation ("shown," "exalted," "filled"), the reverse of the connotations surrounding the verbs that refer to the rich and powerful ("scattered," "put down," "sent away").

Verses 52 and 53 contain antithetical oppositions and are linked by a similar parallelism in 52a and 53. The two verbs are structured in different chiastic forms, making this section the climax of the topic anticipated by the praise of the greatness of God *(Magnalia Dei)* introduced in verse 48. This interconnection of contrasts and opposition resonates with the portrait of God as a martial and militant figure who nonetheless stands with those who are lowly.

<pre>
put down   A   A'   sent empty → mighty   rich
               ✕   ✕
exalted   B   B'   filled ————→ lowly   hungry
</pre>

Note that verse 51 does not have a counterpart. This suggests to me that the tension, the struggle, is not between the mighty and the lowly themselves but between God and the proud. God is the protagonist who with his mighty arm defends "those who fear him." Verse 51b establishes a parallelism with 52a, and 52b with 53a. This concatenation of linking parallels establishes a synonymy of opposition, as follows:

<pre>
Lord ⌉
God │ proud   mighty   rich
Savior│ those who fear   humble   hungry
Mighty └→
</pre>

This war of God against the mighty *(dunástas)* is on behalf of those who fear him. Mary identifies with them. Her humility *(tapeínosis)* places her among the poor of the earth who hope for the mercy of God as the power *(krátos)* that will protect them from the ravages of the mighty of this world. As a matter of fact, of the evangelists, only Luke uses *tapeínosis* (twice) and *krátos* (three times).

The fearful, humble Mary perceives the power of God as a great expression of concern for those who suffer hunger and are poor. Verses 52 and 53 complete the movement of the chiasm in verses 49 and 50:

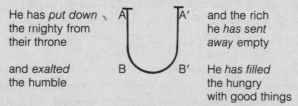

<pre>
He has *put down* A   A'   and the rich
the mighty from   he *has sent*
their throne   away empty

and *exalted*   B   B'   He *has filled*
the humble   the hungry
                                   with good things
</pre>

The figurative language in these central verses speaks of God as the Almighty who does not compromise with the oppressor. He is portrayed with an anthropomorphic figure (with his arm), with a political figure (puts down the mighty), and with a social figure (the rich he sends away empty).

(ii) *The Fulfillment of the Promise, 54-55.* After a profoundly radical and militant climax in which God takes the side of his own (the humble, fearful, poor, hungry), the poem falls into a type of peace and national nostalgia.

Verse 54a serves as a link to the rest of the theme, the mercy of God for the oppressed, ratifying again the cause of Mary's praise. God "comes to the help" of Israel his servant (Isa. 41:8-9). The help of God is a continuation of the act of salvation referred to in verse 47. God is the Savior who remembers the *éleos*, the God who remembered his promises to Abraham and responded to the cries of his oppressed people (Exod. 2:24). Although "servant" *(pais)* has a different etymology than "slave" *(dulé)*, both terms relate to the poor whom God makes his people by pure mercy. This is underscored by the parallelism of "our fathers" and "Abraham." Mary's experience is not an isolated incident but rather part of the merciful remembrance of God who wants to fulfill his promises of salvation. That is why only the descendants *(spérma)* of Abraham will understand and experience the blessedness.

We should note the extent to which mercy is implicit in the framework of the poem, giving cohesion to the text by linking the different ages that are referred to:

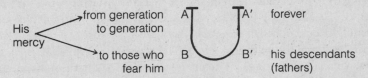

The Magnificat as a whole vibrates with an intensity of rhythm. Oppositions, parallelisms, the thematic "lowliness," "oppression," "exaltation," and "mercy" all lead to a climax, knitting together the parts and giving expression to the acts of God on behalf of those he chooses to save. Like its parts, the whole of the poem reveals two theological foci: the themes of justice for the poor and the action of God in history according to his promise.

salvation (vv. 46-47)   A ⌐   ⌐ A'   memory of the pact (vv. 54-55)

oppression (v. 48)   B │   │ B'   hunger (vv. 52-53)

great things (v. 49)   C ⌐___⌐ C'   feats of his arm (v. 51)

                    D Mercy . . . to those
                    who fear him (v. 50)

We should also consider the temporal aspects of the song more closely. We have already noted the importance of the past-tense verbs not only in making the text more forceful but also in establishing the dynamic of actions that are made evident in history. Mínguez correctly emphasizes the fact that these verbs do not by any means imprison the text in a dead past of remote aorists; that would be to place the events in a "mythical time."[28] Rather, the hymnic expression opens like a fan, an authentically historic resonance of the multifaceted actions of God in the past.

28. Mínguez, "Poética generativa del Magnificat," p. 68.

One cannot lose sight in the *Magnalia Dei* of a continuous present in connection with the Marian *megalúanei*. This exaltation goes beyond the limits of personal experience, beyond the borders of biblical Israel. The "from now on, henceforth" *(apó nún)* marks the beginning of the presence of the "era that was to come" and puts the future generations in eschatological time. All successive generations will continue to experience the mercy of the Mighty (Mic. 7:20). This "from now on" tied to the verb in the future ("will call me blessed") shows, in the context of the whole poem, that with the fruit of her womb (1:35) the Holy Spirit will begin a messianic era for future generations. The time of the just salvation of the "Holy One of Israel" does not remain in a personal past. It reaches into the future, extending from the personal to the general, from the national to the universal, from the chronological to the eschatological.

And we would do well to keep in mind the fact that the whole poem is wrapped in remembered promises. God, the central protagonist, acts sovereignly in Mary because he remembers that his covenant is forever *(eis tón aióna,* 1:32, 55). That is to say, there is a temporal continuity of God's merciful actions on behalf of those who fear him—past (promise), present (remember), and future (fulfillment). The constant praise by Mary and the recognition of his blessings for future generations rests in the remembrance, in the generational memory of the oppressed who, like Mary, trust in the mighty arm of God.

Having considered the text's temporal aspects, we should also examine its spatial aspects. By this I refer not simply to the physical context in which Luke says the Magnificat was sung—a simple home in the hill country of Judea sheltering two women pregnant by the saving action of God (1:39, 56)—but more substantially to the spatial aspects of the text, the horizontal and vertical aspects of the poetic rhythm.

The act of "magnification" so central in the experience of Mary is essentially a concentration on the horizontal space of God in history. She exults in God's mercy on a horizontal plane, his dealing with humanity in the progression of the history of salvation. As a matter of fact, it is this solid horizontal framework that provides the fundamental support for Luke's theology, which emphasizes God's special interest in and compassion for the hungry and the poor from Old Testament times to the present.

But the spatial elements of the text are not exclusively horizontal. The tensions between past and present, promise and remembrance, suggest the presence of very crucial vertical elements in the poem. Similarly, the above-below, high-low, raise-lower dichotomies point to the dynamic vertical (and horizontal) relationship between a transcendant-imminent God and the human beings for which he cares—a relationship underscored by the anthropomorphic expressions used to describe his actions (look, do with his arm, remember). In his saving mercy he acts to change the established order in favor of the poor, of those under, below. Indeed, the change is drastic, of such magnitude as to justify the label convulsion or revolution. This change makes sense only in the context of a sovereign and all-powerful God who chooses to enter history and act on behalf of humanity.

The Theological Approach from Impoverished America

Having reviewed the content of the Magnificat from the perspectives of biblical criticism and structural analysis, I am now ready to express some of the emotion that I've been holding back since the immediate reading of the text. Everything is so clear. If I were now to come upon a Christian singing this poem of Mary in one of the villages of Guatemala, or on a street in San Salvador, or a corner in Bogotá, or perhaps on a Sunday in the marketplace of any of countless other towns in Latin America, I would not be at all surprised if one of those who is always on duty would not prevent the song from being finished, or at least see to it that it would be finished only in jail, assuming the Christian's health permitted.

Luke perceives Mary as a representative of the poor par excellence. She is Mary the poor. The poem has been described as a single act of God in two sequences, in which Mary the poor mother is the eschatological and hierophanic sign, and the Son is the saving fulfillment of God to the oppressed.[29]

Much has been written of the blessedness of Mary. The Catholic position has reduced the width and depth of the Magnificat to a narrow spiritual reading that supports a missionary program that has dehistoricized the liberating experience of Mary from the oppressed peoples of America. The "official" theologies have on the one hand stressed the meekness of Mary, separating her from the conflictive circumstances of her time in an apparent effort to divert the attention of the unfortunate who, like Mary, seek their dignity in God. And on the other hand, these theologies have attempted to make Mary into a bourgeois benefactor of those in privileged positions who do not want her to continue being the Mary of the poor. Perhaps that is why in the Marian devotions the Virgin Mary appears as the great Lady, distanced from the simple people, covered with brocades and glittering with many crowns, looking more like a character in a medieval romance than a real person who speaks to us from the pages of the Bible. One does not hear a country or a laborer's Marian theology but rather a monarchical, verticalistic "Mariology." It is essential that we regain a vision true to the biblical record; as Jesús Espeja reminds us, "Mary is the poor one who listens to and pronounces the song of the poor and the just of all times."[30]

29. See Tannehill, "The Magnificat as Poem," p. 274.
30. Espeja, *Jesucristo: Palabra de Libertad* (Salamanca: Editorial San Estaban, 1979), p. 180; cf. Gregorio Ruíz, "El Magnificat: Dios está con los que pierden," *Sal Terrae* 68 (1980): 781-90.

Mary is presented in the Magnificat as the paradigm of joy in the eschatological era and of confidence in the action of the historical God. God makes his hierophanic expression par excellence in Mary, humanizing his option for the poor.

Protestants are inclined, typically without giving the matter much conscious thought, to view Mary as standing on the threshold of the New Testament unaware of the real significance of what she is singing about. Rejecting much of the Catholic assumptions about the significance of Mary, the great majority of evangelicals picture her as intoning a hymn for a remote and spiritual future. Here again, theological orthodoxy serves the interests of the powerful and proud who exploit the humble and are not interested in listening to the Marian denunciation.

Mary's piety is not ahistoric. She represents all the poor *(anawim)* who wait for the messianic liberation. We have seen that contextually, structurally, and thematically the song unquestionably breathes liberation as the prophetic dimension of the gospel in Luke. The radical and militant similarities of the Magnificat with the songs of Hannah and of Moses are no mere coincidence.

It is clear that Mary holds as the center, the reason, the subject of her blessing God. The *Magnalia Dei* belongs to him as the only Lord. The expectation of the Old Testament is fulfilled in the Mighty. That is why the Magnificat underscores the acts of God as anticipations of the incarnation. Humility and exaltation resound in the fruit of Mary's womb (Phil. 2:5-11), making the poor the parameter of the kingdom of God.

Before the liberating acts of God, the privileged rich lose their dominion, political power decays, the arrogance of the proud disintegrates. The weak, the oppressed, the hungry will experience the justice of the Lord, the Savior and God who humanizes them by himself becoming human. All these actions constitute a radical alteration in human relations. Authority comes to treat people as equals, and riches confer dignity to all by the action of the powerful arm of God. And Mary sings of this revolution as a historic fact growing within her, in the person of Jesus. He is not some abstract hope for the future but an eschatological reality already with us. And yet sadly there are many Christians who do not want to hear that the future is already a reality in the kingdom of God—and this despite the fact that, as Xabier Pikaza points out, Luke speaks more of a present than of a "then." God in Christ brings his salvation in history, now and in the time to come. The fruit of Mary's womb comes forth as the radical realization of the hope for all time of Israel.[31]

We must not underestimate the extent to which the act of God's mercy in Mary was a fulfillment of his covenant promises to Israel. Our tendency to

---

31. Pikaza, in *Teologí de los Evangelios de Jesús,* by Xabier Pikaza and F. de la Calle (Salamanca: Sígueme, 1977), pp. 227-30.

spiritualize the song and its liturgical use has largely emptied it of its militant and radical sense. As John Howard Yoder says, he who was born "is to be an agent of radical social change."[32] We must also be on guard to preserve our awareness of the message that God acts savingly in and for the poor.

The church in Latin America has no alternative if it wants to be a sign of the kingdom of God. If we are to fulfill the task of Christian proclamation, we have no choice but to adopt a lowly lifestyle. We must be sensitive to the millions who live in misery, in the grip of the powerful. God must be magnified in lives of selfless service by Christians who, with Mary, have found grace in his mighty arms.

Conclusion

In conclusion, I must insist that it is a mistake to suppose that the poor, the hungry, and the humble spoken of in the Magnificat are fundamentally the "poor in spirit." There are no dualisms in the psalmody of Mary. Luke placed a clear emphasis on the physical and human realities that the first Christians had to face.

Mary reminds us of the festive character of salvation from God. Even our drained peoples are able to find meaning beyond a mere desire for survival, in the innate joy of the people. It seems to me that in the midst of all of the alienating fiestas, bazaars, and fairs of the rich world, the church should be concerned with rediscovering the psalmodic spirit of Mary. In the face of festivals preserved in alcohol that are designed to divert people from their genuine interests, the church must provide more than mere religious tourism; it must recapture the liberating spirit of the fiesta of Mary who magnifies God. God is the liberator, the true Lord before the chiefs, politicians, dictators, and generals of the day.

Finally, I see Mary as neither timid nor unwilling to risk all. Within the imperialistic regime and before the Roman oppression, she is a symbol of those who have no fear. In this era of aggressions, crimes, kidnappings, and tortures of all kinds, the insecurity and tension are inhuman. It is a relief and a challenge that we can look to Mary, who in a similar environment showed no fear because her confidence was in God her Savior.

32. Yoder, *The Politics of Jesus* (Grand Rapids: Eerdmans, 1975), p. 27.

2.3.3

Report by Douglas Webster and Discussion

Webster: We found Mary's song very relevant for our discussion on hermeneutics. The Magnificat raises the question of Luke's intention in choosing this hymn as an expression of praise to God out of a particular theological and sociological context. We want to understand Mary's song as an integral expression of Luke's theology. It is the dialogical introduction to key themes emphasized throughout Luke and Acts. These themes include God's special regard for the poor, women, and Samaritans and the call to radical discipleship.

We noted that authentic interpretation also must take into account the Old Testament understanding of the pious poor—those who are materially poor, politically put down, and yet open to God, freely acknowledging their dependence upon him for deliverance. Salvation is a holistic reality. We noted in this regard the close affinity between the Magnificat and Hannah's prayer.

We spoke of the importance of interpreting the song eschatologically. Praise springs from God's work, both present and future. God's promise to Mary is realized in her Savior's recognition of her personhood and ministry. Mary's hope in God is spelled out in concrete sociological terms. We had a lengthy discussion concerning how both Roman Catholics and Protestants depersonalize Mary.

We identified the community of believers for which Luke consciously wrote: presumably well-educated, relatively wealthy congregations that may have been faced with the danger of compromising the nature of true discipleship. David Scholer's survey of the exegetical studies of the Magnificat by North Atlantic scholars demonstrates the strange disregard for the sociological dimension of the text up until the mid-seventies. We attempted to understand why this was the case. Several reasons were suggested:

1. Until recently scholars have tended to obscure the distinctive emphases of the individual evangelists. Their concern to harmonize the Gospel accounts prevented them from reading Luke as Luke and from acknowledging his special regard for the disadvantaged.

2. New Testament scholars have tended to be concerned with history understood as facts from the first century. They have focused on the question of how things happened. Today the focus is shifting toward an appreciation of the concrete meaning of the sociological reality in both its original setting and our contemporary situation.

3. Scholars have misread the text in the extent to which they have deemphasized the importance of the Gospels for practical theology. Insufficient regard has been given to the history of Jesus. The Gospels and epistles have been polarized, making them impractical sources for concrete application in the Christian community.

Resisting the temptation to spiritualize the Magnificat raises the important issue of the text's social-ethical implications. What does this text say in our context? How does it shape our situation? What is its relationship to theology and ideology? Hugo Zorrilla's paper stresses the impact that Mary's song has in a Latin American context among people who are downtrodden, hungry, and poor. The identification is practical and sociological as well as theological. The focus of Mary's song is on God. She has heard the good news that God is at work redemptively, powerfully, historically. Ethics begins with theology. Redemption grounds radical discipleship. The gospel brings about change. Without idealizing the poor, the person who shares Mary's praise must identify with the poor. The affluent and the arrogant must repent and turn to God. Ethical sensitivity and practical responsiveness grow out of praise to the God who acts on behalf of the poor. The ethical impact is personal and corporate. Mary praises God out of her individuality, yet sees what God is doing for her in the context of his dealings with the children of Abraham. God's action is personal and corporate, immediate and future, resulting in salvation and judgment. Luke's incorporation of the Magnificat in his Gospel reveals his theological commitment. He has intentionally chosen to emphasize certain points that cause interpreters to look at the social situation from the side of God's concern. He has an agenda that remains authoritative for us. The lack of a specific social agenda only causes us to take more seriously the dialogue between Luke's text and our context.

Hubbard: I'd like to ask a question. Did the group discuss the way in which the Magnificat sounds a theme in the Gospel which is then picked up again and again, thus becoming a mandate for believers? We've talked about the gospel requiring us to involve ourselves in concern for the poor and so forth. Is that part of Luke's own strategy, part of the structure of his Gospel?

Osborne: I'd like to build on that. I think that we should also discuss whether it is actually an intensification of the radical discipleship theme from Mark and Matthew being continued in a much clearer direction concerning what discipleship really means in concrete practice.

Webster: Just initially, that is why we stressed the integral nature of this psalm, which, as David points out in his paper, was not realized really until the mid-seventies.

Watson: We got ourselves into some hot water in this latest session when we put that question to ourselves. I think what we came to was something along the lines of a hermeneutic that has to be Christologically closed but pneumatologically open. Otherwise, if we're to adopt the radical discipleship that Luke speaks of, none of us would be in a position of being able to start. The implications are there. We think of this as a cutting edge to bring us back again and again to what the radical demands of Jesus are.

Fraser: When you talked about the depersonalization of Mary, did you address the significance of this song being Mary's song?

Webster: Yes, we did. We spoke of it in the context of recognizing her personhood, her role in ministry, God's using her.

Fraser: I am not just thinking of her as a woman but as a poor woman, as an oppressed person.

Cummings: There was extensive discussion about that. This concern was obscured until the mid-seventies, as David pointed out.

Fraser: And did you include attention to the theological significance of this—not just the fact of it, but the theological significance—that this is in Mary's mouth?

Cummings: I'm not sure what you mean by that.

Fraser: What do we learn in going beyond the exegesis of the text to the theological significance of this word as a word being spoken by a marginalized member of society?

Webster: We had to contextualize it.

Zorrilla: And as we view the context, what we have to recognize is that this is Luke's composition—Luke's composition in Greek of Mary's tradition. So, what I am trying to say also is that Luke radicalized the discipleship theme, beginning with that woman, in that first chapter of Luke.

Osborne: Did you then, though, discuss the redactional theme of the theology of women as a suffering group, which is so predominant in Luke?

Scholer: We certainly did. And we traced to some extent the ways in which that theme relates to God's throwing down the mighty and rescuing the poor. The succinctness of the report may not offer all the emphases, but it does accurately portray our discussion.

Watson: I would just like to pick up on one of the themes that was very briefly mentioned there—namely, the whole eschatological impact of the Magnificat. It's only in that context that discipleship becomes practical at all. The radical demands in their own right become quite impossible even to attempt, but within the eschatological context they can be understood as the goals of a sort of pilgrimage—an ethical pilgrimage.

Hays: I may have missed something here, but I'm a little surprised to find you talking about this hymn as if it were a kind of prescription for discipleship, because in a formal sense at least it is not a prescription at all, but an ascription of praise to God for what he has done. Did you reflect on that matter?

Webster: No, I think we were saying that this *is* a praise hymn, surely, but it is also a doxological introduction to radical discipleship. It is, in a sense, the preface, the introduction to themes of discipleship that are developed powerfully throughout the Gospel of Luke.

Osborne: And it's more magnificent because it's doxological.

Scholer: I think that Hugo was especially careful to remind us always that God was the protagonist. I don't think we downplayed the doxological setting in any way. This praise introduces the theme of discipleship that is developed through the rest of the Gospel of Luke. One of the major points that we made was that we can't separate the poetic introduction from the rest of Luke. It's all one piece.

Roberts: I'd like to raise the question of what you did with poverty, since that's so critical in liberation theology.

Deiros: In discussing the context of this psalm, we also discussed its context today. Do we start with a text or with today? I think the whole group came to the conclusion that we start here, now, with the poor, the needy, not with the text.

Webster: We also were thinking in terms of the Old Testament understanding of the poor, not wanting to forget the spirituality of Mary and her receptiveness to God—the Isaiah 61 kind of understanding.

Deiros: One of the points that was made had to do with Mary as a representative of the pious, helpless, and needy. This theme is very clear in the whole of Luke's writings, not only in the Gospel but also in Acts. Many crucial issues concerning discipleship, contextualization, God's work in the Messiah, and contemporary ideologies revolve around how one defines the word *poor*.

Members of the 1 Corinthians Study Group

Rolando Gutiérrez-Cortés
Emilio Antoñio Nuñez
Grant Osborne
Aída Bescançon Spencer
William David Spencer
Sze-kar Wan

2.4.1

The Truly Spiritual in Paul: Biblical Background Paper on 1 Corinthians 2:6-16

AÍDA BESANÇON SPENCER AND WILLIAM DAVID SPENCER

Readers of 1 Corinthians 2:6-16 are repeatedly driven by the text to ask what a "spiritual person" is, what an "unspiritual person" is, and how one can become spiritual rather than unspiritual. Sometimes consciously, sometimes inadvertently, the interpreter may assume a certain traditional understanding of Paul's thought. In this paper we would like to show (1) the questions raised by 1 Corinthians 2:6-16, (2) some major traditional understandings of Paul's thought, (3) how Paul answers his questions in the context of chapters 1-4, and (4) some ramifications of our conclusions for a conference addressing context and hermeneutics in the Americas.

1. Questions Raised in 1 Corinthians 2:6-16

In 1 Corinthians 1:18–2:5 Paul disparages the wisdom of the learned sophist, the scribe, and the skillful debater. The one who speaks by means of words of wisdom will lead people to a faith in wisdom, whereas the one who speaks by means of the power of the Spirit will lead people to a faith in that Spirit. The means and the end cannot be separated; every means will lead to its own end. Paul speaks of two wholly unrelated means that lead to two wholly unrelated ends, two separate edifices with no bridge between them. The one edifice is human. Human preaching is characterized by authoritative, high-sounding words and arrogance. It is the wisdom of the learned, which is bound to the physical, or fleshly (2:1, 14; 3:1-3; 4:19; 5:2). The second edifice is godly. To describe this second edifice, Paul uses certain key words: "power," "mystery of God," "Jesus Christ," "crucified," and "preaching" (1:1–2:8, 16; 3:11, 23; 4:1-15). Godly preaching is done in weakness and in fear and trembling by the insignificant, the rejected, the powerless (1:25–2:1-5; 4:9-13). Nevertheless, the preaching has power, through the mystery of the crucified Messiah, who is the power and wisdom of God.

Lest anyone misunderstand, Paul adds in 2:6-16 that he is not opposed to wisdom in general but rather to the wisdom of "this age," the kind of wisdom that renders those who use it ineffective. In contrast to this, Paul and Sosthenes pass on an "of-God wisdom." The placement of the genitive "of God" before the noun "wisdom" accentuates the modifier even more strongly: it is "a *godly* wisdom." What is this "godly wisdom" that had been hidden, that none of the leaders of this age knew? Paul does not immediately answer; he simply states that the leaders of this age proved they did not know the "godly wisdom" when they crucified the Lord of glory (2:7-8). He indirectly raises the same question again in verses 9-10. What is it that "the eye did not see and ear did not hear and did not enter into a human heart which God prepared for those who love God but is now unveiled through the Spirit"? Perhaps 1 Corinthians 2:9 is a paraphrase of Isaiah 64:4, in which we learn that God works "for those who wait for [him]." In the Isaiah passage *ḥākâ* (חָכָה) signifies "wait for," "expect," "long for," which does not contradict the sense of love in 1 Corinthians 2:9. But in Isaiah the emphasis is on the nature of God, whereas in 1 Corinthians the emphasis is on the first word, "what"—what is revealed.

Paul goes on to explain that only the spirit of a person knows the things in a person. They must be revealed to be known. So, too, only the Spirit of God can bridge the gap between the two edifices to bring the things of God to humans. The Spirit is the Means of revelation, the Bringer of the things out of God, the Teacher of God's wisdom words in order that those who love God may see the things he has given them.

But again Paul raises the question in verses 13-16 of what it means to be "taught of the Spirit" rather than "taught of human wisdom words." What does it mean to be spiritual? What kind of truths appear to be "foolishness"?

2. Some Major Traditional Understandings of Paul's Thoughts

Ferdinand Christian Baur has played a pivotal role in New Testament studies. Even if his extreme positions are no longer popular, he was successful in establishing an agenda, in pointing out the questions that must be answered. Baur and many contemporaries treat Paul's thoughts as basically Hellenistic.[1] They would have it that the Greek dichotomy between matter and spirit is implicit in 1 Corinthians 2:6-16, so we can assume that Paul is contrasting the spirit to literal "matter," suggesting that to be spiritual is to be immaterial. In some sense, then, Paul would be agreeing with the gnostic idea of the body as evil. To be "spiritual" then would be to develop a type of individual monastic existence wherein the more one dwells upon God the less one dwells upon one's body. A noun such as "spirituality" might then be appropriately used to describe this quality or state of being. (Incidentally, Paul uses the noun "spirit," the adjective "spiritual," and the adverb "spiritually"; he does not use any term that could be translated "spirituality.")

Other scholars, such as Albert Schweitzer and W. D. Davies, have argued that Paul's thought is basically Hebraic,[2] in which context the spirit would stand in contrast to metaphorical "matter": to be spiritual would be to be prophetic. Paul as Hellenistic would be emphasizing the spirit or wind as an ethereal substance. Paul as Hebraist would be emphasizing the Spirit or wind as power and carrier, as invasive energy distinct from humanity and yet concerned with humanity. In the first chapters of 1 Corinthians Paul accentuates both the power of the Spirit and the Spirit as the Bringer of God's truth. These two ideas are intimately related to the image of "wind." The positive power of the wind would certainly have been seen in its ability to propel ships and, on a smaller scale, to transplant seeds. As the ship is propelled by a wind, so the authentic prophet is moved by the Spirit of God. As the wind carries the pollen from the plant to the soil many miles away, so the Spirit carries God's thoughts to those humans who have been chosen. But then what would it mean to be "prophetic"? Is the prophet the one with charisma? No, Paul declares. The mystery and scandal God has revealed is that true wisdom rests in preaching the crucified Messiah in word and deed. The true prophet is one who lives out Christ crucified.

1. See Baur, *The Church History of the First Three Centuries,* vol. 1, trans. Allan Menzies, 3d ed. (London: Williams & Norgate, 1875); and Walter Schmithals, *Gnosticism in Corinth: An Investigation of the Letters to the Corinthians,* trans. John E. Steely (Nashville: Abingdon Press, 1971). Cf. E. Earle Ellis: "All the 'Greek' reconstructions of Paul have their root in F. C. Baur's interpretation of Paul as the exponent of Gentile Christianity" (*Paul and His Recent Interpreters* [Grand Rapids: Eerdmans, 1961], p. 29).

2. Says Schweitzer, "How could it have been expected that the way to the rich fields of Pauline mysticism should be through the rugged heights of the Late-Jewish Eschatology?" (*The Mysticism of Paul the Apostle,* trans. William Montgomery [New York: Henry Holt, 1931], pp. 165-66; see also p. 380). For Davies's views, see his *Paul and Rabbinic Judaism* (London: SPCK, 1948), pp. 188, 190, 200, 214, 216-17.

3. How Paul Answers His Questions in the Context of Chapters 1-4

One would think that the most likely meaning of "spiritual person" would indeed be a person with the greatest manifestations of God's gifts. Whatever "spiritual" means, however, it is not an adjective Paul employed to describe the Corinthians. Although the Corinthians were enriched in all word and all knowledge (1:5), lacked nothing in the way of *charisma* (1:7), and emphasized the importance of speaking in tongues (chap. 14), Paul could not speak of them as "spiritual." To the contrary, he described them as "earthly" and "immature" (3:1). So to be "spiritual" does not mean simply to have spiritual gifts. Nowhere in 1 Corinthians is there an indication that Paul uses the word "flesh" in a literal sense when he compares it disparagingly to things of the spirit. If anything, he sees matter as significant. Food is not itself evil, even if offered to idols (chap. 8). The apostle also has a right to food and drink (chap. 9) and the saints to a contribution (chap. 16). Although the resurrected body is a "spiritual" one, it is still a body (*soma*, 15:44). So we can see that the letter contains little or nothing to substantiate our understanding the spiritual as immaterial or as charismatic.

The Corinthians were not "spiritual" in Paul's use of that adjective because they neither understood nor appreciated the prophet who lived out Christ crucified. Twice at least Paul describes his own and Apollos's work as that of "servants" (3:5; 4:1). The Corinthians certainly did not understand servanthood and crucifixion as necessary for their leaders or their own manner of living. God chose the weak, low, and despised so that no human might boast in the presence of God (1:27-29). Of such were many of the Corinthians. However, they apparently disparaged their own background (e.g., in 4:8). Paul consciously chose rather to know nothing among them "except Jesus Christ and the crucified one at that" (2:2). If human wisdom were to be used, the cross of Christ would be emptied of its power (1:17). In contrast to looking for signs and wisdom, "we preach Messiah crucified," Paul asserted (1:23), explaining that "Christ, our paschal lamb, has been sacrificed" (5:7). In contrast, the Corinthians lacked unity of mind and purpose (1:10) because they were arrogant, boasting to one another about their gifts (4:6-7). The problem was basically one of worldliness and worldly wisdom. Knowledge had become a basis for assigning superiority and inferiority and therefore generating hostility.

North and South America are separated from each other geographically and by such things as climate, language, and heritage. But they are also separated by the different kinds of knowledge they value and the different lifestyles and values they adopt on the basis of the ways they think. Earthly knowledge is divisive. It separates those who know and therefore hold power from those who do not know and therefore lack power. The Spirit, on the

other hand, unifies people, because its values so transcend those of unspiritual humanity as to appear to be foolishness. This is what unites us. If
the Corinthians were to have embraced in word and lifestyle the message of a
crucified Messiah, then arrogance and disunity would have been impossible
among them.

What does it mean to "preach Messiah crucified"? Paul illustrates such
"preaching" in 4:9-13. To preach Christ crucified is to live "sentenced to
death" as a spectacle to the crowds. The things of the Spirit are "foolishness"
(μωρία) to the unspiritual person (2:14), and true apostles illustrate that
"foolishness" (4:10). To live "sentenced to death" is to look "weak," to be
"unhonored," to be in hunger and in thirst and insufficiently clothed and
beaten and homeless and overworked (4:9-12). (Paul employs polysyndeton
in 4:11, with the repetition of "and," in order to accentuate the exten-
siveness of his list and to have the reader pause at each verb.) If Paul has yet
not made clear to his readers how his lifestyle is like that of the crucified
Messiah, he becomes explicit in 4:12-13: "being insulted, we bestow a
blessing; being persecuted, we are patient; being slandered, we encourage."
Paul has rephrased the concepts in Jesus' sermons on the mount and on the
plain. Even some specific words are repeated: "to be hungry" (πεινάω,
Luke 6:21, Matt. 5:6, 1 Cor. 4:11), "to bestow a blessing" (εὐλέω, Luke
6:28, 1 Cor. 4:12), and "to persecute" (διώκω, Matt. 5:11, 1 Cor. 4:12).
Since Paul has had to be hungry, thirsty, insufficiently clothed, homeless,
and overworked, he certainly can be called "poor" (Luke 6:20).

Paul did not translate Jesus' words into metaphorical language. Paul's
being "beaten" (κολαφίζω, 1 Cor. 4:11) hearkens back to Jesus' "strick-
en" (τύπτω, Luke 6:29). The apostles were "cursed" (λοιδορέω) and
"slandered" (δυαφημέω, 1 Cor. 4:12) even as Jesus had warned (Luke
6:22, Matt. 5:10-11). Nevertheless, Paul had responded with love and
blessings toward his enemies (Luke 6:27-28; 1 Cor. 4:12). He employs
asyndeton in 12b-13a, omitting the "and" in order to move the reader
quickly to his summary in verse 13. The summary rephrases the introduction to the list (v. 9): "as refuse of the world we have become, scum of all,
still." To preach Christ crucified is to live out worldly foolishness, to live
against all the wisdom of this age. One then looks like "refuse": unattractive
and irrelevant. The true apostles' manner of living contradicted completely
the manner of living of the Corinthian Christians. The apostles were still
"scum"; the Corinthians already reigned as kings and queens (4:8).

The significance of the "godly wisdom" described before and after 1 Corinthians 2:6-16 is also echoed within the pericope in 2:8: "If the rulers of
the age had understood the necessity for the Messiah to suffer, they would
never have crucified the Lord of glory." As Luke explains, it was because
Jesus had determined to go to Jerusalem—because he had begun to accentuate the necessity for the Messiah to suffer—that the crowds no longer wel-
comed him (Luke 9:22, 51-53; 13:22-35; 18:31-34; 24:26, 46). Similarly,

neither the rulers of the age nor the crowds comprehended the love that was magnanimous enough to entertain the possibility of having to express itself in so radical a way as crucifixion.

The catalogue of sufferings first presented in 1 Corinthians 4:11-13 to show what "preaching Christ crucified" means is repeated in 2 Corinthians 4:7-11, 6:3-10, and, more emphatically, in 11:23–12:10. "Christ crucified" is synonymous with the "servant of God or Christ" (2 Cor. 6:4; 11:23; 1 Cor. 4:1).

The power of the true prophet is revealed in action such as Paul describes in 1 Corinthians 4:11-13, not merely in "talk" (4:20). Paul's life of suffering in imitation of Christ was his "power," a power that is lacking in others who merely talk rather than share in Christ's sufferings. True apostles establish their authority by the suffering they undergo (though not inflict upon themselves) for the sake of the One who commissions. When Paul tells the Corinthians that he is sending Timothy to remind them of his "ways in Christ" (1 Cor. 4:17), he refers to his list of sufferings, which are both the content and the methodology of his teaching. By suffering he seeks to remove all obstacles to his hearers' learning. Though entitled to material benefits, he forgoes them when he must to promote God's reign (1 Cor. 9:11-12). Paul wants the Corinthians to model themselves on Timothy and on himself, for they have modeled themselves on Christ. Paul preached verbally the fact of Christ's crucifixion, and physically he lived out a life of crucifixion. For as God raised the Messiah, so he would also raise the apostle.

4. Some Ramifications of 1 Corinthians 2:6-16

In conclusion, the larger context of chapters 1-4 helps answer the question of who the spiritual person is. The spiritual person is one who lives out Christ crucified. As one lives in imitation of the crucified Lord, one better comprehends and hears the concerns and insights of the Spirit. To live a "crucified" life does not mean to denigrate the material world. Nor was it for Paul a permanent state. He did not suffer disgrace in all the churches. But he was willing to accept the epithet "foolish" for the sake of the gospel and the well-being of the Corinthians. Nor does what he says denigrate the value of the Spirit's gifts. Paul, for example, said he spoke in tongues more than even the Corinthians (1 Cor. 14:18)! But living a "crucified" life does entail turning away from a life of excessive wealth and being ready to be despised or thought irrelevant if necessary to promote God's reign.

We can be sure that the rulers of this age have entered the church when we hear voices within the church promoting a Christianity of comfort and wealth, whether in participation or simply in appreciation. That is worldly wisdom. We as Christians must listen instead to those whose hermeneutics and therefore interpretation flow from a context that elevates the Messiah crucified, which is foolishness to the rulers of this age. The oppressed Christians of this world in South and North America and elsewhere may well be more "spiritual" than those Christians considered successful by the world because they are already nearer to imitating Paul's example. Moreover, true oppression will not lead to the pitfall of arrogance, another deception of the world. To hear God's Spirit we must live a prophetic life, always ready to follow our crucified Lord; and we must always listen to others who live such lives. This is the context in which God's illuminating wisdom and proper exegesis come.

2.4.2

Report by Grant Osborne and Discussion

Osborne: At first glance we wondered why this passage was chosen for this conference. It is obvious that the other papers deal with the fact and necessity of praxis identification with the oppressed. However, as we studied further, we could see that this passage, perhaps more than any other, helps us to get into the attitude with which we are to perform this praxis. Therefore, it performs an essential function. We decided to begin with a statement of methodology—to try to come to grips with the whole process of interpretation:

> The process of interpretation involves the analysis of the text and the interpretation of the text for our cultural context. Therefore it is a dialogue with the text, as the text draws us into its world, and has two attendant aspects: (1) the determination of its original meaning, and (2) the contextualization of that meaning as we interpret it for our thought world and concretize it in our praxis. At this latter point there will be many meanings derived from what it meant. The original meaning resonates into many complimentary meanings which determine our praxis orientation to the text for our day.

First of all, we discussed the problems among the Corinthians. Paul was probably battling the influence of a group that was characterized by Hellenistic Jewish syncretism of wisdom speculations and proto-gnostic conventions. But more importantly than that, this particular movement resulted in schisms, quibbling over leaders (1:10), and selfish boastings (4:6-7). The opponents stressed worldly wisdom over unity. Paul's answer, found in three categories in this passage, became the body of our discussion: (1) godly versus worldly wisdom, (2) spirit-revealed wisdom, and (3) spirituality or the spiritual person.

1. Wisdom was used in a negative sense and in a positive sense. The wisdom of this age (v. 6) stresses success and self-interest, and it is especially evident in the rulers of this age. After a long discussion we concurred with Cullmann's contention that this is probably the expression of a joining of the

demonic with human institutions. This has tremendous implications for liberation theology because it places worldly wisdom in the category of institutionalized evil eschatologically: "the rulers of this age." In contrast to that, godly wisdom is manifested in weakness and in identification with the crucified Lord. This term, "crucified Lord," has arisen to summarize the entire passage and the entire message, especially in light of 1 Corinthians 1 and 4. This identification, then, is the source of Paul's strength: self is replaced by Christ, demonstrating the spirit and power of God (2:4).

2. We found spirit-revealed wisdom to be at the very core of the passage, for the entire central section. Isaiah 64:4 is used to show the glorious future for the true believers. God reveals this wisdom through the Spirit (v. 10), who reveals the deep truths of God to true believers. Here Paul is turning the proto-gnostic language of his opponents against them. Godly wisdom is hidden, a mystery that brings glory (v. 7). Yet it is now spoken, presented to the mature believer (v. 6). The result is that the Christian life is lived naturally (v. 13) as the mind of Christ (v. 16) gives this hidden wisdom and the power of discernment (v. 15). The spiritual person, as a result, judges all things but is judged by no one. We thought it was very significant that you have the neuter "all things" and then the masculine "no one" in this particular statement (v. 15). We took it to mean that the spiritual person does not take part in manipulating people and therefore is beyond the judgment of people. Rather, living above the external, the spiritual person discerns spiritual realities, and is involved in judging and dealing with those realities concerning God's place in his identification with world. The truths of godly wisdom, then, are revealed only to those in the chosen community (v. 10) who have the Spirit (1:12) and the mind of Christ (v. 16). The paradox is that Paul presupposes a united community here. We felt this was extremely important: he is speaking not purely on the individual level but rather on the community level. This united community takes on the character of Christ and at the same time is the only path by which unity can be achieved. This comes out of weakness—it is foolishness to worldly wisdom (v. 14).

3. The spiritual person (v. 15) is a part of this community that embraces in word and lifestyle the message and paradigm of the Crucified One. This is the central point of Bill and Aída's paper. The spiritual community is not other-worldly but demonstrates the spirit and power of God (v. 4) through a lifestyle controlled by the Spirit. Such a life is characterized by weakness before God rather than success in the eyes of the world. To be wise to the world means to follow its patterns; but to act in such a way is to be despised by God. To participate in God's wisdom is to take part in his liberation— and to be despised by the world. God's wisdom is an absolute and is not open to discussion. To be spiritual, one must humble oneself before God's wisdom.

We then moved from interpretation to contextualization. The basic question of the worldly versus the weak applies not just to the rich versus the poor but to the attitudes of the the leaders of both groups as they seek to contextualize the spiritual life within the larger context of our societal realities. In discussing Latin America and other Third World contexts, we encountered the basic problems of relativism and self-seeking. In this light, we asked a question that our group has not yet answered but that we think all of us should be asking ourselves: Does the liberation theologian have the right to see the passage as a further opiate to the masses and then proceed to change the codes—that is, to change "the wise of the world" to mean "follow the establishment" and change "the weak before God" to mean "take part in liberating the oppressed"? The liberator often becomes the next generation's oppressor. And we believe this difficulty is being addressed in the passage, because that's exactly what happened in Corinth. Therefore we must seek a *kenosis*, a sacrificial love. This was very strongly stressed by Rolando again and again throughout our discussion. I think it is an extremely important point. We seek the sacrificial love and the wisdom of God. He demands not power but servanthood of us in our identification with the poor. Paul is addressing the whole community. He speaks especially to the elite, but he addresses the poor as well as the elite throughout the passage. Weakness, he tells them, turns to strength: it is out of strength that one turns the other cheek. I do not have to kill and revolt. That puts me in the same place as the oppressor. Rather, I take a stand against social evil and then seek to minister to the oppressor as well as the oppressed, as both Christ and Paul did. In the midst of the Pretorium (Phil. 1:13) or Grenada or Nicaragua, God's power is manifest in my weakness and in my servanthood.

Silva: Did I hear you say that you perceived three types of individuals in the passage?

Osborne: Not really. I was referring to separate categories. We would identify the spiritual with godly wisdom. The first category was worldly versus Godly wisdom. The second category concerned the means by which we move from the worldly to the godly—namely, Spirit-revealed truth. Then the third category is the result of that. I was talking about a progression of logic rather than three types of persons.

Stam: When you talk about liberation theologians who switch the terms, were you thinking of someone in particular?

Osborne: No, we were just addressing a question of hermeneutics concerning the extent to which we can contextualize this passage for our time. Since our passage primarily addresses attitudes rather than issues of justice and salvation, we wanted to be more specific on how it relates to our overall discussion.

Zorrilla: A question. Did you say that you had studied this passage in the context of the whole of 1 Corinthians?

Osborne: In their paper, Bill and Aída addressed it in the context of chapters 1 to 4 but also with a consciousness of the whole letter.

Zorrilla: Do you have a clear view of who are the wise and mighty and noble, and who are the weak?

Osborne: We probably spent as much time on that as anything else, discussing the whole question of superapostles and whether the concerns could relate to both Corinthian letters. Bill thought that there are places in chapter 4 where it may. However, the general consensus seemed to be the we probably can't go that far. On the whole we dealt with the problem of leadership.

Costas: So you don't see any socio-economic implication there?

Osborne: Not in this passage. Certainly the implications are obvious in chapters 6 to 8 and in other places in Corinthians, but not in this passage.

Costas: So "mighty" is not social?

Osborne: In this case the mighty were the religious elite. Bill, why don't you address that further?

Spencer: We saw a possible theoretical basis for social categories. We went back and forth between whether this particular passage addressed that or simply provided the theoretical basis that was then overshadowed by issues of religious leadership. We agreed that it did lay a groundwork for the kind of leaders that could be chosen in both religious and secular settings. In that sense, it speaks to the social and economic directions that are tied up with leadership coalitions that contradict salvation. So you're right, Orlando, the seeds are there.

Reid: I'm confused by the way you're construing human wisdom. Because it seems that it is inherently political in the sense that it's a construction of what we take for granted as being of the world. If this is the case, then this is the most political of our passages rather than the least.

Osborne: Yes. I think what we were saying was that it is political but that the passage's context concerns attitudes of the church rather than the confrontation of specific institutions by the church. The institutional side, which comes out in verses 6 and 7, was a hermeneutical control.

Wan: I think I disagree with some of the points that Bill and Aída have raised in this paper. In my opinion, the passage *is* referring to a power play within the church. It was within the church, but it was a problem of political structure, of a hierarchical structure within the church. Paul is tracing the source of these problems back to a kind of an arrogance, a kind of worldly wisdom, and he counters it by bringing forth the witness, the crucified Christ. So to answer some of the questions raised, I thought it was not just a religious problem, but it was a problem that goes through the church, and certainly some of the racial implications are brought out in the later chapters of 1 Corinthians.

Reid: It was my understanding that the Greco-Roman mind attributed a fair amount of political value to human wisdom.

Osborne: It did. Frankly, I wasn't even aware that there was a disagreement.

Spencer: I don't think we really disagree here. Emilio was the one who helped us with the insight that the problem referred to in the passage might be political or, more specifically, ecclesiastical-political.

Osborne: And we easily apply it to everybody but ourselves. But because we felt that this passage *does* address the church concerning this arrogance and our ecclesiastical power plays, we must admit that we are participating in the institutionalized evil that is characteristic of the world.

2.4.3

Final Report from Corinthians Group

SZE-KAR WAN

As a starting point, the study group agreed that the common ground for discussion was our hermeneutical commitment. As a group, we determined that hermeneutics involves both an analysis of the biblical text and an appropriation of the text for our present context. We are engaged in a dialogue with the text as the text draws us into its world. This fusion of horizons has two aspects: first, the determination of its original meaning and, second, the contextualization of that meaning as we interpret it for our thought world and concretize it in our praxis. There are many possible interpretations of what the text "meant," and these many meanings in turn inform our response in praxis.

Paul's Message in 1 Corinthians 2

To understand Paul's message in 1 Corinthians 2:6-16 is not a straight-forward matter, since it is specifically addressed to problems in the Corinthian situation and is couched in paradoxical language. The controversy at Corinth involved schisms among church members and quibbling over leaders (see 1:10-17). Influenced by wisdom speculations and probably proto-gnostic tendencies as well, Paul's opponents valued wisdom more than the unity of the community. They elevated themselves over others with presumptions of spiritual superiority and perhaps also on the grounds of higher social and economic status (see the discussion of the eucharist in 1 Cor. 11). They expressed their elitism directly in boasting and selfishness (4:6-7; cf. 1:28-31).

In response, Paul distinguished sharply between worldly wisdom, which was manifested in the self-aggrandizement of his opponents, and godly wisdom, which he noted is paradoxically manifested in what the world considers foolishness and weakness. The "wisdom of this age" (2:6) revolves around success, self-interest, and power. The worldliness of this wisdom is clearly shown in the ignorance of "the rulers of this age," whose inflated sense of self-importance so blinded them to the true identity of the "Lord of glory" that they proceeded to crucify him (2:8). The power Paul is speaking of goes beyond the merely individual; he links it to institutional evil. The eschatological absolute of God (Isa. 64:3 and 65:16, cited in 2:9) shows such power to be mere illusion; God has already revealed that true power resides in the weakness of a crucified man (2:2). As Paul notes, the condemned man on the cross is none other than the Lord of glory, whose powerlessness demonstrates the "spirit and power" of God (2:4).

The wisdom of God is hidden to some, but revealed to others through the Spirit. Indeed, Paul states that the deep truth of God is revealed only by the Spirit (2:10-11), thereby turning the language of his opponents against them. Godly wisdom is a "mystery," he says, previously hidden but now revealed to the "mature" (2:6). With the benefit of this "hidden wisdom," the Christian lives "in the Spirit" (2:13). The "spiritual" judge all things but are themselves judged by no one. They do not seek to manipulate people; in the Spirit, they are capable of discerning spiritual realities (2:15) and hence are above external judging.

It is a mistake, however, to construe Paul's message along individualistic lines, for he is clearly addressing the entire community. He is saying that the truth of God is revealed only to the chosen *community*, to which is given the Spirit and the mind of Christ (2:16). Moreover, this spirituality is not some otherworldly quality that takes flight into the ethereal; it is expressed in a power and spirit that outsiders can witness (2:4). Spirituality is a matter of the Spirit's control of the community's lifestyle. In unity the community of God embraces in word and action the paradigm of the Crucified One, forsaking the pattern of success that belongs to the wisdom of this age and taking on the weakness of God in humility along with his liberation. This message of self-sacrifice is God's absolute, and as such is not open to discussion. The paradox is that Paul's message presupposes a united community that collectively takes on the character of Christ. Yet he is calling for self-sacrifice to build up and maintain the unity of the community.

Paul's Message in Our Context

The paradox of the crucified Lord recalls the paradox we face in our struggles. The call to surrender such power as we have is at variance with our natural inclination to acquire as much power as possible to produce change, political or otherwise. Similarly, the emphasis on the "foolishness" of God (1 Cor. 1) is jarring to the ear of the highly educated pastor and scholar. We acknowledge that power and education are not omnipotent in themselves, and yet how many times do we not hear of pastors who leave their impoverished homes for theological educations abroad and return in the hope of effecting socio-economic changes to bring relief to the poor only to find that they have in the interim become hopelessly out of touch with their people?

To face this paradox constructively, we once again began by noting that Paul was addressing the whole community. In this context we can see that Paul is calling us to seek a kenotic and sacrificial love in the wisdom of God instead of human wisdom, calling us to servanthood through an identification with the powerless and the poor instead of the empowered. We must not kill and revolt in violence, for that would put us on the same level as the oppressors. Nor should we indulge in the sort of arrogance and power-seeking that are characteristic of party politics, even if our intention in doing so is noble, for to do so is to participate in the institutional evil of the "rulers of this age."

We noted that there are tendencies to relativize the absolute wisdom of God and to seek personal power in the Latin American context. But we are called to manifest God's power in this situation in our weakness and servanthood, standing on the side of those who are constantly ravaged by the Contras in Nicaragua, for example, and of the Granadians invaded by the U.S. Marines. It is an act of strength to turn the other cheek. In Psalm 14 we see the rich and the powerful "in terror" because Yahweh stands with the poor (vv. 5-6).

So, we are not justified in interpreting this passage as a call to abide by the status quo. But neither should we simplistically equate being "wise to the world" with following the establishment or being "weak to God" with liberating the oppressed. The passage is a critique of the view that advocates leadership by power, and it cannot be forced to apply to a context of rich and poor superficially. There is no guarantee, for example, that the liberator of one generation will not become the oppressor of the next, as history so abundantly testifies. We are called to take a stand against social evil, but we must seek to minister to the oppressor as well as the oppressed.

Ultimately we did not resolve the paradox, and probably that is good. Its richness lies in its fruitful ambiguity, which seizes our attention and demands that we reflect on the text and the context afresh in each new situation. We decided that the text cannot be neatly captured and domesticated by our ideological predispositions. It stands above us in judgment whether we are rich or poor.

Members of the Galatians 3 Study Group

Mark Lau Branson
Richard Hays
Linda Mercadante
C. René Padilla
J. Deotis Roberts
Moisés Silva
Valdir Steuernagel

2.5.1

Jesus' Faith and Ours: A Rereading of Galatians 3

RICHARD B. HAYS

1. Faith, Justification, and Christ: Elements of an Exegetical Problem

The doctrine of justification by faith has long been construed as the clear and uncontestable bedrock of Pauline theology. Ever since Martin Luther's paradigmatic hermeneutical breakthrough, it has seemed evident (to Protestant interpreters, at least) that Paul meant something like this: we find acceptance with God not by performing acts of outward obedience but by believing in God's Son, Jesus Christ, who was crucified for our sake. Galatians in particular—one of Luther's favorite texts—appears to be a vehement manifesto of this gospel of justification, affirming the freedom of the Christian from all external requirements: all we need to do in order to be forgiven by God and reconciled to him is to hear and believe.

The extent and consequences of the consensus on this point may be demonstrated by comparing the recent commentaries on Galatians by Hans Dieter Betz and F. F. Bruce.[1] These two very learned New Testament scholars, coming at Galatians from different theological traditions and with

1. Betz, *Galatians*, Hermeneia (Philadelphia: Fortress Press, 1979); F. F. Bruce, *Galatians*, New International Greek Testament Commentary (Grand Rapids: Eerdmans, 1982).

very different methodologies, produce readings of the text that agree on this salient point, that Paul's gospel concerns primarily the justifying of the individual before God. The point is made eloquently in a quotation from Luther that Betz places as the epigraph to his entire commentary.

> Indeed, we are not dealing with political freedom but with a different kind of freedom, which the devil especially hates and attacks. It is that freedom for which Christ has set us free, neither from any human servitude nor from the power of tyrants, but from the eternal wrath of God. Where? In the conscience.[2]

This superscription provides a revealing insight into Betz's hermeneutical perspective. Clearly he intends to locate his interpretation of the letter squarely within the mainstream of Lutheran piety. The gospel is understood here as a liberating word addressed to the (terrified) *conscience* of individuals. The "freedom for which Christ has set us free" is understood as an *internal* freedom from guilt, which must be sharply distinguished from "political freedom." This kind of piety has sometimes played itself out on the stage of modern history with tragic consequences.

Usually theologians seeking to counterbalance such a perspective have not challenged the Reformation's interpretation of Paul. Efforts to assert the gospel's relevance for social ethics have tended to appeal instead to other resources within the canon: Exodus, the prophets, the teachings of Jesus in the synoptic Gospels, and so on—weighty warrants indeed. Recent scholarship on Paul, however, has opened up important new avenues of speculation suggesting that Paul need not—indeed *should* not—be interpreted as a witness for an inward-turned religion dealing primarily with individual guilt.[3] Building upon this work, I will argue in this essay that as long as Paul's gospel is interpreted solely as the means to resolve a soteriological dilemma, that gospel is being severely truncated.

The individualistically oriented reading represented by Betz's commentary severs the relation between theology and ethics in a way Paul would have found most distressing. Consider, for example, Betz's remarkable evaluation of the parenetic section of Galatians:

> Paul does not provide the Galatians with a specifically Christian ethic. The Christian is addressed as an educated and responsible person. He is

2. Luther, in his commentary on Galatians, cited by Betz in *Galatians*, p. v.; translation mine.

3. See, for example, Ernst Käsemann, *New Testament Questions of Today*, trans. W. J. Montague (Philadelphia: Fortress Press, 1969), pp. 168-82; Krister Stendahl, *Paul among Jews and Gentiles* (Philadelphia: Fortress Press, 1976); E. P. Sanders, *Paul and Palestinian Judaism* (Philadelphia: Fortress Press, 1977); Marcus Barth, "The Kerygma of Galatians," *Interpretation* 21 (1967): 131-46; and J. Christiaan Beker, *Paul the Apostle: The Triumph of God in Life and Thought* (Philadelphia: Fortress Press, 1980).

expected to do no more than what would be expected of any other educated person in the Hellenistic culture of the time.[4]

I find this reading of Paul, drastically minimizing the distance between the world and the community of faith as it does, entirely incredible. Did Paul think that God sent the Holy Spirit through Jesus' death on the cross merely in order to empower the church to live in accordance with the conventional standards of popular morality?

Betz has reasons, of course, for interpreting Paul in this fashion. He is able to point to numerous passages from the moral philosophers of Hellenistic antiquity that parallel Paul's exhortations in one way or another. It is neither possible nor necessary to examine these parallels in detail here. In any case, the question is not whether such parallels exist but whether Betz has adequately described the *theological* framework within which Paul's moral exhortations are to be understood. In my judgment, Betz underestimates the extent to which these exhortations became in Paul's hands expressions of an ethic radically transformed by the kerygma of Christ crucified. Thus, the real question is one of theological interpretation.

Betz's reading of Galatians supports Bultmann's influential opinion that Christian obedience entails no particular type of conduct which is specifiably distinct from that of the non-Christian. The theological roots of Bultmann's view on this point are, of course, deeply embedded in the Lutheran "two kingdoms" ethic, which in turn is the logical outworking of Luther's understanding of justification as liberation from guilt.

This theological tradition running from Luther through Bultmann to Betz is wrong—not just because its political consequences may seem unpalatable but because it stems from faulty exegesis. When Galatians is read through the sort of hermeneutical lens provided by the Luther quotation, the result is a gospel that is not merely truncated but distorted. In the final analysis, Betz's enormously erudite commentary overlooks or misrepresents many of Paul's fundamental and explicit concerns in Galatians. Let there be no misunderstanding: I level these serious charges at Betz not to single out his work as an aberration but precisely because his commentary so lucidly exemplifies a widely shared hermeneutical perspective. Betz's commentary is original, even idiosyncratic, in various ways we cannot explore here, but my criticism strikes precisely at the point where Betz speaks for mainline Protestant tradition.

Betz shares the Western proclivity for reading this letter to the Galatian community as though it were a timeless tract addressed to individual believing subjects. He slips casually into treating the parenetic section as if it were addressed to "the Christian" (singular), although in fact it is addressed throughout to the *community*, and its most basic concern is the preservation of unity within the community. (For example, the vice and virtue lists of

4. Betz, *Galatians*, p. 292.

5:16-24 are bracketed by clear admonitions against division within the church in 5:13-15 and 5:25—6:5.)[5]

I would like to concentrate on two other closely intertwined issues that have a crucial bearing on the way we construe the message of Paul's letter to the Galatians. I believe that our received exegetical tradition involves some fundamental errors that have affected our whole interpretation of Pauline theology.

First, what does "faith" (*pistis*) mean, and how is it related to justification)? The popular interpretation is that Paul uses *pistis* to mean "believing," a kind of subjective, cognitive activity that is a prerequisite for justification. That is to say, *pistis* becomes a new kind of work. William Law put the issue bluntly: "Suppose one man to rely on his own faith and another to rely on his own works, then the faith of the one and the works of the other are equally the same worthless filthy rags." Protestant interpreters have often tried to surmount this difficulty by explaining that faith is a gift from God. Certainly that is an edifying idea, but it encounters two serious objections: (1) precisely the same affirmation could be made with reference to "works," and indeed we find that it *is* made in the Qumran Thanksgiving Hymns; (2) in Galatians, as in Romans, Paul never describes faith as a gift. This line of inquiry must lead us to reexamine Paul's discussion of faith in Galatians 3. Does he mean to refer to our activity of believing in Christ, or does he have something else in mind?

Second, how is the figure of Jesus Christ related to "justification by faith"? The popular interpretation of Paul treats Christ as the *object* of our act of believing—that is, it places him "in the passive role of being the object of our justifying faith."[6] From the point of view of systematic theology, this leads to a confusing situation aptly described by Gerhard Ebeling:

> The Reformers' understanding of faith had no effect on the formation of Christology—not, at least, in normal church dogmatics. . . . Hence the difficulty . . . of maintaining the strict inner connection between Christology and the doctrine of justification. The Christology mostly does not lead by any compelling necessity to the doctrine of justification, and the latter in turn usually leaves it an open question how far Christology is really needed as its ground.[7]

The classic illustration of this difficulty is provided by Paul's own discussion in Galatians 3 (and Romans 4) of the figure of Abraham, who was justified not by believing in Jesus Christ but by trusting God. If Abraham is the

5. This is one of the ways in which Paul's parenesis differs most significantly from Betz's parallels.

6. G. M. Taylor, "The Function of *Pistis Christou* in Galatians," *Journal of Biblical Literature* 85 (1966): 74.

7. Ebeling, *Word and Faith* (Philadelphia: Fortress Press, 1963), p. 203.

paradigm of the justified believer, why must we put our faith in Christ in order to be justified? Couldn't we, like Abraham, simply trust God? If so, why was Christ's incarnation and death necessary? Such questions must lead us back to a careful examination of what Paul does and does not say in Galatians 3 about Christ's role in justification.

In the interest of brevity and clarity, I will state my conclusions in the form of theses for disputation, a tactic for which our forefather Luther provided honorable precedent. You will no doubt be relieved to know that my theses number not ninety-five but four, two negative in form and two constructive.

1. Nowhere in Galatians 3 does Paul place any emphasis on the salvific efficacy of the individual activity of "believing."
2. Nowhere in Galatians 3 does Paul speak of Jesus Christ as the object toward which human faith is to be directed. (Gal. 2:16 is another matter, of which more later.)
3. *Pistis Iēsou Christou* in Galatians 3:22 (and 2:20, etc.) refers to "Jesus Christ's faithfulness," his obedience in fulfilling God's redemptive purpose. Paul characteristically insists that we are redeemed/justified not by *our* believing but by Jesus Christ's faithfulness on our behalf.
4. This more Christologically oriented reading of Galatians illuminates in a new way the integral relationship between theology and ethics in Paul's gospel.

Obviously, such claims can be tested only through detailed exegesis. The consequences for our overall understanding of Paul are considerable.[8] Of course, it is not possible here to undertake a complete exegetical study of Galatians 3. I will focus on three verses (3:22, 3:11, and 3:2) and then sketch briefly the implications for our overall understanding of the letter.

2. Galatians 3: Exegetical Probes
a. Galatians 3:22

The easiest place to begin our discussion is Galatians 3:22, because the RSV translation, which reflects the popular reading of Pauline theology, is so clearly strained and implausible. The RSV renders the text as follows: "But the scripture consigned all things to sin, that what was promised to faith in Jesus Christ might be given to those who believe." This translation is unacceptable for several reasons.

8. I develop much of the exegetical work that follows here at greater length in *The Faith of Jesus Christ: An Investigation of the Narrative Substructure of Galatians 3:1–4:11*, Society for Biblical Literature Dissertation Series, no. 56 (Chico, Cal.: Scholars Press, 1983), pp. 139-91. For fuller documentation of the arguments advanced here, I refer the reader to that more technical study.

First, the formulation is redundant. Why does Paul need to say both "to faith in Jesus Christ" and "to those who believe?" He could more easily have written ". . . in order that what was promised might be given to those who believe in Jesus Christ." This suggests that the phrase *ek pisteōs Iēsou Christou* might have some other meaning and function in the sentence.

Second, a very strong case can be made that it is not idiomatic Greek usage to express the object of faith with an objective genitive construction. Users of Hellenistic Greek would more naturally designate the object of faith with the dative case (cf. Gen. 15:6, quoted in Gal. 3:6: *Abraam episteusen tō theō*) or by using the prepositions *epi* or *eis*. Apparent exceptions such as Mark 11:22 can be found, but Paul's usage seems to conform to the more conventional pattern. See, for example, Romans 4:25: *tois pisteuousin epi ton egeiranta Iēsoun ton kyrion hēmōn ek nekrōn* ("to those who believe in the one who raised Jesus our Lord from the dead"). When Paul wants to speak of believing *in* Jesus Christ, as he does in Galatians 2:16, he uses the preposition *eis* (see also Col. 2:5). All of this suggests that the construction *ek pisteōs Iēsou Christou* in Galatians 3:22 should not be interpreted as a reference to "faith in Jesus Christ." Perhaps the most arresting parallel to this phrase appears in Romans 4:16: *ek pisteōs Abraam.* Here Paul certainly does *not* intend to refer to "faith in Abraham"; he means simply "Abraham's faith." In light of this parallel, it would not be unreasonable to suppose that the similar phrase in Galatians 3:22 should be understood to mean "Jesus Christ's faith."

Third, the RSV is almost surely wrong in taking *ek pisteōs Iēsou Christou* as a modifier of the noun *epaggelia* ("promise" or, as the RSV has it, "that which was promised"). Nowhere in Paul's discussion has he alluded to anything that was promised to faith in Jesus Christ. The promise that has been under discussion is the promise to Abraham (see Gen. 17:8), which of course makes no reference to faith in Christ. In fact, Paul has already explicitly insisted that the promise was given only to Abraham and to Christ (3:16). Furthermore, in 2:16 and 3:8, 11, and 24, Paul uses the prepositional phrase *ek pisteōs* adverbially as a modifier of the main verb in a clause rather than adjectivally. These observations taken together suggest that in 3:22 *ek pisteōs Iēsou Christou* should be taken to modify the verb *dothē,* yielding a translation as follows: "in order that what was promised might be given (to) faith in Jesus Christ, to those who believe."

The parentheses in this translation, however, already point to a fourth and final difficulty with the RSV rendering. The preposition *ek* means "out of, from," not "to." By no conceivable stretch of the imagination can it bear the force that the RSV here requires it to bear. In Galatians 3:22 *pistis Iēsou Christou* must designate not the *receiver* of the promise but the *source* out of which or through which the promise is given to those who believe (*tois pisteuousin*).

In light of these observations, we may now propose an alternative translation: "But Scripture locked everything up under sin in order that what was promised might be given through Jesus Christ's faithfulness to those who believe." Note that I have translated *pistis* here as "faithfulness"; the word has a wider semantic range than the English word "faith," and it regularly connotes faithfulness, trust, or reliability. These are its dominant connotations; the notion of cognitive belief is definitely secondary. My interpretation of Galatians 3:22 requires us to suppose that Paul was not writing an awkward, redundant sentence but rather playing upon a double sense of *pistis/pisteuō:* Christ's faithfulness *(pistis)* to God, manifested in his death on the cross "for us" (cf. 3:20, 3:13), becomes the basis upon which those who believe *(hoi pisteuontes)* now receive the blessing promised to Abraham.

Does this interpretation make sense? Is it consonant with the kerygma expressed elsewhere in Paul's letters? Consider, for example, Romans 5:19: "For just as through the disobedience of one man the many were constituted as sinners, so also through the obedience of one man the many were constituted righteous *(dikaioi)*." One could hardly ask for a clearer statement of a Christology that portrays Christ's faithful obedience as soteriologically efficacious on behalf of others. Notice also the extremely interesting passage in Ephesians 3:12 which refers to "Christ Jesus our Lord, in whom we have boldness and confidence of access through his faith *(dia tēs pisteōs autou)*" (translation mine; note again how the RSV's "through our faith in him" contorts the straightforward sense of the Greek). Though I cannot assemble all the evidence here, I think that a very good case can be made that Paul conceived of Jesus Christ as cosmic protagonist *(archegos* in the language of Hebrews) who enacts the destiny of his people; his self-sacrificial faithfulness is vicariously effective on behalf of all who participate in him.

Once we begin to catch the vision represented by this sort of Christology, new exegetical possibilities open up at every turn in Galatians. Consider, for example, Galatians 2:16, which has often been claimed as a definitive proof text for the view that *pistis Iēsou Christou* must mean "faith in Jesus Christ." In the first place, as Betz has rightly observed, this speech of Paul to Cephas (2:14-21) is full of highly condensed formulations, many of them perhaps echoing early Christian confessional language. Paul is here sounding themes he will explicate in the rest of the letter. This means that our interpretation of *pistis* in 2:16 must be shaped by Paul's explicit discussion and usage in chapters 3-6. If 2:16 is interpreted on the analogy of 3:22, in which *pistis* is evidently ascribed both to Christ and to "believers," a very clear sense results: "Knowing that a person is not justified on the basis of works of the law *(ex ergōn nomou)* but through Jesus Christ's faithfulness, we also placed our faith in Christ Jesus in order that we might be justified on the basis of Christ's faithfulness and not on the basis of works of law." Certainly Paul's formulation affirms that "we believed in Christ Jesus *(hēmeis eis Christon Iēsou episteusamen)*"; here Christ is clearly presented as the object of human faith/trust. But the different grammatical construction in 2:16a, c (dia/ek pisteōs Iēsou Christou) signals a different and equally important affirmation: Jesus Christ's faithfulness (not our faith) is the ground of justification.

Likewise, in Galatians 2:20, when Paul declares that "I no longer live, but Christ lives in me," his radical declaration is further explicated by his confession that "I live in/by the faith(fulness) of the Son of God {en pistei zō tē tou huiou tou theou} who loved me and gave himself for me." Paul is certainly not saying here that he lives by virtue of his own act of believing in the Son of God; he has just relinquished any claim to be the acting subject of his own life. Instead, he is affirming that the acting subject is Christ, whose faithfulness is here closely linked with his loving self-sacrifice. The whole context portrays Christ as the active agent and Paul as the instrument through whom and for whom Christ acted and acts. This assertion of the priority of Christ's faithfulness over our willing and acting is the theological heartbeat of the whole letter.

b. Galatians 3:11

In Galatians 3:11 we have a classic example of a text whose meaning has long been obscured in spite of—or perhaps because of—extensive exegetical investigation. The wrong questions have been put to the text. Since the Reformation, interpreters have engaged in long and fruitless debates over the question of whether the phrase ek pisteōs ("by faith") should be taken as a modifier of the verb zēsetai ("shall live") or of the subject of the clause, ho dikaios ("the righteous one"). In order words, should the passage be understood to say "the righteous one shall live by faith" or "the one-who-is-righteous-by-faith shall live?" Despite all the exegetical energy expended in the past on this issue, I would argue that what we have here is a distinction without a difference. If the apostle Paul came and sat down among us today, I suspect that we would have a hard time explaining to him what was at stake in these different translations.

The really interesting question concerning Galatians 3:11 is who ho dikaios is. Who is "the righteous one" about whom Habakkuk prophesied? Generally, our exegetical tradition has assumed unreflectively that the singular adjective dikaios has a generic significance: "the righteous person, whoever he or she may be." The KJV rendered this passage as "the just shall live by faith," as though the Greek text read hoi dikaioi (plural). Indeed, this is how the Habakkuk passage was understood at Qumran, and it is probably a faithful reflection of the meaning of the Hebrew text of Habakkuk. But we must ask how Paul understood this passage. There is compelling evidence to suggest that Paul, who characteristically cites the Septuagint version of OT texts, would have understood this passage from Habakkuk as a messianic prophecy, would have understood ho dikaios as a messianic title: "The Righteous One." The Septuagint rendering of Habakkuk 2:3-4 is unmistakably messianic:

> the vision still awaits its time, and will rise to its fulfillment and not be in vain. If *he* delays, wait for *him,* because *a Coming One* will arrive and will not linger; if he draws back, my soul will have no pleasure in him; but *the Righteous One* shall live by my faith.[9]

C. H. Dodd suggested more than thirty years ago that the logic of Paul's argument in Galatians 3 indicates that Paul is drawing here on a pre-Christian tradition that already recognized this Habakkuk passage as a *testimonium* to the coming of the Messiah. Dodd did not carry his intuition through to the conclusion that *ho dikaios* must be a designation for the Messiah, but that conclusion lies readily at hand, especially when we know that *ho dikaios* was used in this way during the intertestamental period (e.g., in 1 Enoch 38:2) and that it functions as a designation for Christ in several other places in the New Testament (e.g., Acts 3:14; 7:52; 22:14; 1 Pet. 3:18; 1 John 2:1).

Furthermore, there is undeniable evidence in the immediate context that Paul tended to read the Old Testament through messianic eyeglasses. In Galatians 3:16, Paul insists (in a way that appears to us highly arbitrary and tendentious) that the "seed" of Genesis 17:8 is a reference to Christ and *only* to Christ. His point is that God's promise was given to Abraham and to his singular "seed" (the Messiah) and that the Gentiles therefore receive the blessing of Abraham only because they participate "in Christ Jesus" (cf. Gal. 3:14). There is every reason to think, then, that Paul would take the singular form of *dikaios* in Habakkuk 2:4 just as seriously as he takes the singular form of *sperma* in Genesis 17:8. We can imagine him (on the analogy of Gal. 3:16) explicating Habakkuk 2:4 by declaring, "It does not say 'righteous ones,' referring to many; but, referring to one, 'the Righteous One.'" In Paul's eyes, the messianic meaning of Habakkuk 2:4 would have been unavoidable.

What then would be Paul's point in Galatians 3:11? The example of Jesus Christ himself indicates clearly that no one is justified by the law. A paraphrase will make my interpretation clear:

> Now it is evident that no one is justified before God by the law; for, as the Scripture says, even the Messiah, the Righteous One, will find life not by the law but by faith.

Anyone who has worked on this passage knows that Galatians 3:10-12 is full of perplexing exegetical snares; nonetheless, the proposal advanced here goes

9. The translation is that of A. T. Hanson, *Studies in Paul's Technique and Theology* (London: SPCK, 1974), p. 42; the italics are mine. Hanson is one scholar who has argued for the messianic interpretation of *ho dikaios* in Galatians 3:11.

a long way toward clarifying the logic of Paul's argument. The unifying idea throughout this central section of Galatians 3 is that we receive justification (or "the promise") vicariously because we participate in the fate of the Messiah, Jesus Christ, who was vindicated by God and received life/justification not because of "works of law" but because he was faithful even in undergoing a death that made him an accursed outcast in the eyes of the law. As a consequence of his faithfulness, he receives the blessing promised to Abraham, and we share in that blessing because we are "in" him. This way of thinking does not come naturally to most of us, but it is the way that *Paul* thought. If we want to follow his argument, we have to do it on his terms.

c. Galatians 3:2

But what about the very opening of Galatians 3? Is it not true that Paul's rhetorical questions in verses 2-5 make it clear that the Galatians received the Spirit "by hearing with faith"? Once again, I believe that the RSV translation rests upon questionable preconceptions about the shape of Paul's theology and that the Greek text, considered in light of Paul's usage elsewhere, might lead us to a rather different interpretation.

The key phrase, occurring both in verse 2 and verse 5, is *ex akoēs pisteōs*, which the RSV translates as "by hearing with faith." This is certainly a possible translation of the words; here, unlike Galatians 3:22, no violence is done to Paul's language or syntax. The problem, however, is that both nouns in this extremely condensed phrase are ambiguous. *Akoē* can mean either the act of hearing or that which is heard (= "report, message"). *Pistis* can mean either the act of believing or that which is believed (= "the faith"). Although commentators often insist that the objectification of *pistis* as a designation for the context of the Christian proclamation is a phenomenon that occurs only later in the pastoral epistles, the evidence of Galatians 1:23 flatly contradicts this claim: "He who once persecuted us is now preaching the faith *(tēn pistin)* that he once tried to destroy" (see also 3:23-25). Thus we must at least consider the possibility that our phrase in Galatians 3:2 means "by hearing the faith," although the absence of the definite article makes this unlikely.

More crucial is the question about the meaning of *akoē*. Paul uses the word elsewhere in his letters in both of the senses described above. The closest parallels to the present context, however, are found in Romans 10:17 and 1 Thessalonians 2:13. In the former passage, a quotation from Isaiah 53:1, *akoē* unambiguously means "message": "Lord who has believed our message?" In the latter, the sense is somewhat murkier, but the meaning seems to be "you received God's 'word of proclamation' *(logon akoēs)* from us." If these parallels shed light on Galatians 3:2, the upshot would be that Paul is contending that the Galatians received the spirit not through their act of *hearing* the gospel but through the *proclamation* of the gospel to them.

Clearly neither of these interpretations excludes the other in principle, but the difference in emphasis is significant. The reading proposed here is consistent with Paul's well-attested belief that the proclaimed word of the gospel is itself powerful and effectual (cf. Rom. 1:16; 1 Thess. 1:5; 2:13).

The matter can be put another way. The conventional interpretation, reflected in the RSV, attributes to Paul the idea that the Galatians received the Spirit not because they did "X" (performed works) but because they did "Y" (heard and believed). That way of reading the text raises all the problems discussed above, by presenting faith as a human accomplishment that elicits God's approval. The interpretation that I am proposing locates the point of contrast within 3:2 somewhat differently: the contrast is not between two modes of human activity (works/believing) but between human activity (works) and God's activity (the proclaimed message). Readers will have to judge for themselves which way of describing the contrast more faithfully captures Paul's fundamental concerns.

3. Conclusions and Implications

The brief exegetical probes offered here do not yet provide a full account of the logic of Paul's argument in Galatians 3, but they do provide some indication of the way in which I think the thrust of that argument ought to be understood. Paul is not interested in "believing" as a mode of human activity that is somehow inherently salvific, nor does he give more than passing mention (2:16) to the idea that our faith is directed toward Jesus Christ as object. The emphasis of Paul's theological response to the Galatian crisis lies upon Christ's activity for us. This activity of Christ is understood by Paul as a loving, self-sacrificial obedience to God, which is best described by the single word *pistis*, "faithfulness." This faithfulness of Jesus Christ is the efficient cause of the redemption/liberation of God's people.

Paul's objection to the Galatians' flirtation with law is twofold. First, he fears that they will fall into the error of supposing that their own actions are necessary in order to accomplish something Christ has already accomplished. He jealously insists upon both the sufficiency and the priority of Christ's sacrificial self-giving on the cross for us. Second, he fears that the law will become a cause for division and conflict within the church, reestablishing a barrier between Jews and Gentiles that Christ's death had abolished. Our attention to matters of exegetical detail in this paper has precluded sufficient development of this theme, but it must never be forgotten that Galatians is a pastoral letter in which Paul addresses the question of whether the Jewish law is binding on Gentile believers: it is *not* a treatise on how troubled souls can find salvation. Paul's understanding of God's act of deliverance in Christ leads him to a vision of the church as a community in which the divisions between Jew and Greek, slave and free, male and female are reconciled as all become one in Christ (3:28). The meaning of justification is inseparable from the concrete reality of the community in which Christ's love is at work. Self-asserting practices that jeopardize the unity of the community are a de facto denial of Christ and of the reality of grace (5:4).

It is at this point that we can begin to see more clearly the integral relationship between theology and ethics in the letter. Christ's faithful self-giving is not to be understood simply as a magical metaphysical transaction or a superhero's act of rescue that leaves us in an attitude of grateful passivity. "For freedom Christ has set us free" (5:1), and this freedom is to be exercised in serving one another through love (5:14). In other words, our free obedience to God is to take on the shape of Jesus Christ's obedience. That (I would suggest) is what it means to "fulfill the Law of Christ" (6:2)— through bearing one another's burdens. This is likewise what Paul has in mind when he exclaims (4:19), "my little children, with whom I am in travail until Christ be formed among you": not inwardly, in your individual hearts, but concretely in loving community.[10] For these reasons I would insist that, contrary to Betz's assertions, Paul does offer the Galatians a "specifically Christian ethic," an ethic that derives its material norms not from conventional wisdom but from the scandal of a Messiah "publicly proclaimed as crucified" (3:1). Those who believe this message and are incorporated in him will share his destiny; thus, our faith will recapitulate the faithfulness of Jesus Christ.

What are the practical political implications of such a gospel? That question must be answered with prayerful discernment in the various situations in which we find ourselves. One thing is clear, however: there *are* political implications. According to the Reformers, faith in Jesus Christ sets us free from guilt; according to Paul, the faithfulness of Jesus Christ sets us free to serve one another in love. The proclamation of the gospel necessarily leads to the formation of human communities that take the shape of Christ (4:19) and thus embody "faith working through love" (5:6).

10. I consider all these issues concerning the shape and content of Paul's ethics in greater detail in "Christology and Ethics in Galatians: The Law of Christ," an article in *Catholic Biblical Quarterly* (forthcoming).

2.5.2

Report by Linda Mercadante and Richard Hays and Discussion

Mercadante: At first, our discussion focused on some grammatical points and so the two biblical scholars went at it for a while. I appreciated Richard's work, which clearly and successfully led us to consider breaking through traditional ways of understanding Galatians 3.

My exegetical concern revolves around the ambiguity of *pistis Iēsou Christou,* which may be viewed as meaning either *pistenein eis Iēsoun Christon* ("to believe in Jesus Christ") or *Iēsous Christos pistos estin* ("Jesus Christ is faithful"). Since the former expression occurs frequently in Paul, but the latter does not at all, and since ambiguous expressions should be interpreted on the basis of nonambiguous ones, I prefer to take the phrase as an objective genitive ("faith in Jesus Christ").

However, even if we were to reject this part of Hays's interpretation of Galatians 3, his main concern would still stand: ethics—and particularly community ethics—constitutes an essential element in Paul's message to the Galatians. The reason is that the nature of faith includes the radical element of obedience.

René Padilla raised the issue of how one corrects a church that continues to separate theology and ethics. That valuable discussion on the first day led us to three basic issues. How does Scripture function in relationship to contemporary issues? Is the church given a clear mandate to enter into the political arena? How do we bear one another's burdens, especially given the inequities of resources? On the second day, we decided to read Galatians 3 and 5 and part of chapter 6, and—thanks to Dr. Roberts—we focused at first on Galatians 3:28. Some interesting comments were made about the passage, notably one by Mark Branson, asking whether circumcision was the issue there, first raised because of the Gentiles, but having other implications. By doing away with this distinction of circumcision, the distinction between the three groups was done away with. René Padilla mentioned that the personal sins mentioned can also become social problems. We discussed the differences between individual sin and social sin, René saying that there is no social sin without individual sin, and Dr. Roberts talking about the systemic and massive character of social sin, social evil. René commented on the cumulative aspect of the historical dimension of sin and pointed to things in Scripture that confirm what Dr. Roberts had said about this world, principalities and powers, the strength of evil in the world. Richard asked us to work from the passage's reference to circumcision in order to ask what issue serves as a similar distinctive mark for us—what mark does the church use today, rightly or wrongly, to define who is a Christian and who is not a Christian? We all had different answers to that question, but we weren't very successful in clarifying our positions, so rather than dwell on that we will go back into the three questions.

Hays: The first question is: How does Scripture function in relation to contemporary issues? I suppose that our attempt to deal with that question marks our closest approach to something like a consideration of hermeneutics proper, of methodological questions concerning how one takes biblical text and discerns and transfers the meaning into contemporary applications. So far our group has not succeeded in formulating any very helpful guidelines. The one thing that did emerge in the discussions, eliciting a storm of protest if not a groundswell of enthusiastic agreement, was a statement that goes something like the following:

When we look at Paul's letter to the Galatians, we see him addressing particular pastoral problems in his congregation. He does so by working out an ethic within a kind of eschatological tension. This is particularly obvious in Galatians 3:28, in which he says, "in Christ, there is neither Jew nor Greek, slave nor free, male or female." This is a pointer toward an eschatological reality, a new creation which is not in fact yet empirically present in the church's experience. It can't be simply read as a kind of direct blueprint for practical action in the world.

This led us to talk about communities that *have* tried to realize this eschatological reality in particular historical contexts. Linda provided helpful insights into the Shakers, for instance. We concluded that it's inappropriate to use the text in that fashion. But that leaves us with the question of how it *does* function as a norm for shaping the life of the Christian community. Whatever ethical decision Paul made had to be worked out in light of the tension between the situation and the vision, between what the church ought to be and what it in fact is.

So the point then is that Paul's pastoral directive to the churches can't simply be read off the surface of the text of Galatians and applied directly to contemporary situations. Instead we have to move more indirectly by a kind of method of analogy which asks how we are to respond to the situations that confront us while still honoring the spirit of the fundamental theological concerns with which Paul was grappling. We no less than Paul are in a situation of eschatological tension between the already and the not yet.

Mercadante: Contrary to our expectations, we did not find dramatic differences in our readings of the text. Given our different contexts, that was a surprise. We haven't been able to figure out whether that was because we are so different that our communication failed or whether we are in fact very much alike. Theoretically, it seems to me, individuals from different backgrounds should arrive at different observations and interpretations in their study of the text. And yet, although we did talk about different things in our cultures, we didn't encounter significant differences of interpretation or different exegetical results.

Hays: Second question: Is the church given a clear mandate to enter into the political arena? If I have rightly sensed the position of our group, the answer is that it is not at all clear from Paul's letter to the Galatians that the church is given a mandate to enter into the political arena. Though we can easily dispel the kind of popular misconception that Paul was simply an establishment ethicist who sanctioned the status quo, we do not believe he envisioned even the possibility of the church wielding any sort of political clout within the broader society. He was writing for a tiny minority community, and he derived his ethic from the practical situation facing that community. It's a church ethic. It's an ethic for the church as an alternative community called to manifest the values of the kingdom of God.

Father Steuernagel gave us the image of the church as a community of freedom in which people are set free to live without being in bondage to materialism or to idols such as national security. And I think that on the whole there was a kind of agreement in the group that that's an accurate picture of Paul's ethic as it appears in these passages. René suggested to us that it must be very hard to be a Christian in the United States, because citizens of the United States on whole are so comfortably in bondage to materialism that it is difficult to see ourselves as precisely the kind of alternative community that Paul talks about. And Deotis Roberts made the point that the community of black churches in the United States does in fact stand in judgment over against that society and attempts to manifest that kind of alternative vision.

Mercadante: There seemed to be implicit understanding or quiet agreement among everyone that the church, maybe not as an institution but as the body of Christ, has a mandate to enter into the political arena. But as Richard has said, there wasn't anything that people were pointing to in what we read that gives that mandate. What I'm saying is that there wasn't a consensus that there is no such mandate. We just haven't worked it out yet. And that brings us back to the first problem we weren't able to solve, the question of how Scripture functions in relation to contemporary issues.

Hays: The third and final question: How do we bear one another's burdens? I suppose, at that point, we profited the most by hearing from our Latin American members about practical activities that their church communities have been engaging in to try to deal with situations of real need in their midst—establishing ministries in economically downtrodden parts of their cities, working to establish help for farmers, helping people grow gardens. Those are very practical examples of ways that the churches are working to try to bear one another's burdens.

Earlier, in this large group, I posed a question about what we are supposed to do, and how I can avoid being discouraged. I think one of the ways in which my brothers in the study group have ministered to me over the past two days is that they seem to have more hope than I characteristically have about the real power of the Word to effect change in peoples' lives and in the structures that surround them. And I was struck very hard by a verse right at the end of the passage in Galatians we were reading. It says, "let us not grow weary in well-doing, for in due season"—and the Greek word there is *kairos*—"in due season we shall reap if we do not lose heart. So then, as we have opportunity let us do good to all and especially to those who are of the household of faith." So that even there, you see, we have the focus on the community ethic of the household of faith. But there is also the exhortation not to give up, to stay in there and keep plugging, to hold on to hope, and to trust that God will not allow our efforts to be in vain. So to me, personally, that has been an important part of our group process.

Moderator: We have time for a question or two.

Pinnock: On that point you made in the paper about how to translate "by faith in Christ" or "by faithfulness," which was it? Who won? Were you right?

Hays: We didn't reach a consensus on that point, and I think the fact that no final agreement was mentioned in our report on the content of the group discussion is indicative of the difficulty we found in formulating the kind of hermeneutics that allows us to move from exegesis of the text into addressing concrete, particular situations.

Roberts: I think it also needs to be mentioned that in our earlier discussions we did raise the issue of certain preconceptions that exegetes bring to the text. That became a very important part of our discussion.

Costas: I don't quite understand. Were you saying that the group doesn't believe that the church in Galatians received a mandate for political action? How does the group understand the term "political"?

Mercadante: The second question was related to the first. The first was how Scripture relates to contemporary issues, and the second one was about the politcal arena, meaning *our* situation rather than the situation in Galatians. Since we didn't develop a hermeneutic to make that transition, we weren't successful in our investigation of the second topic, deriving contemporary political views from the text, even though we felt the mandate.

Stam: I'd like to add a few questions to the agenda here. Will you find at any point a kind of a *negative* mandate—"keep out of the political arena"? Second, how are we understanding "church" here? And, on an ethical level, is there a mandate or an "antimandate" for the individual Christian that acts in a political arena?

Mercadante: It sounds as though you are still assuming that we don't think that there is a mandate, but that's not the case. We did agree that there is a mandate, but we haven't developed a hermeneutic to work it out, and that, I think, is a problem we all have.

Hays: Let me respond to both of these questions with one answer. You ask about the political arena underlying Paul's letter to the Galatians. I believe that political arena is the Christian church. The political questions being discussed in the epistle involve the relationship between Jews and Gentiles in the church. And if we want to move from that to making affirmations about our political responsibility within a community larger than the church, within society as a whole, then it seems to me we have to extrapolate from that situation in a way Paul himself does not do in the letter. But that is not to say that we can't do it or that it is not legitimate to do it. That was the thrust of my first point.

Costas: If you follow that kind of argument, you end up saying exactly the same thing when you come to the Gospels. The issues there are bound up in the context of the Jewish situation, in a religious cultural setting. So do we then conclude that they have nothing to say to the larger world? I think you need to look into the necessity of transferring the nature of the political sphere into other spheres of society. The mere fact that the political question is limited to the context of the relationship between Jewish and Gentile members of the church does not rule out the relationship of the church to eternal political problems. Politics appears as an internal and an external reality, and I think that to limit it to internal issues is really, quite frankly, copping out.

Hays: Now, wait a minute, Orlando. We are not trying to limit it. We are simply saying that the kinds of moves you're suggesting are not made for us by Paul in the text. Therefore, if we want to make those moves, we have to formulate a constructive hermeneutic that allows us to do that. We are simply giving you a progress report that says that so far in our group discussion of this passage we have not made any notable progress toward doing that.

2.5.3

Postscript: Further Reflections on Galatians 3

RICHARD B. HAYS

Our group discussion yielded a surprisingly high degree of consensus both with regard to issues of hermeneutical method and with regard to substantive matters in the interpretation of Paul's letter to the Galatians. I was particularly glad to find the group in unanimous agreement with my thesis that Paul *does* present the Galatians with a distinctively Christian ethical vision, though I suppose that such agreement among evangelicals is hardly startling. It was also clear that all of us at least intend, whatever our cultural conditioning may be, to allow Scripture to interpret us and to function as an authoritative norm for our theological understanding and our practical living out of the gospel.

Our discussion did raise, however, a number of issues that call for further comment. These may be subdivided into two categories: (1) my response to certain objections raised concerning my interpretation of Galatians, and (2) further reflections stimulated by the discussion, particularly concerning the relevance of my argument for the integrity of the church's witness in Latin America and in situations of prevalent social injustice.

Response to Objections

One of the highlights of our group discussion was Moisés Silva's gentlemanly and collegial disagreement with some of the major points in my essay. I was particularly gratified by his careful response to matters of exegetical detail in my paper, which helped the group as a whole to enter into constructive discussion of the issues. His reservations about my interpretation have not caused me to change my position, but they do offer me the occasion for a response that might serve to clarify my views further. His objections, and those of other members of our discussion group, are basically of two types: exegetical and dogmatic. I will consider these in turn, concentrating primarily on the exegetical issues.

Exegetical Issues

First of all, Silva notes that I have operated with an exegetical methodology that isolates Galatians and reads it "on its own terms," without reference to the other Pauline letters. He suggests that my investigation should seek to interpret particular passages in Galatians in light of their relation to Pauline theology as a whole. In particular, while he grants that my interpretation of Galatians 3:11 makes good sense in its immediate context, he asks whether such a rendering of Habakkuk 2:4 ("the Righteous One shall live by faith") is possible or appropriate in Romans 1:17. If not, my argument would, in his view, be weakened considerably.

Methodological moderation is the course of wisdom here. It is indeed important to read each Pauline letter, at least initially, on its own terms, because Paul is not a perfectly consistent systematic theologian, and he is capable of using the same language differently in different contexts (consider, for example, his contrasting evaluations of the law in Galatians and Romans). So I agree with Silva that we must exercise a concern for consistency: the clear should interpret the unclear, and when Paul quotes the same passage of Scripture in two different places, it is surely reasonable to assume, in the absence of evidence to the contrary, that he understands it in the same sense in both cases. Common sense would suggest that there must be some sort of coherence between Galatians 3:11 and Romans 1:17.

In fact, I believe that there are very strong reasons to interpret Romans 1:17 in a way that is entirely consistent with my interpretation of Galatians 3:11. Thus, I acknowledge the aptness of Silva's proposal about hermeneutical method; my appropriation of it, however, leads to a different result: a reinterpretation of Romans. In Romans, no less than in Galatians, Paul presents Jesus as the faithful one whose obedience to God confers righteousness upon God's people. This is most evident in Romans 5:18-19, but the same idea lies behind Romans 3:21-26, as Luke Johnson has persuasively argued. [1] The recognition of such a theological structure in Romans allows us to assign a clear meaning to Romans 1:17: when Paul writes that the righteousness of God is being revealed *ek pisteōs eis pistin,* he means that the righteousness of God is revealed, through Jesus' faithfulness, for/to those

1. Johnson, "Romans 3:21-26 and the Faith of Jesus," *Catholic Biblical Quarterly* 44 (1982): 77-90. Cf. my discussion in *The Faith of Jesus Christ,* Society for Biblical Literature Dissertation Series, no. 56 (Chico, Cal.: Scholars Press, 1983), pp. 170-74.

who believe. As I suggest in my paper, this reading of Romans 1:17 offers a precise parallel to my treatment of Galatians 3:22. It also suggests that the quotation of Habakkuk 2:4 in Romans 1:17b might carry a double valence: it is both a messianic prophecy and a characterization of the way a person who trusts in Jesus as Messiah will live.

Our discussion also touched on a second problem that would be posed by the attempt to relate my exegesis of Galatians to the overall structure of Pauline theology. Dr. Silva acknowledged in our conversation that the phrase *ek pisteōs Abraam* in Romans 4:16 *does* provide a formidable parallel that seems to suggest that *Iēsou Christou* in the expression *pistis Iēsou Christou* should be read as a subjective genitive. But, he asked, if that is right, would we not be forced to conclude that Paul in Romans attributes to Abraham's faith(fulness) a saving efficacy analogous to the efficacy of Christ's faith(fulness)? Although the question so stated was intended to operate as a *reductio ad absurdum,* I answered, to the surprise of the group, that such a conclusion is indeed a correct interpretation of Paul. I have argued at length elsewhere that Paul understands Abraham's faith, in accordance with the Rabbinic concept of "the merits of the Fathers," as a faith vicariously efficacious for others and therefore as a foreshadowing and precedent of Christ's faith(fulness).[2] Unfortunately, constraints of time prevented us from pursuing this matter further in our conversation. The skeptical and/or interested reader may refer to my article for supporting argument and documentation.

The second exegetical objection raised by Dr. Silva is harder to answer succinctly. He observes that whereas Paul does sometimes make Jesus Christ the object of the verb *pisteuein* ("to believe," e.g., in Gal. 2:16), he never writes a sentence in which "Jesus Christ" is the *subject* of *pisteuō,* nor does he ever describe Jesus Christ as *pistos* ("faithful"). Since the expression *pistis Iēsou Christou* is grammatically ambiguous, Silva argues that the ambiguity should be resolved in favor of the objective genitive interpretation, "faith in Jesus Christ," since the unclear has to be interpreted by the explicit. This argument deserves serious consideration, but in the end I do not find it to be as compelling as the considerations advanced in my paper. In adition to the detailed discussion of the matter I present in *The Faith of Jesus Christ,* I would like to call attention to several Pauline texts that I think undercut the force of Silva's objection.

First of all, there are at least two texts in the Pauline corpus that do explicitly describe Jesus Christ as "faithful." In 2 Thessalonians 3:3 we find the affirmation *pistos de estin ho kyrios* ("but the Lord is faithful"). If anyone should be disposed to question whether *ho kyrios* here really is to be read as a reference to Jesus Christ, we need only point back to 2 Thessalonians 2:16,

2. See my article "'Have we found Abraham to be our forefather according to the flesh?' A Reconsideration of Rom 4:1," *Novum Testamentum* 27 (1985): 76-98.

in which we find the characteristically Pauline reference to "our Lord Jesus Christ." An even clearer instance is found in 2 Timothy 2:13: *ep apistoumen, ekeinos pistos menei* ("if we are faithless, he remains faithful").

The relevance of these passages for the question before us might be disputed for three reasons. First, both occur in letters whose authorship is contested, rather than in the "undisputed" Pauline letters. While there is room here for reasonable doubt, I myself would be content to regard both of these letters as Pauline, as I assume Silva would also. Second, the passage in 2 Timothy appears to be a quotation of an early Christian confession or hymn; therefore, one might question whether it represents Paul's own position. Here I would respond that we should never make the error of underestimating the extent of Paul's dependence upon and harmony with early confessional traditions. He characteristically cites these traditions as warrants for his argumentation (see 1 Cor. 15:1-17, Phil. 2:1-11). It is certainly possible that Paul might quote a tradition containing elements he does not elsewhere emphasize, but it is surely unlikely that he would quote a tradition containing elements he regards as dissonant with his own Christological understanding.[3] A third objection might be that both of these passages appear to emphasize the ongoing faithfulness of the exalted Lord toward his people rather than the faith/obedience of the earthly Jesus in accepting death on a cross. This point is significant, and it is one of the reasons that I did not appeal to these passages in my earlier study. The passages are relevant only as a counterweight to Silva's lexical argument that Jesus Christ is never described in the Pauline letters as "faithful." There is, however, another Pauline text, often overlooked, that does appear to allude to the faith of the earthly Jesus. To that text we must now turn our attention.

In 2 Corinthians 4:13, Paul cites Psalm 116:1 (LXX Ps. 115:1) in a way that presupposes Christ as the speaker of the affirmation *episteusa dio elalēsa* ("I believed; therefore, I spoke"). The Greek text says literally, "having the same spirit of faith (according to what is written: 'I believed; therefore, I spoke') we also believe, and therefore we also speak, knowing that the one who raised the Lord Jesus will also raise us with Jesus and will establish us with him." The RSV interprets the text by supplying the psalmist as the subject of the verbs *episteusa* and *elalēsa*. But, as A. T. Hanson has argued, Paul is surely reading the psalm as a messianic psalm in which Christ himself is the speaker.[4] The whole surrounding context posits a series of parallels between Paul and Christ, and the logic of the argument depends upon the assertion that Paul's own life-pattern recapitulates and participates in the life-pattern of Jesus Christ. Thus, this passage, if Hanson's interpretation of

3. On the whole issue of Paul's relation to early Christian traditions, see my remarks in *The Faith of Jesus Christ*, pp. 254-56.

4. See Hanson, *Paul's Understanding of Jesus* (Hull: University of Hull Press, 1963), pp. 11-13.

it is correct, provides us with an instance in which Paul not only refers to the faith of Jesus but also makes Jesus Christ the subject of the verb *pisteuein*. This would in turn enhance the plausibility of my reading of *pistis Iēsou Christou* in Galatians.

I hope that these exegetical technicalities do not seem wearisome; as René Padilla rightly insisted in our group discussion, a sound interpretation of Paul can only be achieved through this sort of close attention to matters of exegetical detail. In the end, Dr. Silva and I agree that the expression *pistis Iēsou Christou* is ambiguous, that its ambiguity must be resolved by appealing to broader contextual considerations, and that no irrefutable resolution of the ambiguity is possible on either side. We differ with regard to the relative weight that we assign to different contextual considerations, and thus we come down on different sides of the interpretive question. I continue to think that the evidence favors my interpretation; readers will have to come to their own conclusions.

Theological Issues

Apart from the strictly exegetical issues, Silva also brought to our conversations a theological critique of my interpretation. His most potentially damaging charge is that my characterization of "justifying faith" as a "work" fails to appreciate the Reformation's understanding of faith as precisely the *relinquishment* of the effort to seek one's own justification through any means whatever. To this charge I have a three-pronged response. First of all, insofar as Silva's account of the Reformation understanding of faith is accurate, my polemic against the tendency to turn faith into a work is directed not against the Reformers themselves but against their historical successors, particularly twentieth-century evangelicals, among whom this tendency is epidemic. Second, even if the Reformers can be exonerated of the charge of turning faith into a work, as I believe they can be, this still does not show that their understanding of "faith" accurately or fully reflects Paul's. Third, I would contend, at least for the sake of keeping the discussion rolling, that to understand faith primarily as the relinquishment of the effort to seek justification is to misconstrue seriously Paul's understanding of *pistis*, which is for him always "faith *working* through love" (Gal. 5:6), and thus to lapse into precisely that attitude of "grateful passivity" that has tended to make evangelical Protestantism impotent in formulating a social ethic. "Faith," for Paul, because it is defined by the paradigmatic faithfulness of Jesus Christ, always has an active character: it cannot be reduced to a surrender of efforts at self-justification, because it necessarily entails participation in Jesus Christ's sacrificial self-giving for others.

Precisely for that reason, I was puzzled by Silva's other major theological criticism of my reading of Galatians—his contention that it would lead to antinomianism. That danger is always present, of course, in any attempt to offer an interpretation of Paul's gospel, as Paul himself recognized (see Rom. 6). However, I would have thought that my reading of "the faith of Jesus Christ" would provide a safeguard against evangelical antinomianism by stressing that Christ's faithfulness serves as a model that defines "the law of Christ" (Gal. 6:2), the norm whereby the conduct of the Christian community is to be measured.[5] Those who participate in Christ must live in accordance with the pattern that he himself enacted; this I take to be the major burden of the parenetic section of Galatians. Consequently I would sooner have anticipated the accusation of promoting a new legalism than the charge of antinomianism. Perhaps in this area our limited discussion time did not permit sufficient exchange of views for us to come to a clear understanding of one another's positions.

Further Reflections on Justice and the Gospel

My observations about theology and ethics in Paul's letter to the Galatians were addressed to the North American Protestant church, which is the heir of certain Reformation traditions that have made it possible—indeed, nearly inevitable—for Paul to be read and employed as the major canonical witness for a privatized religion of soul-salvation. The burden of my paper was to argue that such a reading of Paul is a catastrophic misreading, that rightly understood Paul offers a vision for community life shaped according to a pattern of obedience exemplified in the self-sacrificial faithfulness of Jesus Christ.

In our discussion, Dr. Silva suggested that there was no necessary connection between my exegesis of Galatians 3 and the community ethic of Galatians 5-6; one could still affirm the letter's ethical emphasis, he contended, without understanding *pistis Iēsou Christou* to mean "the faithfulness of Jesus Christ." There is, of course, some truth in this. The community-oriented exhortations of the letter's final section are plainly there for any reader to see. The history of Western Christianity, however, offers disturbing evidence that readers do not in fact "see" the real thrust of Paul's argument when they understand *pistis Iēsou Christou* primarily as a way of talking about their own disposition toward Christ. Paul's vision for the ordering of the community in Christ derives its cogency and power precisely from its grounding in the pattern of Jesus Christ's own faithfulness. When we lose sight of this pattern, we lose both the theological warrant for and the practical impetus toward the obedience to which the gospel summons us.

René Padilla, speaking in support of my interpretation of Galatians, raised a question for the group that has stayed with me as particularly crucial:

5. I have argued this case at much greater length in "Christology and Ethics in Galatians: The Law of Christ," an article in *Catholic Biblical Quarterly* (forthcoming).

"How do you correct a church that continues to separate theology from ethics?" I came away from our deliberations in Tlayacapan more convinced than ever that the answer to that question lies at least partly in the affirmation that the "faith" of which Paul speaks so passionately is essentially and irreducibly a participation in the faith/obedience of Jesus Christ himself. As long as faith and obedience are in principle distinguished in such a way that faith means "assent" and obedience is regarded as a desirable after-effect of faith, Christians will continue to take refuge in an illusory cheap grace that is in fact a deformed parody of Paul's doctrine of justification.

A moving illustration of this saddening tendency was given us by Dr. Padilla's story of some members of his church in Buenos Aires who steadfastly opposed the church's involvement in mission in a poor part of the city. Despite his diligent pastoral efforts to persuade them that the church has a responsibility to become involved in the lives of the poor, they insisted that the church should confine its activity to "preaching the gospel." In the end, they withdrew from the church because of their displeasure over the issue. This is a story with a disturbingly familiar ring to North American evangelicals, and it points out a truth of which we became aware at many points during our days together in Mexico: Latin American Protestants have unwittingly and regrettably inherited from North American missionaries many of the false spiritualizing dichotomies that have paralyzed and discredited the church in North America. I was very pleased to find that Dr. Padilla and some of his Latin American colleagues saw in my "rereading" of Galatians a potential resource for restoring the integrity of the church's proclamation of the gospel in their cultural setting also.

How do you correct a church that continues to separate theology from ethics? Many kinds of efforts are required. But the *theological* leverage for correcting this kind of church surely must be found in a fixed exegetical stand that refuses to surrender Paul to a tradition that reduces his gospel to a recipe for the alleviation of individual guilt. "The truth of the gospel" (Gal. 2:14) is a truth that must be enacted in the community of faith, a truth that is betrayed by actions that fail to reflect Christ's self-sacrificing love.

There is no "social ethic" in Paul if by that we mean a value system for the state or for "the present evil age" from which Christ delivers us (Gal. 1:4). But there is a social ethic in the sense that Paul sees the church as a society in which the justice of God must prevail. The community of those who are one in Christ must live in accordance with "the law of Christ," which is the law of a love defined by the faithfulness of the Son of God, who gave himself up to death on a cross for us. To point to that faithfulness is not to solve all the problems confronting Christians who live within an unjust social order. But by pointing to it we remind ourselves that the church—Jew and Gentile, North American and Latin American—is called to enact the faith of Jesus Christ.

III

Plenary Discussion of Major Issues

3.1

Theological Education and the Church

Sheppard: I admit, I'm kind of worried. As a young scholar at Union I feel enormous pressure to satisfy my Old Testament discipline in a certain narrow way. With professional academic societies there are attempts to discuss, for example, narrative theology. When the theological students are there, the discussion is on a high dialectical, theological level. When the biblical people come in, the theological students leave. It's sad how that wave washes back and forth. I'm not sure how to defeat it except to undo the whole current paradigm in some way.

Watson: The thing that sticks in my mind from what you said is that some people who go to a seminary like Union are then no good for their denomination afterward. I'd like to ask John Yoder whether he perceives the Mennonite seminaries to be more accountable to his church. The only other denomination where I see scholars and pastors readily interchangeable is the Southern Baptists.

Yoder: I don't think we have a long enough track record to measure. We're different in that our graduate-level schools are young. We still don't hold seminary preparation to be a prerequisite for ordination. There still aren't enough people completing master of divinity degrees to meet the needs of the congregations. But generally speaking, the youth that come out of the seminaries can still be productive in churches. There hasn't been the same distance between academe and church. It's not the same as for Southern Baptists, who have a particular vision of the pastor being at the same time a great scholar and a great preacher. Our model of studies doesn't produce either scholars or preachers but rather the kind of people who can ride with the congregation and do a little of everything. "Enabler" is the term that I use, because it doesn't suggest a lopsided stress on either the skills of preaching or the skills of scholarship.

* * *

Roberts: I have been associated for a long time with three predominantly black seminaries—Howard, Virginia Union, and the Interdenominational

283

Theological Center. In these institutions you have theological education approximating that of the Southern Baptists in the concern for training theological pastors. There's a close relationship between the pastor and the seminary, with a tradition of younger students being apprenticed by older pastors. There is a strong emphasis on biblical preaching, on exegesis, on pastoral care in the oppressed community.

Reid: Jerry spoke about the theological institutions that don't produce graduates that are suitable for the churches. I remember my own experience at Bethany, where seminary was socialization. I too easily began to equate my world with the world of this denomination. Theological education has to help us be part of a community while at the same time helping us to understand the broader community around us. Too often schools do just one or the other.

Sheppard: There are two kinds of seminaries that worry many of us. One could be defined as a special-privilege school which fosters the sort of classicism, elitism, and academic isolation from the churches that tends to lead capable students away from the church. The other, mentioned by Steve, is the homogeneous seminary which lacks a sufficient representation from the ecumenical and confessional part of the church. Against hard realities, I would hope for a situation, perhaps similar to the Interdenominational Theological Center, where the voices of Pentecostals, Methodists, Baptists, and so forth could be heard. Some fears could be broken by the conversations while confessional integrity of the various groups could be retained.

Mercadante: I'd like to focus on the theological and political issue of subscription, which has been implicit in many comments. Many evangelical institutions have a statement of faith and perhaps even a document outlining a lifestyle code that a professor must sign prior to employment. Several of you have said that you can still lose your tenure and be censured or dismissed. The theological issue is not that the statement of faith was not written correctly. Rather, I think the problem is the subscription itself—the effort to encapsule all of the Christian tradition into a little code and then force everyone into it. And this issue of subscription then leads us to our definition of the church. I think the evangelical understanding of the church is that it is a theological voluntary society. But that's not what the church is! The church is the body of Christ, and thus it includes us all. When it is made into a theological voluntary society, similar to a political club, you can be a part only if you hold a certain position.

Watson: To press Linda's point, as we do hermeneutics within these institutions, we need to keep in mind that the academy is one of the demonic systems of our time.

Hays: I would also like to respond to Linda's analysis, because I operate in a very different theological climate. As I teach at Yale, I participate in a radically pluralistic theological setting. There are no confessional standards, no statements of subscription, no institutional guidelines that limit what may be taught, thought, preached, or practiced. I would suggest this raises a number of different difficulties. Within the last year, we have had both witchcraft and goddess worship in chapel. We have also had goddess worship taught in classes. Even accepting a very broad definition of the Christian tradition, some positions are simply unacceptable. If the answer for theological education does not include some concept of subscription and confessional standard, how do we avoid going over the edge on the other side?

Mercadante: My point is not that no confession should be used but that our codes are too tight. Calvin did not write a code. Even Calvinists use the Westminster Confession, which is far longer than most statements of faith used in evangelical institutions today. In North America there is a tendency to want to be efficient, to streamline, to create little boxes. Now we're paying the price for giving in to that sort of inclination. Also, since evangelicals fear the domino effect, this move toward efficiency tends to include a covert exclusionary political view. Words like *inerrancy* are a part of that. *Inerrancy* is a code word, a shibboleth. You either think correctly or you don't. You're in or you're out. That's what I object to.

Nuñez: This carries over into Latin America, where the so-called mission churches are strongly conservative. Bible schools and seminaries are depending on foreign money, and whoever pays gives the orders. This situation is created by the close link between the churches and the seminaries, and it makes it difficult to do serious theological work. We have the advantage, though, of schools that are pastorally oriented—training students for pastoral work and evangelistic work. But the advantage of a close relationship also creates problems for the professors. Still, I am hopeful, because a new generation is coming, and that may allow us to move more seriously into theological work connected to our particular needs in our own context.

Roberts: Howard Divinity School is a concrete model of a university divinity school that maintains a close link with the churches. There is a conscious effort to keep the mission of the church and the training of the minister at the center of the life of the seminary. So you have a strong emphasis on preaching—biblical preaching—on pastoral care, and on continuing education for ministers. Howard, with a university setting, also has academic freedom. There is no discrimination against people from other denominations. Also, at Virginia Union there is no statement to sign, even though I have received such requests in relationship to other seminaries.

Hays: I think you are able to do that because there is a kind of implicit cultural, theological understanding that limits the diversity of people who are involved. If you had a university setting that was really radically pluralistic culturally and theologically, it would be more difficult to do that.

Stam: We do face a problem in Latin America, where the far right fringe of the church is growing. This creates some of the problems Emilio mentioned. It is very different, though, than the situation in North America, where "evangelical" is identified with "inerrancy." In Latin America, "evangelical" can mean simply "Protestant." In Central America, I do not know of any problem historically with liberalism. Nor has it had its own inerrancy debates.

Padilla: However, even though the fundamentalism/liberalism controversy and the inerrancy debate did not arise in Latin America, many missionaries continue to push these issues on the church. They have not been able to understand that these are only political tools for capitalism.

Sánchez-Centina: In the Presbyterian Church seminary in Mexico, I could be very radical and still not make a big impact, because most of our pastors do not go to seminary. This is true for most of the denominations in Mexico. Who is training our pastors? World Vision, Logos, Campus Crusade for Christ.

Padilla: According to recent figures, over 70,000 pastors in Latin America have no formal theological education.

Deiros: Perhaps eighty percent of evangelical pastors in Latin America have had no formal theological training.

Gil: It seems that the common phenomenon among the Americas, and perhaps with the rest of the world, is the middle-class context of our theology. We are all working with a middle-class hermeneutic. To draw on the point David Watson makes in his paper, that the locus of the church is in the world, where are the poor? We are all middle-class. All of our discussions about institutions presupposes our middle-class culture.

Padilla: There is a close relationship between that and our comments about pastors without formal training. It is precisely because most of the pastors belong to the poor classes that they cannot afford going to seminary. In Latin America, most of the seminaries are supported by U.S. denominations. Latin churches could never afford the expense of this seminary training method. This is not true only with evangelicals. I was asked by an ecumenical seminary if my name could be considered for a professorship. When I said Yes, I was asked if I could bring my own support. When I said No, a German professor was hired. I really had no chance. These are the politics of economics, and you don't need to be a Marxist to see it.

* * *

Wan: I would like to address the problem of poverty, because it relates to the cultural assumptions concerning seminaries. I see a phenomenon in Asia that begins with the fact that professors are pastors and pastors are professors. They don't see this as virtue. In fact, they would like to move away from this set-up, eventually to dichotomize themselves as the North Americans have. I think this perspective is tied up with economic issues, which cause many to see the West as the ideal. If one can become a famous professor or a big pastor then one can move away from Asia or from poverty-stricken areas and teach in North America. We do not have a static situation. There is a constant flow of brilliant scholars and pastors from Asia, and from other parts of the world, to North America, because that's where the money is.

* * *

Sheppard: We need to be reminded, also, that in North America there are many churches in which the ministers are not seminary trained, including most of the Pentecostal churches and many of the black churches. At New York Theological Seminary, they are trying to meet a variety of needs by also having a Bible institute. A seminary, with certain goals, is only going to reach a small group of people with a very specific set of concerns. Here in Latin America, seminaries that may have been instituted out of a concern for missions may well be meeting the needs of only the smallest number of those who could most benefit from associating with a fraternity of scholars. We should not underestimate the value of the Bible college/Bible institute system. I teach at a Bible institute in Brooklyn. I believe many North American scholars would do well to teach in these schools and thereby minister in different worlds. We should not contribute to a privatized, classist, elitist system in which the seminaries are held up as trophies—either in North America or in Latin America.

W. Spencer: It is worth remembering, though, that the United States has a system of academic credits. In effect, you may acquire the same education, but without the approved credits you do not have the mobility. In a culture where credits are not normal, that does not matter. But in the U.S. we need a more flexible system to provide both education and acceptable accreditation.

* * *

Osborne: I think we need to discuss the problem of pluralism. Stan Gundry was fired from Moody because his wife wrote a book on biblical feminism. His dismissal was demanded by the constituency. The entire faculty was in favor of his staying, but the president and the board fired him. But the situation with Bob Gundry is the worst of all. Some members of the Evangelical Theological Society moved to dismiss him because of his commentary on Matthew, in which he draws on redaction criticism to make a case for Matthew's use of creative midrash to contextualize events in the life of Jesus. For example, he sees Matthew's account of the Magi as a contextualization of the shepherd story for the Gentiles. Even though he includes a lengthy chapter on how and why he believes in inerrancy, certain members of ETS believe he can no longer sign their statement with credibility. It is a political move that is calculated to purify the church on a subscription basis—but it is much worse because there is no confessional stance. ETS is supposed to be a pluralistic society, and I think that makes it even more serious for them to oust people than it would be for a school.

But, even in the midst of these problems, I believe we must also discuss the god of our age—pluralism. I think pluralism could easily succeed "inerrancy" as the next great issue. There is a place for discipline. John Stam raised the example of justification of faith. We need to come to grips with where discipline belongs.

Stam: I was not pushing for discipline.

Osborne: But is there going to be a place left for discipline if we allow pluralism to control us totally? What's wrong with witchcraft? There's nothing wrong with it in a Yale chapel.

Hays: Now wait a minute. Many people deeply objected. There was a major reaction against it. It's just that there is nothing structurally built into the system to keep it from happening.

Osborne: How can we ever legally or rightfully say something is wrong if pluralism is all we have? We must have some other grounds.

A. Spencer: If you say "Jesus is Lord," you have a subscription. I think the problem lies in the way these statements are written. These abstract terms separate human thinking from action. I see nothing wrong with subscription, but it must be written in a manner that can be fleshed out in life rather than just signed. Even technical biblical approaches can affect our lives as we try to witness. For example, I once taught English to two students from Spain, one of whom had attended seminary in Germany. The one who had not attended seminary asked me if I could show him where the Bible taught that Jesus is God. As we began with several obvious passages, the other student worked to disqualify them on the basis of higher criticism. So with some educated people, witnessing can be affected by these scholarly issues. However, I believe that this is less of a problem in Latin America and with minority persons in the U.S.

One advantage this group has, with such a variety of people, is the opportunity to affect education. The conversation today indicates how we can state our own viewpoints and then comment on how that affects education. For example, when I work in the midst of what I see as an abstract, Greek-based system, I try to introduce different questions regarding practical aspects of an issue. I am often frustrated because such considerations are ignored. It is as if I tossed a stone into the air. A group like this gives me hope.

Steuernagel: I am perhaps one of the few people in Latin America who has been trained theologically under liberal influence. The seminary in Brazil, where I studied, has its feet in Latin America but its head in Germany. On reflection, I believe the main question we should raise regarding theological education is the place of the church. Is it the seminary that controls the church or the church that controls the seminary? When we talk in those terms, we are talking in terms of power. Depending on what kind of church we want, we have to talk about theological education. If we want a church that is concerned with evangelism, with prophetic work, a church that is going to contextualize the message of the gospel, a church that is to be concerned for the poor, then we have to think of a theological institution that will serve that kind of church. That is one approach. Another approach would be to have a seminary that serves an accommodated, comfortable middle-class church.

Watson: Listening to this conversation, I come back to a comment I made earlier. I think those of us from North America have been sensitized to the demonic system of the North American academy. At this moment, Latin American institutions have not yet come to that. In speaking of a "demonic system," I'm not referring to anything that is visible. I'm referring to the sort of loyalties professors pay homage to after only a few years. This is so insidious! I see evangelical students who learn the right language, learn how to quote the right names, learn how to make obeisance to the right articles, all of which seems to me to be an ideology that is demanding loyalties we have no right to give. And if this particular demonic system can in some way be corrected, or at least called back to its true accountability by colleagues in Latin America whose loyalties still are with the gospel, then we have no choice but to make whatever painful adjustments might be required. It's particularly important that such reforms be made because of the tremendous power wielded by the academy in North America. And the power that is wielded is not just power over the careers of teachers. It also determines the curricula that Jerry has outlined, the ways in which we have institutionalized it, whether through demanding subscription or establishing a pluralism that you have to go along with because, after all, they said nice things about your last article. All of this is simply a demonic system. And I think that has been brought very much to light in these last four days.

3.2

Theology in the Contexts of Marginalization

A. Spencer: As I came to this conference, I was hoping that we could avoid a problem most groups have, but I see that it has happened here also. In many groups, including the feminist groups in which I participate, we get together and place all the blame on one side. I saw that happening here as we were talking in another session about the Dominican Republic. I know the U.S. economic interests there are strong, but that doesn't make the Dominicans pure. There is bribery and corruption there, too. People are people. I've just noticed that when we get in a group we always seem to come up with one evil person or group, some demonic figure to blame things on. In our meetings here it's been the United States. We have talked about someone having politics as if only certain groups had politics. Even in our little study groups we have politics. We are always looking to find a scapegoat so we won't have to blame ourselves.

Stam: The issues surrounding the Dominican Republic are all too certain and all too important. We have got to take this into account. I agree that we cannot divide the world into angels and devils, but your comment on their corruption needs a response. In all the countries where I have observed the sort of bribery and corruption you talk about, a small privileged group has been responsible, working with total support from further north. And it is not fair to paint the victims of that corruption with the same brush. In Guatemala, the people who are suffering the most are the Indians, and you can't just say they're guilty too. The truly guilty ones are precisely the ones our U.S. government is supporting. In Nicaragua it is exactly the same thing.

Your comment may be valid and necessary, but there is a danger there too. I hear behind it a plea for a kind of Aristotelian *via media:* let's be moderate, let's keep to the middle. I am not trying to caricature your position; I realize I'm going beyond the substance of your remark, but it puts me in mind of Bethge's biography of Bonhoeffer, where we read that

Bonhoeffer was told two things: don't stick your nose into anybody else's business, because it's better not to know, and there's good on both sides. As the Nicaraguan situation arose, I decided that even if I couldn't do it on a full-time basis, I had to check everything through, talk to the people, look for the facts. Even in talking with Miskito pastors and learning that there is good and evil on both sides, I could not just settle on a Manichean dichotomy. I firmly believe that there is a confrontation between good and evil in Nicaragua even if it is not the case that one force is unqualifiedly evil and another force is divinely and angelically good. There are forces representing life and death there, good and evil, justice and injustice, as they are confronting each other. I am convinced I can decide which side the forces of life and justice are working on: it's the Sandinista government, and I'm with it one hundred percent. I'm in bad trouble for taking that stand, but I'd be in worse trouble if I settled for just saying that there's good and evil on both sides.

A. Spencer: When I worked in a maximum-security prison in New Jersey I would notice the volunteers. When they arrived, the inmates and the administration would pressure them. The prisoners would picture the administration as totally evil, and the administration would picture the prisoners as evil. Although I could easily see that the administration was composed of people who were sinners, there was also some sin in the inmates, and not every administrator was totally evil. As you say, you must be aware of the different issues. In the Dominican Republic, a bribe is not even considered to be corrupt. Now I don't think that every gift is necessarily wrong, but you can't call certain bribes "gifts" and then view those given by Americans as complete corruption.

Stam: Obviously you have created an impossible situation with the adverb *totally*. We live with a very ambiguous history. Blacks have commited evil, as have women. But take the adverb *essentially*. What I feel about Nicaragua is that the Sandinista government is essentially just and that their cause is a cause for justice. And I feel that the Samocista position represented by the Contras and structured around the old officers of the National Guard is essentially evil. And here is where good and evil are confronting. I can't escape from an almost eschatological dialectic right in Nicaragua. I am not saying "totally," but I am saying "essentially."

* * *

Nuñez: I would like to know whether evangelical scholars in North America are doing serious exegetical work in their analysis of liberation theology or whether they are just impressed by the social and political challenge posed by liberation theology. I find two challenges coming from liberation theology. On the one hand there is the theological challenge, the hermeneutical problem—perhaps it would be better to say the exegetical-theological problem. On the other hand there is the social and political challenge. To us in Latin America, of course, the most important challenge is often the political and social challenge, because it appeals to our emotions and often to our pressing needs. It's talking to us about how power operates. So we are confronted by this context of political oppression, underdevelopment, and so on. But what about the exegetical challenge? Are we going to deal seriously from the biblical standpoint with this theology? I want to take liberation theology seriously. I take it not just as a problem, but as a challenge to me personally, and as a challenge to the evangelical church in Latin America.

We want to be enthusiastic about liberation theology and we might consider ourselves the liberators because we're accepting the challenge of liberation theology. At the same time, we might forget that according to liberation theology the only authentic theology is that which is done in solidarity—not just intellectual solidarity but real practical solidarity in this struggle, solidarity with the poor. In other words, it is easy to speak about liberation theology in the abstract, but to be a real liberator, we have to be there in force in the struggle for liberation. I'm afraid that sometimes we Latin Americans, teachers and preachers, might be enthusiastic about the challenge of liberation theology but not enthusiastic enough to get out from behind the desks where we are doing our theology. We forget the challenge of liberation theology. The real liberators according to the original theology are people like Camilo Tores in Colombia, the priest who joined the liberators, and Rumilio Grande, a Jesuit priest in El Salvador who went to work in the fields. They are the ones with the right to speak about liberation theology.

Cummings: It bothers me that many North Americans who talk about and critique liberation theology have not read the books, have not been in these contexts, have not met these theologians. We continue to categorize people just as we have for hundreds of years. We must be very careful about such critiques. This is part of the demystification process. We must have both social research and social analysis to demystify the theological process.

*   *   *

Roberts: This raises the issue of the theological dichotomizing that separates evangelism and social activism. As a black community, we mediate between the two. Too often people believe you must be against something before you can be for something. We are for both. I feel at home in an evangelical situation like this and I feel at home among liberation theologians—and I'm not a split person. I see both dimensions in the gospel. This black tradition is a significant part of the American tradition on these matters.

Cummings: Endemic to our conversations as North Americans and Latin Americans are certain dualisms that the feminists especially have called our attention to: spirituality and activism, theology of grace and theology of works, text and context, whether the seminary controls the church or the church controls the seminary—certain dichotomies that perhaps are unnecessary. For me, some of the most intriguing conversations have been occurring among the black liberationists in North America and Latin American liberation theologians concerning these dualisms. For example, Gustavo Gutiérrez in Lima is both a pastor and a theologian. The professors at the Protestant seminary in Cuba are all pastors. Generally speaking, the tradition of the pastor-scholar is continuing in the black community in the United States.

Second, concerning North America and Latin America on the issues of exegesis and ideology, we could engage in a drawn-out discussion of whether the theologians and intellectuals and exegetes and intellectuals are part of the middle class—but that's not the issue, as has been pointed out many times. The very fact that we can meet here presupposes privilege on our part. Rather we need to ask the question of who the intellectuals are intellectualizing about. There are organic connections among the oppressed—by virtue of ethnicity, race, sex, or whatever. Intellectuals also speak from a particular context.

Sanchez-Centina: It seems to me that during this conference, in several discussions, we are finding that our problems are not necessarily rooted in our theology but in our ideology, and yet we don't want to deal with that openly. Why are we afraid to do that?

Savage: That is directly connected to this issue of culture. I had the privilege of coordinating the Consultation on Gospel and Culture in Bermuda for the Lausanne movement, where we had participants from six continents. And I became aware of a particular problem in doing theology. The British were the imperialists. The first day John Stott was chairing the meeting, I did an analysis of who was talking with whom. Ninety-five percent of the time was occupied by the British scholars talking to each other. I asked myself why it was that Stott as chairman was allowing the British scholars to tie up ninety-five percent of the time. That night I sat down with him and suggested that the Americans and other English-speaking people, such as the Australians, were getting the message that they were considered inferior participants in the conference, that what they had to offer was being suppressed. The next day John raised this concern with the conference, and immediately an African colleague spoke up and said, "Yes, this is what we're feeling. In this conference there's been an oppression at a value level. There are values at play between North Americans and the British in terms of the use of language that affect our communication." Then our African participants started speaking in symbols about elephants and lions, which had the effect of throwing all the North Americans and British out the window. They could not cope with this. How could you describe a serious theological concept with animal terms? This was impossible. This was not real theology. But that is how Africans often speak of theology. Then we began to realize that it was not only the question of abstract versus analogical but also analytical versus intuitive. Anyone who expressed something that was intuitive—a gut feeling—found that those from the North Atlantic could not accept it. And doing theology by quoting a poem—that was heresy! In Latin America we are learning that to do theology we must sing. We have always had theology, even though it has not often been expressed in abstract conceptual terms. Even Gutiérrez's book is not highly analytical and abstract—it is poetical. We struggle with this often, realizing that an intuition that comes during worship often yields deeper theological insights than analytical compositions. During our time here we have had analytical conversations. It is male-oriented, Western, Anglo. We must understand that there are greater dimensions and other forms we can employ. We haven't dramatized theology. We haven't danced theology.

3.3.1

The Role of Women

Nuñez: I am sorry to say that in our Latin American Theological Fraternity we have not gone far in overcoming attitudes characteristic of this machismo culture. We have invited women to present papers at our consultations, but we have accomplished little so far. We are part of a culture in which women are struggling to get their rights, to get the position they deserve in our society.

Cummings: Emilio's mentioning the Fraternity makes me think of another context in which most of the liberation theologians get together—the International and Ecumenical Association of Third World Theologians. There is a very careful and self-conscious concern about the participation of women in this group. The representation from my own black, North American church is always fifty/fifty.

Mercadante: When I heard the gospel, it spoke to me of liberation. When I was at L'Abri, I tried to present this, but they would not listen, as you can imagine. I believe that I was sufficiently articulate, as a college graduate and as a journalist, yet they could not understand. So, in order to be able to speak to them at their level, I decided I needed to go to school. At Regent College I received a good education, but that was not enough. I believe that these evangelicals would not listen to me until I completed eight or nine years of education. The price I had to pay to come here to say these things has been very high. Part of that price has been learning to walk the walk and talk the talk. I don't want these comments to be viewed as an attempt to raise your guilt; I'm simply commenting on what I see. Margaret Mead said that when a woman goes into a male profession, which theology obviously is, she must become an anthropologist. She must see it as an alien culture. As an anthropologist she must learn the language and accommodate herself to that culture. Now, since I have been trained, I can talk to you in those terms. How many women don't have that training? And how women say "let's try another way because this price is too high"? Very few can do what I've done. So I agree with David Watson concerning the ideology of the academy. On day one of my Christian life the gospel spoke to me of liberation. But I had to

295

go through eight years of education and untold psychic battles before I could be heard here.

Scholer: This also relates to what Jerry has said about ideological shifts in U.S. churches. In one denomination (I think it is the Church of the Nazarene in the United States), before 1920 over twenty-five percent of the clergy were women. Now I would guess that the figure is less than two percent. I have talked to ordained women in that denomination who belong to churches pastored by males who will not allow them to participate in pastoral tasks. This attitude can be traced in most cases, I think, to evangelical groups that have polemicized against women in ministry, based on their theological interpretations. They assume that if you accept biblical authority and inerrancy, then you must be against the participation of women in ministry. This has produced dramatic changes in these churches. I think women are the only group in the U.S. subjected to this polemicization, the only group specifically set aside for exclusion with biblical and theological arguments. I would think, George, that part of the reason for the white claim that there are no black scholars, besides prejudice, is simply ignorance of the separate black system of scholars. There was no separate system of women scholars. Only recently have we had a large influx of women into the seminaries. I believe Jerry is right—there have been some major changes. However, there are still relatively few traditional evangelical women who are pursuing classical theological disciplines. That's why most evangelical seminaries still have fewer women. Further, the system that brings people to seminary is still basically the evangelical churches, which do not give women the encouragement they need.

Wan: I'm not quite sure how to react to Linda's comments and examples. On the one hand I empathize with her because I've gone through the same thing. I have often been in seminars where people who are loud and who are very forceful will be heard and the rest will not. At the same time I find it difficult to work her comments into my own situation. I find sometimes in a seminar I really have to emphasize my American side, to show my whole class that I can argue, that I understand what they are saying. But when I do this, I feel guilty for being so fierce and being so un-Chinese. When I take this approach I am not being true to my own heritage.

Pinnock: Wouldn't an American in a Chinese seminar have to contextualize the other way—become quiet and listening?

Wan: The problem is that I'm in an American university, where the rules are laid down by the Americans. I think your case would be valid for an American studying in Taiwan, but perhaps I'm not taking your point.

Pinnock: Well, I'm not sure how you can get around it. If that's the way the culture operates, you have to operate that way.

Padilla: But that begs an important question. Is that in fact the way we should operate in another culture? Do we adopt whatever is currently the norm? If that is what we should do, we would have to say that there is no place for women theologians in Latin America. Why bother about it? That's the way the culture operates.

Mercadante: From what you're saying I'm not sure you understood my point. When I gave my lengthy example, I was not speaking positively. Is that clear? I thought it would become clear. I didn't enjoy that experience, and I hope that I don't perpetuate that. In the classes I've taught, I have not allowed that to take place. And that was good. At least while I was teaching, I had some control and I made sure there was mutual respect. I usually laid it out at the beginning of the class: there *will* be mutual respect; we *will* use inclusive language. If people objected, I'd give them a hearing, but I tried to set some ground rules that were different from those of the typical academic environment so that when they came into that classroom, they could be human beings and not warriors. That is what the seminary trains them to be, but that certainly isn't the pastorate, and it shouldn't be the discipline of theology either.

There are two other points I want to make. One is that I want to add with Sze-kar that I felt extreme guilt at all times doing this. I don't know if it's always a proper guilt but it is guilt. And the second point concerns what David Watson and I observed: on the one hand it is encouraging that there are a lot of women in seminary now, even though it is unfortunate that there aren't as many in the evangelical seminaries. But, on the other hand, when women get out in the field as pastors, they're finding it so hard that many of them are dropping out. And so we have a much larger task than just getting women inside the seminary doors. First of all, the process has to be changed—and indeed many women are working on alternative theological education. And second, within our churches we have to do whatever we can to make it possible for women who are called to survive in their profession. We would be obstructing the call of God if women dropped out because they weren't comfortable or able to exercise that call in the church.

Hays: That gets us to the point I wanted to make, which is the relation of this theme to the conference—hermeneutics. There are really big issues here. If we acknowledge that there are women who are called into ministry, if we acknowledge that they are given by the Holy Spirit gifts and graces that should be exercised in teaching and leadership in the church, that requires a hermeneutic for dealing with the biblical texts that would completely short circuit the traditional evangelical hermeneutics. It means you can't just say, "Oh well, we're going to include women now," and keep on using the Bible the same way we've always used it. It requires a kind of hermeneutical shift that is no less fundamental than the hermeneutical shift that occurred when the early church realized that God had indeed poured out the Spirit upon Gentiles too. It means that we can't just go on using the Bible the same way and make a sort of exception for women. It means we have to rethink the whole business.

Cummings: I think Linda has already said something that I wanted to say—namely, that many women I know believe they ought to develop alternatives. They will not conform to the standards that men have set up. It is unfortunate, but that's the problem.

Roberts: As I've listened to the discussions about the experience of oppression, I've become painfully aware of what Rosemary Ruether called the infrastructure or interrelations of oppressions. This is the kind of experience women have which parallels and intensifies the experiences some of us have with racism. I have been encouraged by the development of a program of black women in church and society under black theologian Jacquelyn Grant. Black women in ministry and in theological training are able to confront the power structure of the church concerning how they handle ordinands and how they deal with women in their own ranks. Also, we have had a group of men and women theologians conversing over a period of four summers who are now ready to publish a book on mutuality between black men and women within ministry. We see this as a very creative way of handling two kinds of oppression which is quite different from the dynamics of the male-female discussions in the white communities. We see this in the context of family, an enlightenment and empowerment of families. We must approach these issues in a comprehensive way.

Savage: I think one of the beautiful things about the Latin American church is that women occupy a very important part in some of the day-to-day ministries of the church. This is more the case in the Pentecostal world than in the faith-mission churches. In many Pentecostal churches women are recognized as pastors, as deaconesses, and they play an active part. Even in faith-mission churches and mainline denominations, the power that really runs the church is the women. This can be seen time and time again. The spirituality, the reality, and the strength within the church itself is to be found and seen in the women. We see this also in the Catholic Church. We must offer a special word for the person who maintains the parish life, that particular devout woman who cultivates the spirituality. It is something that we evangelicals have not faced in Latin America adequately because we have a problem of machismo. This is a neurotic male identity problem that we have not resolved yet at a spiritual, psychological, or pastoral level within our churches. We have not been able to face this adequately yet, and that is part of the reason why the symbolically visible and powerful offices are in the hands of men. However, I believe we have seen some rapid changes during the last fifteen years, with the number of women coming into the universities and holding professional responsibilities. That is producing a major crisis in the family and in the office. Should businesses be run as men run businesses? Should our seminaries be run as men run seminaries?

The whole question of maleness is a very critical problem for us in Latin America because of the thrilling way that women are coming into places of authority. Increasing numbers of women are entering into key ministries and taking up key positions in governments in Latin America. It's something new for us. Unfortunately it's creating quite a crisis for male identity. This can be seen in counseling—the inability of the male to cope with this very aggressive, very open rejection often, of the male identity. And concerns for reactions like these are part of the reason that women graduating from universities feel that they have to decide between marriage and having a professional career.

Branson: We cannot avoid the pragmatic issues here. My comment is partially in response to Clark. We are not going to be able to influence the world around us as often as we wish. Yet in our own lives and in organizations that we influence, we need to learn how to give away power. How do we help those who do not have power? If it is decided that helping someone through the system is appropriate, how can we help provide the power to make that happen? We need to explore various styles of mentoring and of giving away power. If that does not fit our theology, then we have even more work to do!

Gutiérrez-Cortés: Four points. First, in Mexico, we've been graduating women but not giving them work in the churches. Second, in our homiletics class, the men receive credit for homiletics and the women receive credit in speech. Third, the only woman who has graduated from our Baptist Seminary in Mexico with a masters degree was not allowed to preach anywhere except in my church; they didn't even let her preach in the seminary. Fourth, Marco Antoñio Estrada wrote a thesis about women in the New Testament. I published 150 copies and asked him to defend it in two churches. The seminary forbade us to circulate it and they shelved it—but we continued to circulate our own copies. These illustrate the specific, concrete problems we face, both theological and cultural.

Sánchez-Centina: We have learned that we cannot copy the U.S. or other foreign countries regarding such issues. Earlier, I was excited by a course entitled "Women in Church and Society" taught by David Scholer at Gordon-Conwell. We have tried translating books from French, English, and German, but we found that it's not a good idea. The problems we face concerning women in the church are different, because our approach to society and culture is different. Rather than adopt "women's liberation" per se, we must understand the problems in the context of a more holistic struggle for liberation. In speaking with women in the U.S., I have asked, "Aren't you in a position of playing the systems game and forgetting that your struggle is not just an issue within the white middle and upper classes but part of a much larger struggle?" It is hard for me to see how to raise the issue of women's rights in Latin America without losing the reality of the total struggle that we face in our situation.

Hubbard: Richard commented on the need within evangelicalism for a paradigm shift. Historically, this shift may not be as far as we think. A colleague in Denver has studied the magazine that preceded *Moody Monthly*. He observed that the attitude toward women reflected in it and other journals until the early 1920s was much different than in the years that followed. The openness and the freedom with which women ministered in various kinds of positions in that earlier time is quite interesting. Perhaps we are in a sense only just recovering something that has been glossed over because of the modernist-fundamentalist controversy. I realize that this may not make it any easier, but we may in fact be going back to something that was lost quite recently.

Reid: If I go back to a local church and say that we had this conference and concluded that women should have more opportunities in the church, they'll say, "So what? Scripture was not at the conference." Scripture is the major legitimizing force in the evangelical church. If we do not have some way of dealing with the text, then we're suspect. I'd like some help on that.

Gil: I'm also concerned with the question Steve has raised concerning the poor and women. What are we going to do with Scripture? Unless we as evangelicals get down to tough hermeneutical issues, it won't do us any good to go off in one direction intuitively, because a hammer is going to come down on us from the other direction. We have texts that support the poor, but we also have texts that are used to undergird the rich. We have a few texts that support women, but we also have a lot of so-called antiwoman texts. I think we have to grapple with the hermeneutics involved rather than talk as if the texts didn't exist.

Branson: At least this work has begun in the U.S. Even though they're risking their reputations in the evangelical community, a number of biblical and theological scholars have published needed articles and books. I can think of David Scholer and Linda Mercadante here—plus Margaret Howe, Paul Jewett, Patricia Gundry, and Scott Bartchy. Also, several churches have had to listen to excellent and faithful work done by special research committees, even though they may not have heeded the reports. The faithfulness and quality of these contributions shouldn't be ignored.

3.4

Minority Groups

Padilla: Shall we move on to the issue of minority groups—especially those in North America, but also in Latin America. Perhaps we could begin by considering a certain triad that appears repeatedly in the Old Testament— orphans, widows and foreigners. That might help us begin to understand issues of minority groups which are without power.

Wan: Again I would like to express my appreciation for all of you. I have met a lot of new people this week, and with some of you I have begun real friendships, and I appreciate that—especially with Latin Americans here. If you know the Chinese culture, you realize that friendship is very important—it does not come easily. I want to express my appreciation.

I had a difficult time the first two days on interacting with some of the papers. Clark Pinnock, in his paper, dealt with European-Western history. That is something that I only know from books but not from my own heritage. I believe it was a very learned analysis, but it is not one that can help me a lot. René's paper tried to use the historical Jesus as a starting point for Latin American Christology. That too is helpful, but I'm not sure whether in the Chinese culture the historical Jesus by himself would be seen as a superior man. In fact I don't think the historical Jesus would be appreciated in that context. Resurrections are a dime a dozen in Chinese legends. Nor do I think Jesus' personal characteristics and qualities would make him attractive to those in the Chinese culture. So, a North American theologian has missed me on the one hand, and a Latin American has missed me on the other. I think the problem perhaps is because the Chinese culture (and I'm sure this can be applied to other Asian cultures) does not have the same needs as these American cultures. I am not sure whether Asian cultures need liberation theology. I am not even sure whether we are a minority. As Christians we are fragmented, with a few families here, a few families there; we have not come together as a community. So to go from there and to speak about liberation from our oppressors is difficult. We don't even know who the oppressed are.

I think that what we need in the Chinese culture is a theology of integration. The Chinese Christian community and other Asian Christian communities suffer the same problem I observe in the U.S.—fragmentation. In the Chinese community we are divided by our languages, our dialects. We are divided by our place in the world and our political allegiance. We also have the fragmentation that arises from the distance between Chinese culture and Western-American culture. The Chinese in the Americas have not assembled any powerful communities in the Americas apart from those in some of the larger cities like Los Angeles and San Francisco. And of course there is the huge problem of trying to integrate being Chinese and being Christian. I am still not sure whether I can be Chinese and a Christian at the same time. In the seminary, the more I read theology and the more I study, the more I find myself becoming Western. I cannot affirm my Chinese heritage in the way I think some of my American colleagues can affirm theirs. So I think our Chinese culture and Chinese community need a theology of integration, first integrating the different subgroups within the community; second, integrating Chinese life and American life so we can participate in the American process; and third, bringing together Chinese heritage with theological training in the Christian church.

I am speaking here only from the Chinese-American context: what does it mean to be a Chinese Christian? But this is a valid hermeneutical and political issue. In many Chinese and Korean churches, the membership can be very conservative theologically. Unless you are from a seminary like Dallas Theological Seminary, you are not considered orthodox. And I am not sure whether all of the Chinese church leaders have a real understanding of what the issues are. I have seen them manipulate these issues in ways they believe will be beneficial, but I wonder whether it really is. And frankly, I'm not clear on how we can get beyond that. I share all this primarily to solicit help from minority groups such as the blacks and Latin American church leaders who have gone through this, even though their cases may not be precisely parallel.

Branson: I need to speak about lessons I have learned from Asians who are working on this integration of heritage and Christianity. My wife is Chinese-American, second-generation, formerly a university minister and now entering business consultation. I have also worked with Japanese-Americans in Los Angeles. From their work on contextually sensitive hermeneutics, I have learned what the Bible teaches about shame. I've been raised in a culture that focuses on the guilt-concepts about salvation. From these Asian-Americans I have learned that the Bible actually says more about shame than about guilt. So through the eyes of another culture I have been helped to see the Bible in a different way and even have my relationship with God change. I have heard them discuss the heritage of the Japanese samurai and how they can understand and explain Jesus better through some of these images. *Seppuku,* an honorable way to give up one's life to avoid shame in the family and community, and thereby to provide reconciliation, can shed light on

Jesus' death. I realize any cultural analogies have limits, but the point is that my eyes have been opened to richer understandings through the Asian community.

Stam: I want to express my sense of the importance of what Sze-kar said and its relationship to the concerns of another group that has been forgotten—the indigenous people of Latin America. Latin American theology, after five centuries of ostensible Christendom, still can't integrate indigenous culture and Christianity.

Wan: There is not a great deal of interaction between our cultures and questions. I think it is indicative of the problem—that there is no dialogue. And we have too few Asian-American theologians ready to carry on that dialogue. Of course I'm not saying that there are *no* Asian theologians, even in the U.S. But we are enough in a minority that we get into a kind of double bind. I personally have experienced this. In Asia I was not accepted as an Asian, and in the U.S. I am not accepted as an American. So I think Asian-American theologians face a unique problem.

If I were to theologize in my context, if I were to be true to my own heritage—politeness, quietude—I would only listen. If I were to disagree, I would have to disagree politely. It is all a part of the culture, part of the ideals of my Chinese culture. What does one do in such a situation? For those of you who do not understand what I'm saying about the trends and ideals, I would recommend C. S. Song's book *Third Eye Theology.* Song grapples with the issues seriously. Chinese culture is very quiet—not necessarily passive, but quiet—and quietness is perceived as weakness in Western culture. Those who are true to this identity are swallowed alive in the West as a whole, and they will not come out whole even from the seminaries. This is a personal dilemma for me.

Gil: I want to underscore the points that Sze-kar is making. I attended the Christian Conference on Asia meetings that preceded the Melbourne meeting of the World Council of Churches Division on Mission and Evangelism. To my surprise, the Asian theologians there were critical of liberation theology. And the point you brought out is exactly their concern—the need for shalom, for togetherness, for integration. They said that without this they will never have a theology that will be helpful. A lot of liberation emphasis would break down the shalom and integration.

Roberts: In our efforts to understand oppression within black culture, I think history has a lot to say to us. We should take another look at the period in which black consciousness and black power were emerging at the same time. That had a lot to do with the way we went about trying to get blacks into positions where they could participate in decision-making, not simply to be present on the program but to be there from the very beginning of the process, so that they owned whatever happened and could bring their contribution to bear upon the process. This is critical. In the context of black theology I think we have to deal with an epistemological problem, with what I've referred to as the economizing of thought. There was a Christian Platonism implicit in my training, and I found it did not meet my needs any more as I looked at the Afro-American connection and began to think holistically. I have to struggle for a new hermeneutical perspective on the Bible and on systematic theology on the church and faith. That is the great challenge of my career as a theologian.

I'd also like to respond briefly to the issue raised in Jerry's paper which we've discussed privately. It has implications far beyond this group, and it is related to the hermeneutical task. It affects lives and theology. In this paper he has dealt primarily with the black scholars at Union, and he is aware of that limitation in his paper. But what I see happening there—and it's not the first time I've seen it—is that the black theologian is first set on a pedestal and then cut down, and the process of cutting that theologian down destroys everything that all of us are doing.

Let's say James Cone is described as the black theologian par excellence, but then his biblical exegesis is described as precritical and then dismissed as unacceptable on that account. What does that do the rest of us black theologians who do not accept the precritical view? I'm not saying that Cone does accept the precritical view—it's just an example. The point is that we ought to be evaluated on an individual basis, that same way Bultmann and Moltmann and the rest are evaluated. We have an equal right to serious consideration—and that includes the young scholars and those in mid-career, many of whom are doing very significant work in biblical exegesis, who are experts in Old Testament and New Testament theology and so forth. We have to distinguish among the offerings of black theologians in the same way that we have to acknowlege differences among the offerings of those in other theological movements, such as the feminist movement— differences between the perspectives of Mary Daly, say, and Letty Russell and Rosemary Ruether and so forth. Only by doing that can we be fair to a particular theological innovation. I think the time has come for us to take seriously not only the pacesetters in Western theology but the pacesetters that are coming from other persuasions and experiences—the Third World in particular. We have to work to establish real dialogue rather than mono-logue. That's where a real breakthrough, a mutual enrichment can take place.

*   *   *

Cummings: The notion that spirituality and activism go side by side is essential to the black church. This is precisely the point where the politiciza-tion of hermeneutics comes into question. The black church and black theologians have never been included in the discussions that are defining the North American theological and church community. To some degree, black people who consider themselves to be evangelicals have a center that is very different from the predominant culture in terms of spirituality and activism.

That's why we can feel comfortable in both evangelical and liberation discussions. The problem exists because of the fact that when I participate, I end up letting someone else define who I am. I have to sign something or use particular terms or attend a certain school, or else I'm not "in." And that's where the politics come to the fore.

Watson: I would like to ask for assistance, because those of us working in Texas obviously are very much interfacing with the Hispanic culture that has to some extent been detraditionalized. Could I ask how the Chicano community of the U.S. is viewed here? How can we be sensitive to that culture in Texas?

Savage: I attended a border conference of Mexican and U.S. authorities that also included Catholic and Protestant church leaders. This question was raised in terms of power, in terms of culture, in terms of communication, and so forth. The most important issue discussed was that the family is being destroyed on the border. The industries give work to the women but not to the men. So there are hundreds of men in Juarez, El Paso, and elsewhere who cannot find work, while the women get up at four o'clock to prepare meals and go to work. There is no sensitivity to this sort of thing in San Antonio, Dallas, Houston, and Chicago. It is much easier for women than it is for men to find work. The second major issue is that many are not interested in staying in the States. They go there to get money so they can return and build homes. I wish I could take you to several villages in Morelos where you find the homes being built brick by brick. They go straight from a semiliterate, often rural background to find the money in the North. They need to find work and equality in work where they are treated honestly rather than like animals. In Texas and California they are using cowpens to hold these people. Hundreds of them are crossing the border because they can't find work here in Mexico. They've been treated brutally—I've seen it with my own eyes. This is a very emotional issue here in Mexico because we see the oppression of these border areas.

Postscript

Compassion, Vision, and Solidarity

J. DEOTIS ROBERTS

Dear brothers and sisters, it's very good to share with you a few moments of reflection on the meeting and what it means in our ministry. I want to express my gratitude to all those who have been our hosts here, for the wonderful expression of hospitality we have shared in this company. In this setting my colleagues and I have learned from each other, and we will remember this experience for a long time.

In the ninth chapter of the Gospel according to Matthew, around the thirty-fifth verse, Jesus is said to have looked upon the crowd, the multitude, and had real compassion upon them because they seemed to be lost, alienated, scattered, like sheep without a shepherd. I want us to use that passage for reflection this morning.

I think that as a theologian I have neglected certain Scriptures. More recently I have learned a great deal about the importance of biblical studies for the task before me, about the need to return to the habits of my younger years when I did diligently search the Scriptures. As I get older, I get closer and closer to the churches, and so I have a great deal of concern for the relationship between theology and ministry and how what I think and reflect upon affects the life of the church, the witness of the church in the world. The theme of compassion here has a great deal to say to all of us about the nature of our ministry, whatever that ministry happens to be in the world.

I want to think of compassion as love that is deeply felt, that moves one to action. It's not love as a sentimental attitude but love as a kind of solidarity with those who are oppressed. Oppression can take many forms. There is a sense in which all people experience, from time to time, some form of oppression, and there is also a sense in which all of us become oppressors of others. I think we have to take this into account. We aren't being true to our own experience if we press a limited, one-sided approach to oppression, strictly distinguishing between those who are down and out and disinherited on the one hand and the evil oppressor on the other.

We have all been thinking during the course of this conference about the need, as we enter into interpretation of the Scripture, to go beyond a simple investigation of what happened in Palestine two thousand years ago. Of course it is important to try to relive the experience of those who were with Jesus in order to comprehend the nature of his life, his ministry, his death and resurrection, and the benefits of that for us—but we must also translate that in terms of the experience of our time and seek out what it must mean in our world.

Some years ago I studied with some very erudite New Testament scholars. We got down to words, and words have many meanings. But this was another time and another place. Then I came back and got involved in ministry to an oppressed community, and in that context I began to see how much the scholars had missed. They came from a homogenous culture in which everyone looked alike and everyone belonged to the same religious tradition. When one comes into the United States or Latin America, into a clearly multicultural situation, one has to deal with all kinds of problems that impinge upon the lives of people. One has to ask what the text meant and what the text means. One has to move, as Segundo says, in a circle back and forth between the present and the future and past. We have to move from the situation that faces us back to the eternal gospel and apply it in our own time and our own age.

As we look at the text I have chosen, we see that Jesus experiences his compassion for the multitude in their lostness within the context of his activities of healing, raising the dead, giving sight to the blind. Now, when Jesus met a crowd, he very often would single out that individual in its midst who seemed to have the greatest need for healing or salvation. In a sense he tended to individualize his love in this way. We can learn a great deal from this existential approach to dealing with the anxieties and alienations of individuals. It's the sort of thing that we find in the more intimate relationships we have with those in our family, in immediate kinship and friendship relationships. It's very important to remember that Jesus was able to know what is in us, to penetrate the depths of our being, to evaluate the very emotions and motives and dispositions of the heart. It has long been a great source of comfort to black people and other oppressed people to know that Jesus is a divine friend. "What a friend we have in Jesus, all our sins and griefs to bear." It is a very important aspect of faith for all of us to know that Jesus is interested in us, in our personal problems, in our personal needs, and that we can have quiet times in which we can steal away with Jesus. He always expressed his love personally, always conveyed an individualized, personal, very intimate understanding of the needs of the lost ones, the lonely, the forgotten, the anxious, the disinherited, the men and women with their backs against the wall.

But it's also important for us to remember that Jesus somehow knew the psychology of crowds, the sociology of crowds. He could look at a crowd and have compassion on the multitude, seeing them as lost and alienated, in need of comfort, in need of redemption. And it seems to me that in our looking back upon the text and looking at our present situation, the implication is quite clear that we are obliged to follow his example in developing solidarity with the oppressed, making the gospel a living and vital Word, becoming living evangels of the Word in the transformation of the social order.

I want to focus on my primary concerns in terms of three points. One is that we ought to try to view the world as Jesus viewed it. That means developing a compassionate, loving concern for individuals, for crowds, for our families, for all those we hold dear. It also means developing a concern for the larger community, the larger society, and the structural evils that impinge upon individuals and cause many millions of people to weep and moan for the very necessities of life. So we ought to look at the world through the broad lens that Jesus used and see the multiplicity of concerns and problems that make life very difficult for people. And we have to work at making life more human, embracing in our own lives and in the lives of our Christian fellowships the power to make life more human. We must first find the sort of vision that will allow us to see what needs to be done, and then we must proceed to define what it is that we may be able to change.

As we view the world through the eyes of Jesus and feel about it as Jesus felt, we are then moved in a compassionate way to express our love in action—not just pity or sentimental concern about the needs of people in general but in a profound engagement of the issues. And I mean a *profound* engagement of the issues: it will do no good to apply salve to the wounds that require surgery. Some suffering calls for surgery, for transformation, for the active love that the gospel calls us to.

We as a black community are very much involved today in politics. But, as I have mentioned to you before, the progress signaled by the growing number of black mayors in major cities across the country has not been matched by a similar progress in ameliorating the economic plight of black people. In many major cities as few as twenty-five families have practical control of the economic power structure. They can dictate to the city council and the mayor what can and cannot be done. In Atlanta I met with the city manager, who showed me an audio-visual program outlining his plans for the future of the city. That wasn't the mayor's office where the future was being planned; it was the city manager's office. He was the one who was in touch with the business community, including the international corporations with their tremendous economic power. Here was the power that could determine what would happen to people all over the city, what sort of work they could do, where they would live, and where they would die. The people in that city are pawns in the hands of the moneyed classes. And it's the same throughout the United States, throughout the world, not only in terms of those who have power in a particular metropolis, but those who belong to the transnational corporations that control the economy of the world. We are pawns in the hands of those people.

To grapple significantly with the economic realities in this world and to begin to identify with the people who are the real victims of this situation is going to take more than simply voting. As important as that is, we must become wise on the economic front also. As I say to my people, we must become more than consumers; we must learn how to invest and get a share in exercising some of that power. For example, it is very often the case that the substantial amounts of money collected in the black churches are deposited in suburban banks, outside of the black community. We've got to learn to analyze the situation, realize where we have to move in to make our values known, and then act to transform society, to make it more humane for those in the underclass.

This action of bearing witness to Jesus has a great deal to do with what happens to individuals who are broken by the system. A black chaplain told me about a woman, a mother that he was counseling in St. Elizabeth Federal Mental Hospital in Washington. She was there because she had threatened to kill her children. He began to dig into the situation to learn why she had threatened to do that, why she was there in the hospital. Finally he got a confession from her. She did not want to see her children suffer in the same way that she had suffered; she honestly believed they would be better off dead. The illness of this woman is the result of the intolerable pressures society put on her. Her problems could not be solved simply by counseling her as an individual, by trying to deal with her anxieties and loneliness as an individual.

In writing about about theological education in the United States, one of the things I've noticed is that there seems to be a primary emphasis on the pastoral care model, on dealing with the problems of individuals rather than on addressing the larger social problems that produce these personal anxieties. My ministry, on the other hand, presents me with a lot of clear evidence of the structures that oppress people. I think there is an urgent need for us to bring these two dimensions together—a pastoral concern for the problems of the individual and a more overarching concern for all the factors that conspire to produce so many of the personal anxieties in the first place. We've got to feel about the world as Jesus felt and move in a loving way not only to ameliorate the plight of individuals but also to transform the social order. Jesus did not merely stand in the midst of culture; he also stands above it as a Judge, and he gives us the power to transform it and to make its structures more humane.

If we were really to view the world through the eyes of Jesus, we would need no prompting to go out and do some of the things that Jesus did. He healed the sick, he made the blind see, the lame to walk, and the deaf to hear. There was some misunderstanding about the nature of his messiahship, as you know. John sent his own disciples to ask Jesus, "A you really the Christ, or shall we look for somebody else?" Jesus' answer was simply that "where I am the blind see, the lame walk, the deaf hear, and the poor have the gospel preached to them." And so I say that we are called to that kind of ministry, a healing ministry.

We must also hear the prophetic word. Jesus was not only a priest but a prophet, and the prophetic message of the Old Testament also claims us. That is a dimension that we have often not fulfilled. Some time ago Billy Graham was asked why he didn't speak prophetically about racism and other problems in his White House sermons. He said, "I'm a New Testament evangelist, not an Old Testament prophet." (I'm grateful to hear that more recently he has begun to change.) Compare that with the view of Martin Luther King, Jr., who quoted in one breath from Amos, the prophet of social justice, and in the next from Jesus, who was in line with the prophets, who came to deliver the prophetic word, and to carry out a prophetic ministry. In my tradition we have never had the luxury of dividing up the priestly and prophetic dimensions of the gospel. We've had to work with both cutting edges of the gospel, binding up the wounds of those who have been the victims of the structural evil and at the same time seeking to transform the situation, to make life more humane. Viewing the world through the eyes of Jesus means living out a compassionate love in specific action, identifying with those who are in need of our ministry—in short, doing what Jesus did.

On one occasion Jesus took his disciples to the edge of a field that was ripe unto harvest. The wheat had grown and become yellow, and was bowing its head in ripeness. They looked out there and saw only a few reapers casting their sickles into the harvest. He saw a tremendous task to be done but only a few people engaged in gathering in this harvest, and it was very soon that the rains would come and the wheat would be destroyed in the field. So there was a sense of urgency. He said, "Lift up your eyes upon the field and see the field, the grain, is ready to be harvested. The laborers are few, the harvest is great." And so it is that kind of challenge that we face today. There are many problems, personal and social and systemic, that we must confront. We have to pursue our ministries as our Lord pursued his, with the hope that the kingdoms of this world may become the kingdoms of our God and his Christ.

Appendix

Evangelical Theology in the Two Thirds World*

ORLANDO E. COSTAS

The last decades have witnessed a resurgence of evangelical theology and action. Indeed, one could argue that evangelicals have ceased to be a marginal sector of Protestant Christianity and have moved into the mainstream of contemporary society. However, we err if we assume that what Donald G. Bloesch calls the "evangelical renaissance" is solely a Euro-American phenomenon or that it is theologically, culturally, and socially homogeneous.[1] As Emilio Castro, general secretary of the World Council of Churches, stated recently, "in the past . . . evangelical perspectives on spirituality and [theology] came basically from theologians in the North Atlantic region," but today they are coming from all over the world.[2] He also pointed out that evangelicalism is going through the same process and change that the ecumenical movement has experienced in the last decades because of the diverse socio-cultural settings of its adherents. Castro's comment is verified by the published reports of several world gatherings during the last decades and by a growing body of publications.

It is my contention that while evangelicals around the world share a common heritage, their theological expressions are by no means homogeneous. To be sure, evangelicals in the North Atlantic world have had an enormous influence in what I like to call the "Two Thirds World"—that

* This essay, which reflects on several recent international conferences, provides a helpful summary and update on contextual questions in theology. First published in *TSF Bulletin*, September/October 1985, it is reprinted here by permission.

1. Bloesch, *The Evangelical Renaissance* (London: Hodder & Stoughton, 1973).
2. Castro, "Ecumenism and Evangelicalism: Where Are We?" in *Faith and Faithfulness: Essays on Contemporary Ecumenical Themes—A Tribute to Philip A. Potter* (Geneva: World Council of Churches, 1984), p. 9.

part of our planet that is home to most of the poor, powerless, and oppressed people on earth: Africa, Asia, the Pacific, the Caribbean, and continental Latin America. One cannot deny the strong presence and pressures exercised by Euro-American evangelicalism on the Two Thirds World through the missionary movement, literature, the electronic media, and theological institutions. Notwithstanding this reality, however, there seems to be developing in the Two Thirds World a different kind of evangelical theology that addresses questions not usually dealt with by evangelical mainstream theologians in Euro-America, employing a different methodology and drawing different conclusions.

I will begin to make my case by briefly outlining the nature of evangelicalism as I understand it, especially as it has developed in the United States. I will then proceed to analyze the emerging evangelical theological discourse in the Two Thirds World, taking as reference representative statements from several theological conferences held within the last five years. I will conclude with some observations on the mutual challenges of evangelical theology north and south and east and west.

Evangelical Theology in the One Third World

If there is one single characteristic of evangelical theology, it is its missionary intent. Evangelicalism, as its name suggests, has a burning passion for the communication of the gospel, especially in those areas where it has not yet been proclaimed. It is not surprising that the Wesleyan Movement, which made such a dramatic impact in the British Isles during the eighteenth century and in many ways became the basis for Britain's world mission in the nineteenth century, has been described as "the evangelical awakening." Nor is it accidental that Joan Jacobs-Brumberg's scholarly study of the life, career, and family of Adoniram Judson, the American Baptist pioneer foreign missionary, provides the key to her analysis of "evangelical religion" in the U.S. during the nineteenth century. Wesleyan and Baptist preachers, evangelists and missionaries aptly demonstrate the burning passion of the evangelical movement for world mission and evangelism.

The missiological character of evangelicalism is undergirded by four theological principles: the authority of Scripture, salvation by grace through faith, conversion as a distinct experience of faith and a landmark of Christian identity, and the demonstration of "the new life" through piety and moral discipline. The first two are the formal and material principles of the Protestant Reformation. The other two are tied to the so-called Second Reformation (the pietist movement, including the evangelical awakening, which sought to complete the first [theological] Reformation by advocating the reformation of life). The last two principles are also connected with American revivalism and the holiness movement.

These four theological principles have in various ways affected the historical development of the evangelical movement. European Protestant confessional families, including the Lutherans and the Reformed (including Congregationalists and Presbyterians), define their evangelicalism mainly in terms of the first two principles, whereas "pietist" elements, particularly in Lutheranism (who claim to be *with* their churches but never *under* them), stress the latter two a good deal more (at least in practice, though not necessarily in theory). Likewise in North America, those churches and Christians who want to stress the orthodox nature of evangelicalism will point to the Lutheran and Calvinist Reformation, whereas those who stress its practical and experiential side will focus on pietism and revivalism.

Gabriel Fackre has developed a fivefold typology of contemporary North American evangelicalism, using the four principles mentioned above as criteria. He classifies evangelicals into the following groups: (1) Fundamentalists, (2) Old Evangelicals, (3) New Evangelicals, (4) Justice and Peace Evangelicals, and (5) Charismatic Evangelicals. In Fackre's view, Fundamentalists are characterized by their understanding of the authority of Scripture ("plenary verbal inspiration of the original autographs"), their separatist ecclesiology, and their militant opposition of all foes on doctrinal issues. Old Evangelicals are those "who stress the conversion experience and holiness of life and seek to nourish these in the revival tradition and in congregations of fervent piety." New Evangelicals, he says, "insist on the ethical and political relevance of faith as articulated by broad guidelines, stress the intellectual viability of a born-again faith and of orthodox theology, and seek to work out their point of view within, as well as alongside, traditional denominations." Fackre identifies as Justice and Peace Evangelicals the new generation of Christians who "express their faith in more radical political and ecclesiastical idiom," who come from an Anabaptist, Wesleyan, or high Calvinist backgrounds, and who "call into question the accommodation of today's culture and churches to affluence, militarism, and unjust social and economic structures." He identifies Charismatic Evangelicals in terms of their experiential faith, their reaching out "for highly visible signs of the Spirit, primarily the gifts of tongue-speaking (glossolalia) and healing, and intensity of prayer, mercy and communal life."[3]

All of these groups, and their corresponding theological expressions, have made their way in one form or another into the Two Thirds World. In terms of theological production, the most significant group has been the New Evangelicals, and in a lesser way, the Justice and Peace group. The fact that Fackre associates the New Evangelicals with *Christianity Today* (and presumably other theologically similar periodicals, publishing houses, and schools) and links the Justice and Peace Evangelicals with journals such as *Sojourners*

3. Fackre, *The Religious Right and Christian Faith* (Grand Rapids: Eerdmans, 1982), pp. 5-7.

and *The Other Side* is an indication of the theological influence of these two groups.

The New Evangelicals, by and large, represent the North American leadership of the Lausanne Movement, the World Evangelical Fellowship (and its North American counterpart, the National Association of Evangelicals), as well as the two large missionary consortia, the Independent Foreign Missions Association (IFMA) and the Evangelical Foreign Missions Association (EFMA). They also have the most visible presence in theological (and missiological) educational institutions. During the last several decades they have been the largest exporters of North American evangelical theology.

On the other hand, the Justice and Peace Evangelicals represent a new generation of scholars and critics with special interests in and ties to the Two Thirds World. Their criticism of North American religious culture and socio-economic policies, their commitment to a radical discipleship, and their solidarity with the Two Thirds World have made them natural allies of some of the most theologically articulate evangelical voices in that part of the globe. Given the leadership and influence of New Evangelicals in mainstream North American church and society, however, I shall limit my analysis to them.

New Evangelicals and Biblical Authority

For the New Evangelicals, the heart of evangelicalism is its faithfulness to the Reformation's formal principle of biblical authority and its material principle of salvation in Christ through faith. But as Kenneth Kantzer (former editor of *Christianity Today*) has suggested,

> the formal principle of biblical authority is the watershed between most other movements within the broad stream of contemporary Protestantism and the movement (or movements) of twentieth-century Protestantism known as fundamentalism, which is a term often poorly used for the purpose it is intended to serve, or evangelicalism or conservative Protestantism.[4]

Put in other terms, though the New Evangelicals have claimed all the principles of the Reformation, their primary emphasis has been on the principle of biblical authority. This formalistic emphasis does not bypass the need to do theology from the text of Scripture. As Kantzer has also said, "the evangelical . . . seeks to construct his theology on the teaching of the Bible,

4. Kantzer, "Unity and Diversity in Evangelical Faith," in *The Evangelicals,* ed. David F. Wells and John P. Woodbridge (Nashville: Abingdon Press, 1975), p. 39.

the whole Bible, and nothing but the Bible; and the formative principle represents a basic unifying factor throughout the whole contemporary evangelicalism."[5]

In actual practice, nonetheless, the greater energies of evangelical theological formulations, during the last decade at least, have been focused on the formal question of the authority and inspiration of Scripture rather than on its teachings. It is no surprise that the most widely published representative of this brand of evangelicalism, Carl F. H. Henry (another former editor of *Christianity Today*) entitled his six-volume magnum opus *God, Revelation, and Authority.* Nor is it any surprise that Kantzer likens the contemporary debate over the authority and inspiration of Scripture to the debates over the doctrines of the Trinity and of Christ's person in earlier periods of Christian history.

Evangelical Theology in the Two Thirds World

Recognizing that many contemporary evangelical theologians in the Two Thirds World have been formed and informed (and sometimes even deformed!) by New Evangelical theologians, they do not appear to be as concerned over the formal authority question as they are over the material principle. To be sure, one can find evangelical theological formulations in the Two Thirds World that reveal a similar concern over the authority of Scripture. However, such formulations are neither the most authentic expression of evangelical theology in the Two Thirds World nor the most numerous. To validate this assertion, I will turn to the concluding statements from three major theological conferences on evangelical theology in the Two Thirds World held in Thailand (March 1982), Korea (August 1982), and Mexico (June 1984).

The Thailand and Mexico meetings had a missiological thrust and a theological content. They were sponsored by a loose fellowship of evangelical mission theologians from the Two Thirds World. The theme of the Thailand conference was "The Proclamation of Christ in the Two Thirds World." It produced a final document ("Towards a Missiological Christology in the Two Thirds World") and a book *(Sharing Jesus in the Two Thirds World),* published first in India and most recently in the United States. The Mexico meeting focused on the Holy Spirit and evangelical spirituality. It also produced a final statement ("Life in the Holy Spirit") which will be included with the conference papers in a book soon to be published. The Korean Third World Theologians Consultation was sponsored by the Theological Commission of the Association of Evangelicals in Africa and Madagascar, the Asia Theological Association, the Latin American Theological Fraternity, and

5. Kantzer, "Unity and Diversity in Evangelical Faith," p. 52.

the Theological Commission of the World Evangelical Fellowship. Working with the theme "Theology and Bible in Context," it produced the Seoul Declaration ("Toward an Evangelical Theology for the Third World").

All three documents express a clear commitment to Scripture as the source and norm of theology. They express an unambiguous commitment to its authority not only in terms of the content of the faith and the nature of its practice but also in the approach to its interpretation. The Scriptures are normative in the understanding of the faith, the lifestyle of God's people, and the way Christians go about their theological reflection. Yet the Scriptures are not to be heard and obeyed unhistorically. Indeed, the normative and formative roles of Scripture are mediated by our contexts—contexts that are, generally speaking, characterized in these documents as a reality of poverty, powerlessness, and oppression on the one hand, and religious and ideological pluralism on the other. Thus a contextual hermeneutic appears as a *sine qua non* of evangelical theology in the Two Thirds World.

The report on the Thailand conference, for example, states that the participants "worked with a common commitment to Scripture as the norm" but notes that they were also deeply aware that the agenda for theological activity is always dictated to some extent by specific contexts. They agree that such a contextual reading of the Scripture should be equally informed by "the biblical passion for justice, the biblical concern for the 'wholeness' of salvation, and the biblical concept of the universality of Christ."[6] In other words, the Bible has its own contexts and passionate concerns that must be taken seriously into account in the movement from our socio-religious situation to the Scriptures. The text is equally important in the setting of the theological agenda. We ought not simply to come to it with any issue that arises; we should be sensitive to the issues that arise out of the text itself and let the text pose questions to our socio-historical situation.

Thailand's central concern was Christology and its relevance for the proclamation of the gospel in the Two Thirds World. It underscores "the historical reality of Jesus . . . in his concrete socio-economic, political, racial and religious context." It also acknowledges that he is "the Incarnate Word of God" and affirms his "universal lordship." Thus while expressing "solidarity with the poor, the powerless and the oppressed . . . , with those who are followers of other religions and with all people everywhere," it also recognizes the universality of sin and the universal significance of Christ's saving work for all people. "We are all under the sovereignty of the Lord Jesus Christ, whom we are committed to proclaim to all, especially our brothers and sisters in the Two Thirds World."[7] Thailand's Christological concern was, therefore, informed by the historic evangelical passion for the communication of the gospel.

6. See *Sharing Jesus in the Two Thirds World,* ed. Vinay Samuel and Chris Sugden (Grand Rapids: Eerdmans, 1983), p. 277.

7. *Sharing Jesus in the Two Thirds World,* p. 279.

Mexico followed the pattern and perspective of Thailand. It assumed what Thailand had said about Scripture, context, and hermeneutics, affirming the Bible as the fundamental source of knowledge concerning the person and work of the Holy Spirit. Beyond this formal statement, the final report was limited to a summary of how the conference participants understood what the Bible teaches about the Holy Spirit. It demonstrates an overwhelming interest in the *content* of the Scriptures rather than on its formal authority.

The purpose of the Mexico conference was "to understand how the person and work of the Holy Spirit relates to the context of other religious traditions and movements for social transformation." With regard to other religious traditions, the final document states that

> no religion is totally devoid of the Spirit's witness. But no religion is totally receptive to the Spirit's promptings. . . . The Gospel . . . provides a measure to evaluate all religious traditions, that measure being Christ himself (and not any form of Christianity). The encounter of Christian revelation with other religions is therefore not that of mutually exclusive systems. Persons of other faiths have been known to discover in Christ the answer to questions raised within their own traditions. We believe that such experiences indicate the sovereign activity of the Holy Spirit with other religions (Acts 14:14-18; 17:22-31; Rom. 1:18-25; 2:7-16).
>
> Thus, when we bear witness to Christ in dialogue with persons of other faiths, we can accept their integrity whilst we also affirm the ultimacy of Christ.

This posture reflects a positive attitude toward people of other religions. At the same time, it retains a distinctive Christian character and the evangelistic edge so characteristic of evangelical theology.

The Mexico Report points to the category of "justice" as the criterion for evaluating the Spirit's work in movements for social transformation. It states that the Spirit is discerned to be at work in such movements when the transformation they help bring about "results in justice with and on behalf of the poor." The document goes on to assert that "to be faithful bearers of the Spirit who 'comes alongside,' we are called to 'come alongside' such movements not with unqualified acceptance of their agenda, but with the agenda of the Spirit." This agenda is described in terms of "democratization, the socialization of power and the just distribution of wealth." The Spirit calls us as followers of Christ "to serve as witnesses against the self-interests among those involved in . . . struggles for power, and as channels of communication for rival factions having common goals." However, our witness must also "retain its distinctive Christian character and its evangelistic edge."[8]

8. Conference of Evangelical Mission Theologians, "Life in the Holy Spirit" (unpublished report of the Second Conference of Evangelical Theologians in the Two Thirds World, Tlayacapan, Morales, Mexico, 1984), p. 4.

The Korea Consultation, with a much larger participation and external (Euro-American) influence, reflected a concern for the formal aspects of biblical authority. It states emphatically,

> we unequivocally uphold the primacy and authority of the Scriptures. . . . We have concertedly committed ourselves to building our theology on the inspired and infallible Word of God, under the authority of our Lord Jesus Christ, through the illumination of the Holy Spirit. No other sources stand alongside. Despite our varying approaches to doing theology, we wholeheartedly and unanimously subscribe to the primacy of the Scriptures.[9]

Yet the Seoul Declaration also states that the commitment to the authority of Scripture "takes seriously the historical and the cultural contexts of the biblical writings." Moreover, it asserts: "For us, to know is to do, to love is to obey. Evangelical theology must root itself in a life of obedience to the Word of God and submission to the lordship of Jesus Christ." Finally, the Declaration argues that

> a biblical foundation for theology presupposes the church as a hermeneutical community, the witness of the Holy Spirit as the key to the comprehension of the Word of God, and contextualization as the New Testament pattern for transposing the Gospel into different historical situations. We affirm that theology as a purely academic discipline is something we must neither pursue nor import. To be biblical, Evangelical theology must depend on sound exegesis, seek to edify the body of Christ, and motivate it for mission. Biblical theology has to be actualized in the servanthood of a worshipping and witnessing community called to make the Word of God live in our contemporary situations.[10]

Even in those passages where the Seoul Declaration uses formal authority language, it checks it against a contextual and communal hermeneutic and a Christological and pneumatological underpinning: the Scriptures are under the authority of Christ and depend on the Holy Spirit for the communication of their message. Furthermore, the Declaration balances its authority language with its emphasis on Christian obedience, faithfulness to the biblical message and the imperative of mission in the life of the church.

This "material" check and balance helps us understand the twofold theological critique of the Declaration—against Western (i.e., mainstream Euro-American) and Third World theologies, respectively. Western theology, "whether liberal or evangelical, conservative or progressive," is criticized for being, by and large, obsessed with problems of "faith and reason."

9. Third World Theologian's Consultation, "The Seoul Declaration: Toward an Evangelical Theology for the Third World" (Taichung, Taiwan: Asia Theological Association, 1983), p. 3.
10. "The Seoul Declaration," p. 3.

All too often, it has reduced the Christian faith to abstract concepts which may have answered the questions of the past, but which fail to grapple with the issues of today. It has consciously or unconsciously been conformed to the secularistic worldview associated with the Enlightenment. Sometimes it has been utilized as a means to justify colonialism, exploitation, and oppression, or it has done little or nothing to change these situations. Furthermore, having been wrought within Christendom, it hardly addresses the questions of people living in situations characterized by religious pluralism, secularism, resurgent Islam or Marxist totalitarianism.[11]

This statement may lack precision. However, it does articulate a well-known criticism of Western theologies from both the Two Thirds World and minority voices in Europe and North America. Moreover, it has the merit of including the evangelical critique of Euro-American mainstream theologies. This makes all the more meaningful the call for liberation "from [the] captivity to individualism and rationalism of Western theology in order to allow the Word of God to work with full power."[12]

The Seoul Declaration also criticizes some of the emerging theologies of the Two Thirds World, though it does recognize similarities in their respective socio-historical struggles. Both have suffered under colonialism and oppression, are currently struggling against injustice and poverty in situations of religious pluralism, and acknowledge the need "to articulate the Gospel in words and deeds" in their respective contexts. Yet, the Seoul Declaration is equally uneasy with some of the basic premises of these theologies. It is particularly critical of some liberation theologies. While heartily admitting that liberation theologies have raised vital questions that evangelicals cannot afford to ignore, the Declaration nevertheless rejects the tendency "to give primacy to a praxis which is not biblically informed." Likewise, it objects "to the use of a socio-economic analysis as the hermeneutical key to the Scriptures." And finally, it rejects "any ideology which under the guise of science and technology is used as an historical mediation of the Christian faith."[13]

The positive yet critical posture reflected in the final documents of these three meetings demonstrates the authenticity of the evangelical theological reflection that is currently taking place in the Two Thirds World. Evangelical theologians in these parts of the world are appropriating the best of their spiritual tradition and are putting it to use in a constructive critical dialogue with their interlocutors in and outside of their historical context. For them the evangelical tradition is not locked into the socio-cultural experience of the West. They insist that they have the right to articulate

11. "The Seoul Declaration," p. 2.
12. "The Seoul Declaration," p. 2.
13. "The Seoul Declaration," p. 3.

theologically the evangelical tradition in their own terms and in light of their own issues.

Evangelicals North and South, East and West

So far I have argued that evangelical theology emerges out of European and North American Protestant Christianity and has been carried to the Two Thirds World by the missionary movement, theological institutions, and publications and also that there is an identifiable difference between its most influential and visible contemporary expression (New Evangelical theology) and the emerging evangelical theological discourse in the Two Thirds World. This difference lies in the concern of the latter for the formal principle of Protestant theology. The emphasis on the content of the gospel and the teaching of the biblical text rather than on formal questions of authority and the philosophical presuppositions behind a particular doctrine of inspiration is freeing evangelical theology in the Two Thirds World to employ a contextual hermeneutics patterned after the transpositional method witnessed throughout the New Testament. This also explains why evangelicals in the Two Thirds World are more willing to deal with questions of religious pluralism and social, economic, and political oppression than are most evangelical theologians in the One Third World.

Without putting all mainstream evangelicals in the One Third World in the same bag, it seems quite clear to me that mainstream evangelical theologians are too obsessed with the Enlightenment and not enough with the explosive social, economic, political, cultural, and religious reality of most people in the world. As Bernard Ramm has stated quite candidly in the opening pages of his book *After Fundamentalism: The Future of Evangelical Theology,* "the Enlightenment sent shock waves through Christian theology as nothing did before or after. Theology has never been the same since the Enlightenment. And therefore each and every theology, evangelical included, must assess its relationship to the Enlightenment."[14]

It should be pointed out that this obsession with the Enlightenment as an intellectual challenge to faith pertains basically to its seventeenth- and eighteenth-century phase, which focused on the issue of freedom from authority through reason. This obsession is shared by practically all Euro-American theologies. Indeed, it can be argued that all mainstream theologies in Western Europe and North America, from Immanuel Kant to Carl F. H. Henry, have been, by and large, discourses on the reasonableness of faith. Their primary concern has been the skeptic, atheist, materialist-heathen—the nonreligious person. This is why the second phase of the Enlightenment, associated with the nineteenth-century movement of free-

14. Ramm, *After Fundamentalism* (San Francisco: Harper & Row, 1983), p. 4.

dom from political, cultural, economic, and social oppression, has been on the whole a peripheral issue in Euro-American theology, including evangelical theology. Yet, this is an issue of fundamental importance in the theological agenda of the Two Thirds World. For all its missionary passion and experience, mainstream evangelical theology in North America has yet to learn from its missionary heritage how to ask more central questions concerning the destiny of humankind, the future of the world, and even the central concerns of the Scriptures.

In airing this criticism I do not mean to belittle the fact that there are always two sides to the problem of unbelief—the absence of faith and the denial (practical or theoretical) of faith. Theology in North America and Western Europe has been generally concerned with the absence of faith and its theoretical denial. But it must be acknowledged that from the evangelical awakening to the present there have been mainstream Euro-American theologies and theological movements that have sought to address the problem of the practical denial of faith in the unjust treatment of the weak and downtrodden. This is the case with the theology of the Wesley brothers, the Oberlin theology of George Finney, the theology of the Social Gospel, the practical theology of the early Reinhold Niebuhr, the political theology of Jürgen Moltmann and J. B. Metz and the prophetic theologies of mainstream ecumenical theologians, such as Robert McAfee Brown and the Peace and Justice Evangelicals. These theologies have attempted, in varying degrees and in their own peculiar ways, to deal with the problem of social oppression and alienation. In so doing they have built a modest bridge toward a fundamental concern of any theology in the Two Thirds World— namely, the cry of the oppressed and its disclosure of the practical "unbelief" of professing Christians who oppress their neighbors.

It is not my intention here to slight the modest dialogue that has been taking place during the past several years between some mainstream evangelical theologians and their counterparts in the Two Thirds World concerning questions of poverty, powerlessness, oppression, and religious pluralism. Indeed, during the Thailand meeting there were two theologians representing European and North American Evangelical thought.[15] And while they came to the meeting with questions pertaining to traditional theological issues of the North Atlantic, they had to cope with other theological agendas (and did so positively and constructively). They realized that their particular agenda was pertinent to a rather small sector of humankind. They also acknowledged that their agenda was even different from that of the two "minority" participants from North America, whose North

15. Ronald Sider (from the U.S.) presented a paper entitled "Miracles, Methodology and Modern Western Christology," and David Cook presented a paper entitled "Significant Trends in Western Christological Debate" (see *Sharing Jesus in the Two Thirds World*, pp. 237-50 and 251-73).

American evangelical theology was focused on the truth of God's justice. [16]
As one of them commented,

> the issue that divides me from mainstream white evangelicals is not
> whether I believe the Bible to be the Word of God which I do, but . . .
> that I want to . . . read [it] from my situation . . . of oppression. . . .
>
>   I stand in a dialectical tension with the system which has kept my
> people in oppression. . . . I coincide . . . with mainstream white evan-
> gelicals . . . about belief in Jesus Christ. We . . . are committed to Jesus
> Christ [as] . . . Lord and . . . Savior. We . . . are judged by the same
> Word. But when we [ask] what does it mean to believe in Jesus Christ,
> and . . . "who is this Jesus that we confess as . . . Lord and . . . Savior
> and what does [he] command us to do?" at that precise point we start
> departing from one another. [17]

In November 1983, a consultation was held in Tlayacapan, Mexico,
involving several types of evangelical theologians from North America and
their counterparts in Latin America and the minority communities of the
U.S. This "Context and Hermeneutics in the Americas Conference" established a methodology that permitted evangelical scholars to wrestle with
concrete biblical texts and debate such questions as whether our interlocutor
is really the "atheist" (as evangelical theologians who wrestle with the
questions of the first phase of the Enlightenment argue) or the alienated
(i.e., the nonperson who may be religious but has been exploited, marginalized, and dehumanized by religious institutions, as many theologians in
the Two Thirds World and North American minority communities would
argue). The latter issue was not resolved, but the hermeneutical exercises
were very fruitful. Afterward, Grant Osborne, from Trinity Evangelical
Divinity School, wrote that

> everyone present felt that the conference . . . was extremely beneficial.
> Ways of extending the dialogue were suggested. . . . All in all, it was felt
> that North Americans need to enter a Latin American setting and do
> theological reflection in the context of poverty. Those from the North,
> before passing judgment, should be willing to enter a Nicaragua or an
> El Salvador and experience those realities from the inside. [18]

(One might add that this could apply just as well to the urban ghettos of
North America).

16. See George Cummings, "Who Do You Say That I Am? A North American
Minority Answer to the Christological Question," in *Sharing Jesus in the Two Thirds
World*, pp. 217-29.
17. Comment by a minority North American participant in a discussion with
George Cummings, in *Sharing Jesus in the Two Thirds World*, p. 235.
18. Osborne, "Contextual Hermeneutics in the Americas," *TSF Bulletin*,
7 (March/April 1984), p. 22.

Lest I be misunderstood, let me conclude by saying that it has not been my intention to idealize evangelical theology in the Two Thirds World nor endorse the tendency to generalize, avoid precision, or belittle the significance of Western theological debates. I readily admit that evangelical theology in the Two Thirds World is represented by many voices with divergent views. It has a long way to go, and in the process it will have a lot to learn from its counterpart in the One Third World.

However, I submit that the ultimate test of any theological discourse is not erudite precision but transformative power. It is a question of whether or not theology can articulate the faith in a way that it is not only intellectually sound but spiritually energizing and therefore capable of leading the people of God to be transformed in their way of life and to commit themselves to God's mission in the world. As the apostle Paul reminded the Corinthian church many years ago, "the kingdom of God is not talk but power" (1 Cor. 4:20).

DATE DUE